ECONOMIC AND SOCIAL SURVEY OF ASIA AND THE PACIFIC 2011

Sustaining Dynamism and Inclusive Development:

Connectivity in the Region and Productive Capacity in Least Developed Countries

UNITED NATIONS
ESCAP
Economic and Social Commission for Asia and the Pacific

ECONOMIC AND SOCIAL SURVEY OF ASIA AND THE PACIFIC 2011

Sustaining Dynamism and Inclusive Development:
Connectivity in the Region and Productive Capacity
in Least Developed Countries

United Nations publication
Sales No. E.11.II.F.2
Copyright © United Nations 2011
All rights reserved
Printed in Thailand
ISBN: 978-92-1-120622-7
ISSN: 0252-5704
ST/ESCAP/2586

FOREWORD

The dynamism of the Asia-Pacific region was a major factor driving the global economic recovery in 2010, with the developing economies of Asia and the Pacific increasing their rate of growth in gross domestic product from 4.7 per cent in 2009 to an impressive 8.8 per cent. There has also been a strong green component in these efforts. Welcome as this performance has been, the region continues to face serious challenges.

Rising prices of food and energy are at the top of the list. Food costs account for well over a third of household budgets for the region's poor, meaning that the health, education and productivity of these already vulnerable individuals will be affected disproportionately by any erosion in food and nutrition security. Energy is a primary input for the region's massive manufacturing activities; more expensive energy will raise costs and, potentially, make this vital sector less dynamic.

Unemployment remains an additional concern, especially among young people. There is a need to strengthen climate change mitigation and adaptation. And those economies whose exports to developed countries are expected to experience a slowdown in 2011 need to generate alternative sources of demand, including within their own countries.

This *Survey* explores ways the region can sustain dynamism in the medium term. It highlights the importance of greater connectivity in infrastructure and transport, and of more investment in the region's human resources. It also stresses the need to expand and diversify the productive capacity of the least developed countries in order to overcome their structural limitations and take advantage of opportunities arising from globalization. This year's Fourth United Nations Conference on the Least Developed Countries, and next year's UN Conference on Sustainable Development – Rio+20 – are timely and important opportunities to re-think these issues and to set the world on a path of inclusive, clean-energy development that benefits all people, today and tomorrow.

The devastating earthquake and tsunami in Japan have added to the uncertainties that policymakers in the region and beyond must grapple with during 2011. That tragic event has also underscored the need for collective disaster preparedness in the region.

The *2011 Survey* should be of great interest inside and outside the Asia-Pacific region. It aims to help ESCAP economies to implement policies that will protect their hard-won development gains and ensure that progress at the aggregate level translates into far more rapid improvements in the lives of the poor and vulnerable. I commend the information and analysis contained here to a wide global audience.

BAN Ki-moon
Secretary-General of the United Nations

April 2011

PREFACE

The economies of Asia and the Pacific recovered strongly in 2010 from the depths of the "Great Recession" of 2008/09 but they face fresh challenges in 2011. These include rising inflationary pressures, the return of food and fuel crises that are threatening hard-won development gains, sluggish recovery in the advanced economies, and a deluge of short-term capital flows that are causing volatility in capital markets and other problems. Furthermore, the devastation wrought by the recent earthquake and tsunami in Japan provides another stark reminder of the region's vulnerability to natural disasters. These challenges pose significant downside risks to an otherwise robust growth outlook as the region emerges as the growth pole of the global economy.

The key immediate challenge is to address rising food prices that are threatening to seriously undermine the process of poverty reduction. ESCAP projections reported in the *Survey 2011* suggest that as many as 42 million more people could remain in poverty in 2011 as a result, in addition to 19 million already affected in 2010. The challenge has to be addressed through a combination of policies at the national, regional and international levels including tariffs and tax policies, regulation of hoarding and speculative activity in food commodities, disciplining the conversion of food into biofuels, using buffer stocks in a countercyclical manner, and protecting vulnerable households through targeted subsidies. In the medium term, it is critical to increase food supply by paying greater attention to agriculture and rural development and to foster a new green revolution based on sustainable agriculture.

Another fundamental challenge for the medium term will be to boost domestic and regional sources of demand to sustain growth and reduce global macroeconomic imbalances. For that purpose, consumption can be boosted through the creation of employment for men and women and by strengthening social protection programmes, including the establishment of a minimum social floor. In the case of investment, funds should be directed to narrowing development gaps within and across countries, which are particularly large in the area of infrastructure.

The Asia-Pacific region is already moving towards exploiting the potential of regional economic integration for sustaining its dynamism. This is reflected in the rising shares of intra-regional trade and intra-regional foreign direct investment flows, and in improvements in connecting the region through transport, energy and ICT networks. However, much more can and should be done.

On the trade front, the region could leverage its regional trading arrangements so that they become building blocks for the creation of a seamless, broader and unified Asia-Pacific market. In light of the large trade complementarities across subregions, a broader approach to regional integration which focuses not just on deepening integration within subregions but also in fostering trade links across subregions would be fruitful. Promoting cooperation in energy security, strengthening transport connectivity covering not only its *hard* but also its *soft* dimension viz. trade and transport facilitation, and developing mechanisms for the financial intermediation between the region's huge savings and its equally huge investment needs are also key areas which should receive a high priority in the region's policy agenda.

Last but not least, for the benefits of regional integration to truly contribute to a more inclusive and balanced pattern of economic growth, special attention should be paid to the development of the least developed countries of the region. The *Survey* argues that a critical reason for their slow progress is their poor productive capacities, which do not allow them to take advantage of emerging opportunities in the region and beyond. These countries need to be assisted in building capacities-- not only to produce more of the same but to produce and trade new and more sophisticated products. The *Survey* argues that productive capacities can be built through a process of strategic diversification by the combined efforts of the State and the private sector, with a supportive role played by development partners, and it outlines a policy agenda for such an effort in the context of the forthcoming United Nations Conference on Least Developed Countries.

In sum, the Asia-Pacific region emerged from the global financial crisis as a growth driver and anchor of stability of the global economy. It now has the historic opportunity to rebalance its economic structure in favour of itself to sustain its dynamism with strengthened connectivity and balanced regional development and make the twenty-first century a truly Asia-Pacific century. The 2011 edition of the *Survey* reviews some of these issues and policy challenges. I hope that it will help shape the policy debate in the region.

Noeleen Heyzer
Under-Secretary-General of the United Nations and
Executive Secretary, United Nations Economic and Social
   Commission for Asia and the Pacific

EXECUTIVE SUMMARY

The Asia-Pacific developing economies have recovered well in 2010 from the global financial crisis of 2008/09. The dramatic V-shaped recovery witnessed in 2010 by the economies in the region was supported by massive fiscal stimulus packages along with renewed strength in exports. It helped the Asia-Pacific region emerge as a growth pole and a critical anchor for global recovery. As the recovery consolidates in 2011, the economies face fresh challenges, notably the rising inflationary pressures especially with the return of food and fuel crises. Furthermore, many export-driven Asia-Pacific economies could suffer the knock-on effects of sluggish growth in some advanced economies, including the United States of America and the European Union, in which some governments have undertaken drastic programmes to reduce deficits through spending cuts and tax increases. Moreover, there is a risk that some Asia-Pacific economies could be destabilized by volatile flows of speculative capital.

The 2011 earthquakes and tsunami in Japan will also have wide repercussions, though smaller than might have been expected initially. ESCAP estimates that a one percentage point slowdown of economic growth in Japan relative to 2011 baseline growth would result in a 0.1 percentage point slowdown in growth for the Asia-Pacific developing economies as a whole.

In the medium term, governments will also need to consider ways to boost domestic demand and intensify regional integration. In this light, the *Economic and Social Survey of Asia and the Pacific 2011* considers how to improve regional connectivity, and also indicates how the least developed countries can take advantage of this by increasing their productive capacities.

Growth outlook for 2011

The Asia-Pacific developing economies are projected to grow in 2011 at 7.3%, as the recovery process consolidates. This rate is down from the 8.8% growth achieved in 2010 which was high due to a low base, and partly due to the withdrawal of fiscal stimulus policies, adoption of tight money policies and sluggish recovery in the advanced economies. Economic growth in 2011 is expected to be broad-based. Growth projections of developing and transition economies by subregions are as follows: East and North-East Asia at 7.9%, North and Central Asia at 4.8%, the Pacific island developing economies at 5.5%, South and South-West Asia at 6.8%; and South-East Asia at 5.5%.

The region's large developing economies continue to power ahead. The fastest-growing economies in 2011 are expected to be China at 9.5% and India at 8.7% respectively, followed by Indonesia at 6.5%. The economies of India and Indonesia stand to benefit from robust consumption and investment, while China should benefit from the Government's measures to reorient towards a more consumption-driven economy.

However, in 2011 most economies are likely to see an increase in inflation. To some extent, inflationary pressures reflect a resumption in growth. Inflation also results from rising food and energy prices, which would have a particularly damaging impact on the poor and vulnerable populations. Furthermore, there are significant risks associated with the excess liquidity in developed countries, which is resulting in large inflows of speculative capital to Asia and the Pacific. This, in turn, is creating asset price bubbles as well as causing inflation and the appreciation of regional currencies.

The return of the food-fuel crises

Since early 2010, global food and oil prices have been on a sustained and synchronized upward trend. ESCAP estimates that oil price increases will reduce growth by up to one percentage point in some developing Asia-Pacific economies as well as put pressure on inflation and adversely affect current accounts. High oil prices will increase costs for domestic industry and push up the price of imports and reduce demand for exports.

Food prices have increased in various countries by up to 35%. While adverse climatic conditions have affected supply in many countries, increasing conversion of food crops into biofuels, export bans, hoarding and heightened speculative activity in food commodities backed by the massive injection of liquidity in the advanced countries have exaggerated the price surge. Rising food prices are having dire effects on the poor, and reversing hard won development gains. Due to the higher food and energy prices, ESCAP estimates that up to 42 million additional people across Asia and the Pacific may remain in poverty in 2011 in addition to the 19 million already affected in 2010. In the worst-case scenario in which food price inflation doubles in 2011 and the average oil price rises to $130 per barrel, achieving the Millennium Development Goal for many least developed countries would be postponed by up to a half a decade.

Depending on the degree of pass-through of food price inflation to prices of other products, and to related wage demands, governments may respond with monetary policy. However they will also need to address supply-side causes of food price increases. First, international cooperation through the United Nations and the G20 should be stepped up to curb financial speculation in food commodities and to regulate the diversion of food for biofuels. Second, price volatility for food grains should be addressed through the countercyclical use of buffer stocks. Third, vulnerable sections of the population should be protected through public food distribution systems, food vouchers or targeted income transfer schemes. In addition, prices could be reduced by lowering tariffs and/or taxes. Finally, in the medium term, efforts should be made to deliver a supply response by reversing the neglect of agriculture in public policy by enhancing support for agricultural research, development and extension and providing easier access to credit and other inputs in order to foster a new, knowledge-intensive "green revolution". It would also make agriculture more environmentally resilient while enhancing agricultural productivity. Agricultural productivity can also benefit from South-South and triangular cooperation on knowledge and technology transfer.

At the regional level, price shocks can be managed cooperatively by establishing regional food stocks such as the Rice Reserve Initiative of ASEAN+3 and the South Asian Association for Regional Cooperation Food Bank.

Managing capital inflows

Accommodative monetary policies and low interest rates in developed economies are prompting investors to seek higher returns in emerging markets in Asia and the Pacific. As a result, overseas funds are being placed in currency deposits and local bond and equity markets. Equity markets in the Republic of Korea, the Philippines and Thailand, for example, are already at their pre-crisis peaks. Many investors have also turned to the property markets, both in emerging economies such as China and high-income economies, such as Singapore and Hong Kong, China. As a result, the Asia-Pacific region has seen some the world's steepest increases in property prices.

Many economies in the region have current account surpluses, which would tend to put upward pressure on exchange rates. But capital inflows have introduced additional appreciation pressures, including for economies that are running current account deficits such as India. Most major currencies in the region have risen significantly since 2009.

Governments have attempted to insure against volatile capital flows by building up foreign exchange reserves. But this may be inadequate. A vulnerability yardstick developed by ESCAP indicates that the reserves of a number of countries are lower than their overall exposure to these vulnerabilities.

Capital controls should be seen as important elements of the policy tool kit for reducing the volatility of the capital flows, as recommended by ESCAP previously. Some economies in the region have imposed capital controls over the past year, an approach which is now supported even by the International Monetary Fund. Developed economies should also support the imposition of such controls by taking measures that deter capital outflows, such as taxing them or requiring high margin requirements on foreign exchange derivatives that mimic actual outflows.

Unemployment remains a concern for the vulnerable

Growth has supported a recovery in many labour markets but there are still acute concerns about the quality of jobs and the vulnerability of workers. The most serious problems are for young women and men, who are 3.2 times more likely than adults to be unemployed. In South-East Asia and the Pacific, that ratio rises to 4.7 times, the highest among the world's subregions. Across the region, some 1.1 billion workers remain in vulnerable employment. For instance, 47% of workers are living with their families on less than $2 a day, and 23% of workers are living in extreme deprivation on less than $1.25 a day.

As labour markets grow, policy makers need to focus more on quality jobs and incomes. A post-crisis macroeconomic framework should seek full employment for men and women as a core policy goal, besides economic growth targets, inflation and sustainable public finances. As countries in the region reconsider their fiscal policies, and their sustainability, it is critical to incorporate a basic social floor. In addition to reducing insecurity for the poor, improved social protection can support countries in their efforts to rebalance the sources of growth. The crisis has prompted some countries in the region, including Malaysia and the Philippines, to consider establishing unemployment insurance schemes, while India has expanded its national rural employment guarantee scheme.

Support alternative sources of demand

In the medium-term, Asia-Pacific exporting economies will need to generate more aggregate demand in the region to sustain their dynamism in order to mitigate some loss of demand from developed economies as they unwind the global imbalances by restraining debt-fuelled consumption. In particular, an ESCAP analysis finds that East Asian countries need to enhance consumption to drive future growth and investment in South-East Asian countries. With over 950 million people living on less than $1.25 a day, the region has lot of room for expanding consumption. Consumption rates can be enhanced by generating more household income, by such means as raising wages, enhancing employment opportunities or expanding social protection programmes, as discussed earlier.

In the context of enhancing investments, the ESCAP analysis shows that wide infrastructure gaps exist in the region, with the least developed countries particularly lagging behind in infrastructure development. According to estimates, closing these gaps could require annual investments of about $800 billion over the next decade. For this purpose it can not only use domestic resources, but also benefit from the region's considerable foreign exchange reserves. One option for using these would be an infrastructure development fund managed by a regional institution that could assist in intermediating between region's vast foreign exchange reserves and unmet investment needs. Asia-Pacific economies also have the opportunity to develop new greener industries, which would lead to savings on energy and materials, and provide more affordable products to the poor while maintaining growth and enhancing environmental sustainability.

Development-friendly global economic governance

The region must also exert its influence, through the G20 and other forums, in the process of reform of the international financial architecture to make it more development friendly. Important proposals in this regard include: establishing a special drawing rights-based global reserve currency that could be issued counter-cyclically; a global tax on financial transactions to raise resources for achieving the Millennium Development Goals and moderate short-term capital flows; and international regulations to curb excessive risk-taking by the financial sector. The approach adopted by the G20 to address global imbalances by restraining current account imbalances to a certain percentage of GDP is a good start. The G20, as a major forum for global policy coordination on economic issues, should also act decisively to moderate the volatility of oil and food prices which are highly disruptive to efforts to achieve sustainable development. In the area of oil price volatility, the G20, being the group of all major consumers, can match the power exercised over the oil markets by the cartel of producers viz. the OPEC. The two groups may demarcate a benchmark "fair" price of oil and agree to restrict the oil price movement within a band around it. An additional measure to moderate the volatility in the oil market is for the G20 to create a global strategic reserve that would release the oil counter-cyclically. In the case of food price volatility, the G20 may act to regulate the speculative activity in food commodities and discipline the conversion of cereals into biofuels. It may expedite the implementation of the L'Aquila Initiative on Food Security which includes a provision of financing to developing countries for food security. In these and other areas, the Asia-Pacific region can further coordinate its actions through its eight members of the G20 which would ensure that the global economic governance architecture meets the region's developmental needs. G20 can further enhance its credibility and effectiveness by evolving mechanisms for consultation with the non-member countries, as was arranged by ESCAP prior to the Seoul Summit.

Extending regional connectivity

Rapid growth in dynamic economies such as China and India can also benefit smaller and poorer neighbours as it helped in recovery of the region from the crisis. But this cannot be taken for granted. The rising tide of development opportunities will not lift all boats if these are separated by water locks. These obstructions can take the form, for example, of restrictive non-tariff measures, complicated and time-consuming customs procedures, differences in regulations, and poor transport infrastructure. As a result, the enormous opportunities generated by the more dynamic centres may stop at their national borders.

Intraregional trade

Intraregional trade among Asia-Pacific countries has expanded at a faster pace than their global trade bringing its share to nearly 52% in 2008. The analysis presented in the *Survey* shows that the potential of intraregional trade has not been fully exploited partly due to high trade costs and other barriers. The potential for greater trade is evident from the extent of complementarities between and within Asia-Pacific subregions – particularly between East and North-East Asia and South-East Asia, and within East and North-East Asia. Moreover, for four of the five ESCAP subregions trade complementarities were greater with other subregions than within the subregions themselves. Regional integration should, therefore, not just focus on deepening integration within subregions but also on fostering trade links across subregions.

Intraregional foreign direct investment

Trade is closely linked with foreign direct investment (FDI). In the past, inflows to Asia-Pacific countries came from developed countries, but currently, an increasingly larger proportion is coming from other countries in the region, notably China, India, Malaysia, the Russian Federation, and Singapore as these countries have companies that can offer much-needed investment and technological expertise to lower-income countries.

Preferential trading arrangements

The Asia-Pacific countries have been very active in pursuing preferential trading arrangements in recent years and by end of 2010, some 170 such agreement were in place in the region. These agreements tend to be bilateral or subregional in nature and consequently, do not create a seamless, broader and unified Asia-Pacific market. However, they can serve as stepping stones toward achieving that goal. Two important initiatives in that direction are the East Asia Free Trade Agreement (EAFTA) and the Comprehensive Economic Partnership of East Asia (CEPEA). In particular, CEPEA, covering about 80% of the region's population and GDP, and with greater potential of welfare gains for the participants, could constitute the nucleus for an incipient Asia-Pacific-wide free trade area to which other countries in the region could accede in the future. A complementary option would be a regional framework to link various subregional groupings in a preferential arrangement. As a broader regional forum with convening power, ESCAP could facilitate the emergence of such broader arrangements in the region. Considering the diverse levels of development in the region, the regional trading arrangements should not only include special and differential treatment provisions but also incorporate economic cooperation to narrow the development gaps.

Transport links

Rapid export growth has resulted in a sharp pick-up in maritime shipping. As of 2009, Asia had the world's top five container ports – Singapore; Shanghai, China; Hong Kong, China; Shenzhen, China and Busan, Republic of Korea – which accounted for 23% of the world's total container throughput. Much of the economic development has, however, been concentrated around major ports, leaving large hinterland areas relatively underdeveloped. Although land transport networks have improved, moving goods can still be very expensive because of long distances, high operating costs for trucks due to poor roads and ageing vehicles, high transhipment costs, and complex border- crossing procedures. In addition, the Pacific island developing economies face high costs because their small populations and low productive capacities make regular liner services unprofitable.

The Intergovernmental Agreement on the Asian Highway Network (AH) and the Intergovernmental Agreement on the Trans-Asian Railway Network (TAR) signed under the auspices of ESCAP have contributed to infrastructure investment and also triggered several multilateral initiatives. For instance, the Asian Development Bank (ADB), in collaboration with ESCAP, recently initiated a project on the development of priority AH routes and TAR lines. To assist in the integration of networks, ESCAP is developing a third intergovernmental agreement, which focuses on dry ports across the AH and TAR networks.

Trade and transport facilitation

Many countries now realize the importance of streamlining trade procedures. Consequently, they are relying more on electronic data interchange, and are looking to institute national electronic single windows through which traders can submit required documentation, pay duties, and receive clearance. The national single windows considerably help facilitate trade but in order to be effective, it needs to be accepted by all trading partners. Many regional trading arrangements now cover trade facilitation within their scope.

The overall efficiency of transport depends on the harmonization of legal regimes through international conventions. In the Asia-Pacific region, progress in this area has been uneven. The 12 landlocked countries in the region have acceded, on average, to only four of the seven relevant conventions, with their transit partners acceding to an even fewer number, leading to territorial discontinuity, which significantly reduces the conventions' effectiveness.

ICT connectivity

As a result of the rapid diffusion of mobile networks and services, many poor people now have access to telecommunication services. In contrast, the region's developing countries have very low broadband penetration, well below 10%, partly due to the cost of deploying land-based or submarine fibre-optic cables. However, there has been some progress in the Pacific, where some countries have benefited from linkages to existing cables.

In order to boost information and communications technology (ICT) connectivity, governments need to establish regulatory frameworks that promote the development of fair and competitive markets, establish compatible national standards and encourage innovative applications, such as mobile banking. At the regional level, it is important to take into account potential synergies between ICT infrastructure and other physical infrastructure. For example, rights of way for roads and railways, such as those established under the AH and TAR agreements, could also accommodate telecommunications cabling or base stations.

Energy connectivity

As the Asia-Pacific region has both large energy-importing and large energy-exporting countries, energy security would benefit from better physical connectivity between them as well as from institutions to promote cooperation. In this respect, the AH and TAR agreements serve as useful models. A potential regional energy arrangement should also consider issues of pipeline security and safety and explore low carbon paths that place more emphasis on efficiency and take greater advantage of renewable resources. Finally, it is important for the region to develop a deep, liquid and transparent market for crude oil, oil products, and gas. A structured Asia-Pacific regional energy dialogue may be established to foster energy cooperation on a sustained basis.

People-to-people connectivity: migration, overseas education, and tourism

People-to-people connectivity could help promote better mutual understanding, enhanced trust and greater respect for diversity, thus contributing to a culture of peace. The Asia-Pacific region is a growing source as well as destination of migrants for higher education and overseas employment, and is also experiencing rapid growth in tourism. While the majority of migrant workers in Asia and the Pacific leave the region, a significant proportion move within the region – most of them to neighbouring countries within the same subregion. Many of the subregions and countries in Asia and the Pacific have already taken some initiatives towards creating a legal framework for migration. North and Central Asia, ASEAN, and the Pacific have signed multilateral agreements, while some countries have established bilateral memoranda of understanding that establish guidelines and procedures for employment protection and the return of workers.

Financial cooperation

Asia and the Pacific has moved forward with regard to fostering regional cooperation through various initiatives, such as the Chiang Mai Initiative Multilateralization (CMIM), the Asian Bond Fund and the Asian

Bond Market Initiative. However, most of these initiatives are in their early stages and have limited scope and coverage. The region should build on CMIM to create a well-endowed, truly regional crisis response facility by expanding its membership to cover other systemically important countries and increasing its pool of resources. Additional elements of a regional financial architecture, that ESCAP is currently elaborating on include: achieving closer cooperation between central banks, financial institutions and capital markets; creating a large infrastructure development fund, improving exchange rate coordination; and capacity-building for harnessing the public-private partnerships for investment in infrastructure.

Building the productive capacity of the least developed countries

The least developed countries need to increase their productive capacity in order to benefit from greater connectivity and regional integration. Over the past 40 years, however, these countries have remained marginal exporters of manufactured goods. A renewed focus on building the productive capacity of the least developed countries should bring production and productive employment back to the development agenda. However, this should not mean simply producing more of the same goods and services; least developed countries need to expand the range of goods produced.

Diversification, however, is path dependent in the sense that products that a country produces today affect those it will be able to produce tomorrow. Therefore, the least developed countries must keep in mind strategic diversification when choosing new products and select those that would increase the range of possibilities for further diversification. But when left to the market forces alone, least developed countries often do not diversify along the path that would lead to higher possible future returns.

An assessment of the transformation of productive capacities of least developed countries in the Asia-Pacific region shows that these countries have lagged behind in the past two decades; not because they have reduced their productive capacity but because they have progressed more slowly than others. Moreover, few countries have been able to improve their productive capacities starting from levels similar to those of the Asia-Pacific least developed countries. That highlights the special circumstances that these countries face and the need to target assistance and strategies for the improvement of their productive capacities.

The experiences of developed and newly industrialized countries has demonstrated the critical role played by strong and active intervention by the "development State" in the early stages. A pragmatic strategy for least developed countries to build their productive capacities is to let these capacities be generated or acquired as part of the process of strategic diversification through the combined efforts of the State and the private sector with a supportive role played by development partners. The implementation of such strategy, as discussed at the ESCAP high-level policy dialogue on Asia-Pacific least developed countries in Dhaka in January 2010, would involve:

Stable investment-friendly macroeconomic policy framework: Least developed countries need to maintain strong macroeconomic fundamentals to foster productive investments for strong and sustained economic growth leading to expanding employment opportunities. Countries need to utilize the full scope of appropriate countercyclical policies to maintain economic and financial stability in the face of shocks to avoid abrupt economic fluctuations.

Industrial policy and infrastructure development: Active public intervention is required to create infrastructure and promotional measures that are covered under industrial policy, including infant industry protection to domestic industry in the early stages of development. Public investment could play a proactive role in infrastructure development and act as catalyst of public-private partnerships by creating a virtuous cycle of investment and spurring inclusive growth.

Domestic resource mobilization: Least developed countries also need to foster a diversified, well-regulated and inclusive financial system that promotes savings and channels them to productive investments. The domestic supply of long-term capital also needs to be increased by developing domestic capital markets, venture capital funds and term-lending institutions and industrial development banks to provide financing for the creation of new productive capacities. Governments should also provide appropriate and coordinated support to meet the rising demand for microfinance.

Technological upgrading: The scientific, technological and research and development capacities of the least developed countries need to be enhanced through national programmes, and supported by international institutions and programmes. Developed countries should facilitate technology transfer to least developed countries as required under the Article 66.2 of the TRIPS Agreement. It is also timely to consider setting up a technology bank for least developed countries, which could promote the transfer of key technologies, including pro-poor-, green-, agricultural- and renewable energy-related technologies.

Financing for development: The policies aimed at harnessing the development potential of FDI should stimulate productive investment, technological capacities, the development of infrastructure and the strengthening of linkages within and across sectors and between different enterprises. Least developed countries could also adopt associated policies, such as performance requirements, to facilitate technology transfer and diffusion from FDI. Intraregional FDI originating in other developing countries, as observed earlier, enhances the options for them. Development partners could assist in investment promotion through leveraging official development assistance (ODA) and by providing risk cover, and capacity-building for project development, among other policies.

Efforts need to be made to improve the quality of ODA and increase its development impact. There is also a need to set up special purpose thematic funds dedicated to least developed countries, such as a commodity stabilization fund, a technology fund, a diversification fund and environment-related funds. Aid for "new" purposes needs to be truly additional and should not divert resources from other internationally agreed goals.

Market access and aid for trade: Least developed countries need to be provided with enhanced and predictable market access, support for the establishment of export supply capacity that is competitive both in cost and quality, and new trade-related infrastructure. More transparent and simplified rules of origin and more comprehensive product coverage could improve the use and value of Generalized System of Preferences (GSP). In addition, developed countries and developing countries in a position to do so should implement fully the duty-free, quota-free market access as agreed in the Hong Kong WTO Ministerial Declaration.

The focus of aid for trade should be to assist least developed countries in building productive infrastructure and trade capacities to enable them to participate effectively in the multilateral trading system. Aid for trade should be aligned to the national development strategies. In addition, least developed countries should receive priority in the disbursement of funds.

South-South, triangular and regional cooperation: With the rise of emerging countries in the region as the growth poles of the world economy, South-South, triangular and regional cooperation have become viable strategies for development. An increasing number of countries, such as China, India, Malaysia, the Russian Federation, Singapore and Thailand, have well developed programmes for assisting other developing countries, especially their neighbouring least developed countries. Such initiatives should be further promoted and extended.

***

ACKNOWLEDGEMENTS

This report was prepared under the overall direction and guidance of Noeleen Heyzer, Under-Secretary-General of the United Nations and Executive Secretary of the Economic and Social Commission for Asia and the Pacific (ESCAP), and under the substantive direction of Nagesh Kumar, Chief Economist and Director of the Macroeconomic Policy and Development Division. The core team, led by Aynul Hasan, included Shahid Ahmed, Shuvojit Banerjee, Somchai Congtavinsutti, Clovis Freire, Alberto Isgut, Nobuko Kajiura, Daniel Jeongdae Lee, Muhammad Hussain Malik, Jorge Martinez-Navarrete, Margit Molnar, Amitava Mukherjee, Syed Nuruzzaman, Naylin Oo, Pisit Puapan and Marin Yari.

ESCAP staff who contributed substantively include: Hong Peng Liu, Kohji Iwakami and Lee Hu Ti of the Environment and Development Division; Cihat Basocak and Tiziana Bonapace of the Information and Communications Technology and Disaster Risk Reduction Division; Geetha Karandawala and K.V. Ramani of Office of the Executive Secretary; Vanessa Steinmayer of the Social Development Division; Rikke Munk Hansen, Erik Hermouet and Nongnuch Hiranyapaisansakul of the Statistics Division; Yann Duval, Mia Mikic and Marit Nilses of the Trade and Investment Division; Tengfei Wang and Jenny Yamamoto of the Transport Division; Iosefa Maiava, Michal Kuzawinski, Neema Majmudar and David Smith of the ESCAP Pacific Office; Eugene Gherman and Yejin Ha of the ESCAP Subregional Office for East and North-East Asia; Upali Wickramasinghe of the ESCAP Centre for the Alleviation of Poverty through Sustainable Agriculture.

Valuable advice, comments and inputs were received from many staff of the United Nations which include: Kee Beom Kim of the International Labour Organization; Pingfan Hong, Oliver Paddison, Ingo Pitterle and Rob Vos of the Department of Economic and Social Affairs, United Nations, New York; Sumiter Broca of the Food and Agriculture Organization of the United Nations, Bangkok; and Motohiro Kurokawa, Regional Office of the United Nations Industrial Development Organization, Bangkok, Thailand.

The following consultants provided country reports and other inputs: Ron Duncan, Ashima Goyal, Mohammad Kordbache, Alexander Kudrin and Andrey Shastitko.

The report benefited from extensive comments and suggestions from an eminent group of Asian policymakers, scholars and development practitioners, acting as external peer reviewers, namely: Yilmaz Akyüz, Chief Economist, South Centre, Geneva, Switzerland; Ramgopal Agarwala, Distinguished Fellow, Research and Information System for Developing Countries, New Delhi, India; Myrna Austria, Vice-Chancellor for Academics and Research, De La Salle University, Manila, Philippines; Zaid Bakht, Director, Bangladesh Institute of Development Studies, Dhaka, Bangladesh; Nonarit Bisonyabut, Research Fellow, Thailand Development Research Institute, Bangkok, Thailand; Caroline Brassard, Associate Professor, Lee Kuan Yew School of Public Policy, National University of Singapore, Singapore; Chantal Herberholz, Chulalongkorn University, Bangkok, Thailand; Ricardo Hausmann, Director of Harvard University's Center for International Development, Cambridge, Massachusetts, United States; César A. Hidalgo, Assistant Professor, Massachusetts Institute of Technology, Cambridge, Massachusetts, United States; Saman Kelegama, Executive Director, Institute of Policy Studies of Sri Lanka, Colombo, Sri Lanka; Ashfaque H. Khan, Director General and Dean, NUST Business School, National University of Sciences and Technology, Islamabad, Pakistan; Somchai Jitsuchon, Research Director, Thailand Development Research Institute, Bangkok, Thailand; Kyungsoo Kim, Deputy

Governor and Director General, Institute for Monetary and Economic Research, Bank of Korea, Seoul, Republic of Korea; Siwage Dharma Negara, Researcher, the Indonesian Institute of Sciences, Jakarta, Indonesia; Biman C. Prasad, Dean, the University of the South Pacific, Suva, Fiji; Jie Sun, Senior Fellow, Institute of World Economics and Politics, Chinese Academy of Social Sciences, Beijing, China.

Kiatkanid Pongpanich and Amornrut Supornsinchai of the Macroeconomic Policy and Development Division, ESCAP, provided research assistance.

The manuscript was edited by Orestes Plasencia, Alan Cooper, Sanoma Lee Kellogg, John Loftus, Editorial Unit of ESCAP and Peter Stalker. The graphic design was created by Marie Ange Sylvain-Holmgren, and the layout and printing were provided by Clung Wicha Press.

Woranut Sompitayanurak, supported by Metinee Hunkosol, Anong Pattanathanes and Sutinee Yeamkitpibul of the Macroeconomic Policy and Development Division, ESCAP, proofread the manuscript and undertook all administrative processing necessary for the issuance of the publication.

Francyne Harrigan, Thawadi Pachariyangkun and Chavalit Boonthanom of the United Nations ESCAP Strategic Communications and Advocacy Section, Bangkok, coordinated the launch and dissemination of the report.

CONTENTS

CONTENTS *(continued)*

CONTENTS (continued)

CONTENTS *(continued)*

BOXES

FIGURES

FIGURES *(continued)*

FIGURES *(continued)*

FIGURES *(continued)*

TABLES

EXPLANATORY NOTES

Staff analysis in the *Economic and Social Survey of Asia and the Pacific 2011* is based on data and information available up to the middle of April 2011.

The term "ESCAP region" in the present issue of the *Economic and Social Survey of Asia and the Pacific 2011* refers to the group of countries and territories/areas comprising Afghanistan; American Samoa; Armenia; Australia; Azerbaijan; Bangladesh; Bhutan; Brunei Darussalam; Cambodia; China; Cook Islands; Democratic People's Republic of Korea; Fiji; French Polynesia; Georgia; Guam; Hong Kong, China; India; Indonesia; Iran (Islamic Republic of); Japan; Kazakhstan; Kiribati; Kyrgyzstan; Lao People's Democratic Republic; Macao, China; Malaysia; Maldives; Marshall Islands; Micronesia (Federated States of); Mongolia; Myanmar; Nauru; Nepal; New Caledonia; New Zealand; Niue; Northern Mariana Islands; Pakistan; Palau; Papua New Guinea; Philippines; Republic of Korea; Russian Federation; Samoa; Singapore; Solomon Islands; Sri Lanka; Tajikistan; Thailand; Timor-Leste; Tonga; Turkey; Turkmenistan; Tuvalu; Uzbekistan; Vanuatu; and Viet Nam.

The term "developing ESCAP region" in this issue of the *Survey* excludes Australia, Japan, New Zealand and North and Central Asian economies from the above-mentioned grouping. Non-regional members of ESCAP are France, Netherlands, United Kingdom of Great Britain and Northern Ireland and United States of America.

The term "East and North-East Asia" in this issue of the *Survey* refers collectively to China; Hong Kong, China; Democratic People's Republic of Korea; Japan; Macao, China; Mongolia and Republic of Korea.

The term "North and Central Asia" in this issue of the *Survey* refers collectively to Armenia, Azerbaijan, Georgia, Kazakhstan, Kyrgyzstan, Russian Federation, Tajikistan, Turkmenistan and Uzbekistan.

The term "Central Asian countries" in this issue of the *Survey* refers collectively to Armenia, Azerbaijan, Georgia, Kazakhstan, Kyrgyzstan, Tajikistan, Turkmenistan and Uzbekistan.

The term "Pacific" in this issue of the *Survey* refers collectively to American Samoa, Australia, Cook Islands, Fiji, French Polynesia, Guam, Kiribati, Marshall Islands, Micronesia (Federated States of), Nauru, New Caledonia, New Zealand, Niue, Northern Marina Islands, Palau, Papua New Guinea, Samoa, Solomon Islands, Tonga, Tuvalu and Vanuatu.

The term "South and South-West Asia" in this issue of *the Survey* refers collectively to Afghanistan, Bangladesh, Bhutan, India, Islamic Republic of Iran, Maldives, Nepal, Pakistan, Sri Lanka and Turkey.

The term "South-East Asia" in this issue of the *Survey* refers collectively to Brunei Darussalam, Cambodia, Indonesia, Lao People's Democratic Republic, Malaysia, Myanmar, Philippines, Singapore, Thailand, Timor-Leste and Viet Nam.

Bibliographical and other references have not been verified. The United Nations bears no responsibility for the availability or functioning of URLs.

The designations employed and the presentation of the material in this publication do not imply the expression of any opinion whatsoever on the part of the Secretariat of the United Nations concerning the legal status of any country, territory, city or area, or of its authorities, or concerning the delimitation of its frontiers or boundaries.

Mention of firm names and commercial products does not imply the endorsement of the United Nations.

The abbreviated title *Survey* in footnotes refers to the *Economic and Social Survey of Asia and the Pacific* for the year indicated.

Many figures used in the *Survey* are on a fiscal year basis and are assigned to the calendar year which covers the major part or second half of the fiscal year.

Growth rates are on an annual basis, except where indicated otherwise.

Reference to "tons" indicates metric tons.

References to dollars ($) are to United States dollars, unless otherwise stated.

The term "billion" signifies a thousand million. The term "trillion" signifies a million million.

In the tables, two dots (..) indicate that data are not available or are not separately reported; a dash (–) indicates that the amount is nil or negligible; and a blank indicates that the item is not applicable.

In dates, a hyphen (-) is used to signify the full period involved, including the beginning and end years, and a stroke (/) indicates a crop year, fiscal year or plan year. The fiscal years, currencies and 2010 exchange rates of the economies in the ESCAP region are listed in the following table:

Country or area in the ESCAP region	Fiscal year	Currency and abbreviation	Rate of exchange for $1 as at January 2011
Afghanistan	21 March to 20 March	afghani (Af)	45.28
American Samoa	..	United States dollar ($)	1.00
Armenia	1 January to 31 December	dram	363.02
Australia	1 July to 30 June	Australian dollar ($A)	1.01
Azerbaijan	1 January to 31 December	Azerbaijan manat (AZM)	0.80
Bangladesh	1 July to 30 June	taka (Tk)	71.15
Bhutan	1 July to 30 June	ngultrum (Nu)	45.95
Brunei Darussalam	1 January to 31 December	Brunei dollar (B$)	1.29
Cambodia	1 January to 31 December	riel (CR)	4 052.00
China	1 January to 31 December	yuan (Y)	6.59
Cook Islands	1 April to 31 March	New Zealand dollar ($NZ)	1.30
Democratic People's Republic of Korea	..	won (W)	98.10
Fiji	1 January to 31 December	Fiji dollar (F$)	1.83
French Polynesia	..	French Pacific Community franc (FCFP)	87.11
Georgia	1 January to 31 December	lari (L)	1.81
Guam	1 October to 30 September	United States dollar ($)	1.00
Hong Kong, China	1 April to 31 March	Hong Kong dollar (HK$)	7.80
India	1 April to 31 March	Indian rupee (Rs)	45.95
Indonesia	1 April to 31 March	Indonesian rupiah (Rp)	9 057.00
Iran (Islamic Republic of)	21 March to 20 March	Iranian rial (Rls)	10 352.00
Japan	1 April to 31 March	yen (¥)	82.05
Kazakhstan	1 January to 31 December	tenge (T)	146.87
Kiribati	1 January to 31 December	Australian dollar ($A)	1.01
Kyrgyzstan	1 January to 31 December	som (som)	47.27
Lao People's Democratic Republic	1 October to 30 September	new kip (NK)	8 041.23
Macao, China	1 July to 30 June	pataca (P)	8.03
Malaysia	1 January to 31 December	ringgit (M$)	3.06
Maldives	1 January to 31 December	rufiyaa (Rf)	12.80
Marshall Islands	1 October to 30 September	United States dollar ($)	1.00
Micronesia (Federated States of)	1 October to 30 September	United States dollar ($)	1.00
Mongolia	1 January to 31 December	tugrik (Tug)	1 245.01
Myanmar	1 April to 31 March	kyat (K)	5.52[a]
Nauru	1 July to 30 June	Australian dollar ($A)	1.01
Nepal	16 July to 15 July	Nepalese rupee (NRs)	73.15
New Caledonia	..	French Pacific Community franc (FCFP)	87.11
New Zealand	1 April to 31 March	New Zealand dollar ($NZ)	1.30
Niue	1 April to 31 March	New Zealand dollar ($NZ)	1.30
Northern Mariana Islands	1 October to 30 September	United States dollar ($)	1.00
Pakistan	1 July to 30 June	Pakistan rupee (PRs)	85.70
Palau	1 October to 30 September	United States dollar ($)	1.00
Papua New Guinea	1 January to 31 December	kina (K)	2.63
Philippines	1 January to 31 December	Philippine peso (P)	44.09
Republic of Korea	1 January to 31 December	won (W)	1 114.30

Country or area in the ESCAP region	Fiscal year	Currency and abbreviation	Rate of exchange for $1 as at January 2011
Russian Federation	1 January to 31 December	ruble (R)	29.67
Samoa	1 July to 30 June	tala (WS$)	2.36
Singapore	1 April to 31 March	Singapore dollar (S$)	1.29
Solomon Islands	1 January to 31 December	Solomon Islands dollar (SI$)	8.06
Sri Lanka	1 January to 31 December	Sri Lanka rupee (SL Rs)	111.10
Tajikistan	1 January to 31 December	somoni	4.40
Thailand	1 October to 30 September	baht (B)	31.14
Timor-Leste	1 July to 30 June	United States dollar ($)	1.00
Tonga	1 July to 30 June	pa'anga (T$)	1.82
Turkey	1 January to 31 December	Turkish lira (LT)	1.60
Turkmenistan	1 January to 31 December	Turkmen manat (M)	2.85
Tuvalu	1 January to 31 December	Australian dollar ($A)	1.01
Uzbekistan	1 January to 31 December	Uzbek som (som)	1 651.00
Vanuatu	1 January to 31 December	vatu (VT)	93.15[a]
Viet Nam	1 January to 31 December	dong (D)	18 932.00

Sources: United Nations, *Monthly Bulletin of Statistics* website, unstats.un.org/unsd/mbs/app/DataSearchTable.aspx, 5 April 2011; and national sources.

[a] December 2010.

ABBREVIATIONS

ADB	Asian Development Bank
AFTA	ASEAN Free Trade Area
APEC	Asia-Pacific Economic Cooperation
APTA	Asia-Pacific Trade Agreement
ASEAN	Association of Southeast Asian Nations
BIMSTEC	Bay of Bengal Initiative for Multi-Sectoral Technical and Economic Cooperation
CD-ROM	compact disk read-only memory
CEPEA	comprehensive economic partnership for East Asia
c.i.f.	cost, insurance and freight
CIS	Commonwealth of Independent States
CMI	Chiang-Mai Initiative
CMIM	Chiang Mai Initiative Multilateralization
COMTRADE	United Nations Commodity Trade Statistics
CPI	consumer price index
EAFTA	East Asia free trade agreement
ECO	Economic Cooperation Organization
ECOTA	Economic Cooperation Organization Trade Agreement
EPZs	export processing zones
FAO	Food and Agriculture Organization of the United Nations
FDI	foreign direct investment
f.o.b.	free on board
FTAs	free trade agreements
G20	Group of Twenty
G-7	Group of Seven
GDP	gross domestic product
GNI	gross national income
GSP	Generalized System of Preferences
ICT	information and communications technology
IEA	International Energy Agency

ABBREVIATIONS *(continued)*

ILO	International Labour Organization
IMF	International Monetary Fund
JETRO	Japan External Trade Organization
LNG	liquefied natural gas
M1	demand deposit
M2	broad money supply
Mtoe	million tons of oil equivalent
NAFTA	North American Free Trade Agreement
ODA	official development assistance
OECD	Organization for Economic Cooperation and Development
OFDI	outward foreign direct investment
OPEC	Organization of the Petroleum Exporting Countries
RTAs	regional trade agreements
SAARC	South Asian Association for Regional Cooperation
SAFTA	South Asia Free Trade Area
SATIS	SAARC Agreement on Trade in Services
SDRs	special drawing rights
SEACEN	South East Asian Central Banks
SEANZA	South East Asia, Australia and New Zealand
SITC	Standard International Trade Classification
SMEs	small and medium-sized enterprises
TNCs	transnational corporations
TRIPs	Trade-related Aspects of Intellectual Property Rights
UNCTAD	United Nations Conference on Trade and Development
UNESCO	United Nations Educational, Scientific and Cultural Organization
UNNExT	United Nations Network of Experts for Paperless Trade in Asia and the Pacific
VAT	value added tax
WHO	World Health Organization
WTO	World Trade Organization

SOURCES OF QUOTATIONS

(a) Page 1: an excerpt from the speech of Prime Minister Manmohan Singh (India) at the Annual Conference of the Chief Secretaries, February 2011 (source: http://www.indianexpress.com/news/corruption-inflation-hurt-growth-pm/746403/).

(b) Page 51: an excerpt from the speech of President Susilo Bambang Yudhoyono (Indonesia) at Davos World Economic Forum, January 2011 (source: http://www.embassyofindonesia.org/news/2011/01/news124.htm).

(c) Page 107: an excerpt from the statement of President Hu Jintao (China) at G20 Seoul Summit, 12 November 2010 (source: http://www.fmprc.gov.cn/eng/topics/hujintaoG20di5cifenghuiheAPEC18cihuiyi/t769609.htm).

(d) Page 153: an excerpt from the opening statement by Prime Minister Sheikh Hasina (Bangladesh) at the WIPO Regional Forum, 19 July 2010 (source: http://www.pmo.gov.bd/index.php?option=com_content&task=view&id=536&Itemid=353).

(e) Back cover: an excerpt from the Foreword of this *Survey* by Ban Ki-moon, Secretary-General of the United Nations.

"The only lasting solution for food price inflation lies in increasing agricultural productivity ... the public distribution system needs to be strengthened..."
Manmohan Singh, Prime Minister of India

Sustaining Dynamism and Inclusive Development

The Asian and Pacific region has recovered strongly from the 2008/09 recession but it is not out of the woods yet. The global environment in 2011 is turning more difficult than that of 2010, as it will require dealing with a multiplicity of concurrent challenges. As demand from the developed world continues to remain sluggish, the region is being further assailed by a resurgence in food and energy prices, with the repercussions of a host of natural disasters in the region having further impacts on both economic growth and prices. Nevertheless, the divergence in overall growth prospects for the region in the coming years as compared with the developed world suggests a central role for the Asian and Pacific region in driving its own development and, at the same time, being a critical anchor for the global recovery from the recession.

The region's growth recovery has come under pressure in recent months from increasing price pressures, driven by dramatic increases in global food and energy prices as well as the resumption of robust growth after the global crisis. Excess global liquidity has been partly responsible for the commodity price rises, coupled with supply disruptions in key producing economies due to geo-political instability and adverse climatic conditions. This supply-side inflationary pressure has disproportionately hurt the poorest and most vulnerable sections of society in the region and made the ongoing challenge of inclusive development an increasingly urgent issue. High food prices will have the greatest direct impact on livelihoods in developing economies but high energy prices may also substantially affect the region. ESCAP has estimated that high oil prices could lead to a reduction in growth of up to 1 percentage point for some developing ESCAP economies in 2011. High energy prices would increase the input costs for industry in the region, which is more energy intensive than in developed economies. Demand for exports from the region would be affected if the growth recovery in the developed economies is impacted, with the risk of some degree of "stagflation" in the developed world. ESCAP has estimated that high food and energy prices in 2011 may lead to as many as 42 million additional people in the region living in poverty. It is possible that up to half a decade could be lost in the battle to achieve the Millennium Development Goals in many countries of the region, with poverty in some of the least developed countries being among the worst affected by the price rises.

Another key short-term challenge for the region, stemming from the developed countries' recovery measures to stimulate their economies, is the impact of the enormous liquidity injections undertaken by those countries to revive their economies. Favourable growth prospects and comparatively high interest rates in developing economies have attracted large foreign portfolio inflows from international investors to asset markets in the region. These capital inflows have led to potential asset market bubbles in some countries and boosted demand-

side inflationary forces. Additionally, capital inflows have led to pressure for exchange rate appreciation, thereby hampering the recovery of exports from the region.

Exacerbating these short-term threats has been a host of natural disasters that have afflicted the region in the past year. The catastrophic earthquake and tsunami which struck Japan in March 2011 has affected both the country itself and the wider region due to the key role of Japan in the interconnected Asia-Pacific economy. Other major disasters resulting

> *The region's growth recovery has come under pressure in recent months driven by dramatic increases in global food and energy prices*

in loss of life and having a severe impact on domestic economies include flooding in Pakistan and the earthquake in New Zealand. Climatic conditions, such as drought or excess rainfall, have also had impacts on a host of food-producing economies, such as Australia, China, India and Kazakhstan, as well as economies outside the region. The reduction in food supply has been an important element underlying the rise in regional food prices. While specific natural disasters may be difficult to predict, overall trends indicate that Asia and the Pacific as a whole has suffered the maximum losses when compared with different regions of the world suffering from such incidents in recent decades.[1] It is therefore imperative that the possibility of such disasters be integrated as a key downside risk into regional economic and social policymaking while adopting measures to increase the resilience of economies, thereby mitigating the effect of such shocks.

The major medium-term challenge for the region continues to be the slow pace of recovery of the developed world, as many leading developed countries continue to see sluggish GDP growth in 2011. And the likelihood that these countries are unlikely to be as significant a growth driver for the region as before the crisis. The continuing export dependence on developed country markets of many small economies in the region will mean that growth rates in the region will be impacted. Conversely, an increasing trend of intraregional trade with markets characterized by large domestic demand in the region should provide some replacement of the contribution of exports to developed country markets.

The approach to managing these challenges shares a common element: the need for greater regional cooperation. The main alternatives to economic growth which depends on exports to developed countries lie in boosting domestic demand in the large economies of the region and increasing intraregional trade in goods destined for consumption and investment within these economies. Regionally coordinated action to manage foreign portfolio inflows among the affected countries would be fruitful because any particular economy not imposing controls on capital may otherwise be penalized by the financial markets. Furthermore, as put forward by the Group of Twenty (G20) countries, coordination of exit policies, in particular of revoking deposit guarantees, is needed as such a measure could have a significant impact on the flow of capital. The recent lifting of blanket deposit guarantees in

a coordinated fashion by the monetary authorities of Hong Kong, China; Malaysia and Singapore is an example of successful coordination. Regional food prices can be managed through the use of regional food reserves. The cross-country nature of many natural disasters makes regional cooperation critical in mitigating risks and impacts. In these and a host of other areas, it is evident that the time has come for the Asian and Pacific region to further integrate and coordinate its policies, thus not only ensuring its recovery and future dynamism but also supporting the global recovery to the greatest extent possible.

Recovery under pressure

Stellar performance in 2010

The region witnessed a dramatic recovery in economic growth in 2010 following the 2008/09 recession (see figure 1.1). While large economies with significant domestic private demand weathered the crisis with only moderate decreases in growth, many export-oriented economies started moving into positive growth territory only around the third quarter of 2009. The key driver of the private sector recovery for the most adversely affected economies in the region in 2010 was renewed strength in the export and investment

Figure 1.1.   Real growth in gross domestic product, year-on-year, in selected Asian developing economies, 2008-2010

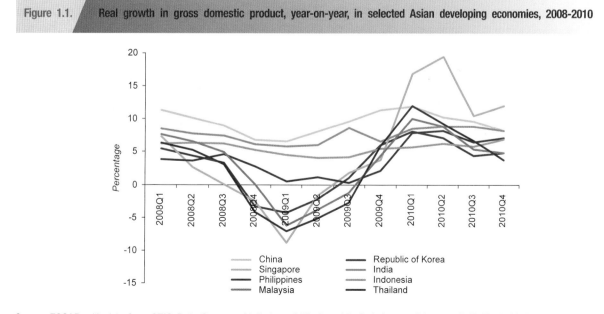

Source: ESCAP, with data from CEIC Data Company Limited, available from http://ceicdata.com/ (accessed 10 March 2011).

sectors, following the initial critical support to growth through massive fiscal stimulus packages. Exporting economies began their recoveries in part through intraregional sales to the large robust economies, particularly China which further spurred its domestic demand with significant stimulus, and eventually to developed economies, which saw improved demand from late 2009 onwards in response to their own stimulus policies.

The past year has seen the recovery of the most adversely affected economies to pre-crisis income levels. Since year-on-year growth numbers in a crisis are influenced by the base effect of low growth in the previous period, absolute gross domestic product (GDP) numbers give a better picture of the extent of recovery in the region. It can be seen that GDP in a number of key export-oriented economies recovered and surpassed pre-crisis GDP levels during late 2009 (see figure 1.2), implying that the income shock at the aggregate level had lasted for approximately one year.

Despite headwinds to growth emerging in 2010 due to the slow recovery in the developed world, growth for the region as a whole remained impressive in global terms. As was the situation in 2009, the Asia-Pacific region was by far the fastest-growing region

in the world, with close to double the growth rate of the next highest growth performers. This brings into stark relief the role of the region as a possible growth locomotive for the global economy.

The growth impact on other regions comes from Asia and the Pacific serving as a source of demand for the goods and, even more so, for the commodities of other regions. Since many manufactured goods are produced within the region as well as in the developed economies of the world, the main impact on other developing regions has come from demand for their commodities which are not available within the region. Thus, producers of manufactured goods in other developing regions may not obtain a significant lift to their growth from demand in the region due to a lack of competitive advantage, whereas commodity producers may obtain a greater impact. The influence of Asia-Pacific demand was seen during 2010, especially in Latin America and Africa, with increased trade and investment in commodity-related sectors. Asia now takes up to 27% of Africa's exports compared with 14% in 2000, with the new figure being similar to the ratio of Africa's exports to its traditional trading partners: the United States of America and Europe.[2] Exports of primary materials to Asia were one of the principal factors underlying the high growth of

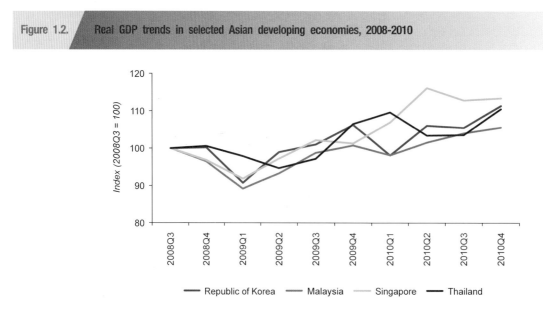

Figure 1.2. Real GDP trends in selected Asian developing economies, 2008-2010

Republic of Korea — Malaysia — Singapore — Thailand

Source: ESCAP, with data from CEIC Data Company Limited, available from http://ceicdata.com/ (accessed 24 February 2011).

exports from the Latin America and the Caribbean region in 2010, with the region's exports to China estimated to have grown by 49%.[3]

Coping with sluggish growth in developed countries

General consumption and specifically demand for exports from developed economies continues to be restrained as the economies' recovery process continues. This can be seen from the fact that absolute GDP in these economies has yet to recover to pre-crisis levels (see figure 1.3). Sluggish recovery in the developed world is partly responsible for the lower export growth numbers being witnessed in the region in recent months (see figure 1.4).

Growth in the United States in the fourth quarter of 2010 remained moderate at 2.8% (year-on-year). The slow recovery has emanated from the lower

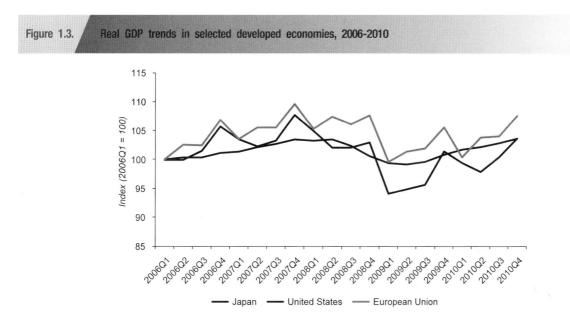

Figure 1.3.   Real GDP trends in selected developed economies, 2006-2010

Source: ESCAP, based on data from CEIC Data Company Limited, available from http://ceicdata.com/ (accessed 22 March 2011).

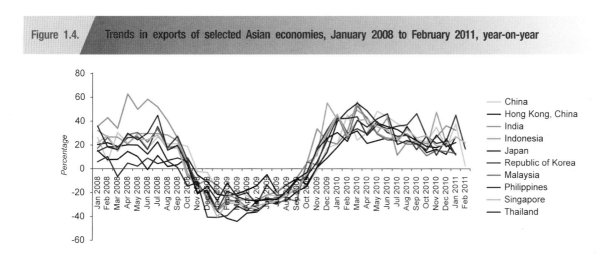

Figure 1.4.   Trends in exports of selected Asian economies, January 2008 to February 2011, year-on-year

Source: ESCAP calculations based on data from CEIC Data Company Limited, available from http://ceicdata.com/ (accessed 23 March 2011).

consumption of households paying off their debt burdens, and the impacts of low house prices and high unemployment rates. On a similar note, growth in the European Union in the fourth quarter of 2010 slowed from 2.1% in the previous quarter to 2.0%, with a wide diversity of performance among economies in the region.[4] Sluggish growth in the United States and the European Union has had a negative impact on export-related growth in Germany, the best performing major economy in the European Union. Growth in other major economies of the European Union continues to be constrained by low consumption, compounded by fiscal retrenchment that will increasingly act as a drag on growth during 2011. The overall close-to-neutral fiscal stance of advanced European countries in 2010 will turn contractionary in 2011.[5]

The growth prospects for Japan are subject to a great deal of uncertainty currently, as the longer-term repercussions of the recent natural disaster in the country become clearer. Prior to the disaster Japan was engaged in some further moderate fiscal stimulus measures, although concerns about the size of the budget deficit restricted the amount of stimulus. However, post-disaster reconstruction will clearly result in enormous additional spending, with careful consideration required on the appropriate financing mix through borrowing and revenue generation in order to ensure both fiscal sustainability and growth recovery. While reconstruction itself is likely to have a stimulative effect on the domestic economy and on the Asia-Pacific region through greater demand for imports, the cost of recovery will impose a high burden on the budget and may have serious macroeconomic repercussions. A raising of taxes to meet the reconstruction costs may dampen consumption while increased borrowing may result in rising interest rates. The short to medium-term concern regarding growth is also due to the possible impact of reconstruction on the Japanese yen. The immediate aftermath of the disaster saw repatriation and speculation regarding such repatriation of money back to Japan, which substantially increased the exchange rate for the yen. Concerted action by the Group of Seven (G-7) countries subsequently

reversed this appreciation, although if such elevated levels of the yen were to re-emerge the country's exports may be significantly affected. Furthermore, production in the economy may be reduced beyond normal levels for an extended period due mainly to energy disruption. The export sector remains critical to the Japanese economy in the presence of continued weak domestic demand, but even before the disaster the sector had been beset by slow United States demand for its high-end products both as direct exports and as inputs for onward export from China. The rate of export growth remained volatile throughout most of 2010, driving the sharp fall in quarterly GDP growth in year-on-year terms in the fourth quarter of 2010.

While there is the risk of below-baseline growth in Japan in 2011 due to the disaster, it is expected that the direct impact on the region will be limited

While there is the risk of slowdown in growth below baseline in Japan in 2011 due to the disaster, it is expected that the direct impact on the region will be limited. ESCAP has estimated that a 1.0 percentage point slowdown in Japan relative to 2011 baseline growth would result in only a 0.1 percentage point slowdown for Asia-Pacific developing economies as a whole (see box 1.1). The economies most adversely affected would be Singapore (an impact of 0.24 percentage point), Indonesia (0.16 percentage point) and Malaysia and Thailand (0.13 percentage point). In terms of the direct impact on export growth numbers, developing Asia-Pacific economies as a whole would see a reduction in export volume growth of 0.35 percentage point, with the economies most affected being Indonesia (an impact of 0.49 percentage point), Malaysia (0.46 percentage point) and China (0.42 percentage point). The economies experiencing the greatest impact on GDP growth are those with the strongest trade ties with Japan and those where their exports to Japan are a more important driver of overall GDP growth. In general, the lack of substantial

Box 1.1. Implications of the earthquake in Japan on developing Asia

The earthquake and tsunami that took place in north-eastern Japan on 11 March 2011 resulted in a devastating death toll, massive destruction of property and the displacement of hundreds of thousands of people. The disaster also damaged nuclear power plants, resulting in several explosions and prompting the evacuation of the surrounding population.

Based on the latest news and assessments of the earthquake and tsunami damage, growth in Japan is expected to lag 0.2-0.3 percentage points behind earlier forecasts in 2011, with the second quarter having the largest reduction in GDP growth. One of the major reasons that the immediate economic damage to Japan is not expected to be significant as the affected region is mostly an agricultural area with some raw material industries, such as oil, steel and pulp, accounting for 6.5% of the country's GDP.   Nonetheless, the underlying assumption is that the national impact of the disaster will be limited so long as major economic centres such as Tokyo avoid prolonged disruption.   Moreover, reconstruction in the affected area should provide an economic boost in the following year. However, the impact of the earthquake and tsunami is likely to have longer-term repercussions in other aspects, particularly domestic supply-chain interruptions. These disasters produced significant aftershocks in the markets for Japanese stocks, government bonds and the yen. They severely interrupted the supply of nuclear power, which accounts for nearly 30% of the total electricity production in Japan, therefore affecting the ability of industries to maintain normal production. Information remains incomplete, but at least 10 reactors automatically shut down in response to the earthquake, meaning that Japan faces a potential loss of around 15%-20% of its total nuclear energy capacity.

In assessing the implications for the Asia-Pacific region of a slowdown in Japan due to the disaster, it is expected that the impact on developing countries in the region should not be substantial. Overall, the ESCAP simulations in the framework of the Oxford Economic Forecasting model, under the assumption of the worst-case scenario that the growth of the Japanese economy would shrink by 1.0 percentage point from the baseline growth in 2011. This suggests that the growth impact for the developing countries of the Asia-Pacific region would be around 0.10 percentage point from the baseline mainly through export linkage, as exhibited in the decline in export volume growth by 0.35 percentage point from the baseline. Despite the overall moderate economic impact, some countries may be more adversely affected than others.   Based on the sensitivity analysis, Singapore may be relatively more affected in terms of economic growth, while Indonesia may experience a relatively greater impact in terms of export performance, due to the scenario of lower Japanese economic growth in 2011. It should be borne in mind that exports for countries in the region may be further affected due to disruption in inputs from Japan as part of regional production chains.

Table. Scenario: Economic growth decline of 1.0 per cent in 2011 in Japan from baseline

	Impact on economic growth	Impact on export growth
China	-0.12	-0.42
India	-0.03	-0.20
Indonesia	-0.16	-0.49
Malaysia	-0.13	-0.46
Philippines	-0.09	-0.41
Republic of Korea	-0.06	-0.23
Singapore	-0.24	-0.28
Thailand	-0.13	-0.35
Developing Asia-Pacific economies	-0.10	-0.35

Notes: Impacts are shown in terms of absolute percentage difference from the baseline; and impacts on exports are based on constant prices in dollars.

Apart from the direct impacts of a slowdown in Japan exerted through the trade channel, the region may be affected through other channels. Developing Asia-Pacific countries still depend significantly on Japanese investment flows, particularly foreign direct investment; it remains to be seen how the disaster would affect the Japanese corporate sector and its investment decisions in the coming months and years.

Source: ESCAP analysis.

impact on the region is related to the diminishing importance of Japan as an export market for the region. However, the effect will be significant on select industries, such as automobiles and electronics, due to disruption of supply chains, although this will be for a limited period. An industry that is likely to face a backlash from the disaster is the nuclear power industry as countries begin to rethink their reliance on this source of power generation in view of safety concerns. It is also likely that any slowdown in Japan due to the disaster will have various other impacts which are not considered in this analysis, such as a slowdown in aid disbursements and foreign direct investment, as both the Government and the private sector redirect funds home from abroad.

The likelihood of further stimulus in the developed economies to support growth is limited due to growing concerns about fiscal sustainability

---

The likelihood of further stimulus in the developed economies to support growth is limited due to growing concerns about fiscal sustainability. For example, while the United States decided on further stimulus measures in December 2010 the amount of stimulus remains limited, especially after discounting the extension of existing tax cuts; actual new fiscal stimulus measures are far lower than the headline figure. Such a moderate amount of new stimulus is unlikely to have a large effect on the speed of recovery. Some European Union member States experienced the greatest pressure to consolidate fiscally. Early 2010 saw the onset of a sovereign debt crisis through a sharp increase in debt financing costs in some European Union economies owing to the lack of confidence of international financial investors in the ability of those Governments to repay their growing debt burdens. This has persuaded the imperiled Governments, as well as other economies under less immediate financial market pressure in the region, to shift from a policy of fiscal stimulus to drastic programmes to reduce deficits through spending cuts and tax increases.

Monetary policy in the United States is unlikely to exert a significant additional impact in supporting the country's growth, while leading to substantial repercussions globally through depreciating the dollar (see section entitled *Managing capital inflows*). Quantitative easing is aimed at boosting domestic demand by increasing asset prices and therefore household wealth, encouraging borrowing through lowering interest rates and encouraging lending through increasing the amount of funds available to the banking sector. However, each of these avenues may not be effective in practice. The household wealth effect of increasing asset prices such as equities may not increase consumer spending when the public is still contending with the major impact of the housing downturn on their wealth, and because the increase in asset prices may be viewed as temporary. Quantitative easing may not increase lending by reducing interest rates significantly to jump-start borrowing, as those rates are already at low levels even with the inclusion of the risk premium to lend to individuals and companies. Such easing is also not appearing to increase the extension of credit from banks to the private sector.

Japan has continued to undertake monetary stimulus through quantitative easing, having taken various moves during the course of 2010 and 2011 to inject funds into the banking sector. Such stimulus had been undertaken partly to revive growth in the economy before the recent earthquake and to maintain economic confidence after the disaster, as well as to exert downward pressure on the yen which had seen rapid appreciation at a time when other major currencies had depreciated sharply. However, as is the case in the United States, the concern for monetary stimulus as a strategy to support growth in Japan is that already-low interest rates could not be decreased substantially and that banks might be unwilling to use any extra liquidity to further increase the extension of credit to the private sector as the banks already possessed sufficient funds and have chosen not to do so. The European Union is unlikely to stimulate economies by monetary easing owing to its central bank being more concerned about potential inflationary pressures as a result of such measures.

Managing the blowback from the European debt crisis

The Asia-Pacific economies should prepare for possible spillovers from the public debt crisis in a number of European economies.[6] In recent months, the bailouts of Greece, Ireland and Portugal, as well as concerns about Spain, have led to credit downgrades across many European economies and increases in the debt servicing costs of those countries. In response, Governments have pledged to decrease their levels of debt in the coming years through stringent programmes of budget cuts, as affirmed by the G20.[7] Global financial markets have yet to be convinced that the affected countries will be able to reduce public debt to a level viewed as sustainable by the financial markets. The worst-case scenario of sovereign debt defaults in one or more European countries at some point remains a concern.

The risk for Governments in Asia and the Pacific lies in the possibility that any financial contagion would spark off another seizure in global inter-bank lending, arising from uncertainty regarding the extent to which banks in developed countries hold financial assets in the affected countries and the possibility of losses through default on some of these assets. The concern is that the scale of investments in financial products would be underestimated and that the full range of transmission mechanisms through which these products could spread contagion between financial institutions would not be recognized until it is too late. While the banking sector in most of the region is healthy at the domestic level, in some economies it is exposed to global shocks due to dependence on borrowings from abroad. In a number of economies, banks are carrying loans that exceed domestic deposits (see figure 1.5), necessitating wholesale funding from foreign banks. As with the subprime crisis, banking operations in such cases have the potential to be disrupted by an international credit crunch during which affected banks in other regions are unwilling or unable to engage in inter-bank lending.[8] There may also be an impact on asset markets in the region, as affected financial institutions in developed countries withdraw

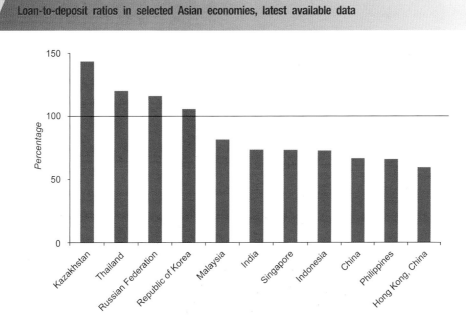

Figure 1.5.   Loan-to-deposit ratios in selected Asian economies, latest available data

Sources: ESCAP, based on data from CEIC Company Limited, available from http://ceicdata.com/ (accessed 15 February 2011); IMF, India: 2010 Article IV Consultation-Staff Report, IMF Country Report No. 11/50 (Washington, D.C., February 2011); Kazakhstan: 2010 Article IV Consultation-Staff Report, IMF Country Report No. 10/241 (Washington, D.C., July 2010); and the Philippines: 2010 Article IV Consultation-Staff Report, IMF Country Report No. 11/59 (Washington, D.C., March 2011).

Notes: Kazakhstan data refer to May 2010. Indonesian data refer to December 2009. Philippine data refer to June 2010. Indian data refer to 2009/10. Republic of Korea and the Russian Federation data refer to Q3 2010. Hong Kong, China; Malaysia and Singapore data refer to October 2010.

from portfolio investments in Asia and the Pacific in an attempt to cash in on profitable investments to offset losses that occurred during the debt crisis.

While the Asia-Pacific region currently has not been affected to a substantial degree by the spillover from the European debt crisis, it is necessary to be watchful as the crisis has the potential to worsen in the coming months, with the risk of possibly greater contagion. In this climate of uncertainty, policymakers in the region should adopt measures to protect their economies against contagion from the debt crisis. Governments that are at risk of sharp withdrawals of external financing and a credit crunch should maintain channels for rapid liquidity support to their financial sectors in the case of a financial shock from abroad. These channels, which were established in the wake of the subprime crisis, are currently being wound up following the region's growth recovery. These measures will be most applicable not only to those economies that are exposed through foreign trade or external financing needs, but also to those that may experience excessive attention from the international investment community in the form of large inflows of speculative capital.

Exports recover strongly in 2010

Since their nadir in mid-2009, the exports of many Asian economies grew strongly until mid-2010,

painting a picture of a V-shaped recovery. The rebound of exports that started in mid-2009 resulted in the quarterly value of exports returning to pre-crisis levels by mid-2010 in most developing economies of Asia (see figure 1.6). There was very little variation in the pace of the export rebound of the countries in the five subregions.[9] Even the countries which prior to the crisis followed somewhat different paths of export growth have started to converge towards the median values, such as Mongolia in East and North-East Asia, Armenia in North and Central Asia, Samoa in the Pacific and Viet Nam in South-East Asia. Similarly, the sectors which traditionally have been labelled as export-oriented, such as electric machinery, footwear and textiles, all grew at a similar pace in most of the dynamic trading economies.

It is clear that intraregional demand was an important factor in export recovery in the initial part of the crisis. The imports of China from major suppliers of parts and components in Asian countries fell sharply and several months prior to the time when the United States began cutting its imports from China[10] (see figure 1.7). Spurred partly by large fiscal stimulus measures, domestic demand in China contributed the vast majority of GDP growth in the economy, that is, 92% in 2010. Robust domestic demand spurred demand for imports, which grew by 38.7% in 2010,[11] thereby boosting the exports of other economies in the region. Prior to a recovery in the exports from

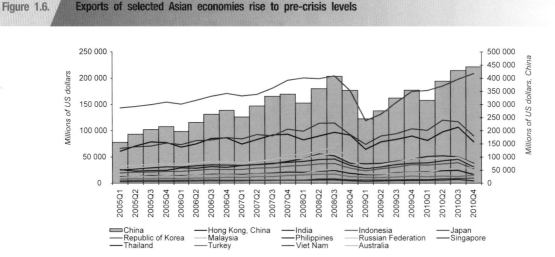

Figure 1.6. Exports of selected Asian economies rise to pre-crisis levels

Source: ESCAP calculations based on data from CEIC Data Company Limited, available from http://ceicdata.com/ (accessed 23 March 2011).

China to the United States, the country had already started to increase its imports from Asian countries (see figure 1.7),[12] and countries exporting goods for final demand in China experienced a faster growth rate for exports than those exporting intermediate goods from the second quarter of 2009. These trends suggest that there have been two engines of growth in the recovery: one involves exports to economies outside the region and the supply of inputs to China for processing and onward export, and the other involves exports intended to satisfy final demand in China which was being fuelled by the strength of domestic demand during the crisis and supported by various stimulus packages. While final demand in China has played an important role in the export recovery of the region, the future role of that economy in providing an alternative source of final demand within the region may be lower due to the withdrawal of fiscal stimulus, albeit on an increasing trend. This outcome will be a continuation of the ongoing process of rebalancing the economy of China, without the temporary contribution of fiscal stimulus measures, as long-term actions to increase domestic consumption continue to bear fruit.

India is playing a growing role in driving the exports of the region.[13] Unlike China, which tends to dominate in manufactured exports of finished goods, India has always been a net importer of goods from countries in the region, except for the Republic of Korea with which it has a positive trade balance. As India continues to grow at robust rates, its imports will provide buoyant demand in the region. Even more significant than net trade figures in the region's trade with India might be the sharp contrast in complementarities of competitive structure. India is a global leader in the export of services, especially commercial services; whereas the comparative advantage for many of the region's trading partners lies in manufactures and commodities. Hence, the Agreement on Trade in Goods under the Framework Agreement on Comprehensive Economic Cooperation between the Association of Southeast Asian Nations and the Republic of India, which went into effect on 1 January 2010, and continuing negotiations in services and investments appear promising for regional integration. The agreement marks intensification of the "Look East" strategy of India and the need for ASEAN countries to engage with rapidly growing markets and to balance their relations with all major Asian economic powers.

Given that export growth has moderated for many economies in recent months, the question is the extent to which future export growth is likely to be hampered. The relevant factors which started to

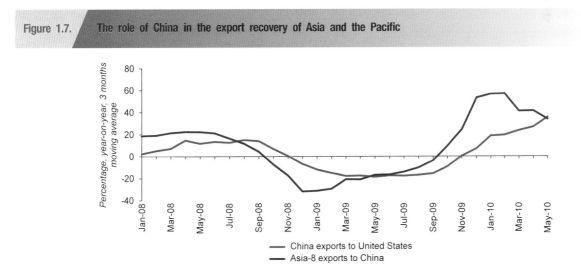

Figure 1.7.   The role of China in the export recovery of Asia and the Pacific

— China exports to United States
— Asia-8 exports to China

Source: ESCAP calculations based on data from CEIC Data Company Limited.

Notes: Export growth rates are expressed in percentages as three-month moving averages, year-on-year. Asia-8 comprises Hong Kong, China; Taiwan Province of China; Republic of Korea; Singapore; Malaysia; Indonesia; Thailand and the Philippines.

take effect about the same time in 2009 to drive the export growth recovery of Asian economies were the following: (a) the need to rebuild inventories in the importing developed economies, as well as in the Asian economies which are hosting major components in the established global and regional supply chains; (b) successful measures to stimulate domestic demand in large regional economies, most importantly China; and (c) continuing competitive strengths of Asian exporters and their ability to diversify.[14] The stylized facts are presented in the rest of the section in support of these arguments.

The "trading-out of crisis" approach used in the past needs modification- traditional markets need to be partially replaced by developing countries and by local demand

---

The source of recovery is of course the key factor in understanding how durable the export sector will be. Some economies in Asia, such as China, India and Indonesia, were able to exploit domestic demand to partially make up for the lack of external demand, but most other economies still depend on exports as an engine of growth. This means that access to "two engines of growth" is not an immediate option for many smaller developing economies and their reliance on exports will continue. Export orientation was one of the key factors of quick rebound from the Asian financial crisis of 1997/98. The then most adversely affected Asian economies were able to continue their expansion of exports to developed country markets, predominantly in the European Union and the United States, which were not affected by the (regional) crisis.[15] During the 2008-2009 crisis, it was the developed countries where demand collapsed, so the "trading-out of crisis" approach used in the past needed modification: traditional destination markets needed to be (partially) replaced by new markets of developing countries (within and outside the region) and by local demand.

An important point is that, even in a switch from traditional to regional markets, it is still exporting

which is relied upon by many economies in the region to sustain their recovery and growth, rather than production for the local (domestic) market. The exploration of trade flows prior to and during the crisis shows that most ESCAP economies saw exports and imports contract both globally and regionally. For the economies where data exist, during the recovery the shares in more recent months changed only slightly in favour of intraregional trade, particularly with China. However, this was in a situation of recovering developed country demand in 2010. If such demand were to stagnate, the resilience of intraregional demand might increase the relative contribution of intraregional exports.

Intraregional flows help foreign direct investment to recover

The region saw strong recovery in foreign direct investment (FDI) flows in 2010 although performance across countries varied greatly. Indonesia, Japan, Malaysia, Thailand, the Republic of Korea and China recorded robust growth rates in FDI inflows of 48%, 41%, 32%, 18%, 14% and 12%, respectively, and Viet Nam posted a 3% increase relative to that of the previous year. In contrast, inflows dropped sharply in some other countries, with a 22% drop in India, 14% in Pakistan and 13% in the Russian Federation (see figure 1.8). The good performance of much of the region is in contrast to that of the global FDI environment, which remains circumspect. It is expected[16] that there will be a slow but steady recovery in global FDI flows. FDI flows in the world are estimated to have increased modestly to about $1.12 trillion in 2010 from $1.11 trillion in 2009. FDI flows in the region, on the other hand, are increasing as a result of the comparatively healthy growth prospects for the region and the increase in South-South investment flows.

While the effects of the global crisis were felt most in the developed countries, which have traditionally been the main FDI source for the region, developing countries in Asia and the Pacific have gained importance and are expected to become an increasingly complementary source of FDI,[17] as

| Figure 1.8. | Percentage growth/decline of FDI inflows of selected Asian economies, 2008/09 versus 2009/10 |

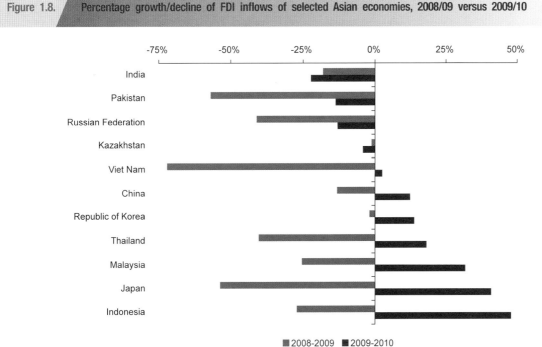

Source: ESCAP calculations based on data from CEIC Data Company Limited, available from http://ceicdata.com/ (accessed 23 March 2011).

Note: All 2009-2010 growth rates are whole year figures, except for Kazakhstan and Malaysia which are for quarters 1-3 only.

described in chapter 3. Comparison with 2000 data reveals that the Asia-Pacific region, particularly East and North-East Asia, has increased its share of FDI inflows to China in 2009, although South-East Asia slightly reduced its share. As a result, both Europe and North America reduced their shares in 2009. While Asian FDI in ASEAN countries dropped from 2007 to 2009, its share in aggregated FDI inflows to the subregion showed an increase in 2009 as compared with that in 2007 (see table 1.1). The European Union and the United States, two traditional FDI sources for ASEAN, reduced both their amounts and shares of FDI in ASEAN in 2009 compared with those in 2007.

There is a growing trend of intraregional FDI inflows to India. The share of Asia-Pacific economies in the FDI inflows to India increased from 8% in 2004 to 20% in 2010. At the same time, both Europe and the United States, two major sources of FDI in India, saw their shares decline significantly (from 36% to 17% for Europe and from 20% to 7% for the

United States), although both increased the amounts of their FDI inflows to India, especially before the outbreak of the recent global economic crisis. Among the subregions in Asia and the Pacific, South-East Asia and East and North-East Asia dominated the FDI inflows to India, posting an approximately 99% share (60% for South-East Asia and 39% for East and North-East Asia) of the total.[18]

Remittance flows to the Asia-Pacific region remain robust

The Asia-Pacific region, in comparison with other major remittance-receiving regions of the world, continued to record positive growth in remittance flows even during the height of the global economic crisis. While all other financial flows to developing countries in the region dropped rapidly, remittance flows remained resilient mainly due to the large and stable stock of labour migrants in a diversified range of host countries, including the countries belonging to the Gulf Cooperation Council (Saudi Arabia, Kuwait,

Table 1.1. Major sources of FDI inflows to ASEAN, 2007-2009

Region/economy	2007 (millions of US dollars)	Share (%)	2008 (millions of US dollars)	Share (%)	2009 (millions of US dollars)	Share (%)
Asia	**25 191**	**34**	**22 005**	**44**	**14 939**	**38**
Japan	8 829	12	4 658	9	5 308	13
ASEAN	9 682	13	10 462	21	4 429	11
Hong Kong, China	1 496	2	1 447	3	1 582	4
China	1 684	2	2 110	4	1 510	4
Republic of Korea	2 716	4	1 583	3	1 422	4
Taiwan Province of China	785	1	1 745	4	688	2
European Union	**17 766**	**24**	**9 520**	**19**	**7 297**	**18**
United States	**8 068**	**11**	**5 133**	**10**	**3 358**	**8**
Offshore financial centres	**4 855**	**7**	**4 664**	**9**	**4 180**	**11**
Others	**18 517**	**25**	**8 178**	**17**	**9 850**	**25**
Total	**74 395**	**100**	**49 500**	**100**	**39 623**	**100**

Source: ESCAP, based on data from the ASEAN Secretariat (2010).

Note: Offshore financial centres include Bermuda and Cayman Islands.

Bahrain, Qatar, the United Arab Emirates, and the Sultanate of Oman) and neighbouring Asia-Pacific economies that fared better in the crisis. Also, in countries such as Pakistan, government initiatives to promote the use of formal channels of remittances led to a remarkable growth in recorded remittance inflows. In addition, remittances for investment purposes would likely have increased during the crisis period when most Asian currencies weakened against the dollar. Overall, in 2010, remittance inflows to South Asia grew by an estimated 10.3%. Similarly, East Asia and the Pacific saw remittances grow by an estimated 6.4% to $91 billion.

In 2010, the Asia-Pacific region remained the world's largest remittance-receiving region. India and China were the largest remittance-receiving countries in the Asia-Pacific region, followed by the Philippines, Bangladesh, Pakistan, Viet Nam and Indonesia (see figure 1.9). Remittance flows to Central Asian countries rebounded in 2010 after experiencing a decline in 2009. Remittances to Central Asian countries were more vulnerable to the impact of the crisis largely owing to their heavy dependence on the Russian Federation as the primary migrant-receiving country. The loss was especially severe for Kyrgyzstan and Tajikistan, given their reliance on remittances.

Remittances are especially significant for small economies. Among the 10 countries in the Asia-Pacific region with the largest remittance-to-GDP ratios in 2010, seven of them were least developed countries, landlocked developing countries or small island developing States. In Tajikistan, although still the country with the highest remittances-to-GDP ratio, the percentage dropped from 49.6% in 2008 to 37% in 2010 due to the large losses in remittances as a result of the global economic crisis. In Nepal and Tonga, remittances became even more important as a result of the crisis.

In 2010, the largest year-on-year growth rates in remittances were experienced by Nepal and the Philippines, while in Bangladesh and Pakistan the growth rates slowed considerably (see figure 1.10). The lower growth rate of remittance inflows in Bangladesh mirrors the drop in migrant worker deployment from that country. Pakistan, on the other hand, saw a surge of remittances in June and July 2010 as a response to the floods that devastated the country.

In looking ahead, while remittances to the Asia-Pacific region grew robustly in 2010, there are a number of factors that could have an impact on future flows to the region. First and foremost, the sluggish recovery and

Figure 1.9.   Top 10 remittance-receiving Asia-Pacific economies, 2008-2010

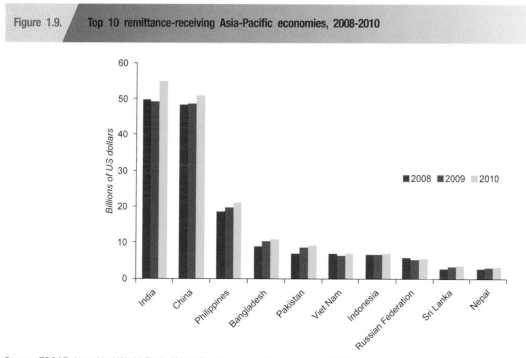

Source: ESCAP, based on World Bank, World Development Indicators online, 2010.

Note: Remittances refer to workers' remittances and compensation of employees.

Figure 1.10.   Remittance growth in selected Asian developing economies, 2008/09 and 2009/10

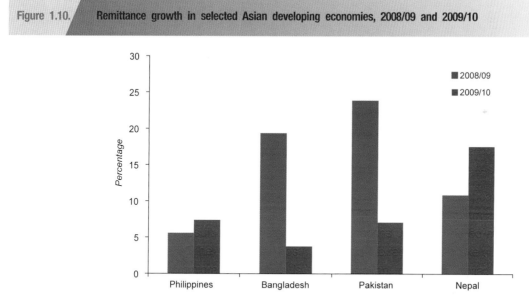

Source: ESCAP, based on World Bank Database, 2010.

soft labour markets in some of the major remittance-sending countries could weigh down the income of migrant workers. Also, as a result of persistently high unemployment in some of the traditional host countries, the risk of further immigration controls is significant. For example, in the United Kingdom of Great Britain and Northern Ireland, the number of immigrants from non-European Union countries has been restricted, and Australia shortened the list of occupations under its skilled migration programme in an effort to reduce the intake of migrants.[19] For workers earning an income in dollar terms, the weakening dollar vis-à-vis their home country currency, coupled with rising inflation in the Asia-Pacific region, could also reduce their incentive for sending remittances home for investment purposes.

One of the ways to offset the impact of negative external factors on remittance flows is to improve the financial infrastructure underlying remittances. Among the critical issues are enhancing remittances by regularizing informal remittance channels, improving regulatory and institutional frameworks, and reducing the money transfer transaction costs. Migrants face several challenges in accessing formal financial institutions. Stringent identification and documentation requirements to open bank accounts compel migrants to divert a larger share of remittance transfers into informal channels.

Remittances, mainly from workers, have generally had a huge impact on small island States. However, the amount remitted has fluctuated over time. Small States, such as Tonga, Haiti, Jamaica, the Dominican Republic, Cape Verde, Kiribati and Guinea-Bissau, were among the top 20 remittance-receiving countries in the world.[20] In the Pacific it has traditionally been Samoa and Tonga which have been the largest recipients of remittances, accounting for about 25% of their GDP. More recently, however, remittances have become increasingly important in other Pacific islands. These include Fiji, Kiribati, Solomon Islands and Vanuatu. Between 2004 and 2007, the remittance receipts of Fiji accounted for about 6% of its GDP. Since then the country's remittance receipts declined in 2007, 2008 and in 2009, coinciding with the global economic crisis. These figures, however, underestimate the true magnitude of receipts since they represent only those officially recorded. A large proportion of remittances is transferred through informal means and these support consumption and to a lesser extent productive investment.[21]

Growth outlook for 2011

Growth to moderate

Growth in developing economies of the region is forecast to be 7.3% in 2011. It represents a decline

compared to 8.8% achieved in 2010. The 2010 growth rates were particularly high, partly because they represented a recovery from a low base or trough due to recession in 2009. Besides the base effect, the 2011 growth slowdown also reflects the effect of withdrawal of fiscal stimulus policies, of tighter monetary policy adopted in some countries to meet the challenge of rising inflation, and also that of sluggish recovery in the developed economies of the world. The slower growth in exports driving some of the growth slowdown in developing economies began to become evident during the course of 2010 and this trend is expected to continue during 2011, with impacts on other components of GDP growth over time, thus driving some of the overall slowdown in growth in exporting economies.

The Asia-Pacific region will remain by far the most dynamic growth region in the world in 2011

The forecast growth rate in 2011 is similar to that experienced by the region in the early part of the previous decade (see figure 1.11). A return to the growth rates seen before the period of pre-crisis debt-driven consumption in the developed economies would indicate the need to look to alternative sources of growth within the region to maintain the dynamism of Asia-Pacific economies. Indeed, the divergence between the growth forecasts (see figure 1.11) of the largest developing economies in the region and the other developing economies also illustrates the potential to benefit from the dynamism of the former.

Despite the moderation in growth in 2011, the Asia-Pacific region will remain by far the most dynamic growth region in the world. As was the case in 2010, the Asia-Pacific region will remain the locomotive of global growth, with its growth rate being nearly one and a half times more than that of any other region of the world (see figure 1.12).

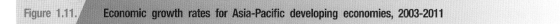

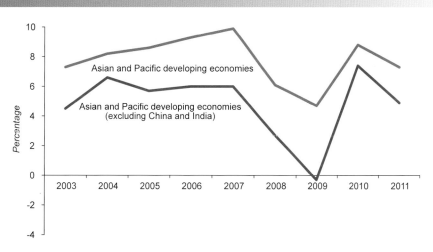

Figure 1.11.   Economic growth rates for Asia-Pacific developing economies, 2003-2011

Sources: ESCAP calculations based on table 1.2.

Note: GDP growth for 2010 and 2011 are estimates and forecasts respectively.

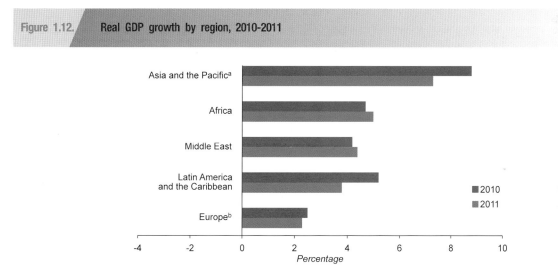

Figure 1.12.   Real GDP growth by region, 2010-2011

Sources: ESCAP calculations based on data from the United Nations regional commissions.

a   Developing economies in the ESCAP region.
b   Developed and developing member countries of the European Economic Commission.

Exporting economies experience greatest impact

Subregions for which exports are a key driver of growth will experience the most significant moderation in growth, after the rapid increase of the previous year. South-East Asia is expected to experience the greatest moderation in growth, from 8.1% in 2010 to 5.5% in 2011 (see figure 1.13). Similarly, the economic growth rate of developing economies in East and North-East Asia is expected to slow from 9.4% in 2010 to 7.9% in 2011. Conversely, subregions where domestic demand is important will see relatively solid growth performance. The South and South-West Asian subregion is forecast to see growth decelerate slightly, from 7.5% in 2010 to 6.8% in 2011. Subregions where commodities play a substantial role are expected to experience robust growth in 2011. North and Central Asia are

Figure 1.13. **Real GDP growth and forecasts of Asia-Pacific economies by subregions, 2008-2011**

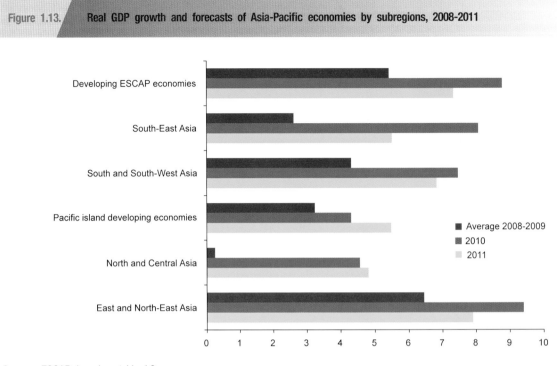

Sources: ESCAP, based on table 1.2.

Notes: Rates of real GDP growth for 2010 are estimates and those for 2011 are forecasts (as of 8 April 2011). Asian and Pacific developing economies comprise 37 economies (excluding those in North and Central Asia). East and North-East Asia in this figure excludes Japan. The calculations are based on the weighted average of GDP figures in dollars in 2009 (at 2000 prices).

expected to see relatively stable growth at 4.8% in 2011. Pacific island developing economies are forecast to see higher growth at 5.5% in 2011 after having grown by 4.3% in 2010.

Large developing economies in the region will continue to grow strongly in 2011. The fastest-growing major economies in the region in 2011 are expected to be China and India, with estimated growth rates of 9.5% and 8.7%, respectively, followed by Indonesia at 6.5% (see table 1.2). Factors that will contribute to their steady performance in 2011 include robust consumption and investment in India and Indonesia, both of which countries are characterized by the increasing wealth of their populations, and in China by gradually increasing consumption due to government measures to reorient the economy towards a more consumption-driven one.

After experiencing a strong rebound driven by export growth and fiscal stimulus measures, export-dependent economies will experience some slow down in 2011. Some deceleration in the region in 2011 would be inevitable, given the especially high growth rates seen in 2010 due to the base effect of low to negative values of growth in 2009. However, the concern is that medium-term growth in the developed economies may remain moderate in coming years as the effects of stimulus end and the economies remain beset by low private consumption and high private and public debt. This indicates the risk that the previous growth model, which was dependent on exports to developed economies, may pose: a reduction in the growth trend for exporting economies in coming years. To replace this loss, there is a compelling need to increase intraregional exports in order to benefit from growth in large domestic demand-led economies, as well as in many cases to increase domestic demand in the exporting economies through investment, which has decreased substantially in many of these economies since the 1997 Asian financial crisis (see figure 1.28).

Table 1.2.   Selected economies of the ESCAP region: rates of economic growth and inflation, 2007-2011

(Percentage)

	Real GDP growth					Inflation[a]				
	2007	2008	2009	2010[b]	2011[c]	2007	2008	2009	2010[b]	2011[c]
East and North-East Asia[d,e]	6.7	2.8	-1.0	6.4	4.5	2.2	3.7	-0.2	1.2	2.4
East and North-East Asia (excluding Japan)[d,e]	11.4	7.1	5.8	9.4	7.9	4.0	5.4	0.0	3.0	4.0
China	14.2	9.6	9.1	10.3	9.5	4.8	5.9	-0.7	3.3	4.5
Democratic People's Republic of Korea	-1.2	3.1	-0.9	..	..	..	..	..	..	..
Hong Kong, China	6.4	2.2	-2.8	6.8	4.9	2.0	4.3	0.5	2.4	4.0
Japan	2.4	-1.2	-6.3	3.9	1.5	0.1	1.4	-1.4	-0.7	0.6
Macao, China	26.0	12.9	1.3	35.0	9.2	5.6	8.6	1.2	2.8	3.4
Mongolia	10.2	8.9	-1.3	6.1	9.0	9.0	25.1	6.3	10.1	16.0
Republic of Korea	5.1	2.3	0.2	6.1	4.5	2.5	4.7	2.8	3.0	3.6
Taiwan Province of China	6.0	0.7	-1.9	10.1	4.7	1.8	3.5	-0.9	1.0	1.5
North and Central Asia[d]	9.1	5.9	-5.4	4.6	4.8	9.6	14.5	10.8	7.1	8.2
Armenia	13.7	6.9	-14.2	2.6	4.0	4.4	9.0	3.4	8.2	7.0
Azerbaijan	25.0	10.8	9.3	5.0	5.5	16.6	20.8	1.5	5.7	7.0
Georgia	12.3	2.1	-3.9	6.0	5.0	9.2	10.0	1.7	7.1	8.0
Kazakhstan	8.9	3.3	1.2	7.0	6.2	10.8	17.2	7.3	7.1	8.0
Kyrgyzstan	8.5	8.4	2.3	-1.4	5.0	10.2	24.5	6.8	8.0	10.5
Russian Federation	8.1	5.6	-7.9	4.0	4.3	9.0	14.1	11.7	6.9	8.0
Tajikistan	7.8	7.9	3.4	6.5	6.0	21.5	20.4	6.5	6.5	9.0
Turkmenistan	11.6	10.5	6.1	8.0	9.5	6.3	13.0	10.0	12.0	14.0
Uzbekistan	9.5	9.0	8.1	8.5	8.5	12.3	12.7	14.1	9.3	10.0
Pacific[d,e]	4.5	2.3	1.2	2.6	2.4	2.3	4.4	1.9	2.7	3.4
Pacific island developing economies[d,e]	5.0	4.3	2.2	4.3	5.5	2.7	10.3	6.7	4.7	6.1
Cook Islands	9.5	-1.2	-0.1	0.5	2.0	2.5	7.8	6.6	3.5	4.2
Fiji	-0.5	-0.1	-3.0	0.1	1.3	4.8	7.7	6.8	4.0	3.0
Kiribati	0.4	-1.1	-0.7	0.5	1.8	4.2	11.0	8.4	0.8	6.7
Marshall Islands	3.3	-2.0	0.0	0.5	1.2	2.6	14.7	0.5	1.0	5.0
Micronesia (Federated States of)	-0.1	-2.9	-1.0	0.5	1.0	3.6	6.8	7.4	3.5	4.0
Nauru	-27.3	1.0	0.0	0.0	4.0	2.3	4.5	2.2	-0.5	2.4
Palau	-0.5	-4.9	-2.1	2.0	2.0	3.2	11.3	5.2	3.8	4.0
Papua New Guinea	7.2	6.6	5.5	7.1	8.0	0.9	10.8	7.0	6.0	8.2
Samoa	2.3	5.0	-4.9	0.0	2.5	4.5	11.5	6.6	1.0	3.0
Solomon Islands	10.3	7.3	-1.2	4.0	7.0	7.7	17.3	7.1	3.0	4.2
Tonga	-1.2	2.0	-0.4	-1.2	0.8	5.1	9.8	5.0	2.0	3.0
Tuvalu	4.9	1.3	-1.7	0.0	0.0	2.2	10.4	0.0	-1.9	1.5
Vanuatu	6.8	6.3	3.8	3.0	4.0	4.1	4.8	4.5	3.4	5.0
Developed countries[d]	4.5	2.2	1.2	2.6	2.3	2.3	4.4	1.8	2.7	3.4
Australia	4.6	2.6	1.3	2.7	2.3	2.3	4.4	1.8	2.7	3.2
New Zealand	3.4	-0.8	0.1	1.5	2.4	2.4	4.0	2.1	2.3	4.6
South and South-West Asia[d,f]	7.6	4.7	3.9	7.5	6.8	8.3	11.4	11.0	10.3	8.6
Afghanistan	16.2	3.4	22.5	8.9	6.8	13.0	26.8	-8.3	8.2	9.5
Bangladesh	6.4	6.2	5.7	5.8	6.4	7.2	9.9	6.7	7.3	7.2
Bhutan	17.9	4.7	6.7	6.8	7.2	5.2	8.8	3.0	6.1	7.5
India	9.2	6.7	8.0	8.6	8.7	6.2	9.1	12.4	11.0	7.4
Iran (Islamic Republic of)	6.9	2.5	1.5	3.0	3.5	18.4	25.4	10.8	12.0	17.0
Maldives	7.2	5.8	-2.3	4.8	4.0	7.4	12.3	4.0	6.0	7.2
Nepal	2.8	5.8	4.0	3.5	4.0	6.4	7.7	13.2	10.7	8.0
Pakistan	6.8	4.1	1.2	4.1	2.8	7.8	12.0	20.8	11.7	15.5
Sri Lanka	6.8	6.0	3.5	8.0	8.0	15.8	22.6	3.4	5.9	7.5
Turkey	4.7	0.7	-4.7	8.1	5.0	8.8	10.4	6.3	8.6	6.0

Table 1.2 *(continued)*

(Percentage)

	Real GDP growth					Inflation[e]				
	2007	2008	2009	2010[b]	2011[c]	2007	2008	2009	2010[b]	2011[c]
South-East Asia[d]	6.6	4.2	1.0	8.1	5.5	4.0	8.8	2.3	4.0	4.8
Brunei Darussalam	0.2	-1.9	-1.8	2.0	1.7	0.3	2.7	1.8	1.8	2.1
Cambodia	10.2	6.7	-2.0	6.0	6.2	7.7	25.0	-0.7	4.1	6.0
Indonesia	6.3	6.0	4.5	6.1	6.5	6.3	10.1	4.8	5.1	6.2
Lao People's Democratic Republic	7.8	7.2	7.6	8.0	8.3	4.5	7.6	0.0	5.4	6.1
Malaysia	6.5	4.7	-1.7	7.2	5.2	2.0	5.4	0.6	1.7	3.0
Myanmar	11.9	3.6	4.9	5.5	5.8	32.9	22.5	8.0	7.9	9.1
Philippines	7.1	3.7	1.1	7.3	5.2	2.8	9.3	3.2	3.8	4.5
Singapore	7.8	1.8	-0.8	14.5	5.0	2.1	6.6	0.6	2.8	3.3
Thailand	4.9	2.5	-2.2	7.8	4.5	2.2	5.5	-0.8	3.3	3.5
Timor-Leste	9.1	11.0	11.6	7.9	8.2	10.3	9.1	0.7	6.5	7.5
Viet Nam	8.5	6.3	5.3	6.8	6.2	8.3	23.1	6.9	9.0	11.0
Memorandum items:										
Developing ESCAP economies[g]	9.9	6.1	4.7	8.8	7.3	5.0	7.3	2.9	4.9	5.2
(excluding China and India)	6.0	2.7	-0.3	7.4	4.9	4.9	8.1	3.6	4.6	5.3
East and North-East Asia	5.8	2.0	-0.9	7.7	4.7	2.3	4.4	1.4	2.3	3.1
(excluding China and Japan)										
North and Central Asia	12.7	7.0	4.0	6.7	6.7	11.7	16.0	7.6	7.8	8.8
(excluding Russian Federation)										
South and South-West Asia	5.7	2.4	-1.0	6.1	4.6	10.8	14.2	9.4	9.6	10.0
(excluding India)										
Developed ESCAP economies[h]	2.6	-0.8	-5.5	3.8	1.6	0.3	1.7	-1.1	-0.3	0.9

Sources: ESCAP, based on national sources; United Nations, Department of Economic and Social Affairs (2011). *World Economic Situation and Prospects 2011*, Sales No. E.11.II.C.2. Available from www.un.org/en/development/desa/policy/wesp/wesp_current/2011wesp.pdf; IMF, International Financial Statistics databases (Washington, D.C., March 2011); ADB, *Key Indicators for Asia and the Pacific 2010* (Manila, 2010); CEIC Data Company Limited; and website of the Interstate Statistical Committee of the Commonwealth of Independent States, www.cisstat.com, 16 February 2011 and ESCAP estimates.

[a] Changes in the consumer price index.
[b] Estimates.
[c] Forecasts (as of 8 April 2011).
[d] Calculations are based on GDP figures at market prices in dollars in 2009 (at 2000 prices) used as weights to calculate the regional and subregional growth rates.
[e] Estimates for 2010 and forecasts for 2011 are available for selected economies.
[f] The estimates and forecasts for countries relate to fiscal years defined as follows: 2009 refers to fiscal year spanning 1 April 2009 to 31 March 2010 in India; 21 March 2009 to 20 March 2010 in the Islamic Republic of Iran; 1 July 2008 to 30 June 2009 in Bangladesh and Pakistan and 16 July 2008 to 15 July 2009 in Nepal.
[g] Developing Asian and Pacific economies comprise 37 economies excluding North and Central Asia.
[h] Developed Asian and Pacific economies comprise Australia, Japan and New Zealand.

Key challenges to the outlook: protecting growth from external headwinds

Rising inflationary pressures create further challenges for sustaining growth momentum

Inflationary pressures are rising in the region in 2011 due both to the growth recovery and to price rises for imported food and energy. Most economies are forecast to see an increase in inflation in 2011 (see figure 1.14). External supply-led increases in food and energy prices are having a damaging effect on economies and on the lives of the poor and vulnerable (see section entitled *Return of food and fuel crises: impacts on income and poverty*). Furthermore, there are significant risks that the excess liquidity resulting from monetary easing in developed economies could spill over into speculative asset price bubbles, as well as general inflation and real currency appreciation due to incomplete sterilization of capital inflows.

For much of the region, headline inflation rose in 2010. Some of the price increases were due

Figure 1.14. Consumer price inflation as measured by changes in consumer price index of selected economies in the ESCAP region, 2009-2011

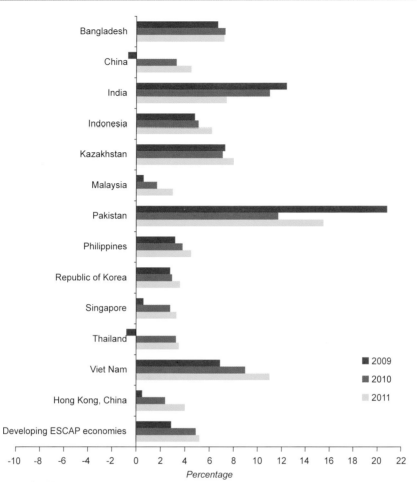

Sources: ESCAP, based on table 1.2.

Notes: Rates of inflation for 2010 are estimates and those for 2011 are forecast (as of 8 April 2011). Developing economies of the region comprise 37 economies (excluding the Central Asian countries) and the calculations are based on the weighted average of GDP figures in 2009 dollars (at 2000 prices).

to normalization in economic activity, particularly for export-oriented economies which had seen sharp declines in economic activity and inflationary pressure during the onset of the crisis. Conversely, some economies where domestic demand plays an important role, which were less affected by slowdown during the crisis, continued to experience relatively high inflation. Inflation in a number of South Asian economies in 2010 was in double digits, or close to such a figure. High budget deficits and accomodative monetary policies in most South Asian economies have contributed to high inflation. Viet Nam saw its inflation rate reach almost 9% in 2010, with import costs rising from currency devaluations and strong credit expansion driving domestic spending.

Inflation in China has been a growing concern, due to strong domestic demand as a result of stimulus measures during the crisis.

In response to growing inflationary pressures, several economies across the region started to tighten monetary policy over the course of 2010 (see figure 1.15). In economies where inflation is a pressing concern, such as China, India and Viet Nam, rates have been raised in recent months. However, for many other economies, such as Malaysia, the Republic of Korea and Thailand, inflation has not yet become a major issue; nevertheless, to counter growing price pressures, those economies also started to raise interest rates. Such monetary tightening will place

Figure 1.15.   Policy rates in selected Asian developing economies, January 2008 to February 2011

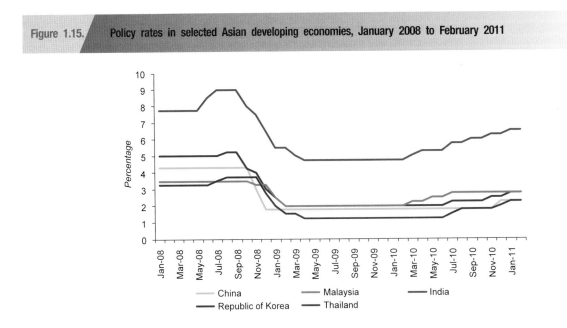

Source: ESCAP calculations based on data from CEIC Data Company Limited, available from http://ceicdata.com/ (accessed 25 March 2011).

Notes: China: policy rate (rediscount rate); India: policy rate (repo rates (Reserve Bank of India)); Republic of Korea: policy rate (base rate (Bank of Korea)); Malaysia: policy rate (overnight policy rate); and Thailand: policy rate.

added pressure on growth in 2011, especially for strongly export-oriented economies that will also see their growth affected by relatively weak demand from the developed economies.

Return of food and fuel crises: impacts on income and poverty

Rising food and energy prices are emerging as an issue of serious concern across much of the region in a manner reminiscent of the 2007-2008 period just before the onset of the financial crisis. Since 2010, global food and oil prices have been on a sustained and synchronized upward trend. The Food Price Index of the Food and Agriculture Organization of the United Nations (FAO) in December 2010 exceeded its previous record value that had been recorded in 2008 (see figure 1.16). Since crossing that record level, the index continued to set new records in subsequent months, with increasingly dire impacts on the livelihoods of the poor and causing social upheaval across the globe. Since 2010, oil prices have also been rising rapidly (see figure 1.16), with increased global demand due to growth recovery in emerging markets coupled with

a number of supply shocks, particularly resulting from geo-political instability in the Middle East. While oil prices, which are denominated in dollars, have been influenced by movements in that currency, it can be seen that oil prices have been on a rising trend even when expressed in terms of a basket of major currencies, such as special drawing rights (SDRs) (see figure 1.17).

Apart from the direct impact on consumption, high food and energy prices have a negative impact on the macroeconomic fundamentals of many developing economies. The key macroeconomic variables affected include inflation, trade balance and fiscal balance. The obvious impact on general inflation of food and energy price rises, especially as such increases pass through from the first-round impact on domestic prices to the second-round impact on wages, would necessitate higher interest rates as part of the macroeconomic toolkit needed to tackle the issue, that would in turn adversely affect investment activity. For food- and energy-importing economies, increased import prices would lead to deterioration in their trade balance and consequent pressure for exchange rate depreciation and increased prices for

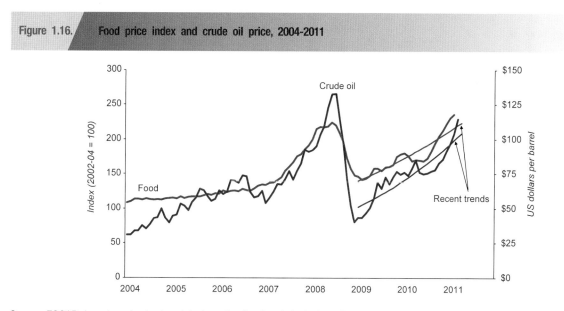

Figure 1.16.   Food price index and crude oil price, 2004-2011

Source: ESCAP, based on food price data from the Food and Agriculture Organization of the United Nations, available from www.fao.org/worldfoodsituation/FoodPricesIndex/en/. Oil price (Europe: Brent spot price), available from the United States Energy Information Administration, www.eia.doe.gov/dnav/pet/pet_pri_spt_s1_d.htm.

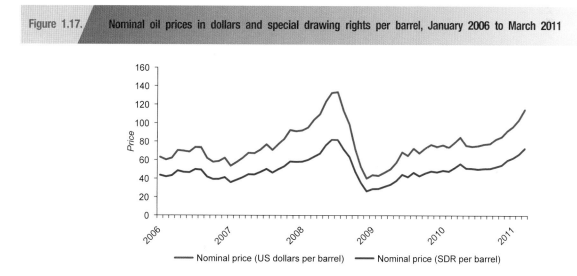

Figure 1.17.   Nominal oil prices in dollars and special drawing rights per barrel, January 2006 to March 2011

Source: ESCAP calculations based on data from CEIC Data Company Limited (accessed 21 April 2011).

Note: Oil prices refer to the price of Brent crude.

other imported consumption goods and inputs for production. The need for government assistance for the poor, such as through income support or price subsidies, would lead to deterioration in fiscal balances. Increased use of government resources for managing the impact of food and energy price rises would lead to reduced availability of government funds for other policies to support growth and poverty reduction. The overall impact of such deterioration in macroeconomic fundamentals for the economies most adversely affected would be a dampening of GDP growth below potential levels. The degree of impact on economies would depend on a number of factors, such as the extent of their dependence on food and energy imports, the amount of government subsidies to offset higher food and energy prices, the relative importance of food based on the income level of the economy, and the relative importance of energy based on the energy efficiency of the economy. Under these criteria, rising food prices would particularly affect a number of economies in the region, such as Bangladesh, Pakistan, the Philippines and Sri Lanka.[22] Similarly, with regard to rising energy prices, economies in the region which may be severely affected include India and Thailand.[23]

ESCAP has estimated that high energy prices would lead to a significant adverse impact on growth, that is, up to 1.0 percentage point in some developing Asia-Pacific economies, as well as upward pressure on inflation and a deterioration of current accounts (see box 1.2). The impacts on these macroeconomic

Box 1.2. Economic impact of oil price increases on the Asia-Pacific region

Given the recent upward trend in crude oil prices, there are increasing concerns about the potential negative impacts on the oil-importing countries in the Asia-Pacific region. Developing countries in the region are especially vulnerable to high oil prices as they still rely heavily on energy-intensive industries and need to import substantial amounts of oil and other energy commodities as essential inputs for economic production.

Energy and food prices have risen substantially starting in the second half of 2010 as the global economy continues on its gradual recovery path and the economic stimulus policies, such as successive rounds of monetary quantitative easing by the major developed economies have resulted in increasing market liquidity, which has contributed to increasing asset and commodity prices. Moreover, geo-political instability in the Middle East has added further upward pressure to prices. As of March 2011, current levels of energy and food prices are much higher than the averages in 2010. In order to assess the impact of higher energy and food prices for 2011, a "what-if" counterfactual scenario has been created under the "optimistic" assumptions of the Brent crude oil price being $90 per barrel and food prices increasing by 10% in 2011, with a comparison of the "current" baseline assumptions of the crude oil price at $105 per barrel and food prices increasing by 27% in 2011. Overall, it was found that the current energy and food price increases (as in the baseline scenario) have adversely affected growth in the developing countries of the Asia-Pacific region compared with the what-if scenario, by 0.47 percentage point, which resulted in additional inflation of 1.09 percentage point, and lowered the current account-to-GDP ratio by 0.53 percentage point of GDP in 2011.

Table a. Impacts from energy and food price increases on developing Asia-Pacific economies in 2011

	Baseline scenario versus counterfactual scenario		
	Output growth	Inflation	Current account to GDP
China	-0.34	0.94	-0.58
India	-0.61	1.96	-0.30
Indonesia	-0.52	0.92	0.49
Malaysia	-0.47	1.10	0.65
Philippines	-0.79	1.24	-0.11
Republic of Korea	-0.60	0.56	-0.82
Singapore	-1.14	1.57	-4.98
Thailand	-0.50	1.11	1.20
Developing Asia-Pacific economies	-0.47	1.09	-0.53

Source: ESCAP computations in the framework of the Oxford Economic Forecasting model.

Notes:
  1. Counterfactual scenario is under the assumptions of the Brent crude oil price being $90 per barrel and food prices increasing by 10% in 2011.
  2. Baseline scenario is under the assumptions of the Brent crude oil price being $105 per barrel and food price increases being 27% in 2011.
  3. Impacts are shown in absolute percentage differences of baseline from counterfactual scenario (i.e. baseline scenario - counterfactual scenario).

In going forward, the macroeconomic implications of high energy prices for the region should be carefully assessed in order to gauge the impacts, as well as to prepare appropriate and timely policies to deal with the situation. Based on the baseline scenario of the crude oil price being $105 per barrel, it was estimated that if the oil price increased to $115 per barrel,

Box 1.2 *(continued)*

overall economic output in the region would be adversely affected by 0.17 percentage point from the baseline scenario in 2011. However, if the average oil price level were to increase further to $130, developing Asia-Pacific countries would experience an even more adverse scenario, with output growth declining from the baseline by 0.47 percentage point.

The impacts of high oil prices would also be evident in other macroeconomic indicators, particularly for headline inflation and the current account balance. For headline inflation, if the oil price were to increase to $115 per barrel, this would generate increasing inflation of an additional 0.31 percentage point. Under the scenario of $130 per barrel, overall headline inflation in the region would increase by an additional 0.87 percentage point. Based on these analyses, the countries most adversely affected in terms of inflationary impact would be Malaysia, the Philippines and Thailand. As for the impact on the current account balance, most developing Asia-Pacific countries have strong external balances that would support the region as a whole so that it is expected to remain resilient against the negative impact of high oil prices. However, oil prices ranging from $115 to $130 would lower the current account-to-GDP position of developing Asia-Pacific countries by 0.25 to 0.73 percentage points. The most impact-sensitive countries are the Republic of Korea and Thailand, the current account positions of which could turn to deficit under the scenario of $130 oil prices. India is the major exception among the major developing Asia-Pacific countries in that it has been steadily recording current account deficits, so the possibility of an upward trend in oil prices could further worsen the external balance of India.

Clearly, higher energy prices offer undesirable scenarios for development in the developing Asia-Pacific region. Given the possibility of sustained high oil prices in the coming years, it is imperative for developing Asia-Pacific countries to promote efficient energy consumption and to expand their energy choices to other alternative energy sources in the future.

Table b. Summary of oil price impacts on macroeconomic variables for developing Asia-Pacific economies

	+10 US dollars oil price increase			+25 US dollars oil price increase		
	Output growth	Inflation	Current account to GDP	Output growth	Inflation	Current account to GDP
China	-0.13	0.28	-0.17	-0.36	0.77	-0.49
India	-0.23	0.52	-0.16	-0.64	1.46	-0.47
Indonesia	-0.18	0.26	-0.06	-0.49	0.73	-0.15
Malaysia	-0.16	0.33	0.23	-0.44	0.92	0.68
Philippines	-0.27	0.39	-0.14	-0.75	1.09	-0.39
Republic of Korea	-0.23	0.34	-0.16	-0.64	1.46	-0.47
Singapore	-0.33	0.26	-0.24	-0.91	0.74	-0.68
Thailand	-0.22	0.19	-0.37	-0.62	0.94	-1.06
Developing Asia-Pacific economies	-0.17	0.31	-0.25	-0.47	0.87	-0.73

Source: ESCAP computations in the framework of the Oxford Economic Forecasting model.

Notes: Under the baseline assumption of the Brent crude oil price being $105 per barrel; Impacts are shown in absolute percentage differences from the baseline scenario.

variables would be through the effects of high oil prices on costs for domestic industries, on the price of imports, and on the demand for exports. The region and emerging economies in general are more energy-intensive in their production than developed economies, leading to a greater proportional impact

of an oil price shock on production costs. In addition to the possible slowdown in production due to higher costs, businesses would be affected by the slowdown in exports to developed economies as a result of higher energy costs. Consumers in the developed world are more dependent on energy than those in developing economies and therefore any substantial price increase would have an impact on consumption and therefore import demand from this region. There is the risk of a return of "stagflation" in the developed world last seen in the 1970s, a phenomenon which was characterized by low growth accompanied by high inflation. At a time when growth in developed economies remains fragile, high oil prices would have a greater impact on their economic growth than would be the case when they are experiencing relatively high growth rates. Additional measures required to restrain inflation related to energy prices would introduce an added constraint to growth in developed economies, such as higher interest rates which would further curb consumption and investment. Therefore, the Asia-Pacific region may face a greater threat to its exports owing to high energy prices than would have been the case if such prices had occurred at a time of robust growth in the developed world.

Of even greater direct impact on the livelihoods of the poor and vulnerable in region would be the effects of rising food prices. Economies in various parts of the region have seen their general food prices increase by as much as 35% since 2009 (see figure 1.18). Higher food prices exert upward pressure on inflation, particularly in lower-income economies where such prices account for a major proportion of the inflation basket. For example, China, India, Indonesia and Thailand have CPI weightings of between 33% and 46% for food. Rising food prices have exceeded headline CPI numbers in many economies in 2010, representing a key factor in the rise in overall CPI (see figure 1.19).[24] Beyond the impact on CPI, rising food prices are of intrinsic concern because they represent a higher proportion of spending for the poorest citizens than for the general population, even in lower-income economies. The 2008 food crisis forced millions into destitution in Asia and the Pacific.[25] As was the case in the 2008 crisis, the poor, both in rural and urban areas, particularly net food buyers, the landless and households headed by females, are the most adversely affected by high food prices.[26]

ESCAP has estimated that an additional 19.4 million people may have remained in poverty due to increased food prices in 2010 (see box 1.3). High prices have prevented 15.6 million people in the region from emerging from·poverty and have pushed another 3.8 million below the poverty line, with the result that a total of 19.4 million additional people are now living in poverty who otherwise would have been above the poverty line, had it not been for the onset of high food prices. ESCAP has estimated the impact on poverty of a number of

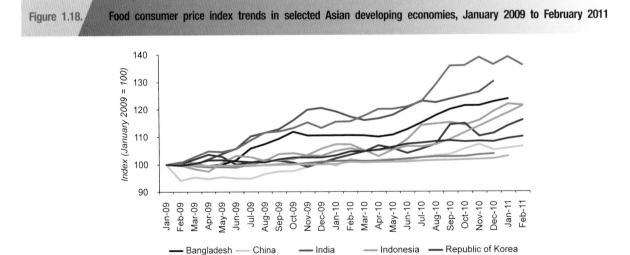

Figure 1.18. Food consumer price index trends in selected Asian developing economies, January 2009 to February 2011

Source: ESCAP calculations based on data from CEIC Data Company Limited, available from http://ceicdata.com/ (accessed 10 March 2011).

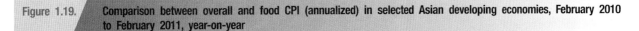

Figure 1.19. Comparison between overall and food CPI (annualized) in selected Asian developing economies, February 2010 to February 2011, year-on-year

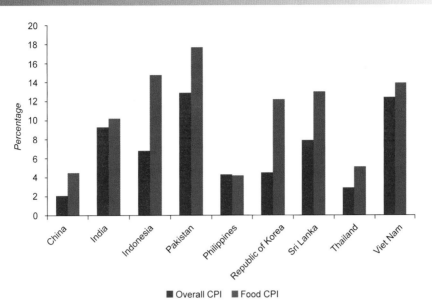

■ Overall CPI   ■ Food CPI

Source: ESCAP calculations based on data from CEIC Data Company Limited, available from http://ceicdata.com/ (accessed 10 March 2011).

Note: Data for India refer to January 2010 to January 2011.

Box 1.3. Impact of food inflation on poverty

There is little argument that food inflation has profound and wide-ranging social and economic impacts, the most fundamental of which is a reduction in food security and an increase in poverty in developing countries. Rising prices of staple food affects the poor in two ways, conditional to their status as net sellers or net buyers of staple food. It increases the income of households that are net sellers and adds to the hardship of poor households that are net buyers. That occurs because the buyers have to expend a larger share of their income on essential food with the result that less is left to expend on other food items which are important as complementary sources of energy and nutrients and on non-food items, including health and education. In general, unexpected rises in the price of staple food items have an immediate negative effect on the urban poor since the majority of them are net buyers of such items. However, the same is true even in rural areas, for example, studies of rural income-generating activities found that 91% of the rural poor in Bangladesh in 2000 were net buyers of main staple food items.[27]

At this stage it is still too early to have definitive empirical evidence of the impact on poverty of the recent rises in food prices. However, it is possible to estimate the magnitude of such impacts at the regional level by using data on staple food prices in domestic markets in 2010. The table below shows, for main urban centres in selected Asia-Pacific countries, the percentage increase in the price of main staple food items, above the CPI inflation, from May 2010 to January 2011, and the percentage of the dietary energy supply that the staples represent. For example, wheat and its products are the main staple foods in many North and Central Asian countries – accounting for half or more of the total dietary supply – and the price of wheat has increased by 14% in the Armenian capital, Yerevan, and by as much as 107% in the capital of Tajikistan, Dushanbe. Price increases in general were lower in the case of rice, which is the staple food in South and South-East Asia. Particularly important for poverty reduction is the lower increase in prices for staples in India and China – about 6% in major cities.

Box 1.3 *(continued)*

Table a. Price changes of staple food items in major cities of selected Asia-Pacific economies

	Percentage price change (real terms)	Percentage of dietary energy supply	Staple
Armenia	14	48	Wheat
Bangladesh	17	71	Rice
China	6	27	Rice
Georgia	69	50	Wheat
Indonesia	16	51	Rice
India	6	21	Wheat
	6	30	Rice
Kyrgyzstan	31	49	Wheat
Lao People's Democratic Republic	20	64	Rice
Mongolia	38	42	Wheat
Nepal	11	34	Rice
Tajikistan	107	58	Wheat
Viet Nam	34	62	Rice

Source: ESCAP, based on data from the FAO Global Information and Early Warning System on national basic food prices. Available from www.fao.org/gviews/pricetool (accessed February 2011).

Note: Second column shows the percentage of change of prices of staple food deflated by the national consumer price index (CPI).

The analysis presented in this box considers the countries listed in the table above and another 15 countries in the Asia-Pacific region, namely Azerbaijan, Bhutan, Cambodia, the Islamic Republic of Iran, Kazakhstan, Malaysia, Pakistan, the Philippines, Papua New Guinea, the Russian Federation, Sri Lanka, Thailand, Turkey, Turkmenistan and Uzbekistan. Together, these countries are home to 96% of the total population of the developing and transition countries in the Asia-Pacific region. When information on price changes in domestic markets was not available, information on the international prices of commodities and the share of the imports of staple food in total consumption was used to estimate the price changes. Based on these data on price changes and information on the distribution pattern and level of consumption as assessed in household surveys, it is possible to estimate the effect on mean consumption expenditures and hence on rates of poverty. In addition, the likely effect of high oil prices on GDP growth is also taken into consideration, since it is expected to slow the rate of poverty reduction.

ESCAP has estimated that high food prices in 2010 kept an additional 19.4 million people in poverty in Asia and the Pacific; they prevented 15.6 million people in the region from emerging from poverty and have pushed another 3.8 million below the poverty line. Given the economic dynamism in Asia and the Pacific, the effect on poverty of the rise in prices of staple food items was not an increase in the total number of poor, but a slowdown in the rate of poverty reduction. Such slowdown in 2010 alone may result in a one-year delay for countries in the region in the achievement of the Millennium Development Goal on eradicating extreme poverty and hunger.

Given the onset of high oil prices and the continued increase in food prices in 2011, estimates of further impacts on poverty were produced using three scenarios (see table below). In the first scenario, if the rise in prices of staple food, above the CPI inflation, continues in 2011 at half the rate of 2010 and the average oil price reaches $105 per barrel, there would be a slowdown in the rate of poverty reduction in the region, with 9.8 million people being adversely affected. Of that number, 8.3 million people would be prevented from rising out of poverty, while an additional 1.5 million people would be pushed into poverty. If prices in 2011 rise above the CPI inflation at the same rate as in 2010 and the average oil price reaches $115 per barrel – a more

Box 1.3 *(continued)*

Table b. Millions of people adversely affected under three scenarios for different prices for staple food items and oil

	Scenario 1 Staple food inflation in 2011 half the 2010 rate and $105 oil price			Scenario 2 Staple food inflation in 2011 same as in 2010 and $115 oil price			Scenario 3 Staple food inflation in 2011 twice the 2010 rate and $130 oil price		
	Urban	Rural	Total	Urban	Rural	Total	Urban	Rural	Total
Pushed into poverty	0.1	1.3	1.5	1.5	3.7	5.1	3.9	13.9	17.8
Prevented to get out of poverty	1.9	6.5	8.3	2.6	12.5	15.1	3.6	21.0	24.6
Total	2.0	7.8	9.8	4.1	16.2	20.2	7.6	34.8	42.4

Source: ESCAP, based on data from the FAO Global Information and Early Warning System website and World Bank's Global Income Distribution Dynamics data set.

Notes: Values may not sum to total due to rounding. See Freire and Isgut (2011) for details about the computation of estimates of number of people affected under the different scenarios.

pessimistic scenario – the resulting slowdown in poverty reduction would be expected to adversely affect 20.2 million people. Of that number, 15.1 million people would be prevented from getting out of poverty, while an additional 5.1 million people would be pushed into poverty. In an alternative scenario in which there are further increases in food inflation and oil prices, with staple food prices in 2011 rising above the CPI inflation at twice the 2010 rate and the average oil price reaching $130 per barrel, the total number of poor in the region would be expected to actually increase, with 42.4 million people being affected. Of that number, 24.6 million people would be prevented from getting out of poverty and 17.8 million would be pushed into poverty. In all three scenarios, the strongest effect is expected to be in preventing people from rising out of poverty and the impact would be more severe in rural areas where the majority of the poor live.

If events similar to those in scenario 3 actually happen in 2011, the achievement of the Millennium Development Goal on eradicating extreme poverty and hunger may be postponed by half a decade in many countries of the region, including Bangladesh, India, the Lao People's Democratic Republic and Nepal.

Source: ESCAP (2011a). "Rising food prices and inflation in the Asia-Pacific region: causes, impact and policy response", MPDD Policy Briefs, No. 7, March 2011.

possible food and energy price scenarios in 2011. The increase in those remaining in poverty consists both of those who are pushed below the $1.25 poverty line in 2011 and those who remain under the poverty line in 2011 who would otherwise have risen above the line in 2011 without the persistence of high food and energy prices.

Under the most pessimistic scenario in which there are further increases in food inflation and oil prices, with staple food prices in 2011 rising above the CPI inflation at twice the 2010 rate and the average oil price reaching $130 per barrel, an additional 42.4 million people could remain in poverty. This would result in a loss of up to 5 years in the efforts of many

countries to achieve the Millennium Development Goal on eradicating extreme poverty, including least developed countries, such as Bangladesh, the Lao People's Democratic Republic and Nepal. The increase would be greatest in rural areas, where the majority of the poor are concentrated, with an increase of up to 34.8 million people remaining in poverty, while in urban areas the increase would be up to 7.6 million people. Conversely, a less dire situation is simulated by halving the rate of food price increase in 2011 above the CPI inflation compared with that of 2010 and assuming an annual average oil price of $105 per barrel. Such a scenario would result in an additional 9.8 million people remaining in poverty.

Causes of rising food prices

Supply shocks. On the supply side, there have been numerous disruptions due to adverse weather events. Harvests of key cereals have been affected by adverse weather events, especially wheat production of major exporters, such as Canada, Kazakhstan, the Russian Federation and Ukraine. Wheat prices (see figure 1.20) were further affected by the announcement made by the Russian Federation in August 2010 of an export ban. While wheat is not a major staple for many countries in the Asia-Pacific region, the impact of wheat prices on the prices for other staples, due to increased demand for substitutes, is of more concern. Export prices of Thai rice, a benchmark for Asia, rose 17% in the fourth quarter of 2010,[28] due to strong demand partially related to the wheat substitution effect, as well as weather-related shocks in Australia, Pakistan, Thailand and Viet Nam. With multiple severe weather events occurring across the globe, it would be prudent not to view such occurrences as random events and instead to factor such disruptions into projections for long-term food supplies.

Conversion of food into biofuels. While market forces play a role in the price behaviour witnessed in recent months, additional man-made factors have exacerbated the price increases and therefore significantly increased

the hardship of the poor and vulnerable. Rising oil prices have been one of the channels through which policies have contributed to further increases in food prices. Critically for the poor in the region, the increases in oil prices would indirectly lead to greater pressure on food prices through the channel of biofuels, and this would have a greater impact on the poor as food expenses account for a higher proportion of spending of the less well-off than energy does. The past few months have seen the return of the food-energy price nexus as oil prices have rebounded from the relatively low levels seen during the crisis. The impact of biofuels was discussed extensively in the *Survey 2008*[29] undertaken in the run-up to the recent crisis. Since biofuels are viable only when the price of oil is high, such fuels have begun to emerge as a competing use for grain crops in recent months and such pressure will increase with any further oil price rise. The use of biofuels had been encouraged in the United States during 2010 by the extension of tax credits for ethanol producers; more than one third of that country's corn production in the year to 31 August 2010 was estimated to have gone into ethanol production.[30]

Role of speculation. The other key channel through which policies have caused the dramatic run-up in food prices is the growing level of financial speculation. It is now increasingly clear that a significant portion

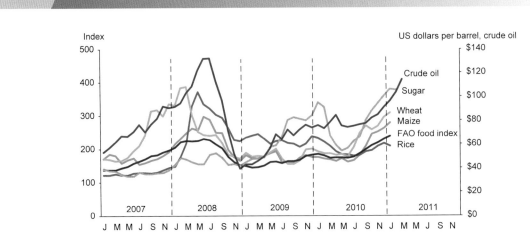

Figure 1.20. Food price index and other selected commodities (index 1998-2000 = 100), 2007-2011

Sources: ESCAP, based on Food and Agriculture Organization of the United Nations, available from www.fao.org/es/esc/prices/PricesServlet.jsp? lang=en; and United States Energy Information Administration, available from http://tonto.eia.doe.gov/dnav/pet/pet_pri_spt_s1_d.htm (accessed 7 April 2011).

of the increases in the price and volatility of food and energy commodities can only be explained by the emergence of a speculative bubble.[31] The argument against the existence of such speculation is that the massive increase in the involvement of financial investors in the commodity markets is only in response to a rising market rather than being the driver of the price rises. However, a number of observations contradict such an interpretation of the current situation in commodity markets.

A significant portion of the increases in the price and volatility of food and energy commodities can only be explained by the emergence of a speculative bubble

---

First, the recent volatility in global prices of items traded on commodity/financial markets cannot be explained solely by movements in demand and supply.[32] The extent of price variation in such a short time suggests that such movements could not have been created by only short-term changes in supply and demand, especially as in world trade the effects of seasonality in a particular region are countered by supplies from other regions, and in any case, there was not a correspondingly significant change in global supply and utilisation for these products over this period.[33] Second, the sheer weight of demand from the new investors in the commodity markets is creating a situation of persistent increase in demand for commodity-based assets as compared with the situation in the past.[34] A key factor underlying the ability of purely financial investors to enter commodity markets was the Commodity Futures Modernization Act of 2000 in the United States, which broke the link between investment and eventual physical delivery of products by permitting traders to take long-term speculative positions through the rolling over of futures contracts. Commodity investments have reached levels not seen even before the start of the financial crisis, with commodity assets under management by financial investors crossing the $300-billion mark for the first time in July 2010.[35] Third, the increasing number of

shocks to food and energy supplies, coupled with recent instances of supply cutbacks by countries that instituted export bans, leads to fear that supplies will be decreased in the future, which therefore encourages the entry of speculators betting on such an outcome. Food supplies have been affected by multiple climatic shocks in producing countries, while oil supplies have been threatened by political instability in the Middle East. The presence of speculation serving to accentuate changes in fundamental factors can be seen, for example, in the case of the wheat market in late 2010. The increase in wheat prices was far higher than that justified by the amount of supply curtailed by the export ban imposed by the Russian Federation, indicating an additional impact of speculation on prices.[36]

This combination of greater demand at any point in time for commodity-based assets due to the presence of speculators as well as the lack of belief among speculators that current stock levels serve as a signal of future supplies can combine to produce periods of self-sustaining increases in commodity prices. Indeed, current data seem to point to such a situation. Prices have been high for a range of commodities despite stocks being more than adequate. For example, the largest production of grain in history was achieved in 2009, but grain prices remained elevated that year.[37] This situation indicates that, in the presence of the current regime of unbridled speculation in commodity markets helped by massive injection of liquidity, the relationship between prices and demand and supply is not operating as would otherwise be expected.

The current pressures for speculation are perhaps even more severe than in the previous period of food price rises immediately preceding the financial crisis. The massive liquidity expansion resulting from easy money policies in the advanced countries in the aftermath of the crisis and the lack of faith in paper money assets of the developed world due to these policies are creating both an increasing stock of investible funds and increasing interest in assets based on tangible goods, such as commodities, including gold and other metals.

The dangers of commodity price changes due to speculation are two-fold: first, that the increase in prices above and beyond the situation dictated by supply and demand will lead to an added burden for the poor, and second, the increased volatility of food prices due to speculation will lead to the likelihood of more extreme falls in prices when the market misjudges the impact of supply curtailments. For example, sugar has gone through a rollercoaster ride in 2010 as prices first rose to record highs in March due to poor harvest warnings for Brazil and India, followed by a halving of prices a month later after production estimates were scaled upwards.[38] Such sharp volatility negatively affects farmers who make their planting decisions on price signals from the markets, which may prove to be fleeting indicators; they thereby suffer eventual losses when harvesting their crops.

The importance of non-demand pull factors in explaining food price increases leads to concerns about utilizing monetary policy as the main tool to combat such increases

---

Addressing the challenge of rising food prices

The importance of non-demand pull factors in explaining food price increases leads to concerns about utilizing monetary policy as the main tool to combat such increases. Monetary policy will be necessary for authorities in some cases depending on the degree of pass-through of food price inflation to other product prices due to higher costs from commodity inputs and higher food price-related wage demands. However, apart from managing inflation pass-through, measures are also required to address the root causes of food price rises. An appropriate approach for policymakers to deal with rising food prices would be to address explicit supply-side factors.

Need for regulation of speculative activity. First, financial speculation in international commodity prices should be addressed through international cooperation. Regulation of commodity markets should be stepped up in order to prevent speculation. In particular, it is important that previously unregulated over-the-counter derivative trades be carried out in public exchanges and that speculative position limits (total number and value of contracts for a given commodity) be established and applied equally to all investors.[39] Such measures are part of the Dodd–Frank Wall Street Reform and Consumer Protection Act passed in 2010 by the United States; however, the challenge will lie in ensuring the implementation of such measures. Moreover, further measures will be required to effectively dampen the quantum of speculation. Legislation in the United States will not be enough, as a significant degree of financial investment in commodity markets is conducted in other economies, such as the European Union. While the European Union is also debating legislation in this sphere, similarly strict criteria and implementation will be required in order to make the legislation effective, and there remains the risk that trading will move to other jurisdictions. Therefore, global legislation would also be necessary as a next step, through forums such as the United Nations or G20.

Second, buffer stocks of food grains should be established and utilized in a countercyclical manner to moderate price volatility. Third, public distribution systems should be strengthened to protect the vulnerable sections of the population from the effects of spiraling prices for food items, besides reducing prices through lowering tariffs and taxes. Social protection should be strengthened through the distribution of food vouchers or targeted income-transfer schemes in order to minimize the impact on the poor due to the higher expenditures people must make for food.[40] Mid-day meal schemes in schools, as implemented in certain parts of the region such as in India, are important means for protecting the nutritional security of children.

Finally, in the medium term, efforts should be made to deliver a supply response through reversing the neglect of agriculture in public policy by enhancing support for agricultural research, development and extension and providing easier access to credit and other inputs in order to foster a new, knowledge-intensive "green revolution". This would also make agriculture more environmentally resilient while enhancing agricultural productivity.[41]

At the regional level, there is scope for cooperation in establishing regional food stocks for use in managing price shocks. An example of such a scheme is the rice reserve initiative of ASEAN+3. In response to the climate of rising price pressure, ASEAN member countries plan to formally establish a permanent ASEAN+3 rice reserve in October 2011, as a follow-up to their ongoing East Asia Emergency Rice Reserve Pilot Project.[42] The plan foresees a total of 787,000 tons of rice for the reserve fund committed by the ASEAN countries and the three East Asian countries in ASEAN+3. Another positive initiative is the agreement made by the South Asian Association for Regional Cooperation (SAARC) in April 2007 to establish the SAARC Food Bank. It would maintain food reserves and support national as well as regional food security through collective action among member countries. The SAARC Food Bank would also foster intercountry partnerships and regional integration.

South-South and "triangular" cooperation on knowledge and technology transfer could play a key role in improving the region's agricultural productivity

---

Finally, South-South and "triangular" cooperation on knowledge and technology transfer could play a key role in improving the region's agricultural productivity. For example, the system of institutes comprising the Consultative Group on International Agricultural Research (CGIAR), which includes the International Rice Research Institute in the Philippines and the International Crops Research Institute for the Semi-Arid Tropics in India, have generated new knowledge and technology in agriculture and made it available to national agricultural research systems for adaptation to their geoclimatic conditions. One recent success story in agricultural transformation based

on knowledge through international cooperation is the New Rice for Africa (NERICA) programme of what is now known as the Africa Rice Center. In 1994 the NERICA programme developed a new rice variety combining the best traits of African and Asian rice varieties. As a major collaborative project, it involved institutions in 17 African countries and CGIAR, with support from the Government of Japan and other multilateral donors. As a result of the growing demand for NERICA rice, cultivated areas have been extended to more than 200,000 hectares in West and Central Africa, exposing hundreds of thousands of African farmers to the new crop and associated technologies, and significantly increasing African rice production. South-South and triangular cooperation can play an equally important role in fostering the second green revolution in Asia and the Pacific.

Managing capital inflows

The Asia-Pacific region is being buffeted by the impact of the accommodative monetary policies undertaken by developed economies as part of their programmes to recover from the recent crisis. The resulting low interest rates in those economies are pushing investors towards developing economies, including those in this region. These economies are attractive because of the better yields offered by their currencies owing to the comparatively high interest rates in the region, as well as the potential capital gains to be realized from asset investments due to the relatively better growth prospects of Asia-Pacific economies. The scale of potential pressure for regional economies can be seen from the disproportionate size of the global fund management industry as compared with the size of most regional economies. The quantum of total global funds under management was estimated at $61.6 trillion in 2008,[43] representing about 100% of global GDP.

Other than reallocation of existing funds by financial institutions, there is once again the burgeoning "carry trade", using borrowings in foreign currencies, such as the Japanese yen, the Swiss franc and to a certain extent the dollar, to invest in higher-yielding currencies in both developed and developing countries. In the initial months of the crisis, risk aversion led to a reversal of the carry trade as investors reverted to so-called safe havens, such as the dollar and yen, despite the low yields of these currencies. The lowering of interest rates by countries with high-yield currencies further accelerated this reversal. However, with a perception among investors of greater stability in global financial markets, the search for high yield has led to a resumption of pre-crisis carry-trade trends, with the destination of choice now being emerging markets. While the size of the current carry trade is difficult to measure with certainty, estimates put it at around $750 billion, approaching the size of the previous carry trade at its peak between 2004 and 2007.[44] Apart from a pure carry trade to take advantage of yield differentials, investment in financial assets in the region is also being driven by prospects for increases in asset values due to comparatively higher economic growth in the region, and expected gains from appreciation in exchange

rates. Interest rate arbitrage is seen most clearly in the case of economies with liberalized debt flows such as those in the middle-income East Asian economies, whereas economies such as India with restrictions on debt inflows have seen foreign inflows concentrated more in equity markets in order to take advantage of good domestic growth prospects. For example, in 2010, India recorded net equity investments by foreign institutional investors of $28.8 billion compared with debt investments of $10.2 billion.[45]

Equity markets in many economies of the region, for example in the Republic of Korea, the Philippines and Thailand, are already at their pre-crisis peaks or have crossed them (see figure 1.21). Foreign investor interest in equity markets of the region is reflected in booming inflows to Asian equity funds (excluding Japan), which stood at $45 billion in 2010, with the greatest interest being in China and India, while developed market equity funds saw an outflow

Figure 1.21. Equity market performance in selected Asian economies, January 2008 to February 2011

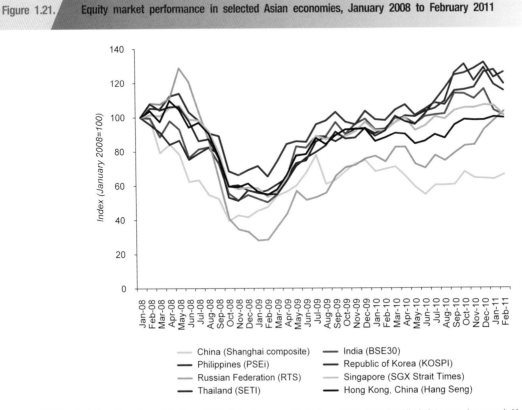

Source: ESCAP calculations based on data from CEIC Data Company Limited, available from http://ceicdata.com (accessed 11 February 2011).

Note: The equity market of each country is noted within parentheses in the legend.

of $62 billion.[46] While price-earnings ratios in the region remain relatively low by historical standards, the steep rise in equity prices for a number of economies indicates the possibility of bubbles building up where equity prices are driven by unreasonable expectations of corporate earnings growth.

ESCAP analysis of the impact of short-term capital flows indicates the role of such flows in building up possible asset bubbles. The economic impact of short-term capital flows on a number of variables for China and India during the period between 1999:Q1 and 2010:Q3 were assessed using the vector auto regression method. Short-term capital flows were seen to have a particularly long-lasting and significant impact on asset prices in these two economies (see figure 1.22).

Another asset class which has seen steep rises is property, both in emerging economies such as China, as well as high-income economies, such as Hong Kong, China; and Singapore. The Asia-Pacific region as a whole has seen the highest price rises of all regions and a number of economies have seen property price increases among the highest in the world up to the third quarter of 2010, with Hong Kong, China seeing the highest increase in the region (21.3% compared with that of a year earlier), followed by China (21.1%) and Singapore (20%).[47]

The immediate impact on economies in the region of the deluge in foreign capital flows has been steep rises in currency values. While many economies in the region have current account surpluses which would put upward pressure on exchange rates, economies are experiencing additional currency appreciation pressure due to capital inflows. Most major currencies in the region have risen significantly since 2009 (see figure 1.23). For example, since the period from January 2009 to 1 March 2011, Indonesia, the Republic of Korea, India and Singapore have seen real effective exchange rate appreciations of 20.1%, 15.9%, 10.7% and 7.5%. A number of countries, such as India, Indonesia and Singapore, are witnessing real effective exchange rates which have already exceeded their pre-crisis values. Surpluses in both the current and financial accounts have resulted in a massive accumulation of foreign exchange reserves (see figure 1.24). Of particular concern is the fact that capital flows are leading to appreciation pressures even on economies with rising current account deficits such as India. Rising currencies make it an even more difficult task to address the challenges of a current account deficit for macroeconomic stability.[48]

Given the large degree of similarity in export structures of several countries in the region, the different extent of appreciation of currencies would result in changing relative competitive positions and thereby affect export performance. To avoid this, a certain

Figure 1.22.   Response of asset prices to short-term capital flows for China and India

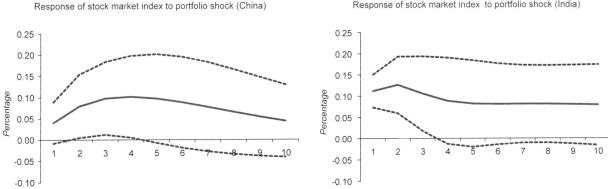

Source: ESCAP analysis.

Note: Response to Cholesky One S.D. Innovations ± 2 S.E.

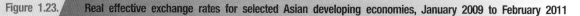

Figure 1.23. Real effective exchange rates for selected Asian developing economies, January 2009 to February 2011

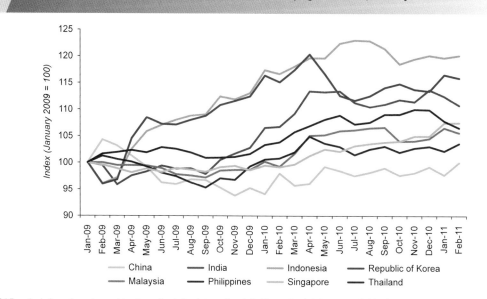

Source: ESCAP calculations based on data from Bank for International Settlements database, available from http://www.bis.org/statistics/eer/index.htm (accessed 14 April 2011).

Note: A positive trend represents appreciation and vice versa.

Figure 1.24. Foreign reserves (excluding gold) in selected Asian developing economies, December 2007 to January 2011

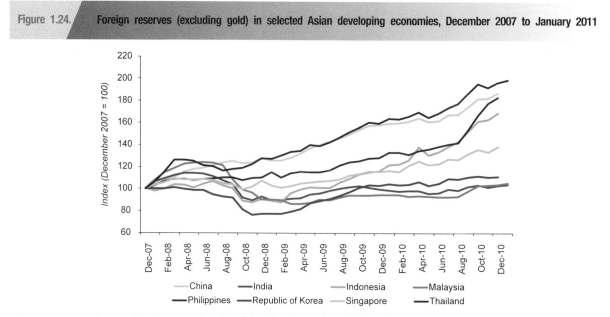

Sources: ESCAP calculations based on data from IMF, International Financial Statistics online, available from www.imfstatistics.org/imf/ (accessed 10 March 2011).

degree of coordination of exchange rate policies is desirable. The recent harmonized movement of exchange rates of some countries suggests that such de facto coordination may already exist.

Protectionist trade policies, such as subsidy programmes and other forms of preferential treat-

ment given as part of bailout packages in many developed countries, could also significantly alter competitive conditions in international markets. As fiscal consolidation proceeds in many developed economies, there may be an additional temptation to replace subsidies and preferential treatments granted in bailout programmes with new trade barriers. Such a scenario of heightened global protectionism is a major concern for the region as it would significantly jeopardize global export recovery and growth.

Economies have attempted to insure themselves against the risk of sudden capital outflows by building up foreign exchange reserves which can be used to defend currencies suffering from capital withdrawal. Despite the high level of reserves in many economies in recent months, there remains the possibility that the quantum of reserves may not be sufficient to defend currencies in the case of sudden capital outflows. The vulnerability yardstick developed by ESCAP[49] indicates that the reserves of a number of countries are substantially exceeded by their overall gross external liabilities which are most clearly reversible and measurable (see figure 1.25). These liabilities are short-term debt, the stock of portfolio inflows and the magnitude of imports over three months. The message is that, even though reserves may appear substantial, their adequacy can be deceptive in view of the scale of various portfolio inflows into the economies of the region. Apart from not being a guaranteed insurance policy,

building up reserves is also a costly and second-best solution for managing capital inflows. Holding reserves is costly because of potential exchange rate losses as well as the loss in interest income incurred from having to invest the funds in foreign currency assets that earn low interest.

Economies in the region are becoming receptive to the view that another solution to managing the deluge of inflows and the consequent risks of outflows lies in various forms of capital controls, as recommended by ESCAP,[50] which alerted policy-makers to the incipient capital heading for the region's shores and recommended the application of controls. It is increasingly accepted that a completely open capital account may not be appropriate from a cost-benefit analytical viewpoint,[51] particularly since research has suggested that the benefits of such openness are ambiguous.[52] Such controls become even more critical when economies are adopting high interest rate policies thereby increasing the attractiveness of the country as a destination for capital flows seeking to benefit from interest rate arbitrage. Thus, increased capital flow may neutralize the effects of interest rate increases. A number

Figure 1.25.   Vulnerability yardstick as a percentage of foreign reserves in selected Asian economies, latest available data

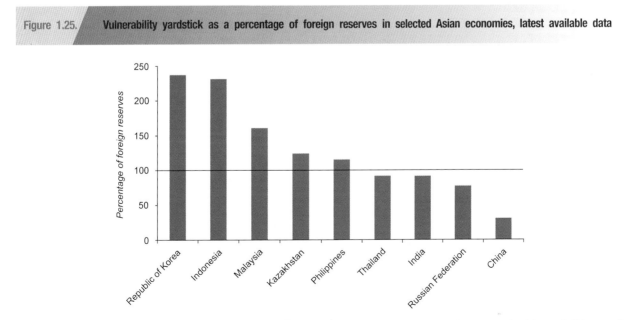

Sources: ESCAP calculations based on data from IMF, International Financial Statistics online, available from www.imfstatistics.org/imf/ (accessed 5 April 2011); World Bank, Quarterly External Debt Statistics databases (accessed 26 February 2011); and CEIC Data Company Limited, available from http://ceicdata.com (accessed 12 April 2011).

Note: The vulnerability yardstick is the sum of short-term debt, imports of the last quarter of the year and stock of equity and debt portfolio capital.

of developing economies as well as multilateral institutions,[53] both within and outside the region, have now realized the value of such controls and have imposed various forms of capital restrictions in recent months. Indonesia recently implemented controls, including a one-month minimum holding period for certain securities. In the Republic of Korea limits have been placed on currency forward positions and equity option contracts, and a tax was reimposed on earnings that foreigners make on government bonds, while Thailand imposed a 15% withholding tax on foreign holders of bonds (see table 1.3).

The recent controls in the region have been designed to reduce the attractiveness of certain types of inflows, such as foreign bank borrowing and short-term bonds. These sectors have been viewed as the most attractive for investors in particular country cases. The intention of the controls is to move investors towards long-term holdings of assets in these sectors. However, there remains the risk that volatility will not decline as a large quantum of reversible capital flows will continue to be attracted into these countries in spite of the type of controls being implemented. This is because the inherent attractiveness of these countries is due to the growth and interest rate differentials with the developed world, which are expected to persist for a long period. It is instructive to look at the case of Brazil, the earliest major developing economy to impose controls in October 2009. That country's 2% tax on foreign investment in equities and debt could not substantially stem the inflow of volatile capital. In response, the country in October 2010 moved to tighten controls further by increasing the tax on debt investments to 4%. Therefore, it is possible that the current controls being applied in the region will result in investors redirecting their investments to reversible holdings in other sectors not covered by the controls. The latter course of action is indeed the finding of numerous assessments of controls imposed by other economies in the past.[54] Indeed, recent data from Indonesia indicate that investors responded to curbs on short-term bonds by retaining their capital flows, but in longer-term bonds which are still inherently volatile. Since the imposition of the controls in early July 2010, by mid-July 2010 there had been a 37% surge in the foreign ownership of longer-term debt, and yields on the short-term bonds rose as foreigners pulled out of these assets.[55]

Table 1.3.	Capital control measures in the Asia-Pacific region, 2010-2011
Indonesia	**7 July 2010:** One-month minimum holding period on one-month Sertifikat Bank Indonesia (SBI) bonds. Increase in the maturity range of debt instruments by issuing longer dated SBIs (9-month and 12-month). New regulations introduced on banks' net foreign exchange open positions.
Republic of Korea	**13 June 2010:** Cap on domestic banks' and non-bank financial institutions' currency forwards and derivatives at 50% of their equity capital. Cap for foreign bank branches set at 250% of equity to account for their lower capital. Limits effectively affect foreign bank branches. Foreign banks' currency derivative positions at that time amounted to just over 300% of capital, while domestic banks' exposure totaled 15.6% of equity capital. Banks will have up to two years to comply fully with the new limits. Tightened the curbs on companies' currency derivative trades announced in November 2009, lowering the ceiling to 100% of the value of their physical foreign trade transactions from the initial 125%. **18 November 2010:** Reimposition of a 14% withholding tax on earnings that foreign investors make on government bonds, which had been removed in early 2009. Scheduled to be finalized in early 2010, the tax is to be levied retroactively on all debt earnings from 12 November 2010. **11 January 2011:** Cap on the positions held by institutional investors in stock option contracts on option expiry days and an obligation for investors to report large holdings of futures and options and major changes in their positions.
Thailand	**12 October 2010:** 15% withholding tax on capital gains and interest payments for government and State-owned company bonds.

Source: ESCAP based on media reports.

Note: Information as of 2 March 2011.

The next steps that may therefore be required by economies seeking to reduce volatile capital inflows would be to impose more widespread quantitative restrictions on foreign portfolio investments and bank non-investment lending. While this would be a strong measure, it may be justified due to the long-term pressure some developing economies face vis-à-vis the developed world. The guiding principle may be to have free entry of foreign investment in the areas which provide funding for the real sector, such as FDI, corporate and bank project lending and corporate equity and new bond issues, while carefully managing the entry of volatile capital for existing portfolio and other assets. Such discrimination between uses of capital would by its nature be difficult to optimize and there would be leakages or reductions in the amount of foreign funds potentially available for real investment. However, in practice this consideration may not be critical as most developing economies which are experiencing impacts from the inflow of volatile capital are arguably either not in significant need of foreign funds for investment or present such attractive investment stories that foreign capital would continue to enter regardless of the restrictions in place.

Developing economies in the region should be encouraged to coordinate and utilize various forms of capital controls as required to manage the influx of destabilizing flows. Such measures would best be implemented in a regionally coordinated manner among the affected countries as no one economy can implement such a policy without a likely exit of capital to comparable economies which have not instituted such controls. However, it remains the case that controls will continue to be dictated, to a large extent, by particular country conditions and therefore a collective response may prove difficult. There is also a need for developed economies to support the imposition of such controls when required by developing economies, especially as these controls have become necessary primarily because of the measures adopted by developed economies during their recovery process. In this regard, the G20 should support the use of capital controls as an additional policy tool at the disposal of developing

countries dealing with this problem.[56] In addition, the G20 could call on the International Monetary Fund (IMF) to provide these countries with technical assistance to help them devise appropriate forms of such controls.[57] In a significant reversal of its policy, the IMF now supports such controls as part of the policy tool kit available to the governments and is developing a 'pragmatic, experience based approach' to help countries manage large capital inflows, now endorsed by its Executive Board.[58]

Apart from measures by target economies to limit capital inflows, the developed economies should also take measures to limit the scale of such flows. Without such measures, there will be sustained pressure on the developing economies affected by capital seeking to move from developed economies into a developing region such as Asia and the Pacific. Furthermore, such measures would help to ensure that extra liquidity created as part of low interest rate policies and quantitative easing remain within the developed economies as intended in order to spur domestic lending. Numerous measures could be taken by the developed economies, such as taxing capital outflows and imposing high margin requirements on foreign exchange derivatives that mimic actual outflows.[59]

Unemployment remains a concern for the vulnerable

The regional unemployment rate is estimated to have fallen only slightly, from 4.6% in 2009 to 4.5% in 2010, driven by positive developments in developing countries in the region.[60] In most developing countries in the region where recent labour market information is available, unemployment levels in 2010 were lower than those in 2009, for example in Indonesia, the Philippines, Sri Lanka and Thailand.[61] In contrast, in many industrialized countries in the region, unemployment rates remained higher than before the crisis. Moreover, youth unemployment continues to be a major issue in the region, with young people being 3.2 times more likely to be unemployed than adults. In particular, the ratio for South-East Asia and the Pacific, at 4.7, is the highest among the world's subregions.[62] In the Philippines, for example, the annual youth unemployment rate in 2010 was 17.6%, compared with 5.1% for adults aged 25-54 years; youth in that country account for 51.1% of total unemployment. The crisis exacerbated the youth unemployment problem elsewhere too, especially in countries that were strongly affected as employers with rebounding output tended to choose from the pool of unemployed workers with experience rather than those without experience. To alleviate this problem, employers could be given incentives to hire young people through measures such as allowing them to pay differentiated (lower) minimum wages, to furnish lower levels of initial employment protection, and to initiate apprenticeship programmes.

Improving labour market conditions in the Asia and the Pacific region also translated into a decrease in the share of workers in vulnerable employment and a decrease in the share of the working poor. Nonetheless, some 1.1 billion workers in the region were in vulnerable employment in 2009. About 46.5% of workers are living with their families on less than $2 a day, and 22.7% of workers are living in conditions of extreme deprivation on less than $1.25 a day.[63]

As the labour markets in the Asian and the Pacific region recover there is a need to focus more on job creation and income growth than in the past.[64]

Rebalancing towards more domestic consumption-driven growth in several countries in the region presupposes robust employment creation, steady growth of disposable incomes and enhanced social protection. Recent data, however, indicate that economic growth has not been job-rich in most countries recording high rates (see table 1.4).[65] During the crisis, real wages in Asia are estimated to have grown by 8.0% in 2009.[66] This regional estimate is heavily influenced by China, which accounts for more than half of total employment in the region, and where real wages are estimated to have grown by 12.8% in 2009. In other countries, such as Malaysia, the Philippines and Thailand, real wages declined during the crisis.

The low employment growth rate is a particular concern for countries in the region which have high rates of labour force growth (see figure 1.26). A post-crisis macroeconomic framework that fosters more inclusive and balanced growth in the region thus calls for a renewed commitment to full employment, for men and women, as a core macroeconomic policy goal. Furthermore, many countries in the region have a large share of workers in the informal economy, where earnings are typically low and protection non-existent. In addition to addressing economic growth targets, inflation and sustainable public

Table 1.4.	Annual growth in GDP and employment in selected Asian economies, 2001-2008

	Average GDP growth (2001-2008)	Average employment growth (2001-2008)
China	10.5	0.9
India	7.0	2.4
Indonesia	5.4	1.7
Japan	1.4	-0.1
Malaysia	5.7	1.8
Mongolia	8.2	3.2
Pakistan	5.3	3.7
Philippines	5.3	2.8
Republic of Korea	4.4	1.4
Sri Lanka	6.0	1.7
Thailand	5.2	1.7
Viet Nam	7.6	2.0

Source: ESCAP, based on ILO, 15th Asia and the Pacific Regional Meeting: Building a sustainable future with decent work in Asia and the Pacific. Available from www.ilo.org/wcmsp5/groups/public/@ed_norm/@relconf/documents/meetingdocument/wcms_151860.pdf; IMF, World Economic Outlook database, October 2009; ILO, LABORSTA Internet; and ILO, Key Indicators of the Labour Market, Sixth Edition (Geneva, 2009).

A post-crisis macroeconomic framework that fosters more inclusive and balanced growth calls for a renewed commitment to full employment for men and women as a core policy goal

finances, the macroeconomic framework needs to ensure that growth is employment-rich and inclusive. In this regard, employment strategies based on employment growth and its gender dimensions are important in underpinning an employment-friendly macroeconomic framework.

In the wake of the global economic crisis, fiscal policies to foster growth and employment in particular have come to the forefront of the policy agenda in many countries in the region and around the world, as evident in the significant fiscal stimulus packages that have been undertaken. As countries in the region reconsider their fiscal policies, including sustainability, it is critical to incorporate into these considerations the issue of a basic social floor. In addition to reducing

Figure 1.26.   Forecast and historical labour force growth in selected Asia-Pacific economies, 2000-2015

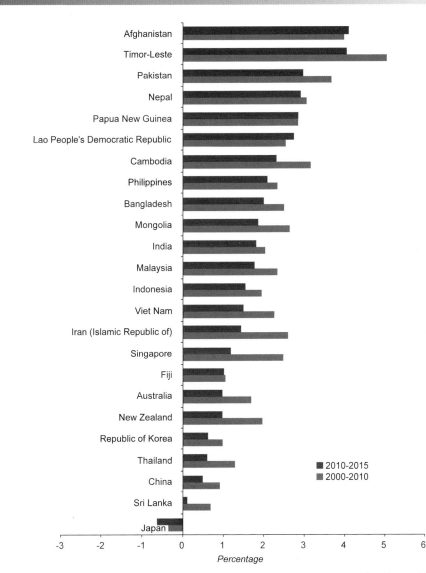

Source: ESCAP, based on ILO, Economically Active Population Estimates and Projections database (5th edition, revision 2009).

insecurity for the poor, improved social protection can support countries in their efforts to rebalance the sources of growth, through the freeing up of excessive precautionary savings for consumption or investment. The 1997/98 Asian financial crisis and the recent economic crisis have starkly brought to the fore the issues of insecurity and vulnerability in employment; they have also demonstrated the urgency of building and strengthening the "automatic stabilizers" of social protection and gradually building a basic social protection floor that includes access to health care, income security for the elderly and persons with disabilities, child benefits and income security combined with public employment guarantee schemes for the unemployed and working poor. Unemployment insurance in particular can function as an automatic stabilizer that cushions the impact of economic shocks and helps maintain aggregate demand. While the majority of countries in the region do not have unemployment insurance systems in place, the crisis has prompted some countries in the region, including Malaysia and the Philippines, to consider establishing unemployment insurance schemes that could be scaled up and expanded quickly during a crisis, while India expanded its national rural employment guarantee scheme.

In addition to strengthening social protection, other measures to improve job quality could support the rebalancing of economies in the region. With the majority of workers in the Asian and Pacific region either in vulnerable employment or working poverty, there is need to sustain growth in labor productivity, which is estimated to have increased by 5.7% in 2010, and ensure that wages keep pace with productivity in order to improve job quality. Education and skills development and ensuring a stronger link between wage and productivity growth are important means through which job quality in the region can be enhanced.

Medium-term challenge is to support alternative sources of demand

In the medium term, the fundamental challenge for the Asia-Pacific economies will be to significantly bolster alternative local sources of demand to replace in some measure the potential loss of demand from developed economies in the coming years.[67] Other than supporting economies in the region by maintaining the growth to be lost through the export channel, such a policy would support the international community in the necessary process of reducing the scale of global imbalances. Such imbalances were a key factor in the onset of the past crisis, with excessive debt-fuelled consumption by developed economies being supported by the purchase of the debt of developed economies by the central banks of developing economies. The likely fall in growth rates of consumption and imports of developed economies during the next few years as debt burdens are worked off, coupled with increasing exports due to depreciated exchange rates of such economies emanating from loose monetary policy, may support a reduction in the current account deficits of these economies. Within the region, a parallel process of expanding domestic demand, due to increasing wealth, as well as supportive government policies, could lead to reductions in current account surpluses as import levels increase in tandem with sluggish exports.

At the national level, reducing the dependence of the region on consumption from the developed world will mean both increasing domestic demand in the major economies and boosting intraregional trade for the region to benefit from the growth of these economies. On a purchasing power parity basis, China, India and Indonesia combined are estimated to have accounted for nearly 80% of the region's GDP in 2010. For these and other economies with significant domestic demand, boosting such demand further would involve placing greater emphasis either on the role of domestic consumption or investment. For instance, in East Asia (see figure 1.27) and, most importantly, in China (see table 1.5), the main shortfall is in consumption. On the other hand, in South-East Asia, the share of investment has declined (see figure 1.28). India, on the other hand, has been sustaining high levels of consumption and investment (see table 1.5) through increasing levels of current account deficits. Measures to increase domestic consumption should be focused on increasing the consumption rates of the poor and vulnerable, such as through raising wages, enhancing employment opportunities, and by increasing social protection programmes which serve to reduce precautionary savings for health and education needs.[68] In the case of investment, funds should be directed towards the bridging of development gaps, most notably in infrastructure, which would serve to increase the productive capacity of economies including those of the least developed economies (see chapter 4). Investment should also be encouraged in environmentally-friendly technologies and products, in line with Green Growth which emphasizes environmentally sustainable consumption and production that fosters low carbon, socially inclusive development. A number of Asia-Pacific countries including Japan, China, India and the Republic of Korea are promoting such innovations as part of their national action plans on climate change.

Figure 1.27. Share of household and government consumption in 10-year GDP growth, 1995-2011

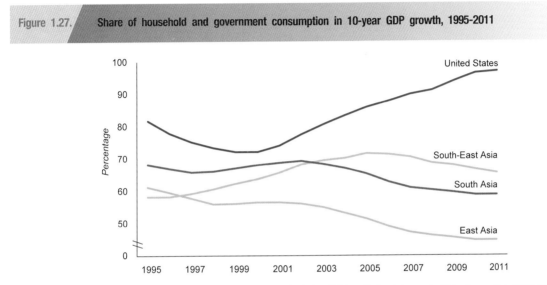

Sources: ESCAP calculations, based on data from United Nations Statistics Division, National Accounts Main Aggregates Database; and Economist Intelligence Unit, Country Data, available from http://countryanalysis.eiu.com/ (accessed 24 September 2010).

Notes: 2010 estimates; 2011 forecasts; see list of countries in table 7 of the Survey 2010 for country groupings.

Figure 1.28. Share of gross capital formation in 10-year GDP growth, 1995-2011

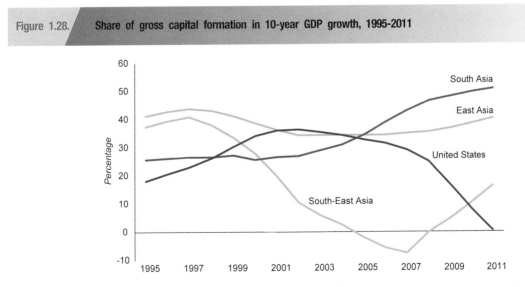

Sources: ESCAP calculations, based on data from United Nations Statistics Division, National Accounts Main Aggregates Database and Economist Intelligence Unit, Country Data, available from http://countryanalysis.eiu.com/ (accessed 24 September 2010).

Notes: 2010 estimates; 2011 forecasts; see list of countries in table 7 of the Survey 2010 for country groupings.

Table 1.5. Contributions of demand components to GDP and GDP growth in selected economies

(Percentage)

	Contributions to GDP				Growth rates of GDP and components			Contributions to GDP growth
	1986	1996	2006	2010	1986-1996	1996-2006	2006-2010	1996-2006
China								
GDP					10.2	9.3	10.3	
C	57.0	45.1	36.7	36.3	7.6	7.0	10.0	30.7
G	16.3	13.2	13.7	12.9	7.9	9.7	8.6	14.1
I	36.2	40.8	41.4	44.1	11.5	9.4	12.0	41.8
X - M	-1.1	1.0	8.2	6.7				13.3
India								
GDP					6.0	6.6	8.1	
C	71.6	63.4	55.7	52.0	4.7	5.2	6.3	47.1
G	12.3	10.7	9.8	10.9	4.6	5.7	11.0	8.8
I	25.5	25.2	38.0	41.5	5.9	11.1	10.5	52.3
X - M	-3.7	-3.1	-9.4	-10.4				-16.4
Indonesia								
GDP					7.6	2.5	5.7	
C	53.5	57.1	60.1	58.4	8.3	3.0	5.0	70.6
G	8.6	6.1	7.0	7.5	4.0	4.0	7.6	10.4
I	31.7	30.1	18.5	19.3	7.0	-2.4	6.8	-23.2
X - M	0.3	0.6	7.0	7.5				30.0
Malaysia								
GDP					9.0	4.4	3.9	
C	48.9	49.0	51.4	56.4	9.0	4.9	6.4	55.9
G	15.2	11.4	14.5	15.7	5.9	6.9	6.0	20.3
I	25.1	45.4	26.1	25.5	15.6	-1.3	3.3	-10.2
X - M	10.9	-5.2	8.6	3.7				34.5
Thailand								
GDP					9.5	2.7	3.6	
C	59.0	53.8	53.0	49.7	8.5	2.5	1.9	50.2
G	12.7	8.9	9.2	9.6	5.7	3.1	4.5	10.4
I	27.2	44.5	24.1	20.3	15.0	-3.4	-0.8	-43.0
X - M	1.7	-10.1	9.1	13.6				72.7
Memo item:								
United States								
GDP					3.4	2.9	0.2	
C	67.1	66.5	71.0	70.4	3.3	3.5	0.0	84.7
G	17.8	14.1	13.4	14.0	1.0	2.4	1.3	11.3
I	18.7	21.7	21.4	17.7	4.9	2.7	-4.4	20.4
X - M	-3.5	-2.1	-6.6	-4.7				-20.7

Source: ESCAP, based on data from the United Nations Statistics Division, National Accounts Main Aggregates Database and the Economist Intelligence Unit, *Country Data* (accessed 1 November 2010).

Notes: Data for 2010 are estimates. Growth rates are average annual growth rates.

Abbreviations: C = consumption; G = government expenditures; I = investments; X-M = net exports.

Other than directing domestic resources towards meeting such infrastructure needs, there is considerable scope for intermediating a portion of the considerable financial resources of the region, as evidenced by its foreign exchange reserves, with its enormous infrastructure requirements, through the establishment of a regional infrastructure financing mechanism. ESCAP analysis shows wide gaps in the levels of infrastructure development across the region (see figure 3.19). Closing these gaps would require huge investments. A recent study has estimated the infrastructure needs of Asia and the Pacific for the period 2011-2020 to be in the order of nearly $8 trillion ($5.4 trillion for new capacity and $2.6 trillion for replacement of old infrastructure).[69] Therefore, an

---

There is considerable scope for intermediating a portion of the considerable financial resources of the region, as evidenced by its foreign exchange reserves, with its enormous infrastructure requirements

---

investment requirement in the order of $800 billion per year is needed, a substantial proportion of which remains unfunded under current arrangements. In this context, the development of a regional financial architecture could facilitate efficient intermediation between a part of the more than $5 trillion in foreign exchange reserves of the Asia-Pacific region and the growing unmet needs for infrastructure development. One option would be to create an infrastructure development fund managed by a regional institution, as discussed in chapter 3.

For the smaller exporting economies in the region, intraregional trade and integration will need to be boosted in order to benefit from the domestic demand of their neighbours. Some of the priority actions that can leverage complementarities across the region and lay the foundations for more inclusive and sustainable development include institutional arrangements for market integration, improved connectivity and the facilitation of the cross-border movement of goods and services, as discussed in chapter 3.

Development-friendly global economic governance

The centrality of growth has been recognized by the adoption in 2009 of the G20 Framework for Strong, Sustainable and Balanced Growth.[70] The Asia-Pacific region could significantly contribute to this framework

by exploiting opportunities for generating additions to global aggregate demand, while also addressing the region's most urgent development needs. The Asia-Pacific region has eight members in G20, namely Australia, China, India, Indonesia, Japan, the Republic of Korea, the Russian Federation and Turkey, which is more than any other region of the world, signifying the systemic importance of Asia and the Pacific in the global economy. The effective coordination of the positions of Asia-Pacific G20 economies would give them greater influence in shaping the direction, content and pace of reform of the international financial architecture so that the reform would be best attuned the region's developmental needs. While G20 has emerged as a major forum for global policy coordination on economic issues, its credibility and effectiveness can be further enhanced by evolving a process of consultation with the non-member countries. In that context, ESCAP organized a high-level consultation in October 2010 with the participation of Asia-Pacific countries on the agenda of the G20 Seoul Summit, to gather their perspectives which were shared with the Summit Chair.

Global issues of importance for the region include proposals such as establishing a special drawing rights-based global reserve currency[71] that would include major developed and developing economy currencies, as well as other stores of value, such as gold, which could be issued countercyclically, supporting a global tax on financial transactions in order to raise resources for financing achievement of the Millennium Development Goals besides moderating short-term capital flows, and instituting international regulations to curb excessive risk-taking by the financial sector, as well as other issues concerning the reform of the international financial architecture that are emerging in the G20, the United Nations and other forums. In particular the approach adopted by the G20, in line with the recommendation of the United Nations,[72] to address global imbalances by restraining current account imbalances to a certain percentage of GDP is a good start. The G20 could also adopt measures to incentivize domestic consumption and investment by economies and discourage running of large surpluses by its member countries. Such a measure would be an important element of the framework for balanced, fair and sustainable growth.

G20, as a major forum for global policy coordination on economic issues, should also act decisively to moderate the volatility of oil and food prices that are highly disruptive of the process of development. In the area of oil price volatility, the G20 being the group of all major consumers can match the power exercised over the oil markets by the cartel of producers viz. the OPEC. OPEC and the G20 may demarcate a benchmark "fair" price of oil and agree to restrict the oil price movement within a band around it. An additional measure to moderate the volatility in the oil markets is for G20 to create a global strategic reserve and release it counter-cyclically. In the case of food price volatility, the G20 may act to regulate the speculative activity in food commodities, and discipline the conversion of cereals into biofuels. It may expedite the implementation of the L'Aquila Initiative on Food Security which included provision of financing to developing countries for food security. In these areas, as well as many others, the Asia-Pacific region has the opportunity to further integrate and coordinate its actions.

Policy agenda for promoting growth and inclusive development

In the year ahead, economies in the region will need to undertake complementary policies which address a number of objectives: protecting macroeconomic fundamentals from global instability, creating new sources of internal and regional growth in the medium-term, and improving the quality of growth to ensure that robust progress at the aggregate level translates into far more rapid improvement in the livelihoods of the poor and vulnerable while also keeping in mind environmental sustainability. The required policy measures should attempt to achieve these objectives in a holistic manner, ensuring that progress in achieving each of these aims does not prove detrimental to the other aims, and indeed serve where possible to support them. The challenges and the recommended approaches to manage them, as highlighted in this chapter, will need to be tackled, depending on their nature, at the national, regional, or global levels. While some actions may be undertaken using existing domestic institutional structures or global arrangements such as the G20, actions at the regional level will in many cases require enhanced and sometimes new cooperative setups to be established. Indeed, the regional aspect of economic and social cooperation is the critical missing piece in ensuring effective policies to safeguard and further support development in the coming years for the region's economies and citizens, particularly economies with special needs and the most poor and vulnerable of the region's peoples. Key elements of the policy agenda for the region are recapitulated below.

National policies

- Combat food and energy price rises with targeted measures to directly impact prices and reduce the burden on the poor. Besides reducing prices through lowering tariffs and taxes, buffer stocks of food should be established and utilized in a countercyclical manner in order to moderate the volatility of food prices, speculative activity in food commodities should be regulated, social protection measures should be undertaken in the form of providing the poor with food vouchers, targeted income transfers should be implemented and school feeding programmes strengthened to minimize the impact on poverty due to higher expenditures on food and energy by the poorer sections of society. In the medium term greater emphasis should be placed on strengthening the supply response by reversing the neglect of agriculture in public policy, raising agricultural productivity through continued support for agricultural research and development, extension services and rural development activities, and instituting a new, knowledge-intensive green revolution which would also make agriculture more environmentally resilient.

- Use monetary policy when required to prevent buildup of demand-side inflationary pressures in fast expanding economies and inflationary pass-through of supply-side food and energy price rises. Demand-side pressures are particularly keen in domestic-demand led economies, while inflationary pass-through will be more prevalent in less-developed and energy-intensive economies where food and energy account for a higher proportion of the consumption and production baskets. In the countries facing large inflows of speculative capital, capital controls may be considered and imposed.

- Enact medium-term policies to foster comple-mentary sources of growth to exports by in-creasing the role of domestic demand. Boost-ing such demand further will involve providing greater emphasis to either the role of domestic consumption or investment. For instance, in East Asia and, most importantly, in China, the main shortfall is in consumption. On the other hand, in South-East Asia, the key drawback is in investment. Measures to increase domestic consumption should be focused on increasing the consumption rates of the poor and vulnerable such as through raising real wages, enhancing employment opportunities, and by increasing social protection programmes which serve to reduce precautionary savings for health and education needs. In the case of investment, funds should be directed to the bridging of development gaps, most notably in infrastructure, which will serve to increase the productive capacity of economies.

Regional policies

- Regional initiatives could play a valuable role in reducing the pressure of food price rises. One such role could be through the establishment of regional food reserves for key staple items, as demonstrated by the ASEAN+3 Emergency Rice Reserve Agreement and the SAARC Food Bank.

- Developing economies in the region should be encouraged to coordinate and utilize various forms of capital controls as required to manage the influx of destabilizing flows. Such measures would best be implemented in a regionally coordinated manner among the affected countries as no one economy can engage in implementing such a policy without a likely exit of capital to comparable economies which have not instituted such controls. However, it remains the case that controls will remain dictated, to a large extent, by particular country conditions and therefore a collective response may prove difficult.

- As a part of rebalancing, regional economic integration should be strengthened to leverage complementarities across the region and lay the foundations for more inclusive and sustain-able development through market integration, improved connectivity and the facilitation of the cross-border movement of goods and services, as discussed in chapter 3.

- It is now widely recognized that a regional financial architecture, elements of which are elaborated in chapter 3, could be a useful complement to the international financial architecture. The Asia-Pacific region is gradually moving towards developing some elements of a regional financial architecture with the Chiang Mai Initiative and regional bond market development. However, with combined foreign exchange reserves of $5 trillion, the region now has the ability to develop a more ambitious regional financial architecture. The economic crisis and subsequent recovery have highlighted the importance of regional options to complement IMF facilities in order to combat global macroeconomic volatility. If governments had access to a well-endowed regional crisis response and prevention facility they would feel less need to build up large foreign exchange reserves to protect their economies against speculative attacks and liquidity crises, and could thus free up reserves for more productive investments. So far, the cooperation in the area has been largely limited to the Chiang Mai Initiative Multilateralization (CMIM). There is a need to extend the scope and coverage of the CMIM to create a real and effective regional crisis prevention and management facility. Enhanced regional cooperation for crisis response and management should not, however, be regarded as an alternative to full participation in global economic relations. Rather it should be seen as a complement to it, filling in the gaps and establishing the building blocks for global multilateral cooperation. The region needs to develop further its financial architecture for development financing, which would include systems of intermediation between its large savings and its unmet investment needs. One option would be to create an infrastructure development fund managed by a regional institution. If this secured just 5% of the region's reserves of nearly $5 trillion it could provide start-up capital of $250 billion besides its ability to borrow from the central banks. This pooling of reserves could assist the region in meeting some of its investment needs estimated to be of order of more than $800 billion per annum in transport, energy, water and telecommunications.Another area where a regional financial architecture could make a positive contribution is in exchange rate coordination. As economies of the region increasingly trade with each other, they will need a currency management system that facilitates trade and macroeconomic stability and discourages beggar-thy-neighbour currency competition. One option worthy of consideration is a basket parity relative to a number of reserve currencies instead of the dollar alone, and a set of weights determined on the basis of regional trade share.

Global policies

- The region should play an active part in reforming the global economic and financial architecture in order to ensure that the reforms best serve the region's development needs. The region should be active in using traditional avenues for global cooperation as well as the increasingly central importance of the G20 process.[73] The Asia-Pacific region has eight members in the G20—Australia, China, India, Indonesia, Japan, the Republic of Korea, the Russian Federation and Turkey—more than any other region, signifying the systemic importance of Asia and the Pacific in the global economy. The effective coordination of the positions of Asia-Pacific G20 economies would give them greater influence in shaping the direction, content and pace of reform of the international financial architecture so that the reform is best attuned to the region's developmental needs.

- Global issues of importance for the region include various proposals such as establishing a special drawing rights-based global reserve currency that includes major developed and developing economy currencies as well as other stores of value, such as gold, which could be issued counter-cyclically, supporting capital controls by the Governments that need them, agreeing to a global tax on financial transactions to raise capital for financing Millennium Development Goals besides moderating short-term capital flows, and instituting international regulations to curb excessive risk-taking by the financial sector, as well as other issues concerning the reform of the international financial architecture that are emerging in the G20, the United Nations and other forums. In particular the approach adopted by the G20, in line with the recommendation of the United Nations,[74] to address global imbalances by restraining current account imbalances to a certain percentage of GDP is a good start. The G20 could also adopt measures to incentivize domestic consumption and investment by economies and discourage running of large surpluses by its member countries. Such a measure would be an important element of the framework for balanced, fair and sustainable growth.

- G20, as a major forum for global policy co-ordination on economic issues, should act decisively to moderate the volatility of oil and food prices that are highly disruptive of the process of development. In the area of oil price volatility, the G20 being the group of all major consumers can match the power exercised over the oil markets by the cartel of producers viz. the OPEC. OPEC and the G20 may demarcate a benchmark "fair" price of oil and agree to restrict the oil price movement within a band around it. An additional measure to moderate the volatility in the oil markets is for the G20 to create a global strategic reserve and release it counter-cyclically. In the case of food price volatility, the G20 may act to regulate the speculative activity in food commodities, and discipline the conversion of cereals into biofuels. It may expedite the implementation of the L'Aquila Initiative on Food Security which included provision of financing to developing countries for food security.

In these areas, as well as many others, the Asia-Pacific region has the opportunity to further integrate and coordinate its actions.

Endnotes

[1] United Nations, Economic and Social Commission for Asia and the Pacific and United Nations International Strategy and Disaster Reduction, 2010.

[2] United Nations, Economic Commission for Africa, 2010.

[3] United Nations, Economic Commission for Latin America and the Caribbean, 2011.

[4] Eurostat, 2011.

[5] International Monetary Fund, 2010a, p. 8.

[6] For further details, see United Nations, Economic and Social Commission for Asia and the Pacific, 2010a.

[7] In G20 Toronto Summit Declaration, 2010. "…recent events highlight the importance of sustainable public finances and the need for our countries to put in place credible, properly phased and growth-friendly plans to deliver fiscal sustainability, differentiated for and tailored to national circumstances".

[8] See, for example, Cetorelli and Goldberg, 2010.

[9] Except for Viet Nam, for first quarter of 2009 and 2010.

[10] United Nations, Economic and Social Commission for Asia and the Pacific, 2009a.

[11] Hang Seng Bank, 2011.

[12] International Monetary Fund, 2010b, figure 1.15, estimates that the exports from Asian countries to China were increasing three times faster than China's exports to the United States and Europe.

[13] See also United Nations, Economic and Social Commission for Asia and the Pacific, 2010b.

[14] See also International Monetary Fund, 2010b.

[15] See, for example, Wang and Whalley, 2010.

[16] United Nations Conference on Trade and Development, 2011.

[17] United Nations, Economic and Social Commission for Asia and the Pacific, 2009a.

[18] ESCAP calculations based on data from CEIC Data Company Limited. Available from http://ceicdata.com/ (accessed 23 March 2011).

[19] Mohapatra, Ratha and Silwal, 2010.

[20] United Nations, Department of Economic and Social Affairs, 2010.

[21] Contributed by Prof. Biman Prasad, Dean, Faculty of Business and Economics, University of the South Pacific, Fiji.

[22] Nomura Global Economics, 2010.

[23] Capital Economics, 2011.

[24] The impact of oil price increases on the consumer price index (CPI) may be limited due to the existence of price controls, price subsidies in many countries as well as to the potential capacity of the oil distribution sector to absorb the costs (by reducing mark-ups) which in turn may be related to the structure and ownership of the industry. ESCAP analysis showed that in China, a 1% increase in oil prices would result in a mere 0.005% increase in core CPI, while the impact would be even smaller in the Philippines and Thailand at around 0.003%. This estimation was done in the framework of augmented Phillips curve of the following form:
$$\Delta \log CPI_t = \alpha + \beta_1 \log GAP_{t-1} + \beta_2 \Delta \log OIL_t + \beta_3 \Delta \log CPI_{t-1} + \varepsilon_t$$
In addition to oil price inflation, past inflation and the cyclical position of the economy also appeared to be important determinants of core inflation. The equation was estimated with a trend.

[25] An estimated 76 million people became undernourished owing to the food crisis of 2008; the proportion of undernourished people jumped by 4 percentage points during the crisis.

[26] Food and Agriculture Organization of the United Nations, 2009.

[27] Food and Agriculture Organization of the United Nations, 2008.

[28] World Bank, 2010.

[29] United Nations, Economic and Social Commission for Asia and the Pacific, 2008a.

[30] Bjerga, 2010.

[31] United Nations, 2010a.

[32] Ghosh, 2010, p. 2.

[33] Ibid.

[34] United Nations Conference on Trade and Development, 2009, chapter 3, p. 26.

[35] Barclays Capital, 2010.

[36] Der Spiegel, 2010.

[37] United Nations Conference on Trade and Development, 2010a, p. 11.

[38] United Kingdom, Department for Environment, Food and Rural Affairs, 2010.

[39] United Nations, Economic and Social Commission for Asia and the Pacific, 2010c.

[40] For further details, see United Nations, Economic and Social Commission for Asia and the Pacific, 2009b.

[41] For further details, see United Nations, Economic and Social Commission for Asia and the Pacific, 2010b.

[42] Khalik, 2011.

[43] International Financial Services London Research, 2009.

[44] Farchy, 2010.

[45] Gupta, 2011.

[46] Yoon, 2010.

[47] Knight Frank, 2010.

[48] See Akyüz, 2011.

[49] For more details, see United Nations, Economic and Social Commission for Asia and the Pacific, 2010b, pp. 21-22.

[50] United Nations, Economic and Social Commission for Asia and the Pacific, 2010b.

[51] Rodrik, 2006.

[52] See, for example, Aizenman and Lee 2007; Jeanne, 2007; Obstfeld, Shambaugh and Talyor, 2008.

[53] International Monetary Fund, 2010c.

[54] See, for example, De Gregorio, Edwards and Valdés, 2000.

[55] Reuters Analysis, 2010.

[56] United Nations, Economic and Social Commission for Asia and the Pacific, 2010c.

[57] United Nations, Economic and Social Commission for Asia and the Pacific, 2010d.

[58] International Monetary Fund, 2011.

[59] See, for example, Griffith-Jones and Gallagher, 2011.

[60] International Labour Organization, 2010a. The region refers to East Asia, South-East Asia and the Pacific and South Asia.

[61] International Labour Organization, 2011a.

[62] International Labour Organization, 2011b.

[63] International Labour Organization, 2010a.

[64] This section draws from International Labour Organization; 2010b; International Labour Organization, 2010c.

[65] International Labour Organization, 2010d.

[66] Ibid.

[67] For a full discussion of the issues summarized in this section, see United Nations, Economic and Social Commission for Asia and the Pacific, 2010b, chap. 3.

[68] See Heyzer, 2010.

[69] Asian Development Bank, 2009.

[70] See Leaders' Statement: The Pittsburgh Summit, 2009.

[71] See United Nations, Economic and Social Commission for Asia and the Pacific, 2011b.

[72] United Nations, Department of Economic and Social Affairs, 2011.

[73] For further details, see United Nations, Economic and Social Commission for Asia and the Pacific, 2010e.

[74] See, United Nations, Department of Economic and Social Affairs 2011, p. 41.

2

"Asia is undergoing a rapid and strong economic, social, cultural and strategic resurgence — the sum of which is certain to redefine global affairs."
Susilo Bambang Yudhoyono, President of Indonesia

Macroeconomic Performance and Policy Challenges at the Subregional Level

While the developing countries of Asia and the Pacific strengthened their growth performance substantially from 4.7% in 2009 to 8.8% in 2010, this region is so vast and diverse that aggregate figures mask the diversity in performance and challenges being faced at the subregion and country levels. Therefore, this chapter provides a more disaggregated analysis of macroeconomic performance and policy challenges at the subregional level with some details at the country level. In the *Survey*, the Asia-Pacific region is divided into five geographic subregions, namely East and North-East Asia, North and Central Asia, Pacific, South and South-West Asia and South-East Asia. An overview of the macroeconomic performance and policy challenges of all the subregions is followed by more detailed analysis.

Divergent performance of subregions

The economic recovery in East and North-East Asia strengthened in 2010, while the primary channels of recovery tended to differ, reflecting the economic diversity in the subregion. Indeed, China emerged as the world's second largest economy in 2010, with its growth increasingly driven by robust domestic demand, particularly investment. The more export-oriented economies of Japan and the Republic of Korea benefited from a recovery in demand for key export products, especially durable consumer goods, while the commodity-based economy of Mongolia grew on the back of rising commodity prices and mining activities. Somewhat worryingly, inflation has also started to rise throughout the subregion, except in Japan. This phenomenon has been mainly due to the rebound in aggregate demand but has also been the result of increases in food and fuel prices driven up, in part, by speculation and excess liquidity in the market. Fiscal policy measures that were part of the stimulus packages introduced in 2008 and 2009 in China and the Republic of Korea are expected to be withdrawn gradually in 2011 so as to restrain the growth in public debt. On the other hand, the Government of Japan will still need to provide further support to the economy through the injection of public spending and other stimulus measures to rebuild the economy in the wake of the devastating earthquake and tsunami.

The North and Central Asian subregion consists of major energy and mineral exporters. Recovery in global demand for oil and gas, gold, cotton and other commodities in 2010, as well as higher prices for them, therefore, gave a strong boost to these economies. Domestic demand in several countries also benefited from a modest recovery in remittance flows from Kazakhstan and the Russian Federation, the two major economies of the subregion. The agricultural sector, however, contracted in several economies of the subregion due to poor weather conditions. Inflation rates were relatively high, over 5% in most countries, although they came down in 2010 in several countries. Countries with large

oil revenues have been able to cushion some of the budgetary shortfalls with transfers from State oil funds, while others have had to rely more on international assistance and are undergoing fiscal consolidation in consultation with the International Monetary Fund (IMF). Although oil and gas exporters continued to enjoy current account and trade surpluses to varying degrees, oil and gas importers have experienced deficits.

In the Pacific subregion, the Pacific island developing economies experienced sharp declines in GDP growth in 2009 on account of the global economic crisis. For 2010, however, the results appear to be mixed, with only Papua New Guinea, Palau and Solomon Islands recording a significantly improved GDP growth performance in 2010. Most of the other economies virtually stagnated, with the economy of Tonga actually contracting. There was some deceleration in inflation in some major economies. Most countries suffered deficits in their current account balances. Available data suggest a mixed picture in terms of budget performance for the economies in 2010 with Kiribati, Papua New Guinea and Solomon Islands recording balanced or surplus budgets while others expecting budget deficits. The economies of both Australia and New Zealand enjoyed positive growth in 2010 following the global economic crisis but with varying impacts on employment. Australia was much more successful in reducing unemployment than New Zealand.

The global economic crisis had a limited impact on the economies of South and South-West Asia because of their greater dependence on domestic than on external demand. With global economic recovery gathering pace in 2010, however, a surge in economic activities was witnessed in several economies, particularly in India, in 2010. Strong growth was driven by a revival in investment and private consumption, a growth in exports, a rise in industrial production and improved performance by the agricultural sector. Sustained high growth is critical to bring down poverty levels, which are still high compared to those in other subregions.

High inflation, however, remains a serious problem in the subregion. While monetary policy has been tightened in some countries to contain inflation, there is a greater need to address supply side issues. Moreover, as budget deficits remain high, there is a clear need for further fiscal consolidation to tackle the problem of inflation.

South-East Asia, after an earlier-than-expected recovery in 2009, once again exceeded expectations with strong, broad-based economic growth in 2010. With rising consumer and investor confidence, the private sector is driving the economies forward. Years of prudent macroeconomic management also paid off well. Unlike many developed economies, South-East Asia was able to sustain fiscal stimulus through much of 2010 until recovery became fully secured. Against the backdrop of an uncertain global outlook, monetary policy was also carefully managed so as to remain accommodative while keeping inflation in check. In some countries, measures were also taken to limit exposure to the short-term foreign capital that flooded the domestic equity, bond, and property markets.

EAST AND NORTH-EAST ASIA

Recovery gains momentum in 2010

The economies of East and North-East Asia, which started to recover from the global economic crisis during the second half of 2009, increased their growth momentum in 2010. The economies rebounded strongly, with manufacturing output and exports returning to near pre-crisis levels by the second quarter of 2010. Government stimulus spending played an important role in boosting economic growth, as did strong domestic demand, which benefited from broader social protection programmes, improvements in the labour markets and rising asset prices. Private investment also picked up, as most economies in the subregion maintained a relatively loose monetary stance to support economic growth. Led by strong growth in China, the subregion grew at 6.4% in 2010, after experiencing a negative growth of 1.0% in 2009 (see table 2.1).

The Chinese economy expanded by a remarkable 10.3% in 2010, after achieving GDP growth of 9.1%

Table 2.1.   Rates of economic growth and inflation in selected East and North-East Asian economies, 2009-2011

(Percentage)

	Real GDP growth			Inflation[a]		
	2009	2010[b]	2011[c]	2009	2010[b]	2011[c]
East and North-East Asia[d]	**-1.0**	**6.4**	**4.5**	**-0.2**	**1.2**	**2.4**
China	9.1	10.3	9.5	-0.7	3.3	4.5
Democratic People's Republic of Korea	-0.9	..	..	..	..	..
Hong Kong, China	-2.8	6.8	4.9	0.5	2.4	4.0
Japan	-6.3	3.9	1.5	-1.4	-0.7	0.6
Macao, China	1.3	35.0	9.2	1.2	2.8	3.4
Mongolia	-1.3	6.1	9.0	6.3	10.1	16.0
Republic of Korea	0.2	6.1	4.5	2.8	3.0	3.6

Sources: ESCAP, based on national sources; and CEIC Data Company Limited; data available from http://ceicdata.com (accessed 25 March 2011).

[a] Changes in the consumer price index.
[b] Estimates.
[c] Forecasts (as of 8 April 2011).
[d] GDP figures at market prices in dollars in 2009 (at 2000 prices) are used as weights to calculate the subregional growth rates.

in 2009. In 2009, urban fixed asset investments fuelled by government spending on infrastructure projects had provided much-needed support to economic expansion. In 2010, fixed asset investment continued to be the main contributor to growth, with real estate development becoming one of the key drivers of investment growth. China's real estate market started to recover during the second half of 2009, buoyed by favourable government policies, such as lower taxes on certain real estate transactions and lower down-payment requirements, as well as rising confidence in China's economic recovery. By the end of 2009, the rapid rise in property prices and concerns over speculative investment, however, prompted the government to reverse the incentive measures. Nonetheless, real estate investment increased by 33.2% in 2010, amid intensified measures to curb overheating. Retail sales of consumer goods increased sharply and the slack in external demand was picked up by domestic demand. Furthermore, in an effort to boost private consumption and promote a more equitable distribution of growth, minimum wages were increased in several provinces across China (for example, Hainan has raised the minimum wage by 37%).[1]

Aided by the strong domestic demand in China and recovery in the rest of the world, Hong Kong, China, rebounded strongly in 2010, with GDP growth reaching 6.8% after the 2.8% contraction recorded in 2009. Domestic demand growth was particularly strong throughout the year and retail sales also benefited from the robust growth of inbound tourism. Residential property sales, which recorded a rise of 28.5% in 2009, continued to increase sharply in 2010. The exchange rate policy of Hong Kong, China, pegging its currency to the dollar, has contributed to the boom in the property market, as the peg requires it to maintain negative real interest rates despite strong domestic growth. In Macao, China, the real GDP growth rate soared to 35.0% in 2010 from 1.3% in 2009, largely owing to a major increase in tourists from mainland China. The tourism and gaming sector constitutes the core of the economy.

Although the Democratic People's Republic of Korea does not publish official statistics, the economy most likely contracted in 2010 due to the negative impact of unusually bad weather on the agricultural sector, which accounts for a large share of GDP. In addition, the economy suffered additional losses from disruptions in trade, aid and tourism from the Republic of Korea in 2010. Trade with the Republic of Korea accounts for approximately 50% of the country's exports.

The adverse economic impact caused by the devastating earthquake and tsunami in Japan will continue to be felt for many years to come

The Japanese economy, which contracted by 6.3% in 2009, bounced back after the second quarter of 2009 and continued to record positive growth in 2010, although the size of the economy still remained well below its pre-crisis level. Economic recovery decelerated in the second half of the year; nevertheless, GDP still grew by 3.9% in 2010. While growth continued to be heavily dependent on net export growth, domestic demand also contributed, albeit weakly. Domestic demand is led by the growth of private consumption, especially of durable goods, reflecting the subsidies for "green" durables as part of the fiscal stimulus. Growth of nominal wage income turned positive in 2010 after recording a more than 7% decline during 2009, thus contributing to the improvement in consumer confidence. Recovery of residential investment has stalled, however, hovering around the 2007 level when residential investment plunged due to regulatory changes. Corporate investment has continued to recover, reflecting an improvement in corporate profits and business sentiment.

Japan was hit by a massive earthquake and a devastating tsunami in March 2011. The Fukushima nuclear power plant crisis, as a result, caused a radioactive contamination scare and disruptions in the electricity supply. It is first and foremost a human tragedy in which thousands of people lost their lives and an even larger number were rendered homeless, but the adverse economic impact caused by the extensive damage inflicted upon the coastal infrastructure in north-eastern Japan will continue to be felt for many years to come. According to some preliminary estimates by the Government, the economic damage could reach $309 billion. Thus, huge resources will be required for reconstruction and rehabilitation activities. While these activities should compensate for some of the losses in GDP growth suffered as a result of the earthquake and tsunami, the enhanced government spending will add to the fiscal deficit and very high public debt. The Bank of Japan has already injected massive funds into the money market to shore up consumer confidence and maintain liquidity.

Mongolia's economy was hit hard in 2009 by collapsing mineral prices, contraction in the construction sector and a steep drop in external demand for major exports, such as cashmere. The contraction of the economy by 1.3% in 2009 was also due, in part, to the underlying weaknesses in the economic environment, as demonstrated by the sudden deterioration in fiscal and external balances and in the quality of bank balance sheets. The strong policy response by the government, however, aided by improved external conditions, particularly the rise in copper and gold prices, led to a rapid turnaround in 2010, with GDP growing by 6.1%. Significant progress has also been made in mining sector reform and development.

The economy of the Republic of Korea grew by 6.1% in 2010, up from 0.2% in 2009. Growth was supported by the recovery in demand for exports, growth in private consumption, fixed asset investment and stock-building. The country was among the first in the Asia-Pacific region to recover from the economic crisis. Economic output stabilized as early as the first quarter of 2009 and by July 2010 manufacturing activity had surpassed pre-crisis levels, with factories operating at 84.8% of capacity, the highest level since October 1987. Inventory-rebuilding, however, which had contributed significantly to economic expansion in early 2010, came to completion towards the beginning of the

third quarter, leading to the subsequent deceleration in economic activity to a more sustainable level. The stock market posted strong gains during the year but the housing market remained flat.

Inflation rises moderately but risks remain

Inflation has picked up in the subregion, although at a modest and manageable rate. Higher international commodity prices, the absorption of excess capacity and strong domestic demand are putting upward pressure on prices but the appreciation of subregional currencies is having a tempering effect on imported inflation. Consumer prices in China and Hong Kong, China, increased by 3.3% and 2.4%, respectively, and inflation in Macao, China, rose to 2.8% in 2010 (see figure 2.1). Within the increase in inflationary pressure, the rapid rise in grain prices and other foodstuffs is a cause for concern. A series of natural disasters has led to poor harvests in many parts of the world. For example, floods along the Yangtze River system and in the north-east have devastated major corn-producing regions in China, and in August 2010, the Russian Federation banned grain exports for the remainder of the year due to the severe drought that had destroyed about 20% of its wheat crop.[2] In the Republic of Korea, inflation rose marginally to 3.0% in 2010, with food prices rising at even higher rates. As Mongolia relies on imports for much of its food and fuel, higher-than-expected rises in food prices had a substantial impact on overall inflation. The Mongolian agricultural sector was also adversely affected by weather conditions, which exacerbated inflationary pressures. In 2010, inflation rose to 10.1% from 6.3% in 2009.

In contrast, deflation has once again become a major concern for the economy in Japan. Consumer prices continued to decline, by 0.7% in 2010, although the pace was slower than the 1.4% decline recorded in 2009. While this current bout of deflation reflects the output gap stemming from the slower economic growth, it also reflects structural factors, such as market deregulation and competitive pressure from China, which is making it more difficult for producers

| Figure 2.1. | Inflation in selected East and North-East Asian economies, 2008-2010 |

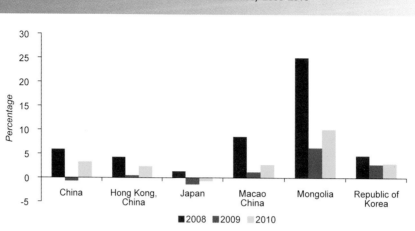

Sources: ESCAP, based on national sources; and CEIC Data Company Limited, data available from http://ceicdata.com (accessed 25 March 2011).

Note: Data for 2010 are estimates.

to increase prices. Other contributing factors include sluggish wage growth and the appreciation of the Japanese currency, which have brought down imported prices in yen terms.

Preparing for a normalization of fiscal policies

China and the Republic of Korea injected fiscal stimulus through spending on infrastructure projects and investment in agriculture, education and health care in 2009 and 2010, but with plans to unwind most of the stimulus spending in 2011. In China, the 2010 budget reflected a shift in focus away from short-term growth towards improving the quality of longer-term growth by strengthening rural sector investments and social welfare programmes. Due to the ongoing rollover of increased spending and reduced tax receipts, budget deficits have increased in China and the Republic of Korea to a slightly higher but manageable level of -2.2% and -1.9% of GDP, respectively (see figure 2.2). Japan, which had accumulated gross Government debt amounting to 217.5% of GDP in 2009, experienced a further rise to 225.0% in 2010. Interest and maturity payments on Government bonds alone came to 20% of the national budget in fiscal year 2010. Despite the growing need to consolidate its fiscal balance, the Government of

Japan launched a fresh fiscal stimulus package in late 2010 called The Three-Step Economic Measures for the Realization of the New Growth Strategy, in view of deflationary pressures and soft labour market conditions. The additional spending coupled with sluggish recovery and reduced tax receipts led the Government budget deficit to increase to 7.5% of GDP in 2010. The Government of Mongolia, which relies heavily on mining-related revenues, saw its fiscal deficit declining substantially in 2010 as a result of recovering commodity prices. The Government also introduced a new fiscal responsibility bill to reduce the budget deficit gradually and keep spending in check as it faces increasing pressure to redistribute the mining revenue to the public.

Monetary tightening begins cautiously

After maintaining low interest rates for a year or longer, monetary policies in the subregional economies have begun to be tightened. Early signs of overheating in the property and stock markets, together with rising inflationary pressure, led the Government of China to increase the benchmark rates several times since October 2010. Similarly, the Bank of Korea adjusted its policy rate upwards from 2.00% to 3.00% in a series of moves beginning in July 2010, after keeping it on hold for 17 months. Going the other way, the

| Figure 2.2. | Budget balance in selected East and North-East Asian economies, 2008-2010 |

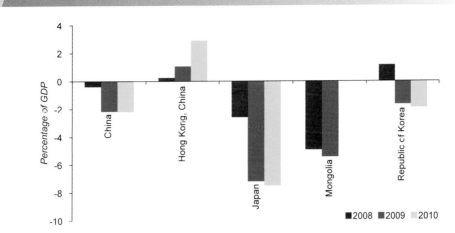

Sources: ESCAP, based on national sources; and CEIC Data Company Limited, data available from http://ceicdata.com (accessed 16 February 2011).

Notes: Data for 2010 are estimates. Budget balance for Mongolia includes grants.

Bank of Japan announced further monetary easing in October 2010. The policy target rate was lowered from 0.1% to a range between 0.0% and 0.1% due to the re-emergence of deflation. The Bank of Japan stated that it would keep rates at virtually zero until prices had stabilized in the medium- to long-term and would consider further temporary measures to inject liquidity into the market, including a buy-back of Government securities and the purchase of other assets, such as corporate bonds and real estate investment. The central bank of Mongolia increased interest rates by 100 basis points in May 2010 to combat the return of double-digit inflation. While economies in the subregion look towards raising interest rates in 2011, a growing concern for the subregion is that rising interest rates are likely to attract an inflow of speculative capital from countries where interest rates are low, pushing asset prices higher and fuelling inflation.

External sector returns to pre-crisis levels

Export growth rates returned rapidly to pre-crisis levels. In China, demand for consumer products, which had been extremely sensitive to the economic downturn, led the growth in exports. Over the years, Hong Kong, China, has moved away from the low-cost manufacturing of clothing and apparel to higher

value-added manufacturing. During this transition, the manufacture and export of a new range of products, including electronic and optical products, machinery and equipment, have increased. Along with strong gains in merchandise exports, the export of services maintained double-digit growth throughout the year, largely due to the increase in tourists from mainland China. Similarly, Macao, China, benefited from a large rise in tourists from mainland China. Japanese exports, which nose-dived at the beginning of 2009, bounced back despite the continued appreciation of the Japanese yen vis-à-vis the dollar. Export growth faltered in the third quarter of 2010, however, as the demand from Asia, which accounts for around half of Japanese exports, experienced a sharp slowdown. Exports from Mongolia increased in line with rising commodity prices. The Republic of Korea, whose key exports include semiconductors, electronics, automobiles, container ships and oil tankers, greatly benefited from the broad-based recovery of the global economy, as well as from specific incentive programmes, both at home and abroad, designed to boost demand for consumer goods, such as "Cash for Clunkers"[3] in the United States.[4] Exports from the Republic of Korea have also been helped by a relatively weak currency compared to the Japanese yen, given that the two economies share a broadly similar export basket.

In China, import growth was particularly strong during the first half of 2010, as restocking demand for raw materials, intermediate inputs and capital equipment increased in response to the global economic recovery. In addition, demand for imported durable consumer goods, such as vehicles and electronics, soared. Due to the large increase in imports, the current account surplus shrank considerably during the first half of 2010 but then bounced back; it did not, however, reach levels seen prior to the crisis. Japan also saw a steady increase of imports since the trough in 2009, although to a lesser extent than exports. The appreciation of the yen against the dollar brought down import prices in yen terms, resulting in a widening of Japan's current account surplus, despite the growth in imports. In contrast to the growth of the merchandize trade surplus, the deficit in services remained modest, with a relatively moderate recovery in overseas travel. Together with a large income surplus reflecting the substantial stock of overseas investment, the current account surplus remained well above 3% of GDP in 2010 (see figure 2.3). While China, Japan and the Republic of Korea were able to maintain a current account surplus in 2010, the strengthening of currencies vis-à-vis the dollar is likely to lead to a narrowing of the surplus in 2011. Mongolia is the exception, as its current account deficit widened as imports rose faster than exports, in part reflecting the need for machinery and equipment for the Oyu Tologi project to develop the copper and gold mine.

Return of capital inflows

Stronger economic fundamentals and expectations of higher returns have led to a rapid recovery in foreign direct investment (FDI) inflows to the subregion. In 2010, China maintained its position as the largest recipient of FDI in the world, with investment inflows increasing 12.0% year-on-year. After mainland China, Hong Kong, China, became the second largest recipient of FDI in Asia and the fourth largest in the world. The Republic of Korea, however, saw inbound FDI drop by 6.7% in the first half of 2010, mainly due to a fall in investment from Japan, the United States and Europe. The decrease in investment from developed countries was partially offset by a large increase in investment from emerging economies, including China and the Middle East. Macao, China, saw a return of FDI to the gaming and hospitality sector, as Mongolia did to its mining sector.

The inflow of portfolio investment is also on the rise, aided by stronger stock market performances in the economies of the subregion. Short-term capital inflows to China and the Republic of Korea were

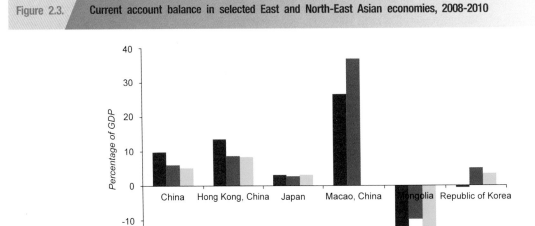

Figure 2.3. Current account balance in selected East and North-East Asian economies, 2008-2010

Sources: ESCAP, based on national sources; and CEIC Data Company Limited, data available from http://ceicdata.com (accessed 16 February 2011).

Note: Data for 2010 are estimates.

particularly strong during the post-crisis period. The position of foreign exchange purchases in China, for example, showed that the Chinese banking system had acquired $78 billion in foreign exchange in October 2010 alone. While the position of foreign exchange purchases stems from both trade and investment flows, the fact that it continued to increase while the trade surplus declined between July and September indicates that short-term capital flows have, indeed, increased. The pattern of capital inflows also appears to be highly correlated with asset (primarily property) prices in China and poses a challenge as the Government attempts to rein in property prices and overall inflation.

Appreciating currencies

All currencies in the subregion gained against the dollar in 2010, with the exception of those of Hong Kong, China, and Macao, China, which are pegged to the dollar (see figure 2.4). The Chinese yuan renminbi started to appreciate gradually following the move by the Government in June 2010 to loosen the dollar/yuan peg that had been in place since

July 2008. Despite weak economic prospects, the Japanese yen strengthened further to 83 yen per dollar in 2010, up by almost 10% since the beginning of the year and an over 30% appreciation since its recent low level of about 120 yen per dollar recorded in 2007. The rapid appreciation of the yen led the Bank of Japan to intervene in the foreign exchange market in September for the first time in six years, but with limited impact. The Mongolian togrog appreciated on the back of rising export values of gold and copper and increased foreign investment in mining activities. In the Republic of Korea, the won continued to experience volatile movements triggered by external events and swings in investor sentiment. In order to curb the potentially destabilizing effects of capital flows on currency movements, the Government of the Republic of Korea instituted capital controls, setting limits on the accumulation of foreign exchange derivatives. On the other hand, the Government of China lifted a series of restrictions that limited the flow of yuan renminbi into Hong Kong, China, resulting in a leap in yuan renminbi deposits in Hong Kong banks.[5] These reforms, together with the growing global significance

| Figure 2.4. | Index of exchange rate movements of domestic currencies against the dollar in selected East and North-East Asian economies, 2009-2010 |

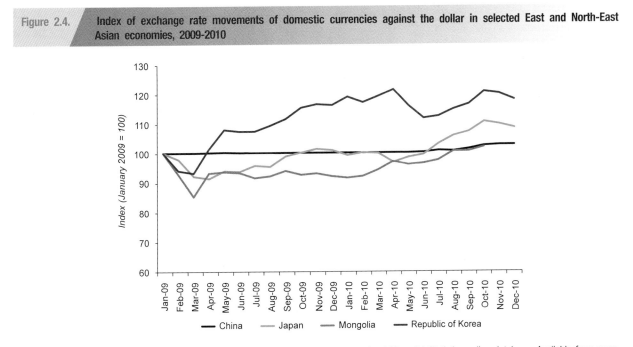

Source: ESCAP calculations based on data from International Monetary Fund, International Financial Statistics online database. Available from www.imfstatistics.org/imf (accessed 16 February 2011).

Note: A positive trend represents appreciation and vice versa.

of the economy of China, are likely to translate into increasing use of the yuan renminbi as a medium of exchange, especially in the subregion.

Future outlook and policy challenges

The strong rebound in economic activity seen in the first half of 2010 for economies in the subregion appears to have decelerated with the slowdown in the global economic recovery, the completion of the inventory cycle and the gradual unwinding of Government stimulus spending. This trend is expected to continue into 2011, with all economies in the subregion forecast to grow at a slower rate. China is expected to grow at 9.5% and, at this rate, should continue to lead growth in the subregion. Hong Kong, China, should revert to its near-trend growth rate of 4.9%. Economic expansion in the Republic of Korea is also expected to decelerate to around 4.5%. On the other hand, Mongolia, whose mining sector is expected to strengthen in 2011 and to profit from the rise in export prices of gold and copper, should grow around 9%. Japan faces the grim prospect of slower economic growth, partly due to the damage caused to the economy by the devastating earthquake and tsunami. Economic growth is expected to slow to 1.5%.

Overall, the East and North-East Asian subregion is expected to continue on a firm recovery path. Nevertheless, a number of downside risks remain. One of the key risks facing the subregion is the rapid inflow of short-term capital due to the loose monetary policies in the developed economies. Short-term capital attracted by higher returns in the region is leading to exchange rate pressure and could spill over into asset bubbles, which fuel inflation and create market distortions. Furthermore, a mass repatriation of capital, once the bubbles deflate, could result in balance of payment problems and inject gratuitous financial instability. The economies in the subregion are already under intense pressure to curb property and stock prices. In this regard, the potential impact of further quantitative easing in the developed countries is a matter of major policy concern for asset prices in the economies of the subregion.

The subregion's dependence on trade with developed countries, in which recovery has been weak, is also an ongoing risk and source of uncertainty. Furthermore, as economies in the subregion increasingly rely on China to replace demand from traditional export markets, China's private sector demand will need to fill the gap left by the withdrawal of Government stimulus in 2011 to ensure continued growth in the subregion. In addition, the subregion also holds the key to rebalancing unsustainably large and increasing trade and current account imbalances in the global economy. For example, during the period 1996-2006, net exports contributed 13% of China's 9.3% growth rate, on average, while during the same period, household consumption growth only averaged 7.7% and the share of domestic consumption as a percentage of GDP was still very low.[6]

The subregion holds the key to rebalancing unsustainably large trade and current account imbalances in the global economy

By enhancing domestic consumption, economies in the subregion have an opportunity to boost their economic development processes while also contributing to the reduction of the global macro-economic imbalances. Furthermore, promoting investments in infrastructure, creating employment and business opportunities for the poor with an emphasis on those living in rural areas, enhancing social protection systems and fostering inclusive financial development are all policies that can contribute to both boosting economic growth and rebalancing the region's trade by enhancing domestic demand. Further loosening of the exchange rate may assist in this. In view of the need to address global imbalances, China is shifting its emphasis towards greater social protection and domestic market growth. In China's twelfth Five-Year Programme on National Economic and Social Development, which covers the period from 2011 to 2015, the expansion of domestic demand and household consumption was emphasized as a long-term growth strategy.

The generation of employment opportunities also remains an important challenge. While the impact of the crisis on labour markets in the subregion appears to have been limited, high unemployment among young people and increases in informal, more vulnerable forms of employment are a major economic and social concern. Moreover, as the official unemployment figures do not take into account those who have given up looking for jobs, actual unemployment rates could be higher when such hidden unemployment is included. In order to promote a more job-rich recovery, policies need to provide greater support, such as access to low-cost finance, to small and medium-sized enterprises, especially in the service sector.

NORTH AND CENTRAL ASIA

GDP growth receives a boost from higher oil and mineral prices

The North and Central Asian subregion registered GDP growth of 4.6% in 2010, in sharp contrast with 2009 when the economies of the subregion contracted by 5.4% (see table 2.2).

After years of strong GDP growth, Armenia's economy saw a sharp contraction of 14.2% in 2009 as a result of the global financial and economic crisis. Although the financial services sector is not internationally exposed to any great extent, the country relies heavily on inflows of remittances and official transfers, and much of its export revenue is generated by commodities, in particular non-ferrous metals, such as copper. In 2010, global recovery led to higher export earnings and remittances and, as a result, industrial output grew by 9.7%. The agricultural sector, however, contracted by 13.5% due to poor weather conditions. GDP grew by 2.6% in 2010. A narrow export base and geographical isolation (closed borders with Turkey and Azerbaijan) are sources of vulnerability.

In recent years, Azerbaijan has enjoyed large and growing oil exports and has been among the fastest growing economies in the subregion. However, as existing oilfields reach their productive capacity, oil output is slowing down. The hydrocarbon sector accounts for some 55% of GDP and over 80% of export earnings and, as such, GDP growth itself slowed to 5% in 2010 from over 9% in the previous two years. Greater efforts are needed to

Table 2.2.   Rates of economic growth and inflation in North and Central Asian economies, 2009-2011

(Percentage)

	Real GDP growth			Inflation[a]		
	2009	2010[b]	2011[c]	2009	2010[b]	2011[c]
North and Central Asia[d]	**-5.4**	**4.6**	**4.8**	**10.8**	**7.1**	**8.2**
Armenia	-14.2	2.6	4.0	3.4	8.2	7.0
Azerbaijan	9.3	5.0	5.5	1.5	5.7	7.0
Georgia	-3.9	6.0	5.0	1.7	7.1	8.0
Kazakhstan	1.2	7.0	6.2	7.3	7.1	8.0
Kyrgyzstan	2.3	-1.4	5.0	6.8	8.0	10.5
Russian Federation	-7.9	4.0	4.3	11.7	6.9	8.0
Tajikistan	3.4	6.5	6.0	6.5	6.5	9.0
Turkmenistan	6.1	8.0	9.5	10.0	12.0	14.0
Uzbekistan	8.1	8.5	8.5	14.1	9.3	10.0

Sources: ESCAP, based on national sources; and data from the Interstate Statistical Committee of the Commonwealth of Independent States. Available from www.cisstat.com (accessed 16 February 2011).

a Changes in the consumer price index.
b Estimates.
c Forecasts (as of 8 April 2011).
d GDP figures at market prices in dollars in 2009 (at 2000 prices) are used as weights to calculate the subregional growth rates.

diversify the economy and institute market-based reforms to boost competitiveness. The agricultural sector has also been adversely affected by poor weather conditions, particularly flooding.

Recovery gathered pace in Georgia after it suffered from military conflict in 2008 and from sharp declines in FDI and remittances in 2009. GDP expanded by 6.0% in 2010, from -3.9% in 2009. Global recovery led to a rebound in exports and remittances and translated into strong manufacturing production and increased domestic demand. All the sectors of the economy expanded except agriculture, which suffered losses. Although far below pre-crisis levels, FDI also began to recover from the second quarter of the year.

In Kazakhstan, a strong Government response was vital in stabilizing the banking sector and turning the economy around. GDP grew by 7.0% in 2010, after a modest 1.2% in 2009. The strong rebound was partly driven by a recovery in external demand for oil and other mineral products. Meanwhile, growth in the non-oil sector, including construction, was more modest, owing to weak domestic demand, which was affected, in turn, by limited credit availability.[7] The agricultural sector and the grain harvest, in particular, were badly affected by a severe drought. As a result, the sector contracted sharply in 2010.

Kyrgyzstan, which suffered from widespread political and social instability in April and June, was the only economy in the subregion to contract in 2010, by 1.4%. Led by strong gold production and construction activity, the economy expanded at a rapid 16.4% in the first quarter, before civil unrest disrupted agriculture, trade and other services. Retail trade, for instance, was hit hard by the closure of the border with Kazakhstan and Uzbekistan. On the bright side, industrial output still managed to grow due to a higher output of gold and improved construction activity. Remittances and international assistance also played a supportive role.

The economy of the Russian Federation, which has a large impact on other economies in the subregion through both trade and remittance channels, began a gradual recovery in 2010 after a 7.9% contraction in 2009. GDP increased by 4.0% in 2010. A large stimulus package and a strong Government response to stabilize the currency and the financial sector laid the groundwork for recovery, which received a boost from strengthening external demand for oil and gas and higher prices for them. Growth began to gain momentum in the second quarter, with tradable goods and manufacturing leading the way. This then translated into more broad-based domestic demand growth in the third quarter, when retail trade and construction expanded by 5.9% and 2.2%, respectively. The firming of the labour market also gave a boost to domestic demand and the unemployment rate fell to 6.7%. The financial sector, however, will take longer to recover due to the large share of bad loans. Despite rapid export growth, the contribution of net exports to GDP growth became less as imports gained rapidly as the year progressed. The agricultural sector was severely affected by the worst drought in decades.

The economy of the Russian Federation, which has a large impact on other economies in the subregion through both trade and remittance channels, began a gradual recovery in 2010

Tajikistan saw economic growth slow to 3.4% in 2009 owing to declines in aluminium exports and remittances. These two main drivers of growth saw a strong rebound in 2010. Aluminium and cotton remain the primary export items, while nearly half of the labour force works abroad, mainly in Kazakhstan and the Russian Federation. GDP grew by 6.5% in 2010. Industry continues to be susceptible to problems in the power sector, with the country facing periodic blackouts.

With sizeable gas and oil resources, Turkmenistan enjoyed over 10% GDP growth for several years, but a disruption in the main gas pipeline to the Russian Federation led to slower growth in 2009. In late 2009 and early 2010, however, new pipelines to China and the Islamic Republic of Iran began to operate and, from the beginning of 2010, gas exports to the Russian Federation resumed. As a result, GDP growth bounced back to 8% in 2010. The hydrocarbon sector continues to drive the economy, but retail trade has also experienced double-digit growth, reflecting strong domestic demand.

Uzbekistan has been the steadiest economy in the subregion, with GDP growing 8.5% in 2010 compared to 8.1% in 2009. Growth was broad-based, supported by both the industrial and services sectors. The agricultural sector also contributed positively to economic growth. Key commodities, such as cotton, gas and gold, received a boost from stronger commodity prices and external demand, while FDI into infrastructure projects and the hydrocarbon sector continued to rise, particularly from joint ventures with China and the Russian Federation.

Inflation remains relatively high despite deceleration in some countries

Growing domestic demand and rising real wages, as well as higher food and energy prices, have put some upward pressure on inflation. In most countries, inflation was above 6% in 2010 (see figure 2.5). Inflation remained high in 2010 in Turkmenistan (12%) and Uzbekistan (9.3%), where Government stimulus measures have continued through 2010 at the risk of overheating.

The severe drought and wildfires in the summer of 2010 fed inflationary pressures in the Russian Federation. The Government introduced a ban on grain exports in order to avoid food price inflation. Consumer price inflation at 6.9% in 2010 was lower than the 11.7% recorded in 2009. The strengthening of the currency, low import prices and sluggish domestic demand, however, kept inflation from rising higher. Consumer price inflation in Kazakhstan reached 7.1% in 2010, within the Government target range

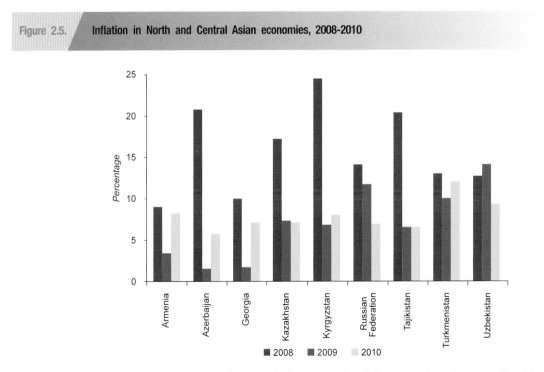

Figure 2.5.   Inflation in North and Central Asian economies, 2008-2010

■ 2008   ■ 2009   ░ 2010

Sources: ESCAP, based on national sources; and data from the Interstate Statistical Committee of the Commonwealth of Independent States. Available from www.cisstat.com (accessed 16 February 2011).

Note: Data for 2010 are estimates.

of 6%-8%. This outcome was helped by a relatively stable exchange rate and food prices. Global food and fuel prices influenced inflation in Tajikistan, as the country is forced to import much of its food and fuel. Consumer price inflation averaged 6.5% in 2010, the same rate recorded in 2009. Rising wages and remittance inflows, however, as well as higher global grain prices, increased inflationary pressure towards the end of 2010.

Kyrgyzstan was unable to avoid price hikes because of a poor domestic harvest and the drought in Kazakhstan and the Russian Federation. Planned increases in utility prices were cancelled, but inflation still reached 8% in 2010. Inflation picked up again in Turkmenistan in 2010 due to higher global prices for food and energy and increased investment in the energy sector. Inflation in Uzbekistan exceeded 9% in 2010 as a result of increased public sector wages and welfare benefits.

Armenia, Azerbaijan and Georgia, which experienced sharp deceleration in inflation during the global economic crisis, witnessed accelerated inflation in 2010. In Armenia, rising prices for imported gas and mineral products exerted upward pressure. Inflation moderated somewhat after monetary tightening at the beginning of 2010 but picked up again in the third quarter. Food prices witnessed a spike in September due to the ban on wheat exports from the Russian Federation. Inflation in Armenia for 2010 is estimated at 8.2%, somewhat higher than the Government target. Azerbaijan saw significant deceleration in inflation from 20.8% in 2008 to 1.5% in 2009, but it rose again to 5.7% in 2010. Higher prices of grain imports from the Russian Federation, among others, have exerted upward pressure, but the stable exchange rate pegged to the dollar and moderate expansion in credit have helped to keep inflation in check. In Georgia, inflation was low at the beginning of 2010 but picked up quickly in the second half of the year due to strong recovery in domestic demand, higher real wages and rising commodity prices. In response, monetary policy was tightened. Inflation rose to 7.1% for the full year.

Fiscal and monetary policy responses

Improvement in fiscal balances

In general, fiscal balances improved in 2010. Oil exporters, particularly the Russian Federation, Kazakhstan and Azerbaijan, received budgetary boosts from stronger global demand and higher oil prices. The Russian Federation saw its deficit fall from 5.9% of GDP in 2009 to 4.1% in 2010. At the same time, the Government has made a commitment to restore the non-oil fiscal balance, which improved only modestly in 2010 after deteriorating sharply in 2009. In addition to drawing support from the National Fund (the sovereign oil wealth fund), Kazakhstan raised export duties by almost 22% to cover additional social spending. Such measures, together with rising tax revenues from the recovery in economic activity, placed the budget deficit at 3.0% of GDP in 2010. The Government of Azerbaijan increased its transfers from the State Oil Fund in order to finance infrastructure and social programmes. While the central Government maintained a large budget surplus, it would be advisable for it to also make efforts to reduce its non-oil fiscal deficit, which stands at over 35% of GDP and is the highest in the subregion.

Oil exporters received budgetary boosts from stronger global demand and higher oil prices

Among the gas exporters, only Turkmenistan and Uzbekistan have surplus budgets. For Uzbekistan, the budget has been in surplus for most of the past decade, but increased infrastructure and social spending, as well as increased public sector wages, narrowed the surplus to near balance in 2010. In Turkmenistan, the budget has been in surplus owing to rapidly growing revenues from the hydrocarbon sector, which remains the main contributor to the government budget.

On the other end of the spectrum, the oil and gas importing countries had to struggle with wide budget deficits. In Armenia, additional public spending and lower revenues widened the budget deficit to 5.2% of GDP in 2010 from 4.7% of GDP in 2009. To contain budget deficit, the Government instituted a three-year programme calling for the suspension of public sector salary increases and a cap on public spending. Efforts to improve the tax and customs administrations are also in place. Nevertheless, subsidies to local communities and expenditures on debt servicing continue to exert pressure. Georgia's budget benefited from strong economic activity and a new excise tax in 2010 and its budget deficit decreased to 6.6% of GDP in 2010.

Despite a significant increase in revenues from aluminium and cotton exports, Tajikistan's overall tax base remained narrow and budgetary support from international donors was needed amid rising levels of social spending. Some deterioration in the budget deficit was estimated for 2010. The budget deficit of Kyrgyzstan widened from 1.5% of GDP in 2009 to 9% in 2010 mainly because of increased spending on wages for State employees, job creation measures, fuel imports and infrastructure improvements. Revenues

suffered from the social unrest in mid-2010, as retail trade underwent a sharp downturn and resulted in a sharp decline in value added tax (VAT) collection. The new tax code introduced in 2009 also reduced the VAT rate from 20% to 12%, and the unified tax on small businesses from 10% to 6%.

Central banks take measures to contain inflationary pressures and maintain exchange rate stability

The economic recovery provided a fresh impetus for the economies in North and Central Asia to focus on their exchange rates, a key policy issue being to maintain a nominally stable rate of exchange against the dollar. The national currencies of several subregional economies depreciated in 2010 (see figure 2.6) owing to downward pressure on foreign-exchange reserves and concerns about the loss of international competitiveness during the economic crisis. However, increasing export earnings, FDI and remittance inflows eased downward pressure. In addition, several central banks widened their trading bands for national currencies in order to rebuild foreign exchange reserves.

| Figure 2.6. | Index of exchange rate movements of domestic currencies against the dollar in selected North and Central Asian economies, 2009-2010 |

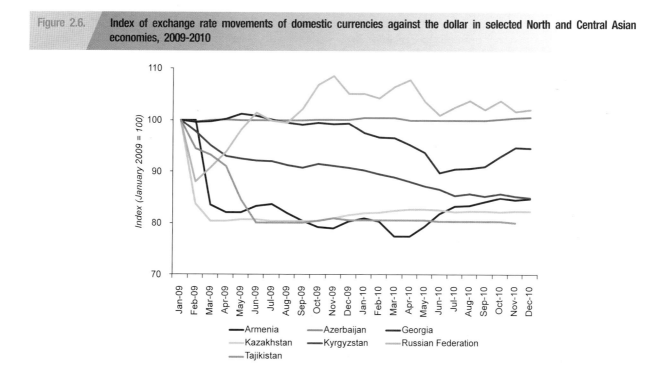

Source: ESCAP calculations based on data from International Monetary Fund, International Financial Statistics online database. Available from www.imfstatistics.org/imf (accessed 16 February 2011).

Note: A positive trend represents appreciation and vice versa.

The Central Bank of Armenia raised its refinancing rate by a total of 275 basis points from January to September and broadened its policy instruments, such as the sale and repurchase of Government securities, in order to deepen the domestic debt market. To enable the domestic currency, the dram, to exchange at a free-floating rate, the Central Bank reduced its intervention in the foreign exchange market in 2010. Georgia's monetary policy in 2010 was aimed at stimulating the economy and reducing the pace of depreciation of the national currency, the lari. Improved economic conditions led the National Bank of Georgia to gradually tighten its monetary policy and resume the use of an inflation-targeting regime after midyear.

In Uzbekistan, the central bank allowed the sum to depreciate in order to support exports and boost the country's competitiveness in both the global and regional markets. Kazakhstan widened the trading band of the national currency from 127.5 to 165.0 tenge per dollar at the beginning of 2010 in order to prevent excessive real exchange rate appreciation. As a result, the tenge appreciated modestly against the dollar by the end of the year. In Kyrgyzstan, the national currency depreciated by more than 11% in 2010 due to a fall in foreign currency inflows and reduced cross-border trade with neighbouring countries from April to July. In response, the national bank made extensive foreign currency sales, an action which also helped it to control the money supply.

The central bank of the Russian Federation maintained a nominally stable rate of exchange for the rouble against a dual-currency basket consisting of 55% dollar and 45% euro. Currency strengthening remained one of the most effective ways to reduce inflationary pressure, which nevertheless led the rouble to strengthen against its target basket in real effective terms in 2010. A reduction of the excessive appreciation of the rouble, however, remained a key monetary policy objective in 2010. By mid-2010, the real effective exchange rate of the rouble was about 9% stronger than at the end of 2009.

Policy rates were raised in Azerbaijan and Tajikistan amid inflationary pressure concerns. The national currencies of the two countries were relatively stable owing to increasing foreign exchange inflows. In Tajikistan, growth in remittances, mainly from Kazakhstan and the Russian Federation, allowed the somoni to remain much more stable in the first half of 2010 than in 2009. Nevertheless, the national currency was around 5% lower against the dollar in annual average terms by the end of 2010.

Economic recovery and continued reform of the financial sector led to greater operational efficiency in the banking sector and increased public confidence

Economic recovery and continued reform of the financial sector led to greater operational efficiency in the banking sector and increased public confidence in 2010. The financial authorities of economies in the subregion committed to maintaining the stability of their banking systems and to ensuring sufficient liquidity in their financial systems, with a view to providing support to economic growth in the short and medium term. In Azerbaijan and Kazakhstan, reserve requirements for commercial banks were lowered to increase liquidity and support economic activities. The banking sector of Georgia increased its lending and started recording a net profit. The level of deposits in the banking system of Tajikistan bounced back rapidly at the beginning of 2010. The currency reform implemented by the Government of Turkmenistan in 2009 benefited the economic and financial development of the country. The banking system of Uzbekistan received an upgrade in Moody's ratings from "negative" to "stable" in 2010.

Strong growth in trade driven by commodity exports

Oil and gas exporters continued to enjoy current account and trade surpluses to varying degrees, while oil and gas importers suffered deficits. In the case of the former, securing alternative export routes (gas pipelines) was important to avoid sharp disruptions in production and exports. In both groups, recovery in remittance inflows provided a modest boost to the current account balance, although the stronger domestic demand that followed led to faster growth in imports in some countries. Remittance inflows from the Russian Federation to the other economies in the subregion also saw a healthy recovery. The non-oil exporting economies in the subregion are still in short supply of FDI, though, and their external debts are high and rising.

In the Russian Federation, the current account surplus improved from 4.0% of GDP in 2009 to 4.5% in 2010 (see figure 2.7). The main country exports of oil and gas, about two thirds of total exports, benefited from higher prices. Kazakhstan turned its 2009 current account deficit into a surplus of 4.5% of GDP in 2010 as a result of rising oil exports. Exports expanded at a much faster rate than imports, resulting in a higher trade surplus. The large current account surplus of Azerbaijan rose further in 2010. Oil and refined petroleum products continue to account for the largest share of export earnings, which grew much faster than imports. Among the largest imports were food products and capital goods, such as machinery, metals and transport equipment.

Turkmenistan saw its current account surplus rise again as oil and gas exports recovered, after disruptions in gas exports to the Russian Federation in 2009 led to a narrowing current account surplus. Imports continue to be dominated by machinery and equipment for the gas sector and construction. The current account surplus of Uzbekistan remained high, at around 18% of GDP, in 2010 owing to a large trade surplus and increasing remittances, mainly from Kazakhstan and the Russian Federation. Rising global prices of principal export commodities, including gold, gas and cotton, increased export revenues by more than 22% in 2010. Hydrocarbons remain an important source of export earnings.

The oil and gas importers—Armenia, Georgia, Kyrgyzstan and Tajikistan—export other commodities, such as non-ferrous metals, aluminium and cotton, and they benefited from rising commodity prices but still suffered current account deficits. Armenia's wide current account deficit narrowed slightly from 16.0% to 14.2% of GDP in 2010, owing to higher prices and demand for metals and mineral products, as well as the economic recovery in the Russian Federation, its largest trading partner. Georgia saw its high current account deficit shrink to 11.7% in 2009, owing to sharp declines in imports. In 2010, the deficit stabilized around the previous year's level

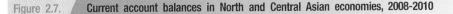

Figure 2.7.   Current account balances in North and Central Asian economies, 2008-2010

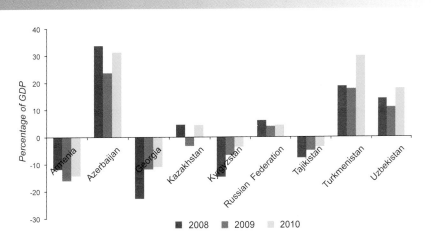

Sources: ESCAP, based on national sources and International Monetary Fund, International Financial Statistics online database. Available from www. imfstatistics.org/imf (accessed 16 February 2011).

Note: Data for 2010 are estimates..

amid a general recovery in imports, as well as higher oil and gas import prices. Georgia's gold and base metal exports also benefited from higher prices, but the overall trade deficit widened. This was partially offset by recovery in remittance inflows.

In Kyrgyzstan, exports grew much faster than imports. The largest imports were food and fuel products, mainly from Kazakhstan and the Russian Federation. Meanwhile, due largely to the economic recovery in the Russian Federation, remittances were reported to have gone up 33% in the first eight months of the year. The country witnessed a reduction in its current account deficit in 2010 as compared to the previous year. The current account deficit of Tajikistan narrowed from 4.9% of GDP in 2009 to 3.6% in 2010, owing to increased remittances from Kazakhstan and the Russian Federation, as well as higher export earnings. The trade deficit narrowed, helped by slower growth in imports. Aluminium, cotton and electrical energy remain Tajikistan's key exports, while its largest imports are food and consumer goods.

Future outlook and policy challenges

Following a long transition from the Soviet-era economic system, North and Central Asian economies have become progressively more integrated in the global economy. A degree of macroeconomic fragility, lack of financial depth and lack of competitiveness, however, make these economies vulnerable to external shocks. In this regard, despite the economic recovery and positive macroeconomic growth prospects following the global economic crisis, there is a risk of some slowdown in a few subregional economies, particularly due to volatile commodity prices and the knock-on effects of slower global economic recovery in the second half of 2010. Economies in the subregion tend to experience sharper declines and upswings due to their heavy reliance on oil and gas, metals and other commodities. Hence, diversifying the sources of economic growth, including through the development of the non-oil sector, will be important not only for future growth but also for greater socio-economic stability.

The economy of the Russian Federation is projected to grow by 4.3% in 2011. Key challenges will be to strengthen the investment climate, improve the situation in the food markets and lower inflation. In Kazakhstan, GDP is projected to expand by 6.2% in 2011, where Government plans to implement a five-year industrial development and diversification plan announced in 2010. The plan envisages diversification of the economy, improvement of labour productivity through investment in training and improvements to infrastructure. The pursuit of broad-based growth and the development of the non-oil sectors are also the principal economic policy challenges of the Governments of Azerbaijan and Turkmenistan. The National Socio-Economic Development Programme of Turkmenistan for 2011-2030 aims to diversify the economy to move it away from its reliance on natural gas, oil, liquefied natural gas, cotton and textiles. A variety of measures are planned to develop a new management cadre and a skilled labour force. GDP is expected to grow by 9.5% in 2011 owing to strong export earnings. In Azerbaijan, the Government is expected to use its State Oil Fund to finance social spending and infrastructure projects, and to increase investment in the non-oil sectors, such as agriculture and manufacturing. The GDP of Azerbaijan is expected to grow by 5.5% in 2011. Uzbekistan is expected to maintain its growth at 8.5%. Assuming political stability holds in Kyrgyzstan, the country is expected to register a positive growth of 5% in 2011, as opposed to 2010, when the economy contracted. Some slowdown in GDP growth in Georgia and Tajikistan is expected.

Rising dependence on imported energy has become a major concern for several economies in North and Central Asia, leading to the expectation that they will develop their energy resources and infrastructure, and increase energy self-sufficiency with technical and financial assistance from the Russian Federation. The entire subregion could, however, benefit from a strengthening of economic cooperation in the energy sector that would facilitate future economic dynamism in the subregion (see box 2.1).

Box 2.1. Energy self-sufficiency and dependency in North and Central Asia

Before 1990, the Central Asian economies were integrated into the single national economy of the Union of Soviet Socialist Republics. While close linkages between these economies and with the Russian Federation continue, Kazakhstan, the Russian Federation and Turkmenistan are also now competitors in the global energy market.

Natural gas

The economies of North and Central Asia provide nearly 29% of world gas exports.[8] The subregion has a common legacy concentrated in physical energy infrastructure—a huge gas transport system connecting Central Asia with the Russian Federation and, further, with the European Union. The common interests of the subregion are the sustainability of gas extraction and gas transit. Gas supply sustainability has three key dimensions: (a) the stability of the gas transmission system; (b) opportunities to diversify routes; and (c) stable demand from China and the European Union, which would justify and support the longer-term investment required in gas exploration in North and Central Asia.

The most extensive gas pipeline system in the subregion starts in Turkmenistan—the country with the highest proven reserves—and has a capacity of approximately 80 billion cubic metres of natural gas per year. An ambitious project in the diversification of gas supplies has been undertaken by Kazakhstan, Turkmenistan and Uzbekistan, together with China, which should allow about 40 billion cubic metres of natural gas to be supplied annually from Central Asia to China as of 2013. The signing of another gas pipeline project by Afghanistan, India, Pakistan and Turkmenistan in December 2010 is expected to bring 33 billion cubic metres of natural gas per year from Turkmenistan to Pakistan and India via Afghanistan.

Electric power

Difficulties with electricity supplies affect all countries in North and Central Asia, particularly Kyrgyzstan and Tajikistan. The problem is in the particular features of the climate and agriculture of the subregion. Kyrgyzstan and Tajikistan generate almost all their electricity using only hydroelectric stations and only at certain times of the year. They now have an opportunity to manage their energy problems by using their hydropower potential more efficiently throughout the year, which could increase the well-being of the entire subregion. The achievement of this goal is connected with investment in new hydroelectric stations; the Russian Federation could play an important role in facilitating this process, both financially and by providing technical expertise.

Oil: balancing diverse interests

Oil production in Central Asia will grow substantially in the next two decades following the development of new oilfields, and much of the additional oil is expected to be exported. The main issues for intraregional relationships are the development of new export routes and timely investment in new projects. There are two giant oilfields currently under development in Kazakhstan that are likely to bring considerable additional volumes of oil to the world market. There is an obvious need to make this possible by renovating the tanker fleets of Kazakhstan's neighbours and enlarging pipeline capacity from Kazakhstan to its markets in China and Europe.

The development of a common infrastructure in the oil and gas industries is a key issue for strengthening cooperation in the energy sector in North and Central Asia. Specific policy areas to be addressed include the efficient management of the existing infrastructure and the creation and implementation of a joint development programme for oil, gas and electricity based on forecasts of subregional energy demand. Most important, it involves looking at the energy infrastructure as a systemic whole and preventing the accumulation of bottlenecks within the subregion.

Source: ESCAP.

Food security was another challenge faced by the North and Central Asian economies in 2010, with adverse weather conditions severely affecting grain production in Kazakhstan and the Russian Federation. The spike in grain prices triggered by crop failure in these economies led to the imposition of export restrictions. In particular, the poor harvest and subsequent wheat export ban by the Russian Federation pushed wheat prices to very high levels. The grain export restrictions were expected to be lifted once the final results of the 2010 harvest were known.

Food security was another challenge faced by the North and Central Asian economies in 2010, with adverse weather conditions severely affecting grain production

---

The Food and Agriculture Organization of the United Nations (FAO) forecasts that global food prices will be sustained at record levels in 2011,[9] which could have a severe impact, especially on the lower income economies of the subregion. In Tajikistan, for instance, the share of household income devoted to food purchases is around 60%. The Government of Tajikistan addressed the issue of food self-sufficiency in a new food security programme and introduced measures aimed at reducing food shortages in the country. Food imports accounted for more than half of all food products in the domestic consumer market in 2010. In addition to a poor domestic harvest in 2010, the economy of Kyrgyzstan suffered from border closures with its neighbouring countries. The Government of Uzbekistan stimulated the agricultural sector to ensure more ample local supplies in rural areas.

PACIFIC

The subregion has been divided into two distinct groups for analytical purposes. One group consists of Pacific island developing economies and the other of Australia and New Zealand.

Pacific island developing economies

Diverse economic performance

There are good prospects for some Pacific island developing economies, particularly those that are resource-driven, but this masks the fact that the majority of them are barely growing. The GDP growth of these economies as a group averaged 4.3% in 2010, up from 2.2% in 2009 (see table 2.3). In recent years, Papua New Guinea, enjoying strong demand and prices for its exports (oil, gold, copper, coffee, cocoa and palm oil), has been the fastest growing economy. Furthermore, driven by the commencement of the Papua New Guinea liquefied natural gas project, the country's GDP grew by 7.1% in 2010 as compared to 5.5% in 2009. Solomon Islands suffered significantly reduced log exports when demand from China declined for some raw material imports. Its economy experienced a contraction of 1.2% in 2009, compared to a growth of 7.3% in 2008. Benefiting from higher commodity prices, particularly for logs, the Solomon Islands economy rebounded by 4.0% in 2010.

Tuvalu's economy contracted by 1.7% in 2009 and recorded no growth in 2010 due to slowdown in remittance flows into the country. Remittances contribute about 15% of Tuvalu's GDP. Vanuatu's GDP growth rate stood at 3.8% in 2009. In 2010, the economy expanded by 3.0%, a downward revision from the 4.6% 2010 budget growth forecast. The revision reflects lower than expected tourist numbers and delays in the implementation of infrastructure projects.

Fiji has experienced declining preferential European Union sugar prices, highly unfavourable weather conditions (severe flooding in early 2009 and the devastating cyclone Tomas in March 2010), a blow to investor confidence from the 2006 military coup and the continuation of the military-led Government.[10] The economy contracted by 3.0% in 2009 and virtually stagnated with a growth of 0.1% in 2010. Samoa continues to recover from the devastation of the September 2009 tsunami, which affected about 20% of its population and killed at least

Table 2.3.   Rates of economic growth and inflation in selected economies in Pacific, 2009-2011

(Percentage)

	Real GDP growth			Inflation[a]		
	2009	2010[b]	2011[c]	2009	2010[b]	2011[c]
Pacific[d]	**1.2**	**2.6**	**2.4**	**1.9**	**2.7**	**3.4**
Pacific island developing economies[d]	**2.2**	**4.3**	**5.5**	**6.7**	**4.7**	**6.1**
Cook Islands	-0.1	0.5	2.0	6.6	3.5	4.2
Fiji	-3.0	0.1	1.3	6.8	4.0	3.0
Kiribati	-0.7	0.5	1.8	8.4	0.8	6.7
Marshall Islands	0.0	0.5	1.2	0.5	1.0	5.0
Micronesia (Federated States of)	-1.0	0.5	1.0	7.4	3.5	4.0
Nauru	0.0	0.0	4.0	2.2	-0.5	2.4
Palau	-2.1	2.0	2.0	5.2	3.8	4.0
Papua New Guinea	5.5	7.1	8.0	7.0	6.0	8.2
Samoa	-4.9	0.0	2.5	6.6	1.0	3.0
Solomon Islands	-1.2	4.0	7.0	7.1	3.0	4.2
Tonga	-0.4	-1.2	0.8	5.0	2.0	3.0
Tuvalu	-1.7	0.0	0.0	0.0	-1.9	1.5
Vanuatu	3.8	3.0	4.0	4.5	3.4	5.0
Developed countries[d]	**1.2**	**2.6**	**2.3**	**1.8**	**2.7**	**3.4**
Australia	1.3	2.7	2.3	1.8	2.7	3.2
New Zealand	0.1	1.5	2.4	2.1	2.3	4.6

Sources: ESCAP, based on data from International Monetary Fund, *2010 Article IV Consultations*. Available from www.imf.org/external/siteindex. htm; Asian Development Bank, *Asian Development Outlook 2010 Update: The Future of Growth in Asia* (Manila, 2010). Available from www.adb. org/Documents/Books/ADO/2010/Update/default.asp; CEIC Data Company Limited, data available from http://ceicdata.com (for Australia and New Zealand) (accessed 25 March 2011).

[a] Changes in the consumer price index.
[b] Estimates.
[c] Forecasts (as of 8 April 2011).
[d] GDP figures at market prices in dollars in 2009 (at 2000 prices) are used as weights to calculate the subregional growth rates.

143 people. Damage and losses to the economy were estimated at $124 million,[11] around 22% of GDP, with an expected contraction in GDP growth of 4.9%. Post-tsunami reconstruction stimulated the economy, as did the increase in remittances recorded after the tsunami. Nevertheless, it will take considerable time for the economic damage to be repaired, particularly that suffered by the tourism sector. Samoa's economy did not grow in 2010. Tonga's economy also continued to struggle to find its way back to full recovery following the tsunami that hit the country in September 2009. Moreover, the global economic crisis, which led to lower remittance inflows and lower tourism demand, has had a significant impact on the Tongan economy, with GDP contracting by 0.4% in 2009 and again by 1.2% in 2010. The Cook Islands was also affected

by natural disasters. After two years of economic contraction, the Cook Islands economy grew by 0.5% in 2010. The destruction caused by Cyclone Pat in February 2010 also hurt the tourism industry in the first quarter of 2010, but it recovered in the second quarter.

Kiribati's economy contracted by 0.7% in 2009 and is estimated to have grown by 0.5% in 2010. The economy of Nauru grew by 1% in 2008 and showed no growth in 2009 and 2010. Nauru continues to be heavily dependent on phosphate exports. Due to damage caused to the export facilities by stormy weather, phosphate exports have been irregular. The economies of the other small islands have also been stagnating in recent years. Tourism, which makes up more than 95% of service exports in Palau, has been doing poorly as a result of the global economic crisis. Palau's economy grew by 2.0% in 2010 as compared to its contraction by 2.1% in 2009. The economies of the Marshall Islands and the Federated States of Micronesia remain flat. The economy of the Marshall Islands recorded no growth in 2009, while a slight improvement of 0.5% in GDP growth was observed for 2010. The economy of the Federated States of Micronesia grew by 0.5% in 2010, after contracting four years in a row. The pickup in activities in 2010 was mainly due to increased infrastructure investments, which increased employment opportunities and domestic demand.

Inflation driven by higher commodity and fuel prices

Inflation has been driven by higher global prices for oil and commodities, and by accelerating price pressures in some of the trading partners of the Pacific island developing economies, particularly Australia and New Zealand. With the exception of the Marshall Islands, the remaining countries recorded lower inflation rates in 2010 as compared with 2009, with inflation pressures actually easing significantly in Kiribati and Samoa.

Papua New Guinea recorded the highest inflation rate in the subregion at 6% in 2010 (see figure 2.8). The global economic recovery in 2010, with higher food and commodity prices and increasing domestic demand associated with the Papua New Guinea liquefied natural gas project, contributed to this outcome. The inflation rate in Fiji declined to 4% in 2010 from 6.8% in 2009. Considering the 20% devaluation of the Fiji dollar in April 2009, the increasing global petroleum price and the increased minimum wage, this was a good performance. In Samoa, the rate of inflation for 2009 reached 6.6% because of the high global prices for food and other

Figure 2.8. Inflation in selected Pacific island developing economies, 2008-2010

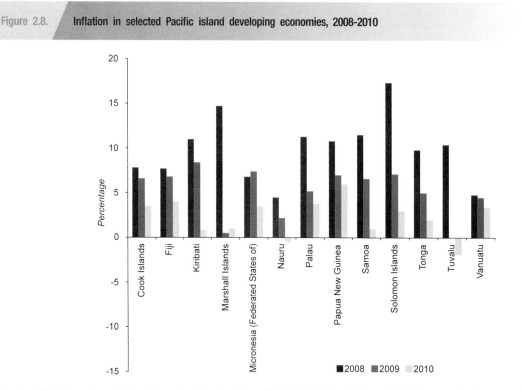

Sources: ESCAP, based on data from International Monetary Fund, *2010 Article IV Consultations*. Available from www.imf.org/external/siteindex.htm; Asian Development Bank, *Asian Development Outlook 2010 Update: The Future of Growth in Asia* (Manila, 2010). Available from www.adb.org/Documents/ Books/ADO/2010/Update/default.asp; International Monetary Fund, International Financial Statistics online database. Available from www.imfstatistics.org/ imf (accessed 15 December 2010).

Note: Data for 2010 are estimates.

commodities, in combination with an expansionary budget. Since Samoa relies heavily on imports of basic food items, such as rice, flour and milk, the impact of inflation on lower-income households was substantial. Inflationary pressures eased significantly in 2010 to about 1%. This significant drop was due to lower international food and commodity prices as well as the tightening of monetary policy to reduce credit growth. In Tonga, inflation came down from 5.0% in 2009 to 2.0% in 2010. The main factors contributing to inflation in 2010 were an increase in transport costs and increases in the prices of food and household commodities. The inflation rate in Solomon Islands declined to 7.1% in 2009 and further to 3% in 2010, partly helped by tight monetary policy in combination with the cutting of government expenditure. In Vanuatu, the inflation rate declined from 4.5% in 2009 to 3.4% in 2010 due to increased international commodity prices.

Key macroeconomic policy responses

Reconstruction efforts lead to increasing budget deficits

Available data suggest a mixed picture in terms of fiscal performance for Pacific island developing economies in 2010, with Samoa and Tuvalu recording larger budget deficits, while others, such as Fiji, Papua New Guinea, Solomon Islands and Tonga, were expecting improved budget performance. In Papua New Guinea, a balanced budget was estimated for 2010 after a small budget deficit of 0.2% of GDP in 2009 (see figure 2.9). In 2009, Vanuatu recorded a budget surplus of 0.7% of GDP. Due to higher-than-forecast grants and lower interest payments, the budget is estimated to have been in deficit of 2.1% of GDP in 2010.

In the 2009 budget, the Government of Fiji introduced some fiscal stimulus measures to respond to the global economic and financial crises. Debt servicing, which had already increased because of the effect of the April 2009 devaluation on foreign loans, increased further due to the higher domestic interest rates on Government bonds. Due to the shortfall in revenue and the widening of the budget deficit, the Government introduced a revised budget in June 2010 to tackle the negative fiscal developments. The budget deficit in Fiji reached 3.6% of GDP in 2010, slightly better than the 2009 budget deficit of 3.8% of GDP. In Samoa, the expansionary 2010 budget was a response to the economic and financial crises. The budget saw capital expenditure

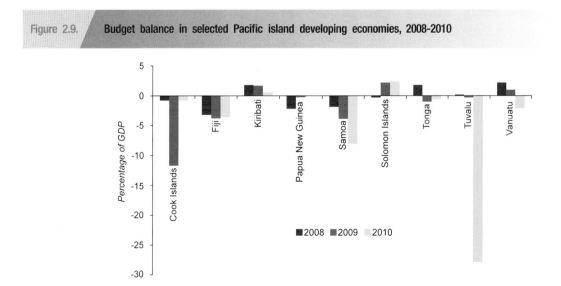

Figure 2.9. Budget balance in selected Pacific island developing economies, 2008-2010

Sources: ESCAP calculations based on data from national sources; Asian Development Bank, *Key Indicators for Asia and the Pacific 2010* (Manila, 2010); and International Monetary Fund, *2010 Article IV Consultations*. Available from www.imf.org/external/siteindex.htm.

Note: Data for 2010 are estimates.

increasing even further, primarily on infrastructure, to be funded by a highly concessional loan from the Asian Development Bank and from donor grants. As a result, the budget deficit for 2010 accelerated to 8.1% of GDP compared to 3.9% of GDP in 2009.

In Tonga, provisional figures from the 2010/11 budget show that revenue and grants declined in 2009/10, mainly because of lower collections of taxes on goods and services. The continuing decline in remittances also played a large role in these falls, through its impact on the retail sector and on imports. In addition, the Government's removal of tariffs on some food items and on fuel for aviation and shipping reduced customs revenue. Due to the continuation of relatively large grant funding, and adjustments on the expenditure side, the overall budget was in deficit equivalent to 0.6% of GDP in 2010 compared to a deficit of 1.0% of GDP in 2009. Tuvalu recently began reform efforts to prepare for freer trade with Australia and New Zealand. The Government introduced a 3% consumption tax, which is set to be gradually adjusted in line with import tariff reductions. Government expenditures increased in 2010; the increase was mainly financed by Australia and New Zealand. Tuvalu's budget deficit increased sharply in 2010. In Solomon Islands, the budget surplus increased slightly from 2.2% of GDP in 2009 to 2.4% of GDP in 2010.

Monetary policy aimed at control of the money supply

Most of the countries in the subregion have used monetary policy measures to boost aggregate demand. As demand for credit is not very responsive to changes in interest rates, central banks in these countries do not place much emphasis on interest rates as a monetary policy instrument. Rather, they try to influence the expansion of the money supply, as seen from action taken on monetary policy in Fiji, Samoa, Solomon Islands and Vanuatu. In addition, commercial banks are encouraged to lend, as was the case in Fiji and Solomon Islands. This is not

a very effective instrument, however, particularly if there are few profitable investment opportunities on offer, and it could lead to the creation of credit bubbles, as it did in Tonga.

As demand for credit is not very responsive to changes in interest rates, central banks in these countries do not place much emphasis on interest rates as a monetary policy instrument

In Papua New Guinea, the Bank of Papua New Guinea has kept its main policy interest rate, the kina facility rate, at 7% since December 2009. The central bank is determined, however, to keep the inflation rate in the single digits, and it is wary of a rise in inflationary pressures owing to the current high level of government spending and the ongoing development of a large liquefied natural gas project. There was also a growing concern of inflationary pressures emanating from imported inflation, with the kina depreciating against its major trading partners and the excess liquidity within the economy. Fiji has faced considerable monetary policy challenges since the 2006 coup, which damaged investor confidence and generally reduced the supply response to any monetary policy actions. The Reserve Bank of Fiji raised the reserve requirement for commercial banks in two stages in June and July 2010 to reduce excess liquidity in the banking system. Credit to the private sector grew by only 1% in 2010, and credit fell in some months. The Reserve Bank of Fiji recognizes that, in the current climate, foreign reserves can be drawn down quickly; therefore the monetary policy stance remains tight.

In Samoa, credit growth slowed in 2010, which helped to slow inflation, as well. With inflation declining and economic output not improving, monetary policy was relaxed later in 2010 in order to increase liquidity in an effort to stimulate economic activity. In Tonga, the credit bubble ended as the banking sector experienced liquidity problems in 2008 and saw a sharp rise in non-performing loans, which represented 20% of outstanding loans by the first quarter of 2009. Following large injections of capital into the two largest banks, the liquidity and the capital positions of the banking sector are now comfortable, but lending to the private sector has declined in recent years. The main reasons for the decline were weaker demand for loans and stricter lending standards. According to the Reserve Bank of Vanuatu, the strong performance of the Government and the fast growth in credit have driven growth in total money supply, which will help the economy as consumer spending increases.

Current account deficits widen

As in previous years, most countries had current account deficits for 2010, with deficits widening for Kiribati, Papua New Guinea and Samoa, as growth in imports of goods and services outpaced that in exports (see figure 2.10). The managed currencies of the countries are linked fairly closely to the dollar.

In 2009 and 2010, the dollar depreciated against most currencies and, as a result, although imports from these sources became more expensive, Pacific tourism became a better bargain. Pacific tourism therefore performed quite well in 2009 and 2010, despite the impact of the global economic crisis on important source markets. For many economies in the subregion, private inflows through home remittances are a more robust source of income than other private financial flows, such as foreign direct investment. Remittances vary hugely in importance among the countries in terms of the share of GDP: from 0.1% in Papua New Guinea to 25.9% in Samoa in 2009.

In Papua New Guinea, the kina was stable against the dollar while it depreciated by 14% against the Australian dollar in 2010. In the first nine months of 2010, total exports increased by 20.8% and imports by 26.3%. Reflecting these developments, the country's current account deficit is estimated to have widened considerably in 2010 to 26.6% of GDP after having been in deficit at 7.3% of GDP in 2009. By early 2009, the level of reserves in

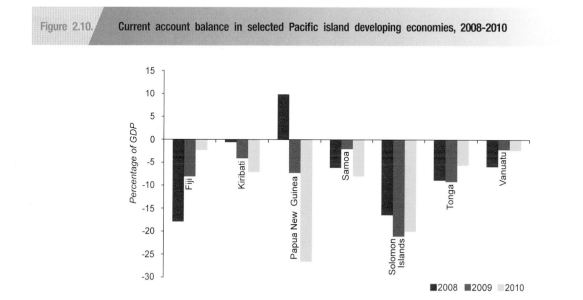

Figure 2.10. **Current account balance in selected Pacific island developing economies, 2008-2010**

■2008 ■2009 □2010

Sources: ESCAP calculations based on data from International Monetary Fund (IMF), International Financial Statistics online database. Available from www.imfstatistics.org/imf; IMF, *2010 Article IV Consultations.* Available from www.imf.org/external/siteindex.htm; and Asian Development Bank, *Key Indicators for Asia and the Pacific 2010* (Manila, 2010).

Note: Data for 2010 are estimates.

Fiji had fallen to about one month of import cover and in April 2009, Fiji devalued its currency. This action has increased tourist arrivals considerably by making Fiji more attractive to tourists from Australia and New Zealand. The devaluation has also helped to offset the decline in the European Union price paid for Fiji's sugar exports, increase the value in Fijian dollar terms of remittances and increase foreign reserves. Exports have grown faster than imports and the current account deficit was 2.3% of GDP for 2010, much lower than for the previous year.

Samoa has only a limited number of export products apart from the automobile wire harnesses assembled for export to Australia. The main import is petroleum products, which accounts for about 30% of the total. The huge merchandise trade deficit is largely offset by remittance inflows. Nevertheless, the current account deficit widened from 2.0% of GDP in 2009 to 8.0% of GDP in 2010. In Tonga, the negative trend in merchandise trade and remittances continued in 2009 and 2010. Estimates indicate that tourist receipts fell by 13.3% in the first six months of 2010. The current account deficit was 5.6% of GDP for 2010 compared to 9.2% of GDP for 2009. The capital account, however, has recently benefited from the injections of capital into the commercial banks and from foreign loans. By the end of June 2010, official reserves had increased to the equivalent of 7.1 months of imports.

A high level of inflation and continuing upward pressure on the real exchange rate, leading to pressure to devalue, has been a long-term problem in Solomon Islands. The exchange rate has not been devalued, however, as pressure on foreign currency reserves has been relieved by injections of donor funds and the general allocation of special drawing rights (SDRs) by IMF in late 2009. As a result, foreign reserves rose to 4.8 months of import cover by October 2009 and to 6-7 months of import cover by mid-2010. Still, the balance of payments outlook remains poor, particularly given the heavy reliance of output and export earnings on log exports and the threat that this industry

faces from over-exploitation. The current account deteriorated further in 2010, with an estimated deficit in excess of 20% of GDP, which is not sustainable and threatens to destabilize the economy. Vanuatu's current account deficit is estimated at 2.4% of GDP for 2010, not much different than the previous year. The country's foreign reserves were equivalent to 5.9 months of merchandise imports at the end of March 2010.

Future outlook and policy challenges

The Pacific island countries are strongly linked to the neighbouring major economies of Australia and New Zealand. Both of these economies are projected to grow in 2011, which contributes to the positive outlook for small island economies. Papua New Guinea is again expected to lead this growth with 8.0% growth as investment accelerates in a large gas export project and several mining projects come on stream. The economy of Solomon Islands is also projected to grow by 7.0% in 2011, largely reflecting higher commodity prices, especially for logs. GDP growth of 4.0% is projected for Vanuatu in 2011. Compared to most other Pacific economies, Vanuatu has made good progress and has shown that the reform of the international air transport sector and of telecommunications, which in turn led to solid tourism growth from both fly-in tourists and visits by cruise liners, can offset the negative external shocks flowing from the global economic and financial crises. Nauru's economy is also expected to grow by 4% in 2011 after zero growth in 2009 and 2010, while Samoa's economy will also rebound with a 2.5% growth in 2011. Similarly, Tonga's economy is forecast to rebound with 0.8% growth in 2011 after contracting in 2010. The main stimulant of the economy is the work on the reconstruction of Nuku'alofa and continuing donor support. The loans (from Australia, China and New Zealand) for reconstruction will be spread over four years and some of the funds will be spent on imports of goods and services related directly to the project; reconstruction overall should have a significant positive impact. Most of the rest of the Pacific island economies are also expected to grow in 2011, but by 2% or less.

Food and oil prices are showing an increasing trend. While the increase in commodity prices is good for producers and bad for consumers, it has to be managed by Governments in a sensible manner. For the larger resource-rich countries, such as Fiji, Papua New Guinea and Solomon Islands, there will be opportunities to increase exports of minerals, timber, and fish. Attention to enhancing the productivity of these industries would be beneficial. On the other hand, food and oil prices could put pressure on the economy and the fiscal balances of the countries. The impact of oil and food price increases could have serious negative consequences for the poor. Therefore, the challenge for Pacific governments would again be to devise appropriate social protection policies to protect the poor. While many governments adopted some good social protection policies in 2009 and 2010, they ought to evaluate further and refine them to ensure the maximum positive impact for the poor.

Tourism has become one of the most important income-generating sectors in many economies of the subregion

---

In recent years, tourism has become one of the most important income-generating sectors in many economies of the subregion. The recent growth in visitor numbers and revenue earnings from tourism has strongly supported economic growth in the Cook Islands, Fiji, Niue, Palau, Samoa, Solomon Islands, Tonga, and Vanuatu. In the medium term, political stability and development of the physical infrastructure and telecommunications would be critical to further expand earnings from tourism. At the same time, another policy challenge for these economies is to build strong linkages between the tourism sector and the local communities so that the benefits of tourism are widely shared among all stakeholders. Increasing dependence on tourism,

however, increases vulnerability to global economic shocks.

Pacific island developing countries face the ever-present challenges of diversifying their economies and developing high-end ecotourism, which puts less strain on the environment. One area that offers potential for diversification is agriculture. A large proportion of the population lives in rural areas and produces largely for a subsistence economy. There are a number of problems which must be addressed as a priority, though, if the productivity of the agricultural sector is to be increased. The involvement of the private sector is crucial. In this connection, the role of the government as a facilitator in improving agricultural productivity is important. Governments need to invest heavily in physical infrastructure (roads, ports, water and electricity) and in research and development. They must also ensure that farmers have access to financing, markets and information on commodity prices.

The impacts of natural disasters continue to affect the economic performance of several economies in the medium term. The effects of climate change and natural disasters on the island economies are well known and, for some of them, the implications are serious, as they not only affect their short-term growth and development prospects but could threaten their very existence if predictions of a rise in sea levels are borne out. Most economies are highly vulnerable to natural disasters. Samoa and Tonga were devastated by a tsunami in September 2009. Fiji experienced damaging flooding in January 2009 and two cyclones in December 2009 and March 2010. These events have and will continue to have a major impact on the economic situation for these small and vulnerable economies. A policy challenge for them is to focus on adapting to climate change and reducing their vulnerability to its effects, particularly in a manner that also mitigates it. In this context, the adoption of a green growth strategy could be one such policy initiative that the Pacific island developing economies could consider (see box 2.2).

Box 2.2. Green growth in the Pacific island developing economies

In recent years, a new paradigm of economic growth combined with environmental sustainability has emerged. Most countries, however, are still grappling with the question of how to continue to grow and lift more people out of poverty. Green growth offers a solution.

Sustainable development and green growth in the Pacific

Achieving sustainable development is critical for the Pacific island developing economies to meet such challenges as climate change, limited resource endowments and vulnerability to external economic shocks. Over time, these economies have faced increased vulnerability while their coping capacity has decreased. The green growth strategy, as articulated by ESCAP, provides a road map to fill the existing gaps while moving towards the achievement of sustainable development. The following six paths provide a useful framework within which each economy can design its unique policies.

Sustainable consumption and production. The green growth approach aims to shape economic incentives to ensure that consumption and production are sustainable. Agriculture and tourism offer the best overall opportunities for combining economic growth and environmental sustainability. Capitalizing on the relatively unspoiled environments of the Pacific, the further development of organic and fair trade certification could allow traditional farming practices to be scaled up into profitable and environmentally sustainable commercial production.[12]

Greening business and the market. The private sector is recognized as the key engine for growth in the Pacific.[13] Nonetheless, the role of government is crucial in creating a more favourable environment for green businesses to prosper. A green rating system for buildings and businesses could be adopted and promoted through tax incentives.

Green tax and budget reform. Green tax reform involves shifting tax revenues by lowering taxes on "goods" and increasing taxes on "bads".[14] The main purpose is increased resource efficiency and environmental improvement, rather than simply raising more revenue.

Sustainable infrastructure. Many community-based projects operate in the Pacific to promote the use of renewable energy, waste-to-energy schemes and rainwater harvesting, and many electricity utilities are experimenting with biofuels. Such schemes need to be replicated widely in the subregion.

Investment in natural capital. Natural capital, such as mangrove forests and oceans, act as a carbon sink and a buffer against climate change impacts.[15] Investment in natural capital is an expenditure that results in more sustainable management of ecosystems and promotes green growth.

Eco-efficiency indicators. Eco-efficiency indicators measure how the environment is used and how it is affected by an economic activity. The development of measures of vulnerability, resilience and progress is currently a focus area for small island developing States. The United Nations is developing vulnerability-resilience country profiles based on a range of previous initiatives in this area. Indicators relating to green growth will be incorporated into this work to improve policies in individual countries.

Effective implementation of the green growth strategy will involve more research on the options for each country. It will also require recognition by policymakers that green objectives are key elements of macroeconomic policy and particularly of fiscal policy.

Source: ESCAP.

Australia and New Zealand

Recovery continues

Australia marked an extraordinary 17 years of continuous economic expansion when its economy grew by 2.7% in 2010 after a growth of 1.3% in 2009 (see figure 2.11). Australia was one of the few developed countries that had weathered the global economic crisis and achieved positive growth during the 2008/09 economic downturn. Moreover, growth in 2010 was broad-based, with the public sector making a major contribution to the process as the result of a sizeable economic stimulus package that buoyed demand and income in both the public and private sectors. Household consumption was also buoyed by the wealth effect of rising asset prices and by employment growth. The relatively strong growth of domestic demand was, however, offset to some extent by the growth of net imports, reflecting both higher consumption demand emanating from households and investment demand from companies, particularly in the mining sector. The expanding Australian economy, which has been driven by strong external demand for raw materials, such as coal and iron ore, helped to generate employment, with the mining sector leading growth in this area. With higher demand for labour in the economy, the unemployment rate fell to a low of 5.1% in December 2010.

The New Zealand economy grew 1.5% in 2010 after virtually stagnating in 2009, although the pace of growth in 2010 decelerated in the middle of the year. The slowdown of growth mainly reflected sluggish private consumption, as households rebalanced their consumption expenditures and mortgage debt in the face of declining house prices and less favourable tax conditions for mortgages. Stagnant house prices also reduced the ability of households to access credit. The resultant weaker private consumption was offset partly by higher levels of investment and partly by export growth, which benefited from an increase in commodity prices. However, a devastating earthquake hit New Zealand's second largest city, Christchurch, in September 2010, with substantial damage to local infrastructure estimated at around 2% of GDP. Given the weakness in private consumption, the unemployment rate in the country remained high, fluctuating between 6% and 7% over much of 2010.

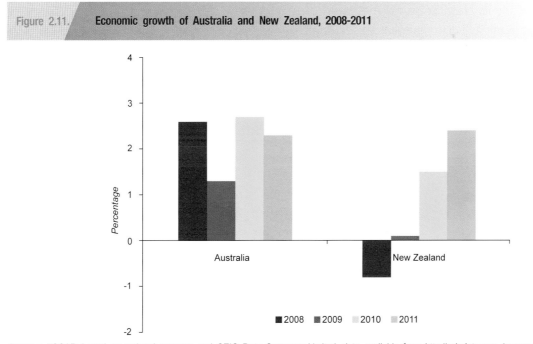

Figure 2.11. **Economic growth of Australia and New Zealand, 2008-2011**

■ 2008 ■ 2009 2010 2011

Sources: ESCAP, based on national sources; and CEIC Data Company Limited, data available from http://ceicdata.com (accessed 25 March 2011).

Note: Real GDP growth rates for 2010 and 2011 are estimates and forecasts respectively.

Modest inflationary pressure

Both Australia and New Zealand witnessed modest increases in inflation in 2010. Inflation in Australia rose to 2.7% in 2010 from 1.8% in 2009, reflecting, in part, the effect of the looser monetary and fiscal policies of the last two years in response to the global economic crisis. In addition, the marked increase in global commodity prices in 2010 fed into domestic price pressures. Import prices have been, by and large, contained due to the strong Australian dollar; consequently, consumer price inflation has been broadly restrained in the economy. Inflation in New Zealand increased to 2.3% in 2010 from 2.1% in 2009. The rate of inflation in non-tradable goods and services went up in 2010, reflecting price rises in rents, house construction and property maintenance, along with the effects of tax changes and of overall economic recovery. Wages have started to rise despite still sluggish employment growth in 2010.

Export growth turns trade balance into surplus

In both Australia and New Zealand, the trade balance turned from deficit to surplus in 2010, buoyed by the strong demand for raw materials and commodities from the Asia-Pacific region aided by higher prices of a wide range of commodities produced by the two countries. The strong growth in exports from Australia reflected acceleration in the growth of export volumes and the strong recovery of commodity prices. Australia's growing trading links with Asia-Pacific countries, led by demand from China, supported the continued growth of its exports even during the economic crisis of 2008/09 in Europe and North America. For instance, China's share in Australia's exports has grown from around 5% to over 20% in the past 10 years. China, Japan and the Republic of Korea together absorbed half of Australia's exports in 2009. New Zealand, too, enjoyed export growth, with buoyant external demand and higher prices for its main commodities, dairy products. Its export growth was also supported by

the growth of the Australian economy, the major export partner of New Zealand.

It should be stressed that, despite its impressive growth and export performance, Australia ran a deficit in its current account of around 2.7% of GDP in 2010. It therefore has to deal with a significant external financing gap whose counterpart is its relatively low domestic savings rate, a matter requiring policy attention in 2011 and beyond. Like Australia, New Zealand, too, has a current account deficit of around 3.4% of GDP. Although financing it has not been an issue in the past, in the more uncertain, risk-averse global financial environment that is likely to persist for some time, access to external financing could potentially become problematic.

The currencies of both countries appreciated against the United States dollar, in line with global trends. The Australian dollar has steadily appreciated against the United States dollar since the beginning of 2009, by over 50% by the end of 2010, while the New Zealand dollar appreciated by 40% over the same period.

Fiscal consolidation policies

Australia's fiscal position has been relatively favourable compared to the dire state of public finances in many other countries of the Organization for Economic Cooperation and Development (OECD), particularly in Europe. The Government ran a budget surplus of about 1.00%-1.75% of GDP for six years prior to the global economic crisis, leaving substantial fiscal space to launch a large fiscal stimulus package to pre-empt the effects of the 2008/09 global recession. Fiscal stimulus in Australia amounted to over 4% of GDP in the two years ending in June 2010, above the G20 average in this regard. The stimulus package led to a budget deficit of about 2.4% of GDP in 2009 and 4.1% in 2010. Damage caused by floods and cyclones in early 2011 will put further pressure on fiscal balance. In New Zealand, the fiscal deficit widened to 5.3% of GDP in 2010 from 3.7% in 2009. Government expenditures are expected to increase in the 2010/11 fiscal year as the Government continues its stimulus package to ensure that the economic recovery and reconstruction of earthquake-hit areas continues apace.

Tightening of monetary policies

In Australia, monetary policy has been progressively tightened since October 2009, much earlier than in other OECD countries. By November 2010, the cash rate had been gradually raised to 4.75%. In the view of the Reserve Bank of Australia, the historically favourable terms of trade, increasing private investment and a firming labour market pose a medium-term risk of higher inflation. In New Zealand, the easing of monetary policy was even more extensive, with the cash rate slashed from 8.25% in June 2008 to 2.50% by April 2009, before it was gradually tightened to 3.00%.[16] The rate was lowered to 2.50% in March 2011 to lessen the adverse economic impact of the devastating earthquake in the country the previous month.

Future outlook

The Australian economy is projected to grow at 2.3% in 2011, driven by continuing investment growth buoyed by the strong demand for mining sector products in the Asia-Pacific countries. Higher investment expenditures, in turn, should have positive knock-on effects for the rest of the economy. Consequential employment and income growth should support continued growth of household consumption. The economic damage and fiscal burden related to the large-scale flooding and cyclones in Australia in the first quarter of 2011 will have a significant impact on the above prospect. The economic losses are expected to run into several billions dollars. The Government introduced a flood tax for reconstruction. The New Zealand economy is expected to strengthen in 2011, with the projected growth of 2.4%, reflecting the continuation of strong export demand, principally from the Asia-Pacific region and, in particular, from Australia. However, the devastating earthquake that occurred in February 2011 could dampen economic growth.

SOUTH AND SOUTH-WEST ASIA

Growth remains strong and accelerates in some major economies

In general, the growth prospects of economies in South and South-West Asia improved in 2010. The subregion is estimated to have grown at 7.5% in 2010 as compared to 3.9% in 2009, with India leading this growth momentum (see table 2.4).

Afghanistan's economy is estimated to have grown by an impressive 8.9% in 2010 despite serious security concerns. This expansion was supported by strong investment in construction, much of which was linked to donor-led projects, and by private consumption. Performance in 2010 follows GDP growth at an exceptional 22.5% in 2009 that was largely driven by the performance of the agricultural sector and greater spending by both the Government and foreign donors. Agriculture grew by 53.0% as a result of good weather in the year and the base effect of a poor harvest in the previous year. Growth in services had also reached double digits in 2009. By contrast, manufacturing and construction growth was modest. The new three year economic programme that was agreed with IMF in July 2010 contains policies to keep inflation low, strengthen banking supervision and regulation, achieve sustained increases in fiscal revenues, ensure transparency in the mining sector and improve efficiency in the budget process and public spending while protecting the poor.

The economy of Bangladesh demonstrated considerable resilience despite the global economic crisis. GDP grew at 5.8% in 2010 on top of the 5.7% growth achieved in 2009. In both years, agriculture expanded by over 4%, helped essentially by favourable weather conditions and the Government's broad-based support for the agricultural sector. Industrial sector growth slightly decelerated from 6.5% in 2009 to 6.0% in 2010, mainly due to sluggish growth in the manufacturing subsector, which was a delayed effect of the global economic recession. The services sector grew by over 6% in both years. The growth of services was broad-based in 2010, with strong growth in key

Table 2.4. **Rates of economic growth and inflation in South and South-West Asian economies, 2009-2011**

(Percentage)

	Real GDP growth			Inflation[a]		
	2009	2010[b]	2011[c]	2009	2010[b]	2011[c]
South and South-West Asia[d,e]	**3.9**	**7.5**	**6.8**	**11.0**	**10.3**	**8.6**
Afghanistan	22.5	8.9	6.8	-8.3	8.2	9.5
Bangladesh	5.7	5.8	6.4	6.7	7.3	7.2
Bhutan	6.7	6.8	7.2	3.0	6.1	7.5
India	8.0	8.6	8.7	12.4	11.0	7.4
Iran (Islamic Republic of)	1.5	3.0	3.5	10.8	12.0	17.0
Maldives	-2.3	4.8	4.0	4.0	6.0	7.2
Nepal	4.0	3.5	4.0	13.2	10.7	8.0
Pakistan	1.2	4.1	2.8	20.8	11.7	15.5
Sri Lanka	3.5	8.0	8.0	3.4	5.9	7.5
Turkey	-4.7	8.1	5.0	6.3	8.6	6.0

Sources: ESCAP, based on national sources.

[a] Changes in the consumer price index.
[b] Estimates.
[c] Forecasts (as of 8 April 2011).
[d] GDP figures at market prices in dollars in 2009 (at 2000 prices) are used as weights to calculate the subregional growth rates.
[e] The estimates and forecasts for countries relate to fiscal years. The fiscal year referred to as 2009 in the table is defined as follows: 21 March 2009 to 20 March 2010 in the Islamic Republic of Iran; 1 April 2009 to 31 March 2010 in India; 1 July 2008 to 30 June 2009 in Bangladesh and Pakistan; and 16 July 2008 to 15 July 2009 in Nepal.

sectors, such as hotels and restaurants, transport and communications, real estate, public administration and defence, education, and health and social services. On the expenditure side, both private and public consumption contributed strongly to growth and the rise in consumption was driven by the remittances of overseas workers, which induced demand. This was supported by a budgetary stimulus package that included higher social safety net spending.

In Bhutan, the completion of the Tala hydroelectric project in 2007 provided a boost to electricity exports to India and, consequently, to Government revenues. As a result, GDP growth had accelerated to a high of 17.9% in 2007 but it returned to a more normal level of 4.7% and 6.7% in 2008 and 2009, respectively. Economic growth rose to 6.8% in 2010 with the start of construction work on two more large hydroelectric projects. A new economic development strategy finalized in March 2010 aims to diversify the economy, generate employment opportunities, promote exports and entrepreneurship, and enhance economic self-

reliance. It also emphasizes sustainable development so that economic growth is not achieved at the cost of environmental degradation.

The economy of India maintained a strong and steady growth momentum throughout the current global economic crisis, unlike many other emerging market economies where growth decelerated sharply and, in some cases, turned negative. GDP growth of 8.0% in 2009 is estimated to have strengthened to 8.6% in 2010. Growth prospects for the agricultural sector were boosted by the relatively good monsoon season, which increased agricultural output in 2010, as the deficient monsoon in 2009 had limited agricultural growth to only 0.4%. The performance of the industrial sector indicates that the 2009 momentum was consolidated, leading the economy to converge rapidly to a longer-term trend towards growth. The industrial production index depicts robust growth of 8.6% over the first nine months of the fiscal year in 2010, while the services sector grew by 9.6% in 2010. With a share of over 57% in GDP, the services sector has been fuelling economic growth.

On the demand side, a rise in savings and investment and a pickup in private consumption contributed to strong GDP growth. Growth in government consumption moderated somewhat, reflecting its fiscal consolidation programme.

The economy of India maintained a strong and steady growth momentum throughout the current global economic crisis

---

The Islamic Republic of Iran is the net oil exporter of the subregion. Its economy remains highly dependent on oil revenues, which provide over 80% of government revenues. Higher oil prices in 2010 contributed to a higher growth rate of GDP at 3.0%, as compared to 1.5% in 2009. The hydrocarbon industry, however, continues to suffer from a lack of foreign investment, which is adversely affecting prospects for a sustainable increase in the output of oil and gas over the long term.

In Maldives, after contracting by 2.3% in 2009, GDP grew at 4.8% in 2010, based on a rebound in tourism and construction. Both of these sectors had registered negative growth in 2009 and their performance in 2010 exhibited significant positive trends in line with broader trends in the subregion and globally.

In Nepal, GDP growth slowed to 3.5% in 2010 from 4.0% in 2009. This relatively low growth rate is partly due to frequent strikes in the country, persistent labour problems and severe electricity shortages. It is also due to adverse weather conditions on account of which growth in the agricultural sector decelerated in 2010. There was some deceleration, too, in the growth of services. On the other hand, the industrial sector expanded by 3.9% in 2010 as compared to the negative growth it experienced in 2009.

In Pakistan, despite challenging security conditions and severe energy shortages, domestic economic activity rebounded to some extent in fiscal year 2010, with economic growth accelerating to 4.1% from

1.2% in 2009.[17] This improved GDP performance was led by a recovery in large-scale manufacturing, a reasonable harvest of major agricultural crops and improved performance in the services sector. On the expenditure side, growth was largely due to a substantial increase in public sector consumption and investment expenditures. Severe floods across the country from August to October 2010, however, added to the existing difficulties of the economy. More than 20 million people (or more than 10% of the population) were affected by the floods, which also severely damaged housing, businesses, agricultural crops and physical infrastructure. Private and public losses due to floods are estimated at $9.7 billion. Indeed, the impact of the floods on the economy will continue to be felt in the coming years as damaged infrastructure will not only need to be repaired but also upgraded to meet the needs of a modern economy.

In Sri Lanka, the economic recovery that began in the second half of 2009 gained momentum and GDP growth is estimated to have accelerated sharply to 8.0% in 2010 from 3.5% in 2009. With the end of the country's civil war in May 2009, the strong recovery is being supported by robust growth in agricultural output and a surge in domestic trade and transport activities. Growth in industrial production has also picked up, supported by strong growth in investment, particularly private investment. Total gross investment is estimated to have increased to 27.8% of GDP in 2010 from 24.5% in 2009.[18] Increased tourist arrivals and reconstruction of the war-torn Eastern and Northern provinces and their integration into the rest of the country also supported growth momentum. Damage caused by heavy rains and widespread floods may affect growth prospects for 2011.

The economy of Turkey, whose trading links are primarily with European Union countries, contracted sharply in 2009 due to the global economic crisis. The sound macroeconomic policy and reforms carried out in the past, however, helped to limit financial system stress by keeping the balance sheets of banks and households strong and successfully containing interest and exchange rate volatility. Business and consumer confidence remained high, which helped the economy to grow faster. The economy grew by 8.1% in 2010, aided by a strong recovery in domestic and external demand, as well as a surge in private investment. The relaxation of fiscal, monetary and financial policies also contributed to the recovery.

High inflation is a major challenge as food prices rise rapidly

Of greater concern in the subregion is high inflation, especially as it concerns food prices. As food inflation affects the poor disproportionately, it is a serious problem for countries with a high incidence of poverty. Reducing inflation is and will remain the key macroeconomic challenge for this subregion.

A sharp increase in inflation in India in 2010 has been a particular cause for concern following a major surge in food prices in 2009 (see figure 2.12). Average inflation in 2009 was in the double digits. Consumer price inflation (for industrial workers) is estimated at 11.0% for the first nine months of fiscal year 2010 and food prices, which are heavily weighted in the consumer price basket, remained elevated in 2010. Deficient monsoon rains in 2009

contributed to higher food inflation. Rapid economic recovery has also generated inflationary pressures due to significant supply-side constraints in the economy. What was initially a process driven by food prices gradually became more generalized, as reflected in the sharp increase in inflation for non-food manufactured products. The increasing generalization of inflation required appropriate policy actions to anchor inflation expectations.[19] It was thus a major challenge for the monetary authorities to moderate inflationary pressures through the judicious use of monetary policy without disrupting the momentum of growth. Monetary policy was tightened gradually and included several policy rate increases. Inflation appears to have stabilized in recent months, although the rate may remain high for some time. The early signs of a downturn in non-food manufacturing inflation suggest that recent monetary actions are having an impact on both inflationary expectations and demand in a non-disruptive manner. In addition, a normal monsoon in 2010 led to a rebound in agricultural output, boosting food supplies and overall GDP growth and easing inflation somewhat in the process. High international oil and commodity prices, however, are keeping upward pressure on inflation.

Figure 2.12. Inflation in selected South and South-West Asian economies, 2008-2010

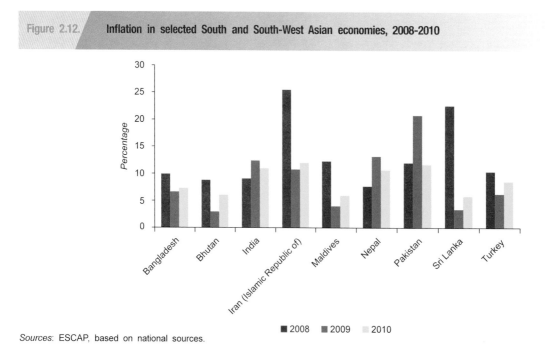

■ 2008 ■ 2009 ■ 2010

Sources: ESCAP, based on national sources.

Notes: Data for 2010 are estimates. Inflation refers to the consumer price index for industrial workers for India and to Colombo for Sri Lanka.

A major challenge for the monetary authorities is to moderate inflationary pressures through the judicious use of monetary policy without disrupting the momentum of growth

Pakistan has been experiencing double-digit inflation over the past three years. In 2010, inflation stood at 11.7%, having decelerated from 20.8% in 2009. Increases in electricity and natural gas charges and upward revisions in petroleum prices influenced production and transport costs, causing prices of other consumer price index items to rise, as well. This cost-push pressure on inflation was the result of a pressing need to reduce government subsidies in order to contain the budget deficit, which has been one of the major factors responsible for high inflation. Ironically, efforts in this case to contain the budget deficit have also led to inflationary pressures. Food prices rose more sharply not only due to the increased cost of transport but also because of a surge in the prices of imported food commodities, mainly pulses, spices and milk powder. Inflationary pressures increased further due to the devastation caused by the floods. Further increases in electricity and natural gas charges and reforms in the generalized sales tax will automatically contribute to keeping inflation high, at least over the medium term.

Inflationary pressures also re-emerged in the Bangladesh economy as the consumer price index increased by 7.3% in 2010 against 6.7% in 2009. The increase in commodity prices, particularly in neighbouring India, contributed to an increase in domestic prices in Bangladesh. Food price inflation rose at an even higher rate. To check this upward trend of prices, the Government took several steps, including ensuring an improved supply of commodities, allowing the sale of essential commodities in open areas, and closely monitoring the price situation and demand-supply gaps. At the same time, the Government attempted to keep inflation at a tolerable level by pursuing a less accommodative

monetary policy by mopping up excess liquidity due to the upsurge of inflows from overseas worker remittances. In addition, the Bangladesh Bank, the central bank of the country, raised its policy rate in May 2010 to contain inflationary pressures.

In Sri Lanka, improved domestic supply conditions and supportive fiscal policies helped to limit inflation to 5.9% in 2010. Domestic supply conditions improved due to improved performance by the agricultural sector and an increased supply of food commodities, mainly from the north and east of the country, due to the improved security situation in those areas. The continued stability of the domestic currency cushioned the price increases of imported commodities, while measures taken by the Government, particularly downward adjustments to tariffs applicable to imported commodities, helped to reduce price pressures further. The unchanged domestic prices for petrol and diesel during the year helped to contain inflation.

Inflation in Bhutan and Nepal is closely linked to inflation in India because of the fixed exchange rates between the currencies of these countries as well as the close economic ties among them. In Nepal, there was some deceleration in inflation in 2010 as compared to the previous year, but it remained high at 10.7%. Moreover, food prices rose at a much higher rate. Inflation increased somewhat in Bhutan in 2010. Inflation in Maldives increased to 6.0% in 2010 from 4.0% in 2009.

Inflation in Turkey also picked up, rising to 8.6% in 2010 as compared to 6.3% in 2009. Large excise tax increases and food price shocks in early 2010 caused a temporary spike in inflation that also raised inflationary expectations. Food prices witnessed sharp increases and volatility over the year. In the Islamic Republic of Iran, which had been experiencing high inflation for several years, inflation fell sharply to 10.8% in 2009 due to lower international commodity prices and a good agricultural crop. Nevertheless, it was in the double digits in 2010, due partly to a gradual reduction in subsidies on consumer goods and partly to the fiscal policy, which continued to be expansionary, albeit not to the extent of previous years.

Monetary and fiscal policy responses

Monetary policy tightened

Governments in South and South-West Asia, as in other subregions, used expansionary monetary policies to counter negative fallout from the global slowdown and moderate the decline in GDP growth. Monetary policy is being tightened in most countries, though, to contain growing inflationary pressures. It was tightened in Bangladesh, India and Pakistan by raising key policy interest rates. In India, policy rates have been raised several times. The Central Bank of Sri Lanka, on the other hand, eased its monetary policy in July 2010 and January 2011 as a result of a deceleration in inflation. In Pakistan, the monetary policy debate has been complicated by the worsening of most macroeconomic aggregates. On the one hand, there is the argument that the central bank should respond to rising inflationary pressures and the excessive increase in the fiscal deficit with higher interest rates; on the other hand, the demand shock stemming from the flood damage argues for

a degree of countervailing easing of monetary policy to help revive the faltering economy.[20]

Budget deficits remain high and fiscal consolidation is taking place in some countries

Although budget deficits were already high prior to the global crisis, governments had little choice but to run up yet higher deficits as a means of countercyclical stabilization (see figure 2.13). Persistent large fiscal deficits, however, carry several adverse macroeconomic risks, including higher inflation, lower savings, crowding-out pressures on private investment, upward pressure on interest rates and a worsening of external imbalances. These concerns may be largely absent in the short term in a phase of economic slowdown that requires the use of fiscal stimulus. In the medium term, however, such risks often materialize if the fiscal deficit is not brought down significantly under a credible fiscal consolidation strategy.

It is important that governments prepare and implement fiscal consolidation plans to contain their budget deficits and growing public debt. India has

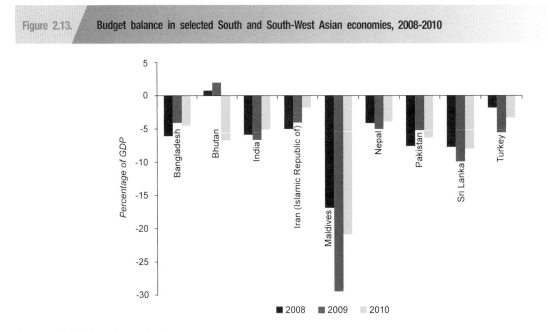

Figure 2.13. Budget balance in selected South and South-West Asian economies, 2008-2010

Sources: ESCAP, based on national sources.

Note: Data for 2010 are estimates.

already devised such a plan, within which a budget deficit of 5.1% of GDP in 2010 was well within the target of 5.5% of GDP. The deficit is expected to come down further to 4.6% of GDP in 2011. In June 2010, the Government of India took a bold decision to decontrol petrol and diesel prices to reform its fuel subsidy programme for fiscal consolidation. Moreover, a higher-than-expected realization on third-generation and broadband wireless access licence auctions combined with buoyant tax revenues helped the budget deficit to perform better than had been targeted in 2010.

In Pakistan, lower revenue generation and higher current expenditures are the underlying reasons for the stressed fiscal position. The tax-to-GDP ratio has fallen to a low of around 10% and, without substantially increasing the resource envelope, it would be difficult to sustain the fiscal deficit at manageable levels. Similarly, the Government must carefully scrutinize and reprioritize spending to create room for public investment to support growth. The budget deficit, at 6.3% of GDP in 2010, will face further pressure in 2011 as a result of the devastation wreaked on the economy by the severe floods and the consequential need for rehabilitation and reconstruction activities.

In Bangladesh, the budget deficit deteriorated slightly to 4.5% of GDP in 2010. The fiscal situation is expected to deteriorate further in 2011 as the Government attempts to tackle a complex array of problems, ranging from shortages of power, gas and water to the need for enhanced welfare spending. The sectoral outlays of public expenditure in the fiscal year 2011 budget contain distinct inclusive features that aim to combat poverty, with one third of total outlays going to social infrastructure, including nearly one fourth for human development (health, education, science and technology, and other related subsectors).

In Sri Lanka, the budget deficit is estimated at 8% of GDP for 2010 as compared to the 2009 deficit of 9.9%. The improvement in the fiscal situation was helped by the considerable recovery in government revenue due to the expansion of economic activities and through savings in government expenditure in certain areas, which was achieved while maintaining public investment at the targeted level. Further reductions in budget deficit are expected in 2011. Defence spending may fall with the improvement in the security situation, but infrastructure projects launched for reconstruction will keep capital spending high.

In Nepal, with growing tax revenues, the tax-to-GDP ratio has been improving and it stood at over 13% in 2010. The budget deficit fell from 5.0% in 2009 to 3.9% of GDP in 2010. Maldives, on the other hand, has been experiencing very high budget deficits in recent years. Some reduction in the budget deficit of 29.4% of GDP in 2009 was expected in 2010 due to an increase in revenue on account of higher import duties and tourism-related revenues associated with the economic recovery.

The Government of the Islamic Republic of Iran has been undertaking measures to strengthen its fiscal position. The system of indirect taxes is being modernized with the introduction of a value added tax and other measures to improve tax policy and administration. The parliament has approved a bill to increase energy prices and phase out subsidies on several other commodities and services. In Turkey, the budget deficit fell to 3.3% of GDP in 2010 from 5.5% of GDP in 2009, helped by indirect tax increases, the favourable impact of low global and domestic interest rates on borrowing costs and the rise in tax revenues resulting from a solid recovery in economic activity.

Exports revive but imports grow more rapidly

In the wake of the global economic crisis, there were unprecedented falls in the merchandise exports and imports of all countries in the subregion. Both exports and imports started to pick up again in late 2009, but growth in imports has been faster than that in exports, leading to widened trade deficits. Large remittances from overseas workers are still growing, albeit at a slower rate; for Bangladesh, growth is estimated at 13.4% in 2010 against 22.4% in 2009.[21] Growing worker remittances will help to contain the current account deficits that are expected to rise somewhat in the subregion (see figure 2.14).

In India, exports and imports began to expand from October/November 2009 after a continuous decline for nearly a year. In fiscal year 2010, export growth exceeded import growth. Due to the significantly larger size of imports, however, the trade deficit widened. The net invisible surplus also shrank. As a result, the current account deficit could increase in 2010 to around 3.0% from 2.8% of GDP in the previous year. Financing of the current deficit was not a problem in 2009 due to stronger capital inflows, but capital inflows in the initial months of fiscal year 2010 moderated somewhat. Given the strong growth outlook of India, capital inflows are expected to accelerate in 2011. In theory, volatile capital flows can be a potential source of instability, as their costs can be alarming for an economy during periods when capital flows are either too small or too large unless they are managed judiciously. To deal with the adverse ramifications of capital flows, India has, in the past, used a mix of a flexible exchange rate, sterilization of the impact

of inflows on domestic liquidity, a cautious approach to the liberalization of the capital account and the cushion of its large foreign exchange reserves. This approach is expected to continue in 2011.

In Pakistan, the external current account deficit came down to 2.0% of GDP in 2010 from 5.7% of GDP in 2009. The improved performance in 2010 was helped by the relatively strong recovery of exports, which grew at 9.4% in 2010, while imports continued to contract, although at the much smaller rate of 0.3%. While the increase in exports was largely due to a higher quantum of goods, the fall in the import bill was mainly a result of lower prices. Overseas worker remittances grew by 14% and reached close to $9 billion in 2010, helping to reduce the current account deficit. The financial account recorded a surplus, mainly due to disbursements by IMF under a standby arrangement. With the overall balance of payments in surplus, foreign exchange reserves reached an all-time high of about $17 billion by the end of fiscal year 2010.

In Bangladesh, after witnessing a slump during the first half of fiscal year 2010, exports picked up in the second half of the year and registered an overall

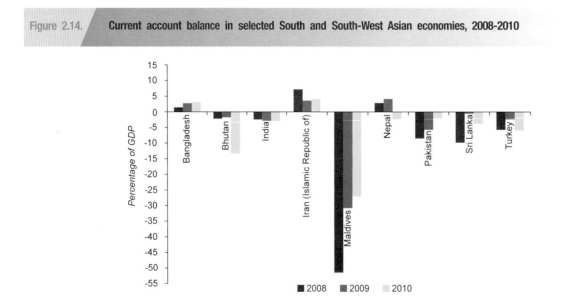

Figure 2.14. **Current account balance in selected South and South-West Asian economies, 2008-2010**

Sources: ESCAP, based on national sources; and International Monetary Fund, International Financial Statistics online database. Available from www.imfstatistics.org/imf (accessed 16 February 2011).

Note: Data for 2010 are estimates.

growth of 4.1% in the full fiscal year. While exports of jute goods, engineering and electronic goods, textiles and garments experienced an increase, exports of chemical products, frozen food and tea fell sharply. Total imports grew faster than exports, thus widening the trade deficit. Remittances from overseas workers continued to grow, albeit at a slower rate. They reached close to $11 billion in 2010 and not only closed the gap on merchandise trade but also helped to post a surplus in the current account balance.

Remittances from overseas workers continued to grow, albeit at a slower rate

---

Foreign trade witnessed a sharp boost in Sri Lanka. While exports grew at a double-digit rate in 2010, import growth was even faster due to increased economic activity and infrastructure investment. Exports grew at 17.3% and imports at 32.4% in 2010. While the growth in exports of textiles and garments was relatively small, agricultural and manufactured goods registered strong growth. On the import side, growth was generally more broad-based, with consumer goods registering the highest growth rate. With recovery in tourism and continued strong worker remittances, the current account deficit was expected to stabilize around 4% of GDP in 2010. Foreign exchange reserves reached $6.6 billion by end of the year

In Nepal, while exports contracted, imports grew at a faster rate in 2010, which led to a wider trade deficit. At the same time, growth in worker remittances slowed. As a result, the current account balance turned into a deficit in 2010 from the surplus of the previous few years. Obstacles in the movement of goods due to strikes, the deterioration of industrial relations and the uncertainty of energy supplies are factors that have been detrimental to export promotion. In Maldives, both exports and imports improved in 2010, the latter at a faster rate. As a result, the current account deficit remained high at about 27% of GDP in 2010. Foreign exchange

reserves, however, are expected to improve with enhanced private capital inflows supplemented by financial support from IMF.

In Turkey, strong growth in imports widened the current account deficit from 2.3% of GDP in 2009 to 5.9% of GDP in 2010. Containing this external imbalance by avoiding a heavy dependence on potentially unstable external financing will be important for sustained economic recovery, given the uncertain global outlook. In contrast, due to higher oil prices, the current account surplus of the Islamic Republic of Iran is expected to widen in 2010 compared to 2009.

As in other subregions, some domestic currencies have appreciated against the dollar. With a strong growth outlook and continued capital inflows, the Indian rupee witnessed some fluctuations over the year but appreciated by about 2% between January and December 2010 but appreciating again in 2011 (see figure 2.15). The Sri Lanka rupee gained marginally while the taka of Bangladesh remained relatively stable over the same period. Deterioration in the macroeconomic aggregates of Pakistan, including higher inflation, contributed to continuous depreciation of the rupee. The Turkish lira fluctuated over the year but the average exchange rate between 2009 and 2010 remained relatively stable. Bhutan and Nepal have pegged their currencies to the Indian rupee and Maldives maintains a fixed exchange rate against the dollar.

Future outlook and policy challenges

Amidst uncertainties surrounding global economic recovery, the subregion is nevertheless expected to maintain its growth momentum into 2011. India will lead this growth dynamism, with its economy projected to grow at 8.7% in fiscal year 2011, with private consumption and investment demand being the two major drivers of growth. In Bangladesh, projected GDP growth for 2011 at 6.4% is ex pected to be supported by improved growth in the agricultural sector, recovery in export growth with diversification into new markets, including the

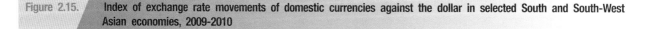

Figure 2.15. Index of exchange rate movements of domestic currencies against the dollar in selected South and South-West Asian economies, 2009-2010

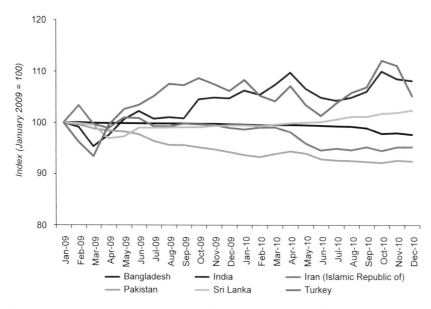

Source: ESCAP calculations based on data from International Monetary Fund, International Financial Statistics online database. Available from www.imfstatistics.org/imf (accessed 16 February 2011).

Note: A positive trend represents appreciation and vice versa.

emerging economies, and an improved situation in power and gas supplies. With the end of the civil war in Sri Lanka, reconstruction activities in the war-torn areas and enhanced tourist arrivals are expected to provide a further boost to economic growth, which should reach 8% in 2011. Damage caused by severe floods in the country in the first quarter of 2011 could have dampening effect on growth, though. In Nepal, GDP is projected to grow at 4% in 2011, somewhat higher than the 2010 rate. Economic revival in the country hinges in large part on the ability of the government to improve law and order, as Nepal's poor security and political instability limit the government's capacity to spend money and boost rural incomes. Devastation caused by severe floods in Pakistan has dampened its immediate growth prospects and GDP growth is expected to fall to 2.8% in 2011. Reconstruction activities should provide some support in achieving even this low growth. A firming of oil prices may help the Islamic Republic of Iran to improve its growth rate in 2011. The current draft of the Fifth Five-Year Development Plan, covering the period of 2011/12-2015/16,

puts forward ambitious macroeconomic objectives, including 8% GDP growth and a comprehensive structural reform agenda. Turkey, which has strong economic ties with European Union countries, may face a slowdown in GDP growth to 5.0% in 2011 as external demand softens.

High inflation rates in the subregion can compromise the achievement of sustained high growth rates

High inflation rates in the subregion can compromise the achievement of sustained high growth rates. Containing inflationary pressures should therefore be a priority in the policy agenda of governments. Both demand- and supply-side factors have contributed to inflationary pressures in the subregion. High budget deficits in most countries have been instrumental in increasing liquidity and have generated price pressures in the face of supply constraints. There is an urgent need to bring budget deficits down to a more sustainable level. Some countries have been tightening monetary policy to alleviate pressures on inflation from the demand side but a combination of monetary, fiscal and other measures is needed to reduce price pressures in the subregion (see box 2.3). Repeated supply shocks pose a constant challenge to sustaining a low inflation regime. A more medium-term approach is needed in order to augment the supply of items of mass consumption by addressing structural supply constraints. Moreover, food prices are, in part, being driven by structural imbalances between demand and supply as, for instance, increasingly affluent consumers diversify their dietary patterns away from cereals towards protein sources, which calls for an effort to increase the supply of such items rapidly. The success of this effort will largely determine the longer-term outlook for food price inflation.

Strong and sustained growth momentum is needed in the subregion to tackle the long-term problem of widespread poverty. Over the past few years, most countries have made progress in reducing poverty. Even today, however, at least one in every three persons in South Asia is classified as poor. The fight against poverty therefore must continue. Countries need to continue pursuing economic reforms to improve productivity, strengthen public institutions, improve economic governance, and build social safety nets to protect the more vulnerable segments of the population. To promote more inclusive growth, the provision of basic services such as health and education and the generation of ample employment opportunities should remain the principal priority in the policy agenda of the governments. Growth cannot be sustained in the long run if it is not inclusive.

Remittances from overseas workers are quite large and play an important role in the economies of South Asian countries. A large number of South Asian workers (more than 5 million, most of whom are unskilled or low-skilled) are employed in oil-rich Middle Eastern countries. Despite the global economic crisis, remittances from these countries have been growing in recent years, although the rate of growth is slowing. One of the main issues that should be addressed is the transfer of these remittances through informal channels. To take full advantage of these resources, policymakers need to take steps to promote the use of formal channels by lowering their transaction costs. There is also need to create a commission that can present a united stance of countries in the subregion to oversee migration and enhance its positive aspects.[22] The South Asian Commission can help in protecting workers' rights and enhancing their social protection. The Commission can also work to ensure that the workers' remittances and their savings when they return can be invested in productive areas. The South Asian countries need to provide a diverse pool of investment and savings options for this purpose.

To promote more inclusive growth, the provision of basic services such as health and education and the generation of ample employment opportunities should remain the principal priority in the policy agenda of the governments

---

On the physical infrastructure side, one of the biggest challenges being faced by several countries is improving the electricity supply. Electricity supply disruptions are common in Bangladesh, Nepal and Pakistan. Electricity outages that last many hours have been affecting productivity in all sectors of these economies. Businesses and even households use small electricity generators, operated on imported fuel, to meet their electricity needs. This raises the cost of production, which leads to higher inflation and adds to the import bill. Exports from these countries are also being affected due to high production costs and low outputs. Disruptions in the electricity supply are adversely affecting both the quality of life and the development of human capital. Without addressing the severe electricity problem, the full potential of economic growth in some of these countries cannot be realized.

Box 2.3. Some policy options to contain inflationary pressures in South Asia[23]

Spikes in food and fuel prices in 2008 caused inflation rates to increase in most Asian countries. With the onset of the global financial crisis in 2008/09, however, price pressures subsided rapidly across the region, except in South Asia. Indeed, India and Pakistan are experiencing double-digit inflation driven mainly by food. Given the high incidence of poverty in the region, higher food and overall inflation rates disproportionately affect the poor. Moreover, because of the large share of food in the average household consumption budget, a sustained rise in food prices tends to put upward pressure on wages and, with a time lag, on general inflation.

Causative factors of inflation

An analytical and empirical examination of the causative factors of inflation can be divided broadly into two categories, demand and supply. The analysis shows that demand components have tended to fluctuate with output levels and growth rates but they have not been major independent sources of price shocks. The major sources of price volatility have been from the supply side. Although longer-run aggregate supply in South Asian countries is elastic given youthful populations in transition to more productive occupations, it is subject to frequent negative supply shocks (see figure). Demand contractions tend to amplify these shocks. South Asian economies are supply constrained in the sense that, while output is largely determined by demand, inefficiencies on the supply side tend to perpetuate inflation by creating shortages of goods and services from time to time.

Figure. Aggregate demand and supply

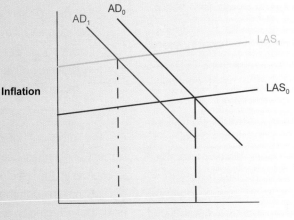

With a supply shock, the aggregate supply curve in the figure shifts upward, leading to higher inflation. If, in response, a demand contraction shifts the aggregate demand curve downward, this reduces inflation only marginally and at a high cost in terms of output lost. Therefore, the use of restrictive demand-side policies to tackle inflation when its causes are primarily on the supply side may not help much in reducing overall inflationary pressures. Both formal econometric tests and analysis of shock episodes based on Indian data support this analysis.

In South Asia, the food price-wage cycle is an important mechanism for propagating price shocks and creating inflationary expectations in response to a supply shock, which acts as an inflation trigger. The political economy of farm price support, consumption subsidies and wage support, with built-in waste, inefficiencies and corruption, contributes to chronic cost-push

Box 2.3 *(continued)*

pressures. Poor targeting of consumption subsidies implies nominal wages rising with a time lag, pushing up costs and generating second-round inflationary pressures from a temporary supply shock.

The political economy of the subregion informally indexes wages with food price inflation. If the rise in average wages exceeds that of agricultural productivity, however, prices of food will inevitably go up, propagating more generalized inflation. Populist policies that provide short-term subsidies but raise indirect costs also contribute to cost-push pressures. For example, neglected infrastructure and poor public services increase overall costs in the economy. The power shortages from which most South Asian countries suffer are a case in point.

Virtually all countries in the subregion have shifted to more flexible exchange rates that are managed to varying degrees. Bangladesh and Sri Lanka avoided significant exchange rate depreciation during the global crisis and their inflation rates dropped into the low single digits in 2009. Elsewhere, however, food inflation has remained high. These differential outcomes indicate a more strategic use of exchange rates in anti-inflation policy.

Policy options

Once the nature and structure of shocks and elasticities of aggregate demand and supply are identified, certain policy implications follow: a shift down the supply curve in response to a supply shock; avoidance of an excessively large demand contraction; and the identification and removal of propagation mechanisms. Above all, a hasty tightening of monetary policy will, in all likelihood, involve a large output cost with little effect on inflation.

Temporary shocks

Mild but early monetary tightening after a supply shock can prevent inflationary wage expectations from becoming entrenched and further pushing up the supply curve. Given this, a first-round price increase from a supply shock might be allowed, but a second-round wage-price increase should be prevented inasmuch as possible. A nominal appreciation of the exchange rate can serve to push down the supply curve.

Short-term fiscal policies to push down the supply curve include tax and tariff cuts and freer imports. These policies can also lower inflationary expectations. Trade policy works best for individual country shocks that are not globally correlated. Nimble private trade can defeat speculative hoarders. It should be stressed that short-run policies are likely to work only for a temporary shock. A long-lasting shock requires a longer-term productivity response.

Preventing chronic cost-push

Food prices play a central role in propagation mechanisms since they raise nominal wages with a time lag. A fundamental reason for chronic supply-side inflation is that real wages tend to exceed labour productivity. The solution is to raise labour productivity, especially in agriculture.

Following liberalization, as farm produce has become part of the wider traded economy, border prices have begun to affect domestic food prices. In such a situation, the exchange rate can affect food prices and overall inflation. Conflict between a depreciated exchange rate to encourage exports and an appreciated exchange rate to increase real wages can contribute to a wage-price cycle, with depreciation raising nominal wages and prices and leading to real appreciation. Attempts to dampen exchange rate appreciation sustain the cycle. Only improvements in productivity can close the demand-supply gap and break this inflation propagation mechanism.

Box 2.3 *(continued)*

Capital inflows will tend to appreciate the exchange rate, thus satisfying the wage target, and finance the accompanying rise in imports. But a widening current account deficit is risky even though it might allow gross investment to exceed domestic savings. It would be preferable to set a sustainable current account deficit and meet it by raising productivity in the economy. Rising productivity increases the level of capital inflows that can be safely absorbed at a reasonable current account deficit. In this regard, better governance and improved delivery of public services improve productivity in the economy and, within the corpus of governance, reform of food policy is especially urgent given the economy-wide impact of food inflation.

Governance in food policy

Developing East Asian countries with large food components in household budgets have successfully moderated food inflation by focusing on raising agricultural productivity. India moved early to agricultural subsidies together with implicit taxes generated through the imposition of restrictions on different activities within the agricultural sector, including public distribution schemes. Procurement prices were raised with the rise in border prices but did not fall with them, thus imparting generalized cost-push pressures in the economy and creating unnecessarily large food stocks in costly and dysfunctional food support programmes. If

the procurement price becomes a true support price, food stocks should come down in a bad agricultural season when market prices rise and go up as market prices fall in a good year. Through such a policy, farmers would receive some assured income support even as a removal of restrictions on the movement and marketing of agricultural goods and better infrastructure allowed them to diversify their crops.

With lower average stocks, the public distribution scheme should focus more on remote, inaccessible areas. Food coupons or cash transfers directed primarily to female members of households can provide food security to the poor while allowing them to diversify their food consumption basket. Since the income elasticity of demand for food is still high, more moderate nominal price increases could serve to incentivize higher agricultural output and income growth.

Political jostling when deciding on food policy, in general, and procurement prices, in particular, ignores their negative long-term effects. Poor coordination means that multiple agencies do not factor in each other's costs or consider the wider picture. Until thorough food policy reform occurs, a possible nominal appreciation of the nominal exchange rate can prevent a sharp rise in border prices from triggering multiple interest group actions resulting in complex domestic distortions.

International

Emerging markets must find non-distortionary ways to respond to spikes in food and commodity prices. Large global spikes imply distortions beyond supply shocks, which should be prevented. Policies that are driving up prices across all asset categories, such as excessive liquidity creation in some of the developed countries that is directing large funds into commodities, might be re-examined at a subregional or regional level and its impact modified through some form of collective action.

Futures markets help output planning through better information on future demand and supply and the hedging of risk, but any overreaction implies that prices in financial markets do not reflect their real determinants. The answer is not to ban such markets but to improve their working and regulation. Progressive convergence towards common global regulatory standards can prevent arbitrage. Participation by more diverse groups in commodity trading could be encouraged within a framework of rules that discourage market abuses and thereby limit volatility.

Source: ESCAP.

Both short-term and long-term measures are needed to tackle the electricity problem. To boost electricity supply in the short term, Bangladesh and Pakistan are implementing rental power projects, where the private sector quickly installs small thermal power generation units and sells electricity to the government. This is clearly an expensive stop-gap option and, in the long term, much greater attention would need to be paid to renewable sources of energy. It is useful to note that the Government of Bangladesh plans to generate 5% of its total electricity from renewable energy sources by 2015 and 10% by 2020. In the subregion, transmission and distribution losses vary from 20% to 40% in different countries and theft of electricity is a major problem. There is therefore a need for greater efficiency on both the generation and distribution sides.

Promotion of regional cooperation in the energy sector can benefit the participating countries enormously

---

Concerning electricity pricing, some countries have been providing substantial subsidies, but they are being withdrawn. This process has been raising the cost of living, though, and there is a need to provide some form of protection to the poor. Tariff rates somehow need to be kept affordable for small consumers. It is also worth considering a more targeted approach to providing subsidies following the pattern of food stamps, where electricity stamps or coupons can be given to the poor to pay their electricity bills.

Finally, the promotion of regional cooperation in the energy sector can benefit the participating countries enormously. The signing of a gas pipeline project in December 2010 by Afghanistan, India, Pakistan and Turkmenistan will bring 3.2 billion cubic feet of natural gas per day from Turkmenistan to Pakistan and India via Afghanistan. Along with economic benefits, this project should contribute to peace and stability in the region.

SOUTH-EAST ASIA

Growth remains robust despite some cooling off

In 2009, South-East Asia posted a mere 1% GDP growth. With the recovery in global trade and boosted by bold stimulus packages, however, GDP growth steadily improved over the second half of 2009 and reached its peak in the first half of 2010, when such countries as Singapore and Thailand grew by over 10%. Due to a lower base effect and weaker demand for exports, growth decelerated in the second half of the year. Nevertheless, domestic demand remained robust and the 11 South-East Asian economies grew by an estimated 8.1%, on average, in 2010 (see table 2.5).

After three years of weak growth and contraction, Brunei Darussalam saw its economy expand by 2.0% in 2010, supported by small increases in oil and gas production, which accounts for some 50% of real GDP, 95% of total exports and 90% of government revenue. Stronger economic expansion from higher global oil and gas prices should be taken as an opportunity to accelerate investment in the non-energy sector, which remained subdued despite fiscal stimulus measures. Some early progress was seen with a new methanol plant in 2010.

One of the hardest hit economies in 2009, Cambodia, benefited from a rapid recovery in tourism, a modest rebound in garment exports and higher agricultural output in 2010, when the economy expanded by 6.0%. The construction sector, however, which contracted by some 40% in 2009, remained subdued due to delays in major property projects. Government efforts to strengthen trade ties with neighbouring Asian countries need to be accelerated, as a narrow export base with heavy reliance on the markets of developed countries in the West poses significant risks. Export items could also be diversified into areas of comparative advantage, including rice, footwear and low-end electronics. The rice harvest, for instance, was reported to have reached nearly 8 million tons in 2010, but suffered from a shortage of processing facilities.

Table 2.5. Rates of economic growth and inflation in South-East Asian economies, 2009-2011

(Percentage)

	Real GDP growth			Inflation[a]		
	2009	2010[b]	2011[c]	2009	2010[b]	2011[c]
South-East Asia[d]	**1.0**	**8.1**	**5.5**	**2.3**	**4.0**	**4.8**
Brunei Darussalam	-1.8	2.0	1.7	1.8	1.8	2.1
Cambodia	-2.0	6.0	6.2	-0.7	4.1	6.0
Indonesia	4.5	6.1	6.5	4.8	5.1	6.2
Lao People's Democratic Republic	7.6	8.0	8.3	0.0	5.4	6.1
Malaysia	-1.7	7.2	5.2	0.6	1.7	3.0
Myanmar	4.9	5.5	5.8	8.0	7.9	9.1
Philippines	1.1	7.3	5.2	3.2	3.8	4.5
Singapore	-0.8	14.5	5.0	0.6	2.8	3.3
Thailand	-2.2	7.8	4.5	-0.8	3.3	3.5
Timor-Leste	11.6	7.9	8.2	0.7	6.5	7.5
Viet Nam	5.3	6.8	6.2	6.9	9.0	11.0

Sources: ESCAP, based on national sources; and CEIC Data Company Limited, data available from http://ceicdata.com (accessed 25 March 2011).

[a] Changes in the consumer price index.
[b] Estimates.
[c] Forecasts (as of 8 April 2011).
[d] GDP figures at market prices in dollars in 2009 (at 2000 prices) are used as weights to calculate the subregional growth rates.

Indonesia, with its large domestic market, was among the fastest growing major economies in 2009 at 4.5% and grew even faster, by 6.1%, in 2010. The economy benefited from continued strength in household consumption, robust exports and improving investment. Private consumption was supported by the availability of consumer financing and low household debt and mounting consumer optimism. Meanwhile, investment benefited from a recovery in lending to the private sector as well as increased FDI inflows. On the production side, the services sector, including retail and telecommunications, saw a sharp rebound compared to the more modest and steady recovery in industry. Overall confidence in the economy also increased, as reflected in the credit rating upgrades. Strong capital inflows and rising commodity prices, if well managed, should provide additional resources to narrow the social and infrastructure gaps.

The Lao People's Democratic Republic has been enjoying steady growth in recent years, with most of its trade done with neighbouring China, Thailand and Viet Nam. The economy, which expanded by 8.0% in 2010, received a boost from a surge in the global price of minerals, especially gold and copper, which together account for over half of export earnings, and from a new hydropower facility which began to operate in March. These developments, in turn, helped to attract further inflows of private investment and donor aid. As the only landlocked country in the subregion, the Lao People's Democratic Republic stands to gain from rising intraregional trade as a "land-linking" country, but customs modernization and upgrading of railways need to be accelerated.

After contracting in 2009, the economy of Malaysia expanded by 7.2% in 2010, with double-digit growth in exports and manufacturing in the first half of the year. Amid concerns over currency appreciation and weak demand from the United States, growth clearly moderated in the second half. Private consumption remained strong, however, and on the supply side, services continued to grow robustly, bolstered by retail trading as well as financial and insurance activities. Expenditure on machinery and equipment also picked up. Gross domestic investment, however, remains low at some 20% of GDP, behind other major economies in the subregion. This is a key challenge for Malaysia, and implementation of structural reforms as envisioned in the Government's New Economic Model will be vital for its future growth.

Myanmar saw its economy slow down sharply in 2009, but with new foreign investments in oil and gas, electric power and mining, growth picked up again and reached 5.5% in 2010. It was reported that FDI, mostly from Asia, reached a record $16 billion in the first 11 months of 2010.[24] A special economic zone law was enacted in January 2011 in a bid to attract more foreign capital. Plans are also under way to promote tourism and to expand banking, telecommunications, shipping and agriculture. Nevertheless, the overall domestic economy still suffers from restrictive measures, such as licensing, which pose barriers to the agricultural and manufacturing sectors in gaining access to inputs and equipment.

After a modest 1.1% growth in 2009, the Philippines benefited from a revival of exports and manufacturing, especially in electronic goods, which account for over 60% of its export earnings. The economy exceeded expectations with a 7.3% growth in 2010, despite adverse weather conditions hitting the agricultural sector and rice production hard. Private consumption, which accounts for over 70% of GDP, received a boost from strong remittance inflows and pre-election spending as well as an accommodative monetary policy. Early progress in the new administration's efforts to improve the fiscal balance has also led to improved investor perceptions. The business process outsourcing industry also continued to grow rapidly. Gross domestic investment remains among the lowest in the subregion, however, and greater efforts are needed to improve the business environment and basic infrastructure.

Singapore, one of the most open economies in the world, was also one of the fastest growing in 2010 at 14.5% after contracting by 0.8% in 2009. A sharp revival in exports led to over 40%

growth in manufacturing in the first half of 2010 and this, in turn, had positive effects on the large services sector, including wholesale trade, transport and financial services. Industry growth markedly decelerated in the third quarter but bounced back in the fourth quarter, led by the biomedical industry. Singapore continues to rank at the top in terms of competitiveness and enjoys prudent macroeconomic management. The Government plans to focus more on productivity growth, for example by strengthening human capital development.

Thailand, which suffered a 2.2% contraction in 2009, grew robustly by 7.8% in 2010. The economy benefited from a revival in merchandise exports and decisive policy responses, including a record low policy rate and an estimated fiscal stimulus of 3% of GDP.[25] There was a minor bit of a time lag, but private consumption and investment eventually began to expand from the second quarter and remained robust despite the political instability in May. Services were hit hard, however, albeit temporarily, with hotels and restaurants posting a sharp drop. Growth decelerated in the third quarter, owing to slowing demand for exports and a drop in agricultural production due to bad weather and plant diseases. The economy picked up again in the fourth quarter owing to the continued strong performance of the major trading partners in Asia and a steady high level of future orders for key exports items.

Boosted by oil revenues, the economy of Timor-Leste has been growing steadily in recent years and expanded by 7.9% in 2010. Public spending accounts for about half of non-oil and gas GDP and plays a critical role in effectively spreading the benefit of its petroleum wealth to the wider population. The national oil fund was reported to stand at about $7 billion. Sound management of the fund will be important in achieving the national development plan, which envisions sharp reductions in the poverty rate.

Viet Nam, which came out strongly in 2009 with 5.3% growth, continued to expand at a faster pace throughout 2010 amid concerns about the economy overheating. Manufacturing benefited from the global recovery in demand for exports but also from the growing domestic consumer market. Production of garments, shoes, motorcycles, refrigerators and air conditioners all grew at a rapid pace, while the value of retail sales expanded by 24.5% for the full year. With high inflation, however, there are clear signs of overheating. Large public sector-led investments in the areas of transportation and industry and trade, while contributing much to economic growth, have also resulted in fiscal deterioration and raised questions over the quality of investments. The economy grew by 6.8% in 2010 but could benefit more if accompanied by macroeconomic stability, which would further boost business confidence.

Price stability remains vital to rising confidence

With the narrowing of output gaps, inflation picked up across the subregion, but at an overall modest and manageable rate (see figure 2.16). Inflation is not the primary challenge for South-East Asia at the moment, except in Viet Nam. There is no doubt, however, that buoyant domestic demand and rising consumer and investor confidence were possible because of price stability. Moreover, given that several countries in the subregion have recent histories of high inflation,[26] it is possible that confidence could be easily affected even by signs of its modest resurgence. As such, any risk factors should be carefully monitored and necessary actions taken in a timely manner.

Driven by a credit expansion boom, inflation in Viet Nam was at 28.3% as recently as mid-2008. After moderating to 6.9% in 2009, prices began to climb up again to reach an average 9.0% in 2010, with the December figure hitting a 22-month high at 11.9%. Inflationary pressure is also rising in Indonesia amid surging food prices and rises in transportation costs. Inflation in December 2010 reached around 7.0%, although the average for the year was 5.1%. Food commodities, in particularly rice, dominate the list of commodities contributing most to inflation. Rise in electricity tariffs have also led to some upward pressure. Inflation in Malaysia is among the lowest in the subregion, but the phasing out of price controls and subsidies could result in upward pressure in 2011.

After experiencing relative stability in 2009, food prices increased across the subregion in 2010, partly due to lower agricultural output caused by adverse weather conditions. Food accounts for a large portion of consumption in low-income households, and governments should be vigilant against a possible resurgence of food price pressure hikes. In the

Figure 2.16. Inflation in South-East Asian economies, 2008-2010

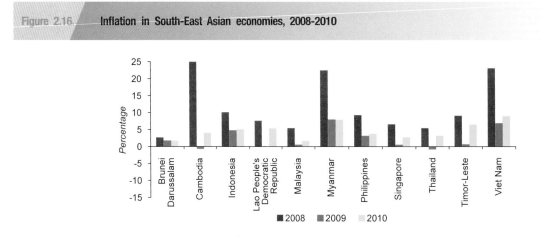

Sources: ESCAP, based on national sources; and CEIC Data Company Limited, data available from http://ceicdata.com (accessed 25 March 2011).

Note: Data for 2010 are estimates..

After experiencing relative stability in 2009, food prices increased across the subregion in 2010

Philippines, the Government was able to alleviate upward pressure on food prices by supplementing national stocks with a record 2.45 million tons of rice imports in 2010. The Indonesian Government is also beginning to scale up rice imports. Rice import duties were suspended in January 2011 in a bid to boost rice stockpiles to 2 million tons from 1.5 million tons.[27] In contrast, prices of foodstuffs rose in Myanmar when the Government closed the border-trade checkpoint with Thailand. High inflation in the Lao People's Democratic Republic was also affected by high food prices, in addition to strong money supply growth fuelled by foreign investment in the extractive sector.

In several economies, the steady appreciation of local currencies since mid-2009 has helped to contain imported inflation, including in commodities. In contrast, Viet Nam has been more vulnerable to imported inflation due to their weak currencies and wide current account deficits. Viet Nam risked further inflation by devaluing its currency twice in 2010 and again in February 2011.

Fiscal and monetary policies remain supportive of growth

Fiscal policy

The South-East Asian countries at large were able to implement bold stimulus packages through 2009 and much of 2010, thanks to healthy fiscal balance sheets. Such measures were vital in supporting domestic demand in the face of external demand shocks. A number of countries, including Malaysia and Thailand, introduced a second stimulus package following the initial one launched in early 2009. As the recovery became more entrenched, several countries started a gradual exit from policy support in 2010, although in some cases, it was postponed until 2011. In addition, such countries as Indonesia and the Philippines are aiming to front-load public expenditure in 2011, as their economies in the first half of the year are generally expected to be more sluggish than in the second half, when exports and manufacturing activities are expected to bounce back.

Even with recent fiscal expansions, fiscal positions remain relatively sound in most countries, and deficits narrowed as economic expansion led by the private sector set in (see figure 2.17). Nevertheless, efforts have been under way to rebuild the buffers for future crises and, moreover, to create fiscal space to finance growing social programmes and address infrastructure gaps. Some countries are also pushing for fiscal consolidation to further reduce public debt. To this end, most Governments included in their 2011 budget plans to strengthen the tax administration and, in some cases, to increase taxes and/or introduce new taxes.

In addition, a number of countries have plans to reorient public expenditure away from poorly targeted subsidies and tax breaks to a more direct delivery of education, health and anti-poverty programmes. The implementation of such plans will require not only strong political will, however, but also capacity-building of the civil service.

Thailand's large fiscal support programme known as "Strong Thailand (TKK)" focuses on infrastructure, agriculture, education and health. It is estimated to have added some 2.3 percentage points to economic growth in 2010 and is expected to continue to contribute to growth in 2011.[28] To finance such programmes, the Government may need to cut down on a number of tax breaks and allowances, particularly those favouring the relatively wealthy. With a view to boosting its competitiveness and balancing its budget by 2020, Malaysia is gradually reducing its subsidy bills, starting with sugar and energy, and reviewing all areas of government expenditure to prevent waste from inefficiency. In an effort to widen its tax base,[29] it further plans to gradually implement a value added tax.

Figure 2.17. Budget balance in selected South-East Asian economies, 2008-2010

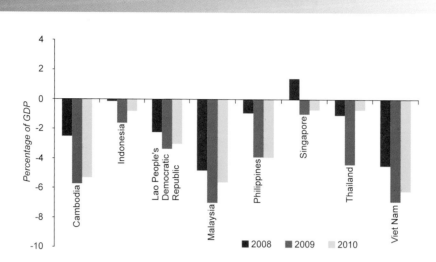

Sources: ESCAP, based on national sources; and CEIC Data Company Limited, data available from http://ceicdata.com (accessed 16 February 2011).

Note: Data for 2010 are estimates.

In the Philippines, government efforts to rein in tax evasion saw early progress in the second half of 2010. Government revenue is still low as a proportion of GDP and it may be necessary to introduce new taxes to boost revenues and continue making progress in reducing public debt, which is still above 50% of GDP. The Government also introduced plans to rationalize spending by cutting down on inefficient programmes and instead putting in place a larger conditional cash transfer programme. Indonesia has successfully reduced its public external debt to below 30% of GDP from almost 90% in the past decade. The fiscal deficit is also gradually narrowing to near balance, making it cheaper for the Government to raise funds. In 2010, it began to take steps to reduce the subsidy bill, which took up 4% of GDP, on average, from 2007 to 2009. The Government has also proposed boosting capital expenditure to finance infrastructure development and continue pro-poor social programmes.

Viet Nam has the highest fiscal deficit in the subregion and a growing public debt, which now exceeds 50% of GDP. Much of this debt can be attributed to economic growth, which is largely driven by public investment that is often channelled through inefficient State-owned enterprises in need of streamlining. These enterprises account for some 40% of GDP, and questions about their solvency led to a credit downgrade at the end of 2010. The Government aims to reduce its fiscal deficit from some 6.2% of GDP in 2010 to 4.5% by 2015. In Cambodia, the Government introduced a tax on property and doubled the road tax on vehicles. The Lao People's Democratic Republic has also been more proactive in its revenue-raising efforts, with the VAT reinstated in January 2010 and plans for taxes on land and inheritances. In addition, the new hydropower dam is expected to contribute significantly to the national budget. There are no timely fiscal data on Myanmar, but it is likely that the country is continuing to run a large fiscal deficit.

Monetary policy and financial markets

The aggressive easing of monetary policy through lowered policy interest rates and bank reserve requirements was also vital in sustaining domestic demand amid external demand shocks. As output gaps narrow, inflationary pressures have returned and the focus of monetary policy has largely been refocused on maintaining price stability even as authorities are careful not to disrupt the recovery amid uncertainties in the global economy. Simultaneously, major economies in the subregion are facing massive capital inflows resulting in a surge in equity and property prices, with most stock markets in the subregion reaching record levels in 2010.

In response to the faster- and stronger-than-expected recovery, Malaysia quickly raised its policy rate three times between March and July 2010, by a total of 75 basis points. Thailand also raised its policy rate five times between July 2010 and March 2011 by a total 125 basis points. Further tightening could take place, but with concerns in both countries that further increases in interest rates could attract even greater foreign capital inflows and that growth in the key export markets remains subdued, there will need to be a careful balancing act in this area. Meanwhile, Singapore has allowed a gradual rise in the nominal effective exchange rate to curb inflationary pressure.

Boosted by strong foreign capital inflows, South-East Asian stock exchanges were among the best performers in the Asia-Pacific region in 2010

Indonesia and the Philippines, on the other hand, kept policy interest rates unchanged through 2010 at record low levels. In Indonesia, bank reserve requirements were raised from 5% to 8% in November 2010, but the policy rate remained at 6.5% until February 2011, when a 25 basis point hike took place amid concerns over rising inflation. To encourage banks with sufficient reserves to continue lending, including to micro-, small and medium-sized enterprises, banks with loan-deposit ratios below 78% face a penalty beginning in March 2011. In the Philippines, the policy interest rate remained unchanged, but other measures to increase credit flow, such as lower bank reserve requirements, were rolled back at the beginning of 2010. In Viet Nam, despite signs of

excessive credit in the economy, the base interest rate was left unchanged through most of 2010. As inflationary pressure mounted, however, strong policy measures were introduces between November 2010 and March 2011, including significant hikes in the refinancing and discount rates.

Boosted by strong foreign capital inflows, South-East Asian stock exchanges were among the best performers in the Asia-Pacific region in 2010. Indonesia's stock market surged 46%, Thailand was up 41%, the Philippines 38% and Malaysia 19%. Singapore's Straits Times Index gained 10%. In January 2011, however, stocks dropped in major stock markets as capital outflows led to a weaker baht in Thailand and fear of rising inflation led to a sell-off in Indonesia. Meanwhile, Viet Nam did not benefit from strong capital inflows in 2010 due to such risk factors as declining foreign exchange reserves, high inflation and a weak currency. In the Lao Peoples Democratic Republic, the first stock exchange began to operate in January 2011, initially with two State-owned companies listed. Similarly, Cambodia is expected to the launch its first stock exchange in July 2011.

External sector poised for rebalancing, with strong currencies and intraregional trade

Current account balances

Most countries in South-East Asia used to have current account deficits until the Asian financial crisis resulted in a turnaround in surpluses and sharp declines in investment rates (while savings rates remained roughly the same). Due to their high reliance on exports, however, countries suffered more from the recent fluctuation in global demand, which has led to renewed interest among policy-makers in rebalancing strategies geared toward boosting domestic demand, both consumption and investment.

There is early evidence that rebalancing is taking place in South-East Asia in the post-crisis period.

Current account surpluses narrowed, on average, in 2010, owing to a faster rise in imports supported by robust domestic demand as well as recovery in exports requiring imported inputs. At the same time, gross domestic investment is also rising or is expected to rise due to brighter economic prospects, increased public infrastructure spending and capital inflows.

Malaysia and Singapore continued to post large current account surpluses of over 13% of GDP, while the Philippines and Thailand maintained surpluses at more modest levels in 2010 (see figure 2.18). Thailand saw its current account surplus cut by half from 2009, due to strong domestic demand and input demand for electronics and vehicle exports. As for the Philippines, merchandise trade was in deficit but there was a large surplus in services from overseas worker remittances. Indonesia saw its trade surplus rise in 2010, but with rapidly growing imports driven by a large and buoyant domestic market, the current account balance may turn negative within a few years.

On the other end of the spectrum, Cambodia and Viet Nam continued to post large current account

deficits in 2010, while the Lao People's Democratic Republic recorded more modest deficit. Viet Nam's trade deficit rose slightly from 2009 levels, despite the fact that the dong was devalued twice in 2010. In Myanmar, major foreign investment projects rapidly increased capital imports in 2010, so the current account was likely to be in deficit.

Broader trends affecting South-East Asian exports are sluggish demand in the developed countries, offset by rising demand from China and India. This holds true even after taking into account that a bulk of the electronic parts and components are eventually re-exported from China to the United States and Europe. In particular, under the Association of Southeast Asian Nations (ASEAN)-China free trade agreement, which came into effect in January 2010, South-East Asian countries are likely to see an increase in raw materials, food and natural resource-based exports to China. There are also concerns, however, that cheaper manufacturing goods from China will threaten the development of domestic industries in the subregion. What has received less attention is the rising trade with India, which actually ran a larger trade deficit than China with the six largest South-East Asian economies[30]

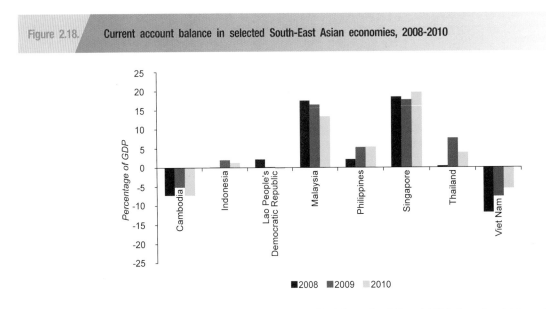

Figure 2.18. Current account balance in selected South-East Asian economies, 2008-2010

2008 2009 2010

Sources: ESCAP, based on national sources; and International Monetary Fund, International Financial Statistics online database. Available from www. imfstatistics.org/imf (accessed 16 February 2011).

Note: Data for 2010 are estimates.

in 2009.[31]   While China's total trade with South-East Asia is almost five times that of India's, given India's rapidly expanding economy, the country will increasingly become a key source of export growth for South-East Asia. Finally, intra-ASEAN trade is continuing to rise rapidly. Trade cooperation among Cambodia, the Lao Peoples Democratic Republic and Viet Nam is also increasing.

Capital flows and foreign reserves

In some countries, measures were also taken to limit exposure to short-term foreign capital, which flooded the domestic equity, bond and property markets. Indonesia introduced restrictions on foreign purchases of short-term bonds issued by the central bank in June 2010, followed by additional measures to slow the currency appreciation introduced in December 2010. Similarly, Thailand reinstated a tax on foreign investors' capital gains and interest from bonds issued by the Government, State-owned enterprises and the central bank in October 2010. It is more difficult, however, to curb the flows into equities, and regional stock exchanges are expected to see further, albeit smaller, rises in 2011, not least due to the second round of quantitative easing in the United States.

After suffering a decline in 2009, FDI is also returning to South-East Asia. In Indonesia, FDI inflows more than doubled to $12.8 billion in 2010 from $4.9 billion in 2009, while Malaysia saw a rise from $1.4 billion to $7 billion over the same period. In fact, in a sign of resilience, its share of global FDI actually increased from 2.8% in 2008 to 3.6% in 2009, even as the amount itself was down during the global economic crisis.[32]   In 2009, countries in the subregion received about $40 billion in FDI, with approximately half of it coming from OECD countries. South-East Asia is enjoying a rise in South-South investment, with intra-ASEAN direct investment becoming more prominent in recent years and China also becoming an important source of investment as observed in chapter 1.

Official development assistance (ODA) remains important for the least developed countries in the subregion, which benefit less from private capital inflows than the emerging market economies. In 2008, ODA was equivalent to about 16% of GDP in Timor-Leste and about 9% in Cambodia and the Lao People's Democratic Republic. ODA to Myanmar doubled after Cyclone Nargis in 2008 to around 2% of GDP, but it is still relatively low compared to the amount received by other least developed countries. Although Viet Nam is not a least developed country, it received ODA equivalent to approximately 4% of GDP.

Official development assistance remains important for the least developed countries in the subregion

With surpluses in both current and capital accounts, several South-East Asian economies saw their official foreign reserves rise rapidly in 2010. With a few exceptions, such as Viet Nam, most countries are at comfortable levels and are able to cover several months of imports and servicing of official external debt. In particular, Thailand saw its reserves more than double between 2008 and 2010. Indonesia, Malaysia, the Philippines, Singapore and Thailand together have some $630 billion[33] in reserves, which is comparable to the total reserves of about $710 billion in the entire euro region.

Exchange rates

Fuelled by massive capital inflows, the ASEAN-5 economies saw their currencies appreciate substantially against the dollar in 2010: the Malaysian ringgit gained 11.8%, the Thai baht 11.0%, the Singapore dollar 9.6%, the Philippine peso 5.7% and the Indonesian rupiah 4.6% (see figure 2.19). In the case of Indonesia, currency appreciation was more modest in 2010 after sharper rises in 2009. The currencies of major South-East Asian economies are expected to see further appreciation in 2011.

Currency appreciation has raised concerns about losing competitiveness, but the slowdown in export

| Figure 2.19. | Index of exchange rate movements of domestic currencies against the dollar in South-East Asian economies, 2009-2010 |

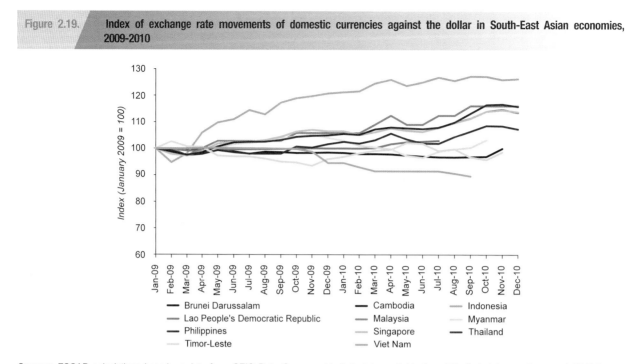

Sources: ESCAP calculations based on data from CEIC Data Company Limited, data available from http://ceicdata.com (accessed 16 February 2011); and International Monetary Fund, International Financial Statistics online database). Available from www.imfstatistics.org/imf (accessed 16 February 2011).

Note: A positive trend represents appreciation and vice versa.

growth in the third quarter of 2010 appears to be due more to weaker demand in the developed countries. Nevertheless, certain sectors and small business exporters were hit harder than others and several governments introduced support measures, such as encouraging State banks to offer dollar loans and to help companies with forward contracts. At the same time, however, currency appreciation has its positive side. In addition to taming imported inflation, stronger local currencies, if they are broadly in line with fundamentals, could provide an opportunity to develop the domestic market and replace old plants and machineries to boost productivity. This, in turn, should help to rebalance the global economy, which is desirable.

The Vietnamese dong, on the other hand, was devalued for the fourth time since November 2009 in February 2011, weakened by a cumulative 13.6% against the dollar, making it the sharpest depreciating Asian currency. The Cambodian riel appreciated slightly against the dollar in 2010, despite its large

current account deficit. Lao People's Democratic Republic, which also saw the kip gain against the dollar, tried to maintain a stable exchange rate vis-à-vis the Thai baht. These economies are also highly dollarized,[34] and a weaker dollar could mean a loss of purchasing power and higher imported inflation from neighbouring countries whose currencies have strengthened against the dollar. Meanwhile, in Myanmar, the multiple exchange rate system continues to create economic distortions and an inefficient allocation of resources.

Future outlook and policy challenges

South-East Asian countries will continue to see their economies expand at healthy rates in the coming years. Of course, there are risk factors which could upset the positive momentum. As one of the most open areas in the world, the subregion will inevitably be affected if there is a slowdown in the United States or turbulence in the European financial markets. China's possible slowdown due to monetary tightening to curb inflation could also affect the subregion's growth. On the other hand, currency appreciations may be less of a problem if they are in line with the fundamentals and supportive of rebalancing. Domestic sources of risk vary from country to country. For instance, Thailand could suffer a fall in investor and consumer confidence if political instability rises again, while in Viet Nam, high inflation and wide fiscal and trade deficits continue to be sources of instability.

In 2011, Indonesia is expected to see growth accelerate slightly to 6.5%. The more export-driven economies of Malaysia, Singapore and Thailand are likely to see growth slow more in the first half of the year than in the second. Malaysia and Singapore are forecast to see around 5.0% growth in 2011, while Thailand is expected to see 4.5% growth. The Philippines, after posting strong growth in 2010, will see growth moderate to 5.2%. Growth in Viet Nam is expected to slow slightly to 6.2%, which is still higher than the subregional average. Cambodia is expected to grow faster at 6.2% as recovery gains hold, while the Lao People's Democratic Republic will maintain high growth at 8.3%. The projection for Myanmar is 5.8%, but this could improve if substantial reforms are introduced in the wake of the general elections in November 2010. The oil-driven economies of Brunei Darussalam and Timor-Leste are expected to see growth at 1.7% and 8.2%, respectively.

If the priority during the economic crisis was to keep jobs, in the post-crisis period the focus should be on improving the quality of jobs

---

Growth dynamics are closely related to the labour market. While unemployment has fallen to pre-crisis levels in many countries, the formal sector has seen less improvement, as many of the workers who had been laid off were absorbed by the informal sector during the crisis. For instance, a 2010 labour survey in the Philippines found that the ratio of workers earning wages and salaries—as opposed to

the self-employed and unpaid family workers—had fallen from 55.3% a year earlier to 53.2%.[35] In several countries, including Malaysia, Indonesia and Viet Nam, this change was often reflected in a decline in employment in the high value added manufacturing jobs and a rise in low value added activities in services and agriculture.

The informal sector, however, suffers from lower productivity, lower wages, poorer working conditions, lower employment protection and minimum levels of social protection. The International Labour Organization (ILO) estimated that over 60% of all workers in ASEAN countries were in the informal sector in 2009. From 2007 to 2009, average annual labour productivity in the subregion contracted by 0.3%, while the ratio of the working poor (earning less than $2 per day) in the total labour force rose from 51% to 57%.[36] This implies that informal sector employment has had serious implications not only for poverty but also for the future growth potential of the subregion. Hence, if the priority during the economic crisis was to keep jobs, in the post-crisis period the focus should be on improving the quality of jobs.

To this end, human resources and skills development—including strengthened education, technical and vocational training and lifelong learning—is vital for sustained dynamism in South-East Asia. Such efforts will also help to tackle high youth unemployment in the subregion. For instance, Thailand's youth unemployment rate was 3.6 times higher than the total unemployment rate in 2009. Moreover, considering that labour is one of the few assets of the poor, creating more and better jobs will help the poor to earn their way out of poverty. In this regard, economic policies should be tailored towards expanding opportunities for poor workers to move into better jobs in the formal and non-agricultural sectors.

Endnotes

[1] Xin, 2010.

[2] Hernandez, Robles and Terero, 2010.

[3] The Consumer Assistance to Recycle and Save Act of 2009, or "Cash for Clunkers", offered consumers in the United States up to $4,500 when they traded in their older vehicles for more fuel efficient models.

[4] Crawley, 2010.

[5] Cooks, 2010.

[6] ESCAP calculations (also see United Nations, Economic and Social Commission for Asia and the Pacific, 2010b).

[7] Non-performing loans remained high, at 25.8% of total loans, as of September 2010.

[8] International Energy Agency, 2010a..

[9] Hornby, 2011.

[10] Prasad, 2010.

[11] Samoa, 2009.

[12] Earth Systems, 2010.

[13] Pacific Islands Forum Secretariat, 2010.

[14] Koo, 2006.

[15] United Nations, Economic and Social Commission for Asia and the Pacific, 2009c.

[16] New Zealand, Reserve Bank of New Zealand, n.d.

[17] Pakistan, Ministry of Finance, 2010.

[18] Sri Lanka, Central Bank of Sri Lanka, 2010.

[19] India, Reserve Bank of India, 2010.

[20] Pakistan, State Bank of Pakistan, 2010.

[21] Bangladesh, Bangladesh Bank, 2010.

[22] Kelegama, 2011.

[23] This box is based on detailed analysis contained in Goyal, 2011.

[24] Myanmar, Central Statistical Organization, n.d.

[25] After a first stimulus package worth $3.4 billion, a bigger and more medium-term targeted second package named "Strong Thailand" was introduced in October 2009.

[26] During the 2008 global food and fuel crisis, Cambodia, Myanmar and Viet Nam had inflation rates higher than 20%. Prices were also unstable in Indonesia in the years preceding the global financial crisis, with inflation exceeding 10% in 2005, 2006 and 2008.

[27] Chatterjee, 2011.

[28] Estimate of the National Economic and Social Development Board of Thailand, as quoted in Theparat, 2010.

[29] At present, the national oil company, Petronas, supplies over 40% of fiscal revenues.

[30] Indonesia, Malaysia, the Philippines, Singapore, Thailand and Viet Nam.

[31] Hui, 2010.

[32] United Nations Conference on Trade and Development, 2010b.

[33] At the end of 2010, Singapore had $207 billion, Thailand had $174 billion, Malaysia had $106.5 billion, Indonesia had $96.2 billion and the Philippines $54 billion.

[34] About 20% of all currencies in circulation in Viet Nam are foreign currencies (mostly the dollar), as are 50% in the Lao People's Democratic Republic and 90% in Cambodia, according to a recent Asian Development Bank publication (Capannelli and Menon, 2010).

[35] Philippines, Bureau of Labor and Employment Statistics, 2010.

[36] International Labour Organization, 2010c.

3

Regional Connectivity and Economic Integration

In view of the uncertain prospects for a speedy and strong recovery in the industrial countries and the need to unwind the global imbalances indicated in chapter 1, the economies of Asia and the Pacific will need to rely more on domestic and regional demand. Regional economic integration could enhance regional demand, driven by populous and rapidly growing economies, such as China and India, the dynamic domestic markets of which could also benefit their smaller and poorer neighbours. However, such a desirable outcome cannot be taken for granted. The rising tide of development opportunities will not lift all boats if these are separated by water locks. These obstructions can take the form, for example, of restrictive non-tariff measures, complicated and time-consuming customs procedures, cross-country differences in legal and regulatory regimes and poor transport infrastructure. As a result, the enormous opportunities generated by the more dynamic economic growth centres may stop at their national borders.

Connectivity to boost regional integration

Economic development involves expanding not just production and consumption but also the kind of exchange activities that are enabled by the growth of cities and by the development of long-distance transport, telecommunication and energy networks. In this chapter the term "connectivity" refers to the degree to which exchange activities are facilitated, both within and across countries.

This term has often been associated with cross-country connectivity or regional connectivity. According to the Master Plan on ASEAN Connectivity the term refers to "the physical, institutional and people-to-people linkages that comprise the foundational support and facilitative means to achieve the economic, political-security and socio-cultural pillars towards realising the vision of an integrated ASEAN Community".[1] Similarly, the Heads of Governments of the South

Asian Association for Regional Cooperation (SAARC) agreed at their 14th summit to improve intraregional connectivity – particularly physical, economic and people-to-people connectivity – as a stepping stone towards a vision of a South Asian community "where there was smooth flow of goods, services, peoples, technologies, knowledge, capital, culture and ideas".[2] Examples across the SAARC subregion include the recent initiative of Bangladesh to sell seaport services to Bhutan, India and Nepal, and the $1 billion soft loan that India granted to Bangladesh to help it upgrade its transport infrastructure.

However, it is important to keep in mind that physical transport, telecommunications and energy infrastructure connectivity take place mostly within countries, where these factors are closely related to economic development. This is illustrated in figure 3.1, which shows the relationship between the ESCAP infrastructure index, a composite measure of infrastructure development in countries of the region,

| Figure 3.1. | Infrastructure and gross domestic product per capita in Asia and the Pacific, 2007 |

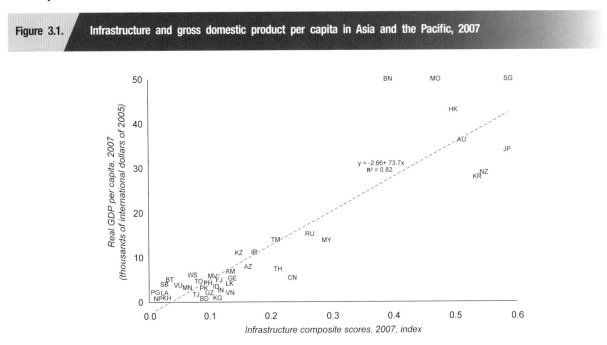

Source: ESCAP, based on data from the World Bank, World Development Indicators Database.

Note: The composite measure of infrastructure development is based on eight physical infrastructure indicators covering 40 ESCAP member countries for 2007. See ESCAP (2010b, p. 143) for details.

Abbreviations: AM=Armenia; AU=Australia; AZ=Azerbaijan; BD=Bangladesh; BT=Bhutan; BN=Brunei Darussalam; CN=China; FJ=Fiji; GE=Georgia; HK=Hong Kong, China; ID=Indonesia; IN=India; IR=Iran (Islamic Republic of); JP=Japan; KG=Kyrgyzstan; KH=Cambodia; KR=Republic of Korea; KZ=Kazakhstan; LA=Lao People's Democratic Republic; LK=Sri Lanka; MN=Mongolia; MO=Macao, China; MV=Maldives; MY=Malaysia; NP=Nepal; NZ=New Zealand; PG=Papua New Guinea; PH=Philippines; PK=Pakistan; RU=Russian Federation; SB=Solomon Islands; SG=Singapore; TH=Thailand; TJ=Tajikistan; TM=Turkmenistan; TO=Tonga; UZ=Uzbekistan; VN=Viet Nam; VU=Vanuatu; WS=Samoa.

and GDP per capita. There is also robust evidence of the importance of infrastructure for increasing productivity and reducing income inequality.[3]

The rising tide of regional development opportunities will not lift all boats if these are separated by water locks

---

Enhancing connectivity requires a two-pronged approach. On one hand, it is necessary to build strong regional institutions for planning, managing and funding major cross-country initiatives – in physical infrastructure, trade, transport and harmonization of rules and regulations. At the same time it is important to provide specific support to the region's least developed countries, landlocked developing countries and small island developing States so that they can take full advantage of better regional connectivity. This chapter considers these issues starting with assessments of connectivity in trade, investment, transport and information and communications technology. It also discusses the roles of regional and subregional institutions, as well as national policies, and their potential for promoting regional connectivity.

Intraregional trade

According to a common model known as the "gravity equation", the value of bilateral trade increases with the economic size of the trading partners, measured by their GDP, and decreases with their distance apart.[4] The model usually includes additional variables, such as the use of a common language or a common land border, although it omits other significant determinants, including sources of comparative advantage and trade policy regimes. According to this model about half of Asia-Pacific trade should be intraregional.

This is illustrated in figure 3.2 for the period 1993-2009, which compares modelled and actual data. In both cases the trend has been upwards. Between 1998 and 2008 the proportion of trade that was intraregional increased from 46.7% to 51.5%, and the modelled value from 44.7% to 53.6%. Until 2003, the actual shares exceeded the modelled values, but subsequently have been lower. This could reflect large trade surpluses. Between 1999 and 2008, the region accumulated a $3 trillion surplus with the United States and a $2 trillion surplus with the European Union, which during that period represented 20% of the region's imports. In comparison, between 1993

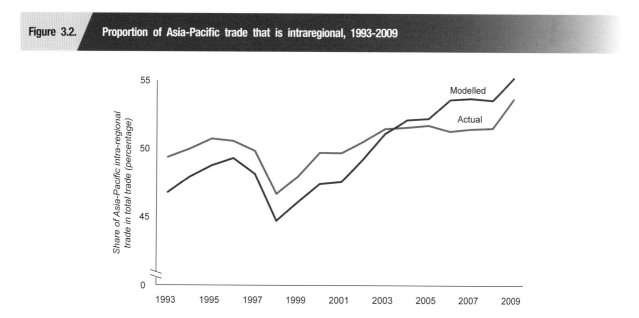

Figure 3.2.   Proportion of Asia-Pacific trade that is intraregional, 1993-2009

Source: ESCAP computations based on data from International Monetary Fund, Direction of Trade Statistics, CD-ROM, August 2010; United Nations Statistics Division, National Accounts Main Aggregates Database; CEPII, Bilateral Distances Dataset, www.cepii.fr/anglaisgraph/bdd/distances.htm.

and 1997 the region's trade surpluses represented only 6% of its imports.

The trends in both modelled and actual intraregional trade suggest that the region could become an increasingly important market for its own exports, particularly if its GDP continues growing faster than that of the rest of the world. However, it may be asked: will this be supported by the region's physical connectivity? Will Governments of countries in the region be able to dismantle non-tariff measures and harmonize and simplify regulations?

The extent to which countries trade with partners within a region as vast as that of Asia and the Pacific can also be expected to differ across subregions. The proportion of trade of each subregion conducted within Asia and the Pacific is indicated in figure 3.3, panel A. Over the period 2006-2009 it varied from 66% for both the Pacific and South-East Asia to a low of 31% for North and Central Asia, the countries of which are, on average, closer to Europe than to the rest of the Asia-Pacific region. The low figure of 38% for South and South-West Asia can also be explained by its proximity to Europe and the Middle East.

Over the period 2006-2009, the actual intraregional trade shares for North and Central Asia, South and South-West Asia, and East and North-East Asia were lower than modelled, suggesting that these subregions have room for expanding intraregional trade. In the Pacific, on the other hand, the actual share was greater than modelled, probably as a result of the long distances between countries in that subregion and those in the rest of the world, which creates an incentive for them to trade more with each other.[5]

> *The trends in both modelled and actual intraregional trade suggest that the region could become an increasingly important market for its own exports*

Between the periods 1993-1996 and 2006-2009 both modelled and actual intraregional trade shares increased significantly. The greatest modelled increase, 8 percentage points, was in East and North-East Asia, while the greatest actual increase, again 8 percentage points, was in South-East Asia,

Figure 3.3. Intraregional trade shares of the Asia-Pacific subregions, 1993-1996 and 2006-2009

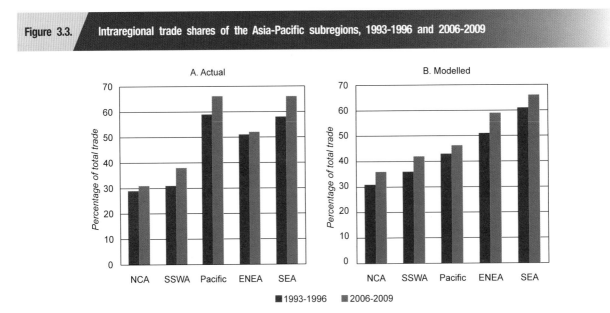

A. Actual   B. Modelled

1993-1996   2006-2009

Source: ESCAP computations based on data from International Monetary Fund, Direction of Trade Statistics, CD-ROM, August 2010; United Nations Statistics Division, National Accounts Main Aggregates Database; CEPII, Bilateral Distances Dataset, www.cepii.fr/anglaisgraph/bdd/distances.htm.

Abbreviations: ENEA=East and North-East Asia; NCA=North and Central Asia; SEA=South-East Asia; SSWA=South and South-West Asia.

followed by South and South-West Asia and the Pacific (7 percentage points each).

To offer more insights, table 3.1 decomposes intraregional trade shares of the Asia-Pacific subregions by partner subregion; the data should be read horizontally. For instance, the intraregional trade share of East and North-East Asia (51.9%) is decomposed as 32% with itself, 2.2% with North and Central Asia, 3.2% with the Pacific, 3.4% with South and South-West Asia and 11.1% with South-East Asia. The table shows that the East and North-East Asian subregion was the most important trading partner not just for itself but also for the other four subregions.

The numbers in parentheses in the table 3.1 show the modelled shares. The cells highlighted in yellow are those in which the actual trade shares exceed the modelled shares by 2 percentage points or more, indicating that trade is significantly larger than might be expected on the basis of the trading partners' GDP and their distance apart. This may be the result of preferential trade agreements, good

transport infrastructure, proper transport and trade facilitation, or complementarities that make trade particularly attractive. Conversely, cells highlighted in red are those in which the actual trade shares are less than the modelled ones by 2 percentage points or more, which could be explained by the lack of effective preferential trade agreements, insufficient transport infrastructure, high trading costs, poor trade facilitation or the lack of complementarities.

The main cases in which actual trade exceeds that indicated by the gravity model are within South-East Asia, within North and Central Asia, between East and North-East Asia and South-East Asia and between the Pacific and both East and North-East Asia and South-East Asia. Possible explanations include the trade and investment promotion institutions of ASEAN, infrastructure links in Central Asian countries that were developed in the former Union of Soviet Socialist Republics, the deployment of supply chains linking South-East Asia with North and North-East Asia and complementarities in production. Also significant are the relatively shorter distances from the Pacific to South-East Asia and

Table 3.1.   Decomposition of intraregional trade shares of the Asia-Pacific subregions, by partner subregions, 2006-2009

Subregion \ Partner subregion	East and North East-Asia	North and Central Asia	Pacific	South and South-West Asia	South-East Asia	Asia and the Pacific
East and North East-Asia	32.0 (38.8)	2.2 (3.1)	3.2 (3.3)	3.4 (6.7)	11.1 (7.7)	51.9 (59.5)
North and Central Asia	14.9 (18.2)	8.3 (4.6)	0.2 (1.4)	6.5 (8.6)	1.4 (2.6)	31.3 (35.5)
Pacific	37.6 (22.6)	0.3 (1.7)	8.8 (7.5)	3.6 (5.5)	15.5 (9.2)	65.8 (46.6)
South and South-West Asia	17.4 (20.1)	4.9 (4.3)	1.5 (9.8)	8.1 (9.8)	6.3 (5.2)	38.4 (41.7)
South-East Asia	32.7 (30.5)	0.6 (1.8)	3.8 (5.3)	3.7 (7.0)	25.0 (21.2)	65.9 (65.7)
Asia and the Pacific	29.3 (31.3)	2.6 (3.1)	3.1 (3.5)	4.3 (7.4)	12.6 (8.7)	51.9 (54.0)

Source: ESCAP computations based on data from International Monetary Fund, Direction of Trade Statistics, CD-ROM, August 2010; United Nations Statistics Division, National Accounts Main Aggregates Database; CEPII, Bilateral Distances Dataset, www.cepii.fr/anglaisgraph/bdd/distances.htm.

Notes: Modelled shares are shown in parentheses within each cell. Cells where the actual intraregional trade share exceeds the modelled share by 2 percentage points or more are highlighted in yellow. Cells where the actual share is less than the modelled share by two percentage points or more are highlighted in red. See Isgut (2011) for details on the computation of modelled shares.

North and North-East Asia –7,700 and 7,300 km respectively – compared with 11,400 km to North America and 15,400 km to Western Europe.

The table highlights in red cases in which actual trade is less than the gravity model suggests. These include trade between East and North-East Asia and West and South-West Asia, trade within East and North-East Asia, and trade between North and Central Asia and East and North-East Asia – all of which suggest unexploited opportunities.

The region could benefit from a broader approach to regional integration which focuses not just on deepening integration within subregions but also on fostering trade links across subregions

---

Although the gravity model provides useful insights about potential trade, it overlooks the product composition of exports and imports, which could play a role in determining the volumes of bilateral trade. To complement this analysis, box 3.1

shows calculations of the complementarity index between and within Asia-Pacific subregions. This index measures the degree to which the export pattern of one subregion matches the import pattern of another. A high value of the index for a pair of subregions indicates that there is high potential for them to trade with each other. The results suggest that the region could benefit from a broader approach to regional integration, which focuses not just on deepening integration within subregions but also on fostering trade links across subregions.

Trade costs

The volume of trade could be adversely affected by various costs, including import tariffs, export taxes, costs related to fulfilling regulatory import and export requirements, and domestic and international shipping and logistics costs. In particular, the costs associated with completing documents and other import and export procedures for international trade can account for up to 15% of the value of traded goods.[6] The analysis of this section is based on a broad measure of trade costs, drawn from the ESCAP Trade Cost Database.[7]

Box 3.1. Complementarities in products

Since many Asia-Pacific countries export the same products as others in the region they may have less potential for trade with each other. The World Bank (2000) and Chen and Liao (2005) argue that the export structures of East Asian countries were becoming increasingly similar towards the mid-1990s and early 2000s, although a more recent study by Shirotori and Molina (2009) shows evidence of increasing trade complementarities among Asian developing countries.

To assess the degree of complementarities across Asia-Pacific subregions, values of the complementarity index between their exports and imports for 2007 are shown below. The index is calculated as follows:

$$CI_{ij} = \left[1 - \frac{\sum_p \left| s_{ip}^X - s_{jp}^M \right|}{2} \right] * 100,$$

where s_{ip}^X is the share of product p in subregion i's exports and s_{jp}^M is the share of product p in subregion j's imports. In the hypothetical case where both shares coincide for all products, the summation is 0 and the value of the index is 100. If, instead, there is no overlapping between one subregion's exports and the other subregion's imports, the summation is 2 and the value of the index is 0. It should be noted that in general $CI_{ij} \neq CI_{ji}$ (except when $i = j$), so one subregion's exports

Box 3.1 *(continued)*

can be complementary with another subregion's imports even if the second subregion's exports are not complementary with the first subregion's imports. This could happen, for example, if the first subregion exports a wide array of products but the second subregion is very specialized in a few export products. In this calculation, the products are defined at the five-digit level of the Standard International Trade Classification (rev. 2) and the unit of analysis is the subregion.

Table. Complementarity index for trade between and within Asia-Pacific subregions, 2007

Complementarity index between exports of Subregion 1...	... and imports of subregion 2					Average of the complementarity index between exports of subregion 1 and imports of other subregions
	ENEA	NCA	Pacific	SEA	SSWA	
ENEA	64	49	55	55	44	51
NCA	33	24	23	34	42	33
Pacific	39	31	34	32	41	36
SEA	60	41	46	51	44	48
SSWA	40	36	39	37	37	38

Source: ESCAP based on data from the United Nations Commodity Trade Statistics Database (COMTRADE) for 2007.

Note: The exports (imports) of a subregion are the sum of exports (imports) of all its countries.

Abbreviations: ENEA=East and North-East Asia; NCA=North and Central Asia; SEA=South-East Asia; SSWA=South and South-West Asia.

The results of this calculation, shown in the table above, suggest that there is an important degree of complementarity between the Asia-Pacific subregions. The pair of subregions with the most complementarities are East and North-East Asia (ENEA) and South-East Asia (SEA), with $CI_{ENEA,SEA}$ = 60 and $CI_{SEA,ENEA}$ = 55. The table also shows the complementarity index for trade within subregions (shaded). Interestingly, it shows that the highest degree of complementarity is within the East and North-East Asia subregion, the economies of which, as seen above, are trading less than expected (see table 3.1 above) and are characterized by high trade costs (see table 3.2 below). It is also noteworthy that, with the exception of East and North-East Asia, the value of the complementarity index is lower for trade within a subregion than for trade between that and other subregions. For instance, the exports of North and Central Asia are more complementary with the imports of South-East Asia and South and South-West Asia than with imports from the North and Central Asia subregion itself. Similarly, exports from South and South-West Asia are more complementary with imports from East and North-East Asia and the Pacific. The case of East and North-East Asia suggests that there are important gains from trade to be realized from further regional integration within this subregion. The case of the rest of the Asia-Pacific subregions suggests the desirability of pursuing a broader approach to regional integration, which focuses not just on deepening integration within subregions but also in fostering trade links across subregions.

Finally, it should be emphasized that the index is based on historical data for 2007, and that the pattern of comparative advantage changes over time, as countries develop and diversify their exports. For instance, a similar calculation for 1995 reveals that South and South-West Asia increased substantially its complementarities with other Asia-Pacific subregions, from an average of 31 in 1995 to 38 in 2007. Such an increase in the index was particularly sharp for exports from South and South-West Asia to South-East Asia (from 23 in 1995 to 37 in 2007), but was also important for exports from South and South-West Asia to East and North-East Asia (from 34 in 1995 to 40 in 2007). It is expected that these trends will continue in the future and not just for South and South-West Asia. If progress in regional integration and connectivity accelerate in the years to come, countries in the region will be able to greatly benefit from trade opportunities.

Source: ESCAP.

For illustration, figure 3.4 shows the costs for trading with Japan for a range of Asia-Pacific countries, along with those of two other trading partners: Germany and the United States. Expressed as an ad valorem tariff equivalent, the median value is 158%, ranging from 45% for Malaysia to a high of 328% for Kyrgyzstan. Distance is one factor: trading costs with Japan are lower for neighbouring countries, such as China and the Republic of Korea, as well as for Australia, Indonesia, Malaysia, Thailand and Viet Nam. However, distance is not the main factor. For instance, the distance from Bhutan to Japan is roughly the same as that to Thailand – about 4,500 km– but the cost of trade is almost five times higher. In general, trade costs are significantly higher for landlocked countries, such as Afghanistan, Armenia, Bhutan, Georgia and Kyrgyzstan, as well as for Pacific island developing economies, such as Fiji, Samoa, Tonga and Vanuatu.

Other costs include documents, administrative fees for customs clearance and technical control, customs broker fees, terminal handling charges and inland transport. These are reflected in the World Bank's Doing Business database. For instance, in 2010 the average cost of importing a 20-foot container for China, Malaysia, the Republic of Korea, Thailand and Viet Nam was $645, compared with $2,630 for Afghanistan, Armenia, Bhutan, Georgia and Kyrgyzstan. Similarly, the average number of days to import was 15.8 for the first group of countries and 43.6 for the second.

Across Asia and the Pacific there are also significant differences in trade costs within and between subregions. As indicated in table 3.2, the trade efficiency of ASEAN is comparable to that of the North American Free Trade Agreement (NAFTA) and the European Union. But trade costs are more

| Figure 3.4. | Comprehensive international trade costs between selected Asia-Pacific countries and Japan |

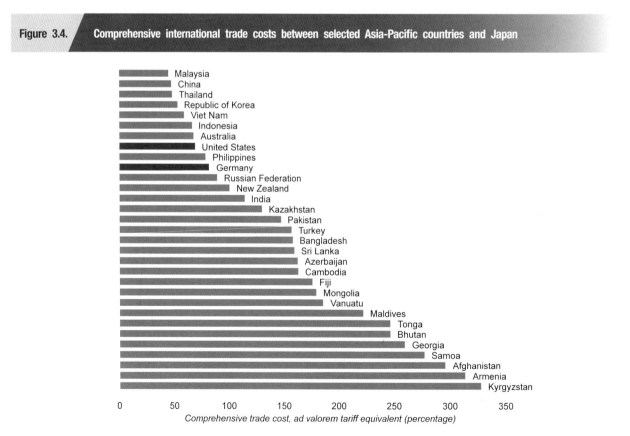

Source: ESCAP Trade Cost Database.

Note: The data are for the latest available year, 2008 in most cases. Germany and the United States are included for reference.

Table 3.2.   Ad valorem intra- and extra-subregional trade costs, 2007

Percentage

Partner / Reporter	ASEAN4	SAARC4	East and North East-Asia	North and Central Asia	AUS-NZL	EU5	NAFTA
ASEAN4	53						
SAARC4	139	138					
East and North East-Asia	141	227	113				
North and Central Asia	280	282	204	149			
AUS-NZL	90	168	155	329	61		
EU5	113	139	135	166	129	59	
NAFTA	109	162	122	259	130	107	50

Source: ESCAP Trade Cost Database, www.unescap.org/tid/artnet/tcdb.asp.

Notes: ASEAN4 comprises Indonesia, Malaysia, the Philippines and Thailand; SAARC4 comprises Bangladesh, India, Pakistan and Sri Lanka; and EU5 comprises France, Germany, Italy, Spain and the United Kingdom of Great Britain and Northern Ireland; ASEAN = Association of Southeast Asian Nations; AUS-NZL = Australia and New Zealand; EU = European Union; NAFTA = North American Free Trade Agreement; SAARC = South Asian Association for Regional Cooperation.

than twice as high for SAARC, East and North-East Asia, and North and Central Asia. In general, trade costs are lower within subregions because of geographic proximity as well as similarities in language and culture.

For SAARC, however, intra-subregional trade costs remain high: they are only 1% lower than those between SAARC and ASEAN or those between SAARC and the European Union. Trade is similarly expensive within North and Central Asian countries – only 10% less than between this subregion and the European Union. And trade costs within East and North-East Asia are only 9% lower than those between this subregion and NAFTA. It should also be noted that the costs of trade between Asian subregions are also high. For example, trade costs between ASEAN and SAARC are nearly 30% higher than those between ASEAN and NAFTA. Similarly, trade costs between North and Central Asia and SAARC are 70% higher than those between North and Central Asia and the European Union.

On a more positive note, the time spent in moving goods from factory to ship at the nearest seaport – or vice versa – fell on average by about 16% in ESCAP developing economies between 2005 and 2010, although the experience varied greatly from country to country.[8] The greatest progress was in South-East Asia, which cut its average time to only 19 days; Cambodia and Thailand cut their trade time by over 40%. India and Pakistan achieved similar improvements, although in South and South-West Asia trade procedures still take 50% more time to complete than in South-East Asia. The North and Central Asian subregion, with its many landlocked countries, made small improvements, but procedures employed in moving goods to a seaport from most countries remain extremely lengthy (52 days on average). And no significant progress was made in the Pacific. Overall it still takes three times longer to complete trade procedures in ESCAP developing economies than in ESCAP developed economies.

However, in most ESCAP economies the inflation-adjusted cost of trade procedures has marginally increased. This may be attributed partially to the increased cost of labour or to the greater demand for logistics and transport services as trade volumes increase. Between 2005 and 2010 the biggest increases in the average cost of moving goods from factory to seaport by container were for South and South-West Asia (17%), and North and Central Asia (9%).

Trade costs are also affected by restrictions on the movement of vehicles and trains across borders.

For example, many countries allow only international transport by road within 30 to 100 km of their borders, or along limited routes, and designate only a few loading and unloading points. In addition, there are restrictions on the number of transport permits issued per year and on the length of their validity. In 2008 and 2009, the International Road Transport Union monitored road freight from the borders that China shares with Central Asian countries to Western and Central Europe and estimated that 40% of the overall travel time was being spent at national borders. These delays, together with the relatively high level of official and non-official payments at borders, act as deterrents to land-based road transport.

Finally, it is clear from available statistics and consultations that logistics account for a substantial component of production costs. In Indonesia, for example, logistics comprise 14% of total production costs compared with 5% in Japan.[9] In China in 2004, logistics costs accounted for 21.3% of the total GDP, while in Thailand, the logistics costs in 2007 were equivalent to 18.9% of GDP.[10] Better logistics can provide a substantial boost to competitiveness and trade. For example, it has been estimated that, in Cambodia and the Lao People's Democratic Republic, a 20% reduction in logistics costs could increase the trade-to-GDP ratio by more than 10%.[11]

Intraregional foreign direct investment

Another important cross-border economic activity is foreign direct investment. In the past, most foreign direct investment (FDI) inflows to Asia-Pacific countries came from developed countries, but nowadays increasingly larger proportions come from developing countries. According to the United Nations Conference on Trade and Development (UNCTAD), between 1985-1989 and 2005-2009 those flows increased from an annual average of $9.5 billion to $234.7 billion – or from 5% to 15% of the global FDI outflows.[12]

This trend is roughly consistent with the "investment development path theory", which states that, as countries develop, some of their firms acquire ownership advantages that enable them to compete successfully outside their home markets – either to access a larger market or to relocate some production to countries where costs are lower.[13]

However, FDI now seems to be increasing more rapidly than predicted by theory. This is partly due to intense competition in home markets and more liberal investment policies and privatization, along with the need for fast-growing economies, such as China and India, to secure key resources. Many developing countries also believe that by investing overseas domestic firms can catch up with established players and offset their latecomer status.[14]

Companies from Asia-Pacific developing countries can contribute investment and technology to enhance the productive capabilities of lower-income countries in the region

Over the last two decades, ESCAP developing economies have been the source of two significant waves of outward foreign direct investment (OFDI) (see figure 3.5). The first was between 1993 and 1997 (up to the start of the Asian financial crisis), when these countries accounted for 12.8% of global OFDI flows. Of this amount, almost 80% came from the "newly industrialized economies": Hong Kong, China; the Republic of Korea; Singapore; and Taiwan Province of China. The second wave started in 2004: from 2004 to 2008, ESCAP developing economies accounted for an average of 10.5% of the global flows. During this second period, however, only 50% came from Asian newly industrialized economies. In fact, between 1993-1997 and 2004-2008, China and India increased their joint share from 5% to 20% and the Russian Federation increased its share from 1% to 18%.

Companies from Asian and Pacific developing countries can have a significant impact in the

Figure 3.5.	Share of ESCAP developed and developing economies in global outward foreign direct investment flows, 1992-2009

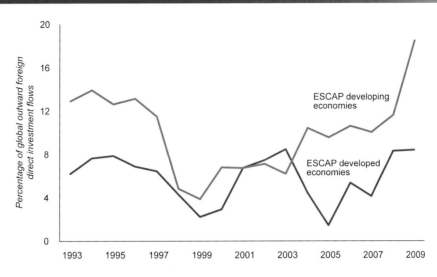

Source: ESCAP based on data from UNCTAD (2010b).

Note: ESCAP developed economies consist of Australia, Japan and New Zealand.

region's lower-income countries. They tend to invest in neighbouring countries that have similar economic conditions and institutions. These firms have an advantage over companies from developed countries because their technologies are more appropriate to the factor endowments and market sizes of the recipient developing countries. The smaller technological gap puts these firms in a good position to transfer and diffuse knowledge and competencies.[15] Such firms can contribute much-needed investment and technological expertise to enhance the productive capabilities of lower-income countries.

Many low-income countries in Asia and the Pacific now get most of their FDI from other developing countries in the region. In Nepal, for instance, India (in manufacturing and services) and China (in manufacturing) account for more than half of FDI; in Sri Lanka, many of the foreign manufacturing firms are Indian; in Mongolia, most of the FDI comes from China and the Russian Federation.[16] An important contribution to such flows has been the development of regional production networks. As a result, China and Malaysia, for example, have been investing in emerging countries such as Viet Nam. Industries that have benefited from intraregional FDI

flows are electronics, steel and automotives. Banking has also been expanding: for example, a Chinese commercial bank, the Industrial and Commercial Bank of China, has recently acquired financial institutions in Indonesia and Thailand.

OFDI not only benefits the destination countries but also boosts the competitiveness and performance of firms and industries in the source country. To encourage this type of investment, Asian countries have therefore been liberalizing regulations on capital account outflows and, in some cases, providing financing for domestic firms seeking to invest abroad.[17] In China, for example, the Government has declared its intention to develop national champions that can compete on the global stage.[18] Similarly, the Government of India has gradually liberalized its OFDI policies, initially raising the threshold for the automatic approval of proposals and then in 2004 removing the limit and allowing Indian enterprises to invest abroad up to 100% of their net worth.[19]

Regarding investment facilitation, a number of bilateral and subregional free trade agreements (FTAs) have provisions for investment liberalization, besides numerous bilateral treaties that are generally confined to investment promotion and protection, and to frameworks for the settlement of disputes. In addition a network of bilateral double tax avoidance treaties has been signed by a number of countries in the region to facilitate investments. In the Asia-Pacific region, ASEAN has the most developed provisions on intraregional investment promotion and facilitation.

Preferential trading arrangements

As discussed above, the last decade has witnessed a steady increase in intraregional trade flows, a trend that is expected to deepen in the future as a result of the higher rate of economic growth of Asia-Pacific countries compared with the rest of the world. However, important differences in the cost of trade across countries and subregions remain. In this context, the significantly lower costs of trade among ASEAN countries compared with other subregions in Asia and the Pacific suggest that preferential trading arrangements may play a role in stimulating trade. Therefore, expanding such arrangements region-wide could result in reduced trade costs and increasing volumes of trade across the region. Lowering trade costs is particularly important to enable smaller countries to extend their markets and reap efficiency gains by exploiting economies of scale and specialization. Such process of efficiency-seeking industrial restructuring also facilitates the creation of supply capabilities in relatively poorer countries and their convergence to higher levels of development.[20] This section provides an overview of the region's preferential trading arrangements and suggests possible ways to creating a unified regional market to foster efficiency-seeking industrial restructuring.

Countries in Asia and the Pacific have been late starters in exploiting the potential of preferential trade agreements, as they tended to rely more on the multilateral trading system. Before the turn of the century, preferential trading arrangements in the region were limited to a few between countries in Central Asia, others in the Pacific subregion, the Bangkok Agreement (later known as the Asia-Pacific Trade Agreement, or APTA), a framework agreement

on the ASEAN FTA, and bilateral agreements between India and Nepal and between the Lao People's Democratic Republic and Thailand. At the turn of the century, bilateral FTAs and regional trade agreements (RTAs) were given due recognition in the trade policy of the Asia-Pacific region because of two factors. One was the growing importance of RTAs in the Western world, which started with the formation of the Single European Market in 1992 and the North American Free Trade Agreement (NAFTA) in 1994. That trend was followed by the implementation of similar arrangements in the rest of the world, such as the Southern Common Market (Mercosur) in South America and the Common Market for Eastern and Southern Africa (COMESA), leading to more than half of global trade being conducted on a preferential rather than most favoured nation basis. The second factor was the recognition of the importance of regional economic interdependence in the aftermath of the 1997/98 Asian financial crisis, which led to the formation of the ASEAN+3 (China, Japan and the Republic of Korea) grouping. Such recognition also contributed to strengthening the ASEAN dialogue partnership process, which has brought together the leaders of the 10 ASEAN countries with those of Australia, China, India, Japan, New Zealand and the Republic of Korea for annual summits on the sidelines of the ASEAN summits, and to the creation of a new annual forum, the East Asia Summit.[21] These interactions have led to the negotiation and implementation of multiple FTAs between ASEAN countries, both individually and as a grouping, and their dialogue partners, creating a veritable Asia-Pacific RTA "noodle bowl".

One decade later, at the end of 2010, there were 170 preferential agreements involving at least one ESCAP member State, 115 of which were in force, 16 were pending country ratification and 39 were under negotiation. Of these 170 agreements, 125 were bilateral FTAs and 95 were signed between an Asia-Pacific country and a country outside the region. Subregional trade agreements include the ASEAN Free Trade Area (AFTA), the Bay of Bengal Initiative for Multi-Sectoral Technical and Economic Cooperation (BIMSTEC) FTA, the Economic

Cooperation Organization Trade Agreement (ECOTA) and the South Asia Free Trade Area (SAFTA).

Most RTAs with members from the Asia-Pacific region only are aimed at eliminating tariffs and other trade barriers. Trade agreements include rules of origin to avoid trade deflection to unintended partners. For some, especially the most recent ones, their scope extends beyond trade in goods to cover trade in services, investments and economic cooperation, in order to exploit the full potential of regionalism. While liberalization of trade in goods is generally on a negative list basis, that is, covering all products except those on a small exclusion list, trade in services and investment are liberalized generally on a progressive or positive list basis. However, some FTAs, such as the Japan-Singapore Economic Agreement for a New Age Partnership, include investment liberalization on a negative list basis as well, and a few have provisions for the movement of natural persons, such as the Japan-Philippines Economic Partnership Agreement, which allows the movement of medical caregivers to Japan, subject to a limit.

Because of their bilateral and subregional nature, trading arrangements in Asia and the Pacific are not contributing to the creation of a seamless, larger market in the region

The process of ASEAN economic integration is the most advanced in the region. It covers a progressive deepening, with AFTA being complemented by a number of agreements, including the ASEAN Framework Agreement on Trade in Services (AFAS), the ASEAN Industrial Cooperation scheme and the ASEAN Investment Area, with the goal to form an ASEAN economic community, comprising a single market, by 2015. Following the ASEAN lead, SAARC also adopted the SAARC Agreement on Trade in Services (SATIS) in 2010 to complement its SAFTA and it is working on an investment agreement.

Agreements such as AFTA, SAFTA, BIMSTEC, Pacific Island Countries Trade Agreement and APTA provide room for special and differential treatment for least developed countries, offering them longer periods for tariff elimination, along with special measures regarding rules of origin.

The Asia-Pacific network of FTAs and RTAs, summarized in figure 3.6, presents a picture of a dense web of trade arrangements criss-crossing the region mostly within the subregions but also linking subregions. For instance, ECOTA links some Central Asian countries with some South and West-Asian countries and BIMSTEC links South Asian countries with some South-East Asian countries. The figure shows that North and Central Asia and the Pacific island developing economies are mostly unconnected with the rest of the region. It also shows that some countries, such as Australia, China, India, Japan, Malaysia, New Zealand, the Republic of Korea, Singapore and Thailand, are important hubs, with bilateral agreements linking them with other countries in their subregion and in three other subregions. ASEAN is the only subregional grouping that has trade agreements with countries in other subregions. The emerging ASEAN+3 (EAFTA) and ASEAN+6 (CEPEA) agreements, while not yet formally under negotiation, are included for reference.

While these agreements provide incentives to increase trade among their members, their bilateral and subregional nature does not contribute to the creation of a seamless, larger market in the region. One of the key components of a scheme of economic integration is to create a larger integrated market through trade liberalization and trade facilitation that would enable businesses in the region to be restructured on the most efficient basis and to exploit economies of scale, scope and specialization. This process of efficiency-seeking industrial restructuring could offer substantial welfare gains for participating countries. The benefits of extended markets could be particularly significant for smaller economies. Indeed, the diversity in the levels of development across the region makes regional economic integration particularly fruitful as

Figure 3.6. The Asia-Pacific network of preferential trading arrangements

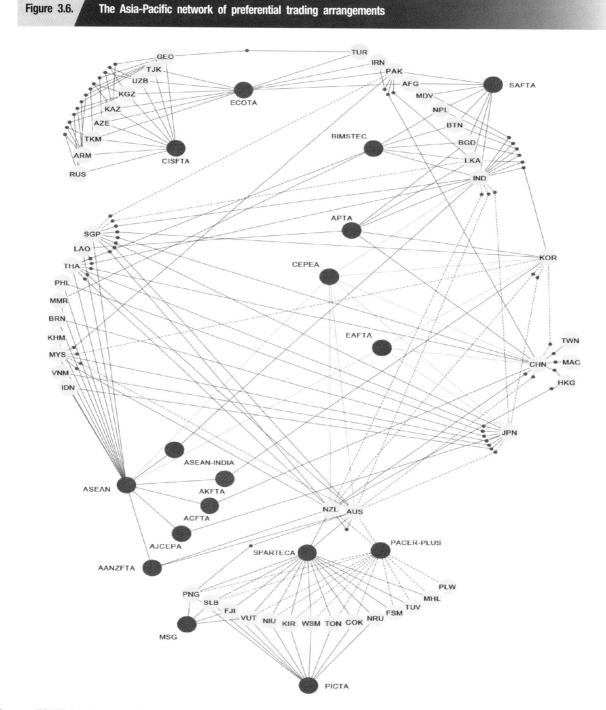

Sources: ESCAP, based on data from the Asia-Pacific Trade and Investment Agreements Database, available from www.unescap.org/tid/aptiad/agg_db.aspx.

Notes: This figure represents 78 trade agreements among 51 ESCAP Asia-Pacific countries. Only agreements in which all the members are Asia-Pacific countries are included. Yellow circles represent countries, small red circles represent bilateral agreements and large red circles represent subregional agreements. Dashed lines represent agreements under negotiation and dotted lines represent emerging agreements (EAFTA and CEPEA). The figure was created using the program Cytoscape, which is available from www.cytoscape.org.

Abbreviations: AFG=Afghanistan; ARM=Armenia; AUS=Australia; AZE=Azerbaijan; BGD=Bangladesh; BTN=Bhutan; BRN=Brunei Darussalam; KHM=Cambodia; CHN=China; COK=Cook Islands; FJI=Fiji; GEO=Georgia; HKG=Hong Kong, China; IND=India; IDN=Indonesia; IRN=Iran (Islamic Republic of); JPN=Japan; KAZ=Kazakhstan; KIR=Kiribati; KGZ=Kyrgyzstan; LAO=Lao People's Democratic Republic; MAC=Macao, China; MYS=Malaysia; MDV=Maldives; MHL=Marshall Islands; FSM=Micronesia (Federated States of); MMR=Myanmar; NRU=Nauru; NPL=Nepal; NZL=New Zealand; NIU=Niue; PAK=Pakistan; PLW=Palau; PNG=Papua New Guinea; PHL=Philippines; KOR=Republic of Korea; RUS=Russian Federation; WSM=Samoa; SGP=Singapore; SLB=Solomon Islands; LKA=Sri Lanka; TWN=Taiwan Province of China; TJK=Tajikistan; THA=Thailand; TON=Tonga; TUR=Turkey; TKM=Turkmenistan; TUV=Tuvalu; UZB=Uzbekistan; VUT=Vanuatu; VNM=Viet Nam.

the synergies between factor endowments, production structures and specializations provide for mutually beneficial exchanges as highlighted by the analysis of complementarities reported above. The region is becoming aware of the potential for broader regional economic integration as a number of leaders, including those from Australia, India, Japan and the Philippines, have articulated visions of broader pan-Asian economic communities.

CEPEA, which represents about 80% of the region's population and GDP, could constitute the nucleus for an incipient Asia-Pacific-wide free trade area to which other countries in the region could accede in the future

---

In the context of broader regional economic integration, two initiatives resulting from the ASEAN dialogue partnership could serve as stepping stones to a broader, unified Asia-Pacific market and economic community: an East Asia free trade agreement (EAFTA) proposed within the framework of the ASEAN+3 Summit, and the comprehensive economic partnership of East Asia (CEPEA) proposed within the framework of the East Asia Summit combining ASEAN+6 countries. Feasibility studies on these two proposals were conducted in parallel by track-II study groups and their reports were presented to the respective leaders at the Fifteenth East Asia Summit held in Cha-Am/Hua Hin, Thailand, in October 2009. Four ASEAN-plus working groups were appointed by the leaders of the respective countries to work further in parallel on the recommendations of the EAFTA and CEPEA studies. Independent simulation studies using computable general equilibrium models show that the EAFTA and CEPEA proposals would offer significant welfare gains for their member countries. Higher welfare gains were reported for CEPEA compared with alternative options probably because of synergies brought by additional members, such as Australia, India and New Zealand, and indeed a much larger market.[22]

In particular, CEPEA, which represents about 80% of the region's population and GDP, could constitute the nucleus for an incipient Asia-Pacific-wide free trade area to which other countries in the region could accede in the future.

A complementary option could be to set up a regional framework to enable members of subregional groupings to exchange market access on a reciprocal basis. A good example of such a framework could be the European Economic Area (EEA) through which three of the four members of the European Free Trade Association, namely Iceland, Liechtenstein and Norway, entered a free trade agreement with the European Union. Given the large number of subregional groupings that exist in the Asia-Pacific region, a regional framework to facilitate the signing of agreements, such as the European Economic Area, among them could be useful. A broad regional organization with convening power in Asia and the Pacific, such as ESCAP, could provide a platform and a forum to assist in evolving such a framework.

Finally, in view of the wide developmental gaps in the Asia-Pacific region, an important objective of a broader economic integration in the region should be to bring about convergence in the levels of economic development of all countries through the optimum deployment of the region's resources. However, there is some evidence suggesting that increased trade by itself, even if balanced, does not always ensure economic development. Complementary policies on investment in infrastructure and public goods such as education and research and development, as well as regional and sectoral programmes, are also needed.

Transport links

Merchandise trade depends on effective transport links. Today, Asia is home to the world's top five container ports: Singapore; Shanghai, China; Hong Kong, China; Shenzhen, China; and Busan, Republic of Korea. Together they account for 23% of global container throughput. Over the past three decades

China in particular has dramatically increased its port throughput: between 1983 and 2005 such throughput rose from 1 million to 43.6 million 20-foot equivalent units.

The most important liner routes from Asia are still to Europe and North America. However, there has been a substantial increase in intra-Asian container shipping, particularly between China, Japan and the Republic of Korea, and between these countries and those in South-East Asia. China now tops the UNCTAD liner shipping connectivity index, followed by Hong Kong, China; and Singapore. Other Asian economies, namely India, Japan, Malaysia, the Republic of Korea, Sri Lanka, Taiwan Province of China and Thailand, were among the top-25 economies (see figure 3.7).

Many Governments of countries in the region have established special economic zones or export processing zones near their maritime ports. Such facilities, combined with the liberalization of some manufacturing sectors, the reduction of shipping costs, dedicated industrial infrastructure and

improvements in communication technologies and Internet connectivity, have opened up a broader range of potential manufacturing locations. Transnational corporations can now break down production into discrete functions and carry them out in the most cost-effective locations, taking advantage of access to resources and capabilities, thus enabling them to gain competitive advantage to better penetrate important growth markets.

These factors have helped to disperse productive capacities across the region, but have also increased the significance of transport and logistics costs. As a result, much of the new growth has been concentrated in coastal areas, leaving large hinterland areas relatively underdeveloped.

The region's land transport networks have strengthened since the 1990s, although, as elsewhere in the world, this phenomenon has been more rapid for road than for rail networks. In most countries road networks have increased faster than the population. Between 1993-1997 and 2003-2007 road networks increased fastest for China, at an annual average

Figure 3.7. Liner shipping connectivity index, 2004 and 2010

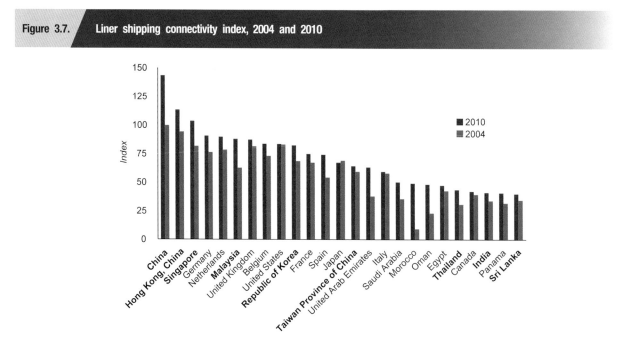

Source: UNCTAD, unctadstat.unctad.org/TableViewer/tableView.aspx?ReportId=92.

Notes: The index has five components: (a) number of ships; (b) the container carrying capacity of those ships in 20-foot equivalent units; (c) the number of companies; (d) the number of services; and (e) the maximum ship size, always referring to the ships that are deployed to provide liner shipping services to a country's port(s).

growth rate of 9.3%, followed by Viet Nam (7.2%) and the Russian Federation (5.9%) (see figure 3.8). The increase in rail networks was slower: in China, it was at an annual rate of 1.2%, followed by the Republic of Korea (0.8%) and Viet Nam (0.5%). The faster expansion of roads probably reflects the significantly higher costs of extending rail networks; it might also reflect the rising demand among the middle classes for using automobiles.[23]

In recent years, regional transport has benefited from intergovernmental frameworks (see figures 3.9 and 3.10). The Intergovernmental Agreement on the Asian Highway Network,[24] for example, which entered into force in 2005 under the ESCAP auspices, sets out the route alignment for roads of international importance and defines technical standards. While the infrastructure along the Asian Highway is of varying quality it has been improving: between 2004 and 2008, the proportion of the roads under class III (2 lanes, paved) fell from 16% to 8%.[25]

Similarly, ESCAP facilitated the Intergovernmental Agreement on the Trans-Asian Railway Network, which entered into force in 2009, aims at constructing missing links and dealing with the problem of differences in track gauges between countries. The latter are being overcome by improvements in logistical capacity and equipment.

Despite these efforts, it is still often expensive to move goods to the hinterlands and across countries. This reflects not just the distances involved but also high operating costs for trucks due to poor roads and ageing vehicles, high transshipment costs and delays at border crossings due to complex procedures. At a particular disadvantage are the landlocked countries in Central Asia, for which reaching external markets involves multiple border crossings. The Pacific island developing economies face other challenges. Not only are they far from major ports, but with small populations and low productive capacities they do not warrant regular liner services, so they face high transport costs and low profits.[26]

Some countries are overcoming the problems posed by geography and economic size by developing air transport. Indeed, the International Air Transport Association reported that, despite the global economic downturn, airlines in Asia and the Pacific outperformed the industry average. The Association

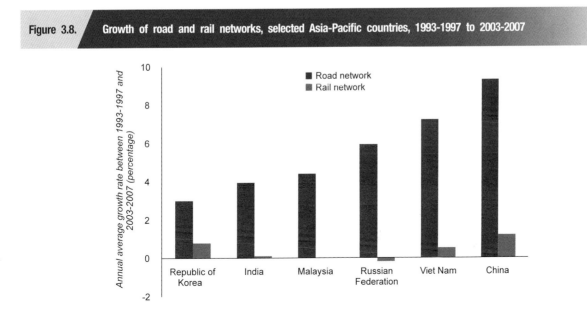

Figure 3.8.   Growth of road and rail networks, selected Asia-Pacific countries, 1993-1997 to 2003-2007

Source: ESCAP, based on World Bank, World Development Indicators.

Note: The figure shows the annual average growth rates in the number of kilometres of roads and railroads between the periods 1993-1997 and 2003-2007.

Figure 3.9. **Asian highway network**

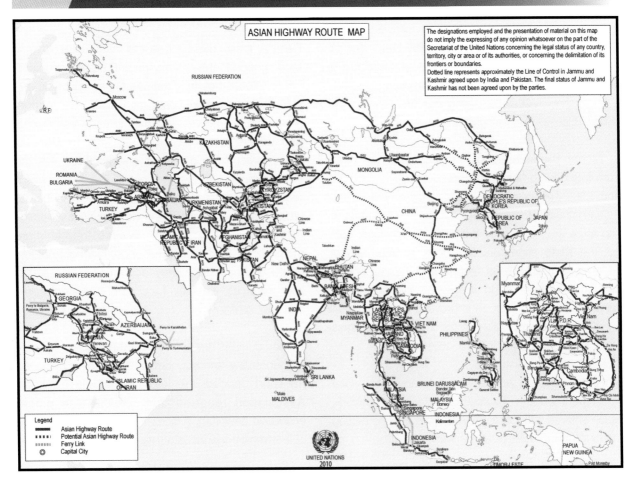

Source: ESCAP.

of Asia Pacific Airlines estimated that in October 2010 year-on-year traffic was up by 8.2% for passengers and by 16.6% for freight. Much of this growth is attributed to strong demand on intraregional routes. However, the high cost of air transport limits its use to low-weight, low-volume, high-value products, such as organic foods for European markets.

Between 1993-1997 and 2003-2007, most Asia-Pacific countries saw a significant increase in both the number of air passengers and the volume of air freight. For those included in figure 3.11, the median annual rate of growth was about 4%; compared to 2.5% for the world. The annual rate of growth in the number of air passengers was highest in China (11.1%), Viet Nam (9.2%), India (7.9%) and

the Islamic Republic of Iran (5.4%). The volume of air freight increased spectacularly in China (16.4% per annum), followed by Viet Nam (8.8%), Malaysia (8.6%) and the Russian Federation (5.6%).

Developing an integrated international transport network

The Intergovernmental Agreement on the Asian Highway Network and the Intergovernmental Agreement on the Trans-Asian Railway Network have contributed to infrastructure investment and also triggered several multilateral initiatives. For instance, the Asian Development Bank (ADB) recently initiated a project on the development of priority Asian Highway routes and Trans-Asian Railway

Figure 3.10.   **Trans-Asian railway network**

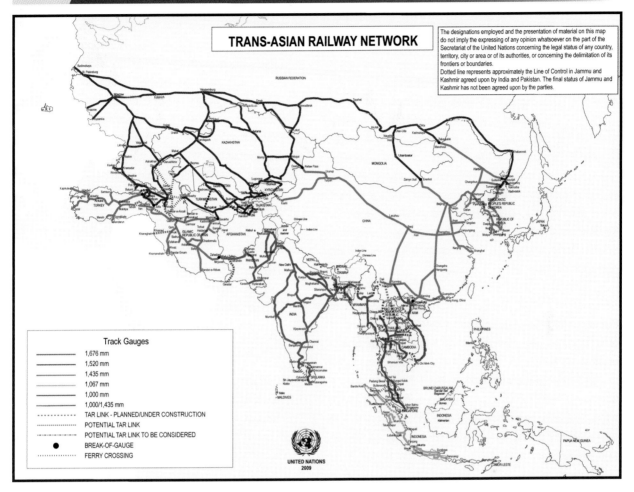

Source: ESCAP.

lines in collaboration with ESCAP. The networks are forming the basis of infrastructure cooperation through other subregional organizations, such as ASEAN, Economic Cooperation Organization (ECO) and SAARC. In addition, the Trans-Asian Railway network is increasingly being used for cross-border movements of container block trains.

The main challenge for transport connectivity now is to improve linkages between modes, for example, between ports, roads and railways. It will also be important to extend routes to hinterland areas and through landlocked countries and transit countries, as well as to small island developing States in the Pacific. To assist in the integration of the networks, ESCAP is developing a third intergovernmental agreement focusing on international dry ports along the Asian Highway and Trans-Asian Railway networks (see box 3.2).

Another approach is the development of transport corridors. The Central Asia Regional Cooperation programme of ADB, for example, has identified a number of priority corridors and is planning to combine infrastructure investments with activities to streamline cross-border procedures. Corridor-based approaches also lend themselves to railway services. For example, in 2009 there was a trial run of a container block train on the 6,500-km rail route from Islamabad to Istanbul, Turkey, via Tehran. These demonstration runs have shown a clear time advantage.

Transport and trade facilitation

While building physical transport infrastructure is important to facilitate trade across borders, a geographical simulation study found that border costs constitute a much more serious obstacle.[27] Reducing these trade costs is a great challenge because transport and trade facilitation measures are wide-ranging in complexity and resource requirements, and to be effective they depend on the level of infrastructure and the quality of the business regulatory environment. However, many countries in the region have fully realized the importance of streamlining procedures and are now engaged in the implementation of advanced facilitation measures, often taking advantage of modern information and communications technologies.

Streamlining trade documents. The preparation of documents takes about four times the amount of time needed for customs clearance and technical control at borders.[28] Most countries now rely more on electronic data interchange; the long-term goal is to set up national electronic single windows through which traders can submit all the information online and also pay duties and receive relevant authorization and clearance. Hong Kong, China; the Republic of Korea; and Singapore are world leaders in the use of single windows. However, their full benefits cannot be realized until the electronic data and documents in a national single window can be accepted by authorities in partner economies. Although international standards have been developed to address technical issues related to cross-border data exchange, there has been little progress in developing an international legal framework. Even the pioneering ASEAN Single Window Initiative, which is aimed at creating a regional single window by 2012, has struggled to establish the necessary legal basis for electronic exchange.

> *The full benefits of single windows cannot be realized until the electronic data and documents in a national single window can be accepted by authorities in partner economies.*

To build capacity for single windows and paperless trade, ESCAP and the Economic Commission for Europe in 2009 established a community of knowledge and practice: the United Nations Network of Experts on Paperless Trade for Asia and the

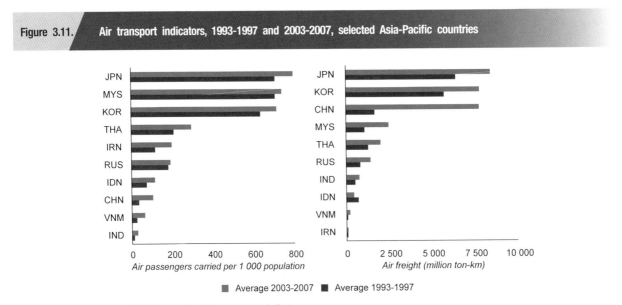

Figure 3.11. Air transport indicators, 1993-1997 and 2003-2007, selected Asia-Pacific countries

■ Average 2003-2007 ■ Average 1993-1997

Source: ESCAP based on World Bank, World Development Indicators.

Abbreviations: CHN=China; IND=India; IDN=Indonesia; IRN=Iran (Islamic Republic of); JPN=Japan; KOR=Republic of Korea; MYS=Malaysia; RUS=Russia; THA=Thailand; VNM=Viet Nam.

Box 3.2. Developing dry ports

In the past, inland freight facilities were designed to handle simple functions, such as temporary container storage. However, now they are offering a wider range of services to support the transport and logistics needs of companies engaged in international trade. A dry port, for example, provides services for containers, as well as bulk cargoes entering by any mode of transport. According to ESCAP, dry ports should also, whenever possible, offer full customs and related services, such as inspections of cargos for export and import.

Dry ports enable goods to be transferred efficiently between transport modes. They can also serve as magnets for investment in manufacturing, agricultural processing and associated transport services, thereby stimulating local development and increasing employment. The ESCAP region has a number of successful dry ports, such as the Uiwang Inland Container Depot near Seoul and those of the Container Corporation of India which has 59 inland container depots, of which 49 are export-import depots.

Dry ports can add value to the logistics chain by offering single-window facilities to the various agencies involved in containerized cargo, such as customs, railways, road hauliers, freight forwarders and shipping lines.

A comprehensive regional strategy to develop dry ports at key locations would ensure more evenly spread economic growth and may also encourage modal shifts from road to rail and to inland waterways. In this regard, ESCAP will continue to collaborate with member States in 2011 and 2012 to define and finalize an intergovernmental agreement on dry ports along the routes of the Asian Highway and the Trans-Asian Railway networks.

Source: ESCAP.

Pacific (UNNExT). Some of the UNNExT tools, such as the Business Process Analysis Guide to Simplify Trade Procedures, have already been applied in almost a dozen countries.

Most regional trade agreements now include provisions for trade facilitation. For example, the latest ASEAN Trade in Goods Agreement, which came into force in 2010, includes an entire chapter on trade facilitation, while the third round of negotiations on APTA also resulted in a trade facilitation framework agreement in 2009 among China, India and other members of APTA. There have also been less formal approaches, such as the voluntary but systematic preparation by Asia-Pacific Economic Cooperation (APEC) members of an individual trade facilitation action plan and annual reporting of progress. This provides a potentially useful model for strengthening regional cooperation among all ESCAP members, by providing an inventory of trade facilitation measures and highlighting examples of effective practice.

Facilitating border crossing. In the area of transport facilitation, the harmonization of legal regimes related to international transport is a prerequisite to ensuring the smooth movement of goods through national borders and optimizing the overall efficiency of international transport. According to the Almaty Programme of Action, Addressing the Special Needs of Landlocked Developing Countries within a New Global Framework for Transit Transport Cooperation for Landlocked and Transit Developing Countries,[29] international conventions in the area of international transport and transit, as well as regional and bilateral agreements, should be considered by landlocked developing countries as the main vehicles by which harmonization, simplification and standardization could be achieved. However, progress in implementing Commission resolution 48/11 of 23 April 1992, which recommended that countries in the ESCAP region accede to seven international conventions, has been uneven. The 12 landlocked countries in the region have acceded, on average, to only 4 of the 7 conventions, and only 2 countries, Kyrgyzstan and Uzbekistan, have acceded to all of them. Furthermore, some transit countries neighbouring the region's landlocked countries have acceded to even fewer conventions, leading to a territorial discontinuity in their application, which significantly affects their effectiveness. The barriers hindering accession to the international conventions include costs of adjustment to meet their requirements, difficulties in implementation and inadequate national capacities.

Barriers of access to international transport and transit conventions include costs of adjustment to meet their requirements, difficulties in implementation and inadequate national capacities.

In recent years, subregional organizations have been actively promoting subregional agreements on cross-border or transit transport. ASEAN, for example, has adopted the Framework Agreement on the Facilitation of Goods in Transit and the Framework Agreement on the Facilitation of Inter-State Transport, while a subset of ASEAN member States plus China has also adopted the Agreement on Facilitation of Cross-border Transport of Goods and People in the Greater Mekong Subregion. ECO member States have also adopted a wide-reaching transit transport framework agreement. In recent years ESCAP has been providing technical support for the formulation of an agreement among members of the Shanghai Cooperation Organization on Facilitation of International Road Transport. The effectiveness of these agreements will partly depend on the harmonization of arrangements for cross-border and transit transport across subregions.

Improving logistics and freight forwarding. Efficient movement of goods also depends on the performance of the logistics and freight forwarding industry. Some countries monitor the industry quite closely, requiring bonds and compulsory training and certification. However, many countries have yet to establish liability regimes for loss of, or damage to, goods while in the custody of service providers. Such liability regimes are based on a combination of the United Nations Convention on International Multimodal Transport of Goods of 1980, which has

not yet entered into force, and the UNCTAD/ICC (International Chamber of Commerce) Rules for Multimodal Transport Documents.

Many ESCAP member countries have recognized the importance of logistics services and reflected this in their national development plans. For example, China has included measures to promote the rapid development of logistics in its eleventh five-year plan. In support of ASEAN Vision 2020 strategies for economic integration, the economic ministers of the Association resolved that logistics should be the ASEAN Economic Community's twelfth priority sector for integration. Further efforts should be directed towards improving all aspects of logistics systems, including transport and communications infrastructure and equipment; international, regional and national rules, policies and institutions; and the professionalism of all actors.

Improving cooperation and coordination. Trade facilitation could benefit from better inter-agency cooperation and consultation with the private sector, more use of information and communications technologies and generally a more integrated approach to trade, transport and connectivity. While these issues are national they also affect connectivity with neighbours and the rest of the region. At the national level, Governments need to strengthen institutional mechanisms to remove bottlenecks, based on high-level political support and the involvement of multiple agencies and the private sector. One option is to designate single national lead agencies for transport and trade facilitation. Governments can declare their determination eventually to establish full fledged single windows and make a start on a detailed analysis of the processes to be streamlined.

At the regional level, such measures can be accompanied by a harmonized framework for electronic exchange of trade data and documents. This could involve, for example, creating an Asia-Pacific coordination mechanism that brings together representatives of key regional and subregional organizations, such as ADB, APEC, ASEAN, ESCAP and SAARC. It could also involve bilateral and global donors and be linked with the annual Asia-Pacific Trade Facilitation Forum organized by ESCAP in collaboration with ADB and many other organizations.

All these activities need to take place in an integrated manner. An electronic single window, for example, will not be successful if the basic ICT infrastructure is not already in place. Similarly, there will be little progress in corridor approaches without accompanying legal and regulatory changes at the national level. In addition, boosting trade will require improvement in the business environment which includes, for example, ready access to credit information and the capacity to enforce contracts.

Information and communications technology connectivity

Information and communications technologies (ICT) have revolutionized the way in which people and businesses communicate and exchange information. ICT connectivity infrastructure can be categorized as wired, wireless and satellite. Fibre-optic wired connectivity occurs via submarine or terrestrial cables. For submarine cables, the Asia-Pacific region relies almost exclusively on those installed by various consortia; however, for terrestrial cables,

countries have been building up their own networks to expand backhaul services.

For the poor, who are gaining access to telecommunication services for the first time, mobile technology is a tool for economic empowerment

The most astounding development in the region's ICT connectivity, however, has been the rapid diffusion of mobile telephone networks and services (see figure 3.12). For the poorest countries almost all telephone lines are now mobile, as in Afghanistan (99%), Bangladesh (97%), Bhutan (92%) and Cambodia (99%). Just as important, access to mobile telephones has become more equal. Between 2000 and 2009, the Gini coefficient of the distribution of mobile telephone subscriptions across countries decreased from 0.75 to 0.55.

For the poor, who are gaining access to tele-communication services for the first time, mobile technology is a tool for economic empowerment.[30] For instance, after the introduction of mobile telephones in Kerala, India, in 1997, fishermen started telephoning

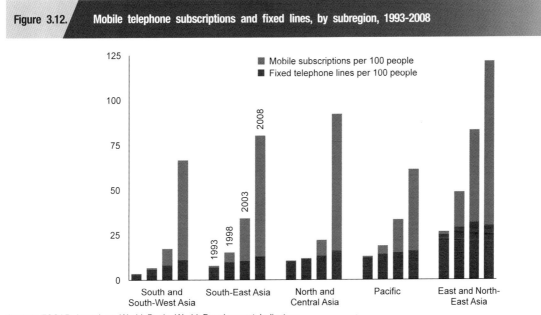

Figure 3.12. Mobile telephone subscriptions and fixed lines, by subregion, 1993-2008

Source: ESCAP, based on World Bank, World Development Indicators.

Note: Figures are simple averages for the countries in each subregion.

while still on their boats to choose the best beach market for selling their catch. This has benefited both fishermen and consumers, evening out the price of fish along the coast and reducing waste.[31]

Nevertheless there is still significant inequality in ICT connectivity. The least developed countries and the Pacific island developing economies have on average fewer than 28 mobile telephone subscriptions per 100 persons, compared with an average of 99 in high-income countries. Internet usage remains low: 1 per 100 people in least developed countries, 6 in

Pacific island developing economies and only 19 in the middle-income countries, compared with 78 in high-income countries. In addition, despite several countries having announced national plans for setting up broadband services, broadband penetration rates remain well below 10% of the population in developing countries of the region. Moreover, the data on international Internet bandwidth, which measures the contracted capacity of international connections between countries for transmitting Internet traffic, reveals that great inequalities exist across countries in the Asia-Pacific region (see figure 3.13).

Figure 3.13. International Internet bandwidth per capita in Asia and the Pacific, 2007, selected countries

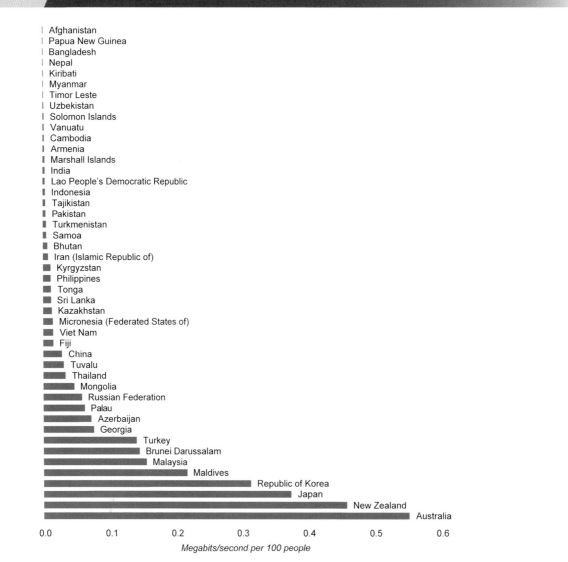

Megabits/second per 100 people

Source: ESCAP, based on data from the International Telecommunication Union, World Telecommunication/ICT Indicators Database, 2010.

Deficiencies in broadband Internet services are hampering efforts to increase cost efficiency and productivity, particularly among small and medium-sized enterprises, which typically operate in highly competitive environments. Inadequate services reduce the opportunities for synergies among telecommunications, electricity, water and transportation grids, which could enable, for example, the design of "smart buildings" that use ICT innovations to control energy consumption. They also reduce the possibility of communities to access images, video and audio through the Internet, which could reach even illiterate people and children.

An important obstacle is the cost of deploying land-based fibre-optic cables. This is especially difficult in countries such as Mongolia, with widely dispersed populations, or in countries such as the Lao People's Democratic Republic and Nepal, with their difficult terrain, or in remote island countries in the Pacific. Such countries can instead use satellites, although connections are slow and more expensive. With limited purchasing power, small economies have less bargaining strength in dealing with international service providers, although they can improve their positions through coordination and group negotiations.[32] Other areas of possible cooperation include sharing ground facilities for satellite antennae, as well as for servers and information systems.

Across the region, there have been a number of initiatives on land-based, fibre-optic cabling. Progress continues, for example, in completing and upgrading the national sections of the Greater Mekong Subregion Information Superhighway Network. Similarly, the South Asia Subregional Economic Cooperation Information Highway Project is aimed at enhancing connectivity between Bangladesh, Bhutan, India and Nepal. The Trans-Eurasia Information Network provides high-capacity connectivity between research institutions in Australia, China, India, Indonesia, Japan, the Lao People's Democratic Republic, Malaysia, Nepal, Pakistan, the Philippines, the Republic of Korea, Singapore, Sri Lanka, Taiwan Province of China, Thailand and Viet Nam and is expanding into Bangladesh, Bhutan and Cambodia. The Central

Asia Research and Education Network, which has been operating since 2010, connects Kyrgyzstan, Tajikistan and Turkmenistan and is expected to be extended into Kazakhstan and Uzbekistan.

Deficiencies in broadband Internet services are hampering efforts to increase cost efficiency and productivity

There has also been some progress in the Pacific, where some least developed countries have become connected by building linkages to existing cables. For example, Samoa and American Samoa are now connected through the American Samoa-Hawaii submarine cable, and Marshall Islands and the Federated States of Micronesia are connected via Guam through the HANTRU-1 submarine cable. Other Pacific island developing economies connected via submarine cables are French Polynesia through the Honotua cable to Hawaii, New Caledonia through Australia using the Gondwana-1 cable, and Fiji through the Southern Cross Cable Network (see figure 3.14). Fostering regional cooperation on submarine cabling and other infrastructure arrangements is one of the priorities of the Framework for Action on ICT for Development in the Pacific of the Secretariat of the Pacific Community.[33]

The private sector has been playing an increasingly more important role in ICT connectivity. At the end of 2009, of the world's top 30 telecommunications service providers by revenue, 9 were from Asia and the Pacific.[34] Although some of these companies are government-controlled, they are all listed in stock exchanges and have large numbers of private shareholders. As a result, increasing shareholders' returns is an important priority for them. Private companies are also playing an important role in ICT infrastructure investment. For example, since 2009 there has been a terrestrial link between China and India established by Reliance Communications and China Telecom. In 2011 one of the Tata companies in India and China Telecom will roll out

Figure 3.14. Submarine telecommunications cables in the Pacific

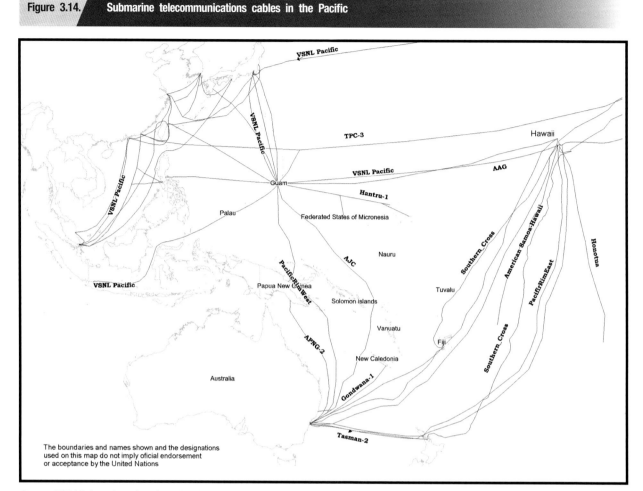

Source: ESCAP, based on data from the *Final Report for the Pacific Islands Forum Secretariat: Review of Pacific Regional Digital Strategy, 2010,* Annex C: Submarine cable connectivity. Available from: www.forumsec.org.fj/resources/uploads/attachments/documents/Review%20of%20Digital%20 Strategy_PartA.pdf.

a 500-km fibre-optic terrestrial cable linking the two countries. As well as linking the region's largest and fastest-growing economies these cables will provide additional high-speed connectivity between Europe and Asia, thus helping to increase network redundancy and security.

Boosting ICT connectivity

In order to boost ICT connectivity, policies at both the national and regional levels are needed. At the national level, policymakers need to adapt quickly to a rapidly changing technological environment, working with the private sector to promote economic growth while protecting consumers. Thus, they will need to foster fair and competitive markets, through transparent licensing practices, while establishing standards to ensure interoperability between service providers. They will also want to encourage innovative applications such as mobile banking.

For these purposes it is important to establish independent regulators. Acting in the best interests of both the State and end-users, independent regulators can also encourage investment and innovation by service providers, as well as stimulating competition between them. Between 1990 and 2009 the number of independent regulators around the world increased from 12 to 153.[35]

While promoting investments in ICT infrastructure, Governments need to take into account not just private returns but also social returns by, for example, connecting schools, health facilities and rural government offices to the Internet, establishing disaster early-warning systems and enhancing access to public information. Policymakers should also consider potential synergies with other types of infrastructure investments. For example, rights of ways established for roads and railways can also accommodate telecommunications cabling or base stations. This is particularly important at the regional level, where rights of way established under the Intergovernmental Agreement on the Asian Highway Network and the Intergovernmental Agreement on the Trans-Asian Railway Network could accommodate investment in ICT infrastructure. In fact, the linkages between ICT, energy and transport have been considered at the Joint Ministers Meeting for Energy, ICT and Transport that took place in Noumea in April 2011 under the auspices of the Secretariat of the Pacific Community.

Policymakers should consider potential synergies between ICT and other types of infrastructure such as rights of ways established for roads and railways

---

Another major concern is affordability and access. For this purpose Governments can, for example, consider taxing service providers to create universal obligation funds to develop infrastructure in underserved areas. Policymakers also need to consider the appropriate level of import tariffs on ICT equipment and services to ensure that the required materials are available at competitive prices.

Taking full advantage of ICT does not depend, however, only on the availability of physical infrastructure. Countries also need people with adequate skills – from government officials, to private entrepreneurs, to school teachers. At the same time they need to protect the integrity of their infrastructure, with appropriate policies for both cybersecurity and physical security to ensure that ICT gains are not reversed by natural or man-made disasters.

For these purposes, small and low-income countries should also be able to rely on partnerships with development agencies and donor countries. They can also work together on the basis of regional or subregional cooperation to share resources, maximize the use of existing investments and improve their bargaining power with commercial service providers. A number of country groupings, such as ASEAN, SAARC and ECO, have working groups and committees for improving subregional connectivity through harmonization of their policies and regulations and through the exchange of good practices.[36] For example, the Master Plan on ASEAN Connectivity, developed with the assistance of ESCAP and ADB, emphasizes the need to narrow the digital divide between lagging regions and urban areas, as well as between countries.[37] Similarly, the Pacific Islands Telecommunications Association and the Secretariat of the Pacific Community are trying to assist member countries in improving ICT services. In June 2010, the Pacific Regional Information and Communication Technology Ministers' Meeting adopted the Tonga Declaration, ICT for Development, Governance and Sustainable Livelihoods, recognizing the potential of ICT for socio-economic development; the ministers also endorsed the Framework for Action on ICT for Development in the Pacific. ICT connectivity could enable these countries to overcome the disadvantages of distance by expanding their trade in services (see box 3.3).

Energy connectivity

Between 1992 and 2008, demand for primary energy from ESCAP economies rose from 36.7% to 45.2% of the global total. China, India, Japan and the Russian Federation were among the top five consumers, accounting for 71% of Asia-Pacific consumption and 32% of the world's consumption. Only a few countries satisfy their needs from their own resources; the region as a whole is a net importer of primary energy. Nevertheless, by global standards the region's net imports are relatively small: 83 million tons of oil equivalent (Mtoe) in 2008 compared with 477 Mtoe for North America and 1,020 Mtoe for Europe. However, this average hides

Box 3.3. Information and communications technology overcomes the disadvantages of distance

ICT has created many new opportunities for cross-border trade in services. The ability to transmit documents and data instantly has enabled companies to shift some operations from Europe, Japan and the United States to lower-cost locations. There they can offer services such as software design and development, customer helpdesks, hosting data centres, accounting, administration, graphic design and other business processes. By 2009, India was the global leader for business processing offshore with 35% of the trade, followed by Canada, 21%; the Philippines, 15%; Ireland, 4%; China, 3%; and Central and Eastern Europe, 6%. Smaller and more remote countries however have also joined in. In Nepal, for example, entrepreneurs have established a state-of-the-art facility to produce animation and visual effects for the global movie industry.

Another country starting to make inroads into this market is Fiji where English is the language of education. In 2009, part of the Emirates Group, Dnata Mindpearl, established a call centre with capacity for 1,000 operators to serve the airline industry. According to the company, the country selected had to have three key characteristics: (a) a first-world telecommunications infrastructure; (b) people with the ability to speak English that would be easily understood by customers in Canada, the United Kingdom of Great Britain and Northern Ireland and the United States of America; and (c) readily available staff. Fiji was found to have all three characteristics.[38]

Some countries in the Pacific have also generated ICT-related revenues by creatively using their Internet domain codes. Tuvalu, with a population of 10,000, sells the use of the country code ".tv"; Time Warner Inc., for example, has registered the domain name TNT.tv. Other countries and territories in that subregion have used their code to gain global recognition, as well as revenue. For example, the territory of Tokelau competes globally with large countries, such as China and the Russian Federation, in the number of websites registered under its code ".tk".[39] At no cost, users can register a convenient website name, such as "escap.tk", to redirect traffic to an existing web page that has a much longer address.

Smaller countries also use the Internet effectively to promote tourism. Samoa, for example, with a population of 180,000, displays six hotels in expedia.com, with room charges ranging from $100 to $300 and can thus compete in the global tourism marketplace.

Source: ESCAP.

---

large net surpluses and deficits across subregions. As shown in figure 3.15 for the period 1992-2008 the main energy trading subregions were North and Central Asia, whose surplus increased from 382 to 767 Mtoe, and East and North-East Asia, whose deficit increased from 550 to 947 Mtoe. The Pacific and South-East Asia have relatively small surpluses that have changed little over time. Net exports of South and South-West Asia deteriorated from a small surplus of 48 Mtoe to a deficit of 134 Mtoe.

The region's largest exporter of primary energy is the Russian Federation (see figure 3.16). In 2008, its net exports of 589 Mtoe represented 77% of the total for North and Central Asia. Other important net exporters from that subregion are Kazakhstan (84 Mtoe), Turkmenistan (50 Mtoe) and Azerbaijan (46 Mtoe). Other significant net exporters from the Asian and Pacific region are Australia (155 Mtoe), Indonesia (154 Mtoe) and the Islamic Republic of Iran (130 Mtoe).

In contrast, in East and North-East Asia all the major economies are net importers: Japan (462 Mtoe), the Republic of Korea (208 Mtoe), China (148 Mtoe) and Taiwan Province of China (102 Mtoe). South-East Asia has net exporters, such as Brunei Darussalam, Indonesia, Malaysia and Myanmar, as well as net importers, such as the Philippines, Singapore, Thailand and Viet Nam. Except for the Islamic Republic of Iran, most countries in South and South-West Asia are net importers, among which the most significant are India (157 Mtoe) and Turkey (77 Mtoe).

Oil. In 2008 the region imported 1,132 million tons of crude oil, or 42% of the world's imports. That year, the combined oil imports of China, India and Japan alone amounted to 612 million tons, an amount comparable to the imports of the United States or the European Union. The largest source is the Middle East, which provides more than 60% of the total. While most of the oil trade is by maritime transport, there are two important oil pipelines. The Sino-Kazhak pipeline, opened in May 2006, transports oil from Kazakhstan and the Russian Federation to China, and the Russia-China oil pipeline, which opened in January of 2011, is part of the Eastern Siberia–Pacific Ocean oil pipeline that is designed to pump up to 1.6 million barrels of crude oil per day from Siberia in the Russian Federation to China. The construction of another important oil pipeline, as well as a gas pipeline, connecting Myanmar with Yunnan Province of China started in mid-2010.

Gas pipelines. In 2008, Asia and the Pacific exported by pipeline 183 billion cubic metres (bcm) of gas, representing 31% of the world's total. The Russian Federation, the main exporter from the region, exported 154 bcm to European countries and Turkey. Other Asia-Pacific exporters of natural gas are the Islamic Republic of Iran (to Turkey and Armenia), Turkmenistan (to the Islamic Republic of Iran), Myanmar (to Thailand) and Indonesia and Malaysia (to Singapore). The region's natural gas imports by pipeline accounted for less than 10% of the global total in 2008 and were sourced only from within the region. However, a number of pipeline construction projects, some of which are already operational, are expected to increase this figure considerably. Among them is a new 1,000-mile pipeline which in 2009 started pumping liquefied natural gas from Turkmenistan to north-western China. During its first year of operation, this pipeline pumped 4 bcm, a figure that is expected to triple in the future, furnishing 50% of the gas imported by China.

| Figure 3.15. | Production minus consumption of total primary energy, by subregion, 1992-2008 |

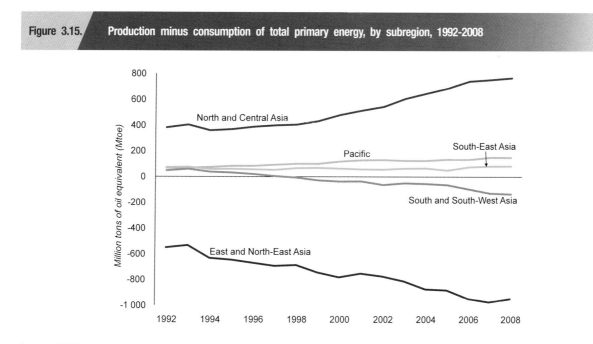

Source: ESCAP, based on data from International Energy Statistics, United States Energy Information Administration.

Notes: Total primary energy comprises crude oil, natural gas and coal, plus net generation of nuclear, hydroelectric and non-hydroelectric renewable electricity. The original data, expressed in quadrillion British thermal units (BTUs), were converted into million metric tons of oil equivalent (Mtoe) using the conversion factor 1 quadrillion BTUs = 24.9 Mtoe.

In 2008 the combined oil imports of China, India and Japan alone amounted to 612 million tons, as much as the imports of the United States or the European Union

Recent initiatives include gas pipelines linking the Russian Federation with China; Myanmar with Bangladesh and India; the Islamic Republic of Iran with Pakistan; and Turkmenistan with Afghanistan, India and Pakistan. Construction for the Russia-China pipeline, which will go through the Altai area in southern Siberia, will start in 2011; it is expected to supply China with 30 bcm annually. In 2009, Bangladesh agreed to allow the passage through its territory of the Myanmar-Bangladesh-India tri-nation pipeline that would enable regional gas trade, but construction has yet to start. The Iran-Pakistan-India gas pipeline project was launched in the 1990s, but after long years of negotiations, from which India virtually withdrew after the terror

attacks in Mumbai in 2008, the Islamic Republic of Iran and Pakistan agreed in March 2010 to build a 7.5 bcm pipeline by 2015. Finally, the 1,640-km Turkmenistan-Afghanistan-Pakistan-India pipeline, which will cost $7.6 billion, could inaugurate a new era of cooperation and solidarity in the region; it has been labelled by the Prime Minister of India as the "peace pipeline".

Liquefied natural gas. Gas is also traded by ship as liquefied natural gas (LNG). The Asia-Pacific region is a net importer of LNG. In 2008 it exported 86 bcm, but it imported 161 bcm, which accounted for more than 70% of total LNG trade worldwide. More than half of this amount went to Japan. Other significant LNG importers from the region are China, India, the Republic of Korea, Taiwan Province of China and Turkey. More than half the region's LNG imports come from Australia, Brunei Darussalam, Indonesia and Malaysia. These countries export LNG only within the region, and in 2008 their exports represented 38% of total LNG trade.

Figure 3.16. Production minus consumption of total primary energy, by economy, 2008

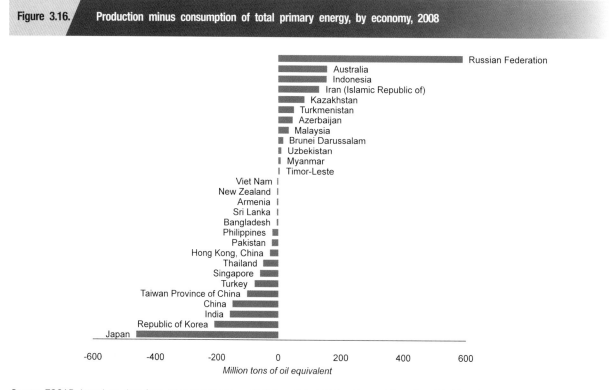

Source: ESCAP, based on data from International Energy Statistics, United States Energy Information Administration.

Coal. The Asia-Pacific region is a net coal exporter. Its exports reached 751 million short tons in 2007, 71% of the global trade in coal, and its imports amounted to 599 million short tons, or 59% of the world's total. The region's largest exporters are Australia. Indonesia and the Russian Federation, with combined exports in 2007 of 491 million short tons. The region's largest importers are China, India, Japan, the Republic of Korea and Taiwan Province of China.

In 2008 Asia and the Pacific exported by pipeline 183 billion cubic metres of gas, 31% of the world's total

---

Electricity. Trade in electricity usually takes place among countries that share a common border. Just over half the electricity trade in Asia and the Pacific is currently taking place in North and Central Asia, facilitated by a collective system of electricity management established in the period of the former Union of Soviet Socialist Republics. Within this system, the Russian Federation buys electricity from Kyrgyzstan and Tajikistan and supplies its own electricity to the northern regions of Kazakhstan. In addition, these countries, plus Uzbekistan and Turkmenistan, have had equal stakes in a public company based in Tashkent – the Central Asian United Dispatch Centre – which maintains a synchronized and balanced system for the transfer and distribution of electricity for member countries. However, electricity transmission within the region remains a major problem. There are a number of reasons for this: the absence of connections between certain regions within each country; considerable energy losses owing to the poor state of lines; and a lack of financing for constructing new lines or repairing old ones.

In addition, China has been exporting electricity to Hong Kong, China; Macao, China; and Viet Nam, and importing electricity from the Russian Federation. In South-East Asia the electricity grid of Thailand is connected with those of the Lao People's Democratic Republic, Malaysia and Singapore. In South and South-West Asia electricity trade is relatively small, but Bhutan exports 75% of its hydroelectricity to India; Afghanistan imports electricity from the Islamic Republic of Iran, Turkmenistan, Uzbekistan and Tajikistan; Pakistan imports electricity from the Islamic Republic of Iran to the isolated grid of Baluchistan; the power system of Nepal is interconnected with the power systems of the states of Uttar Pradesh and Bihar in India, and talks are under way to set up a 130-km power transmission link connecting Behrampur in India and Bheramara in Bangladesh.

Between 1993-1997 and 2003-2007, per capita electricity consumption of the median Asia-Pacific country grew by close to 50%. Growth has been even faster for large energy importers, such as China (140%) and the Republic of Korea (100%). By contrast, some countries in the region have extremely low levels of electricity consumption. For instance, during the period 2003-2007 Bangladesh, Cambodia, Myanmar and Nepal consumed less than 138 KWh per capita – among the lowest consumers of electricity in the world. Similarly, the average annual electricity consumption per capita of India, Indonesia, Pakistan and Sri Lanka during that period was 508 KWh or less, placing these countries in the bottom 20% of such consumers in the world. Clearly, as development proceeds all these countries will increase their consumption of electricity substantially, giving rise to further opportunities for energy trade.

Towards a regional framework for energy connectivity

Because energy is a critical production input, and disruptions to either its availability or price can have serious economic consequences, energy security – understood as both a stable supply for importing countries and a stable demand for exporting countries – is a fundamental goal. As discussed above and shown in figure 3.17, the Asia-Pacific region includes both large energy-importing and large energy-exporting countries. Therefore, the region's

Figure 3.17. **Asia-Pacific energy imbalances**

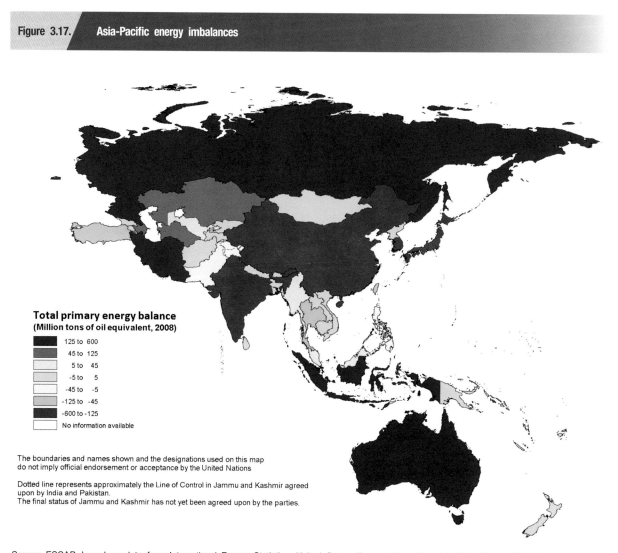

Total primary energy balance
(Million tons of oil equivalent, 2008)

■	125 to 600
■	45 to 125
□	5 to 45
□	-5 to 5
□	-45 to -5
■	-125 to -45
■	-600 to -125
□	No information available

The boundaries and names shown and the designations used on this map do not imply official endorsement or acceptance by the United Nations

Dotted line represents approximately the Line of Control in Jammu and Kashmir agreed upon by India and Pakistan.
The final status of Jammu and Kashmir has not yet been agreed upon by the parties.

Source: ESCAP, based on data from International Energy Statistics, United States Energy Information Administration, available from www.eia.doe.gov/cfapps/ipdbproject/IEDIndex3.cfm?tid=44&pid=44&aid=1 (accessed on 24 January 2011).

energy security could be increased by enhancing physical connectivity and building institutions to promote cooperation between the region's energy importers and energy exporters.

While no region-wide institutions currently exist, a number of subregional initiatives could serve as building blocks for a regional energy cooperation framework. A subregion that has built strong institutions over the years for cross-country energy cooperation is South-East Asia (see box 3.4). Because, as mentioned above, this subregion includes both net exporters and net importers of energy, cooperation among them has been

particularly fruitful. In several Asia-Pacific countries, there is a predominance of net exporters or net importers that provides opportunities for a region-wide cooperation on energy matters. For this reason, the development of a regional Asia-Pacific Energy Forum is essential to ensure the consolidation of subregional efforts towards developing regional connectivity and enhancing energy security. Such a regional forum could provide the basis for institutional cooperation, the harmonization policies, exchanges of knowledge and facilitating physical connectivity.

Enhancing physical connectivity infrastructure across countries is one important objective of regional

---

Box 3.4. Association of Southeast Asian Nations institutions for energy cooperation

Since the 1970s, South-East Asia has built institutions to promote energy cooperation. In 1976, for example, the Association of Southeast Asian Nations (ASEAN) established the ASEAN Council on Petroleum to promote collaboration in the development of petroleum resources. In 1981 it established a task force involving the Heads of ASEAN Public Utilities/Authorities to establish cooperation on power grid connections and avoid supply disruptions. In 1986 the ASEAN Petroleum Security Agreement obliged ASEAN members to provide oil/petroleum products to a member in distress because of a sudden shortfall in supply.[40]

Since the 1990s, cooperation has extended beyond energy security to issues such as energy efficiency and environmental impacts. For instance, the ASEAN Plan of Action for Energy Cooperation included six programme areas: (a) Trans-ASEAN Gas Pipeline; (b) ASEAN Power Grid; (c) coal, including clean-coal, technologies; (d) energy efficiency and conservation; (e) new and renewable sources of energy; and (f) regional energy outlook, energy policy and environmental analysis. These initiatives are coordinated through the ASEAN Centre for Energy established in 1999.[41]

Among these programmes, the ASEAN Power Grid was created in 1997 to enhance trade in electricity across borders, optimize energy generation and development, and encourage reserve sharing. One important challenge will be to connect the power grids of Cambodia, the Lao People's Democratic Republic, Myanmar and Viet Nam. Although the projects are technically viable they have yet to be accepted by participating economies.[42]

The Trans-ASEAN Gas Pipeline programme is aimed at developing a regional gas grid by 2020. With the completion in 2013 of the offshore Block M9 pipeline from Myanmar to Thailand, ASEAN will have 3,020 km of pipeline in place. The Trans-ASEAN Gas Pipeline will encounter substantial financial and legal complexities. The main challenges include high investment costs, synchronizing national technical and security regulation requirements and addressing differences in the supply, distribution and management of natural gas across countries. Countries also need to overcome the issues of political trust common in energy market cooperation.[43]

Source: ESCAP.

---

energy cooperation. As the number of pipelines planned or currently being constructed increases, it may be useful to identify missing infrastructure links and investment needs from a region-wide perspective, taking into account projected increases in the demand for energy within the region. In this respect, the modalities developed for the previously mentioned intergovernmental agreements on the Asian Highway and on the Trans-Asia Railway networks could provide useful models.

In addition, a region-wide energy cooperation framework could encourage joint investments by buyers and sellers in the region to create a pan-Asian gas grid linking multiple demand and supply sources. Cooperation could also be greatly beneficial for undertaking longer-term multilateral projects, such as joint research on energy technologies

relevant to the region, or for the formation of joint ventures of regional energy companies for joint prospecting and exploration. Further, regional cooperation could play an important role for the development, commercialization and dissemination of energy-efficient technologies, including solar panels, wind turbines and other technologies that take advantage of renewable resources. Such an approach will be increasingly needed, given the region's economic dynamism, the imperative of making energy available to all and the expectation that the price of crude oil will continue increasing over the next two decades.[44]

In order to promote energy cooperation and trade in the region, it is also necessary to develop a deep, liquid and transparent market for crude oil, petroleum products and gas. Building blocks of such a market include identifying a benchmark price for crude oil or marker crude that is relevant for the region, obtaining support from key buyers and sellers to ensure adequate trading volumes, securing adequate physical storage infrastructure, establishing a conducive regulatory framework and being able to access robust financial markets to support hedging and tradings.[45] Other fruitful areas for regional energy cooperation include sharing detailed information on demand, supply and inventory positions and building emergency response mechanisms by increasing physical supply security in Asia and the Pacific through strategic reserves and cross-border inventories.

The region's energy security could be increased by enhancing physical connectivity and building institutions to promote cooperation between its energy importers and exporters

---

Overall, a region-wide framework could encourage further investments in energy infrastructure with a more systematic involvement of the private sector, resulting in increasing volumes of intraregional energy trade and enhanced energy security for both importing and exporting countries.

People-to-people connectivity

Exchange activities across countries can be classified into two kinds: those in which the parties to the transaction exchange goods, services, money, or information across the border but without leaving their respective countries, and those in which one of the parties moves to another country to provide a service and/or consume goods and services there. Short-term and long-term labour migration by both skilled and less skilled workers is a prime example of an exchange activity that involves people moving to another country to provide a service. International tourism and studying abroad are examples of exchange activities that involve people moving to another country to consume services. Such activities

result in economic benefits for both countries. The country of origin often benefits from remittances sent by migrant workers to their families and the recipient country benefits from the purchases of goods and services by migrants, tourists and international students. In addition, such economic activities, which are often referred to as people-to-people connectivity, could help promote better mutual understanding, enhanced trust and greater respect for diversity, thus contributing to a culture of peace.[46] This section provides a succinct overview of the state of people-to-people connectivity in the areas of labour migration, education and tourism.

Migration

International migration of both skilled and less skilled workers is driven by three basic factors: income differences across countries, proximity and networks.[47] Income differences are due to differences across countries in economic growth, technological progress, levels and distribution of skills and population dynamics, which result in imbalances across their labour markets and create employment opportunities for migrants. Proximity between the countries of origin and destination of migrants reduces the financial and cultural costs of migration and enables migrants to be in closer contact with family and friends left behind in their country of origin. Immigrant networks often facilitate the search for employment for new migrants and, by creating a sense of community, their adaptation to live in a different country.

Migration flows are difficult to capture because of the variety of types of flows and channels to migrate and because a large number of migrants actually remain unrecorded. The most comprehensive data set of bilateral migration, prepared by researchers of the World Bank and the University of Sussex and updated to 2010, is based on stocks rather than flows. One problem of these data that should be kept in mind is that some countries define immigrants as "foreign born" individuals while others define them as "foreigners", which include people born in the country but who are not citizens.

Figure 3.18. Destination of Asia-Pacific migrants and origins of migrants to Asia and the Pacific, 2010

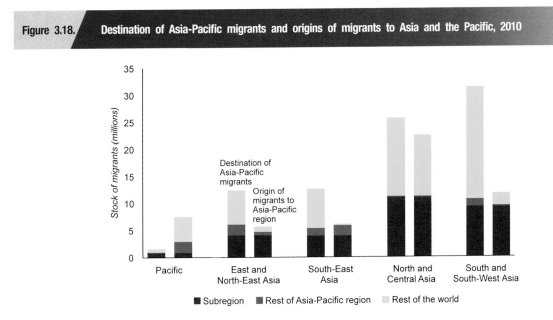

Source: ESCAP, based on data from World Bank, International Migration and Remittances, 2010.

Another problem is that the stock data show the accumulation of past migration flows, but those flows could have occurred a long time ago. As a result, data on migrant stocks are more useful to measure long-term trends. With these caveats in mind, this section uses that data set to explore the degree to which the Asia-Pacific region is connected with itself and with other selected regions of the world through migration.

Economic activities such as labour migration, studying abroad and tourism could promote better mutual understanding, enhanced trust and greater respect for diversity, contributing to a culture of peace

The data show that the Asia-Pacific region has been a net sender of migrants to the rest of the world, with a stock of 49.4 million Asia-Pacific migrants living in the rest of the world compared with 19.4 million migrants from the rest of the world living in Asia and the Pacific. As shown in figure 3.18, four of the five Asia-Pacific subregions have been net senders of migrants to the rest of the world.

South and South-West Asia is the subregion with the most migrants in the rest of the world (20.8 million), followed by North and Central Asia (14.5 million), South-East Asia (7.3 million) and East and North-East Asia (6.3 million). The Pacific is the only subregion in Asia and the Pacific that has been a net receiver of immigrants.

The World Bank data show that approximately 34 million Asia-Pacific migrants live in other countries in the region. They represent 41% of the stock of migrants from the region and 64% of the stock of migrants to the region. Much of this movement is within subregions. Intra-subregional migration ranges from 30% of the stock of migrants in South and South-West Asia to 57% in the Pacific. Such migration could be partially attributed to historical ties and geographic proximity. In contrast, there has been less migration between subregions. East and North-East Asia and South and South-West Asia have been net senders of migrants to the rest of the Asian and Pacific region, while the Pacific and South-East Asia have been net receivers of migrants from the rest of the region.

Some of the key migration corridors within the region extend from South-East Asia to East and North-East

Asia or to migrant-receiving countries in South-East Asia, such as Brunei Darussalam, Malaysia, Singapore and Thailand. For instance, as of 2010, there was a stock of 1.4 million Indonesians living in Malaysia and 1 million Malaysians living in Singapore. Meanwhile, workers from Central Asian countries migrate easily to Kazakhstan and the Russian Federation through a visa-free regime among most of the countries of the Commonwealth of Independent States (CIS). As of 2010, there was a stock of about 6.6 million migrant workers from Central Asia in the Russian Federation and a stock of about 2.2 million from the Russian Federation in Kazakhstan. These numbers, however, include migration flows that took place while these countries were part of the former Union of Soviet Socialist Republics. Another important migration route is from China to other East and North-East Asian countries (3.4 million) and to South-East Asia (1 million). Finally, in South Asia 5.2 million migrants from Bangladesh, Nepal, Pakistan and Sri Lanka reside in India, while 2.2 million migrants from India reside in Bangladesh, Nepal and Sri Lanka.

Table 3.3 shows the origins and destinations of migrants for the five ESCAP subregions and selected regions elsewhere in the rest of the world. The main destination of migrants from East and North-East Asia and from South-East Asia has been North America.

In contrast, the main destinations of migrants from South and South-West Asia have been the Middle East and North Africa, followed closely by the South and South-West Asia subregion itself. For North and Central Asia, the most important destination is that subregion itself. The same is true for the Pacific, although, as mentioned above, this subregion has been the only net receiver of migrants in the Asia-Pacific region, mostly from countries that are currently part of the European Union.

A major limitation of migration data is that they do not account properly for irregular migration. It is virtually impossible to accurately estimate irregular migration flows, which often are revealed only in regularization campaigns that register irregular migrants in order to offer them amnesty. Migrants may have an irregular status owing to unauthorized entry, unauthorized employment, or a change in employment status, such as working for a different employer than the one specified in the employee's work permit. Many irregular migrants, particularly in ASEAN countries, cross borders legally but work without permits.

Studying abroad

An important form of cross-border exchange of people is for education, especially at the tertiary level. This

Table 3.3. Bilateral migrant stocks, by Asia-Pacific subregions and selected regions in the world, millions, 2010

Origin \ Destination	East and North East-Asia	North and Central Asia	Pacific	South and South-West Asia	South-East Asia	Middle East and North Africa	EU 15	North America
East and North East-Asia	4.09	0.00	0.68	0.04	1.24	0.08	1.17	4.59
North and Central Asia	0.02	11.06	0.03	0.07	0.00	1.04	0.88	0.67
Pacific	0.02	0.00	0.91	0.01	0.03	0.00	0.26	0.35
South and South-West Asia	0.09	0.13	0.50	9.28	0.62	9.66	6.56	3.70
South-East Asia	0.46	0.00	0.82	0.07	3.97	1.38	1.37	4.32
Middle East and North Africa	0.00	0.01	0.26	0.43	0.01	9.91	5.27	1.32
EU 15	0.05	0.19	2.35	0.49	0.10	0.22	10.31	4.63
North America	0.11	0.00	0.19	0.02	0.07	0.12	0.84	13.35

Source: ESCAP, based on data from World Bank, Bilateral Migration and Remittances, 2010, go.worldbank.org/JITC7NYTT0.

Note: EU15 = Austria, Belgium, Denmark, Finland, France, Germany, Greece, Ireland, Italy, Luxembourg, Netherlands, Portugal, Spain, Sweden and United Kingdom.

is becoming an increasingly attractive option for students who also want to familiarize themselves with the language and culture of the destination country. It may also result eventually in longer-term migration. Countries such as Australia, interested in attracting skilled immigrants, often facilitate the long-term settlement in the country of foreign students who completed their studies there. According to data from the UNESCO Institute for Statistics, the Asian countries that sent the most students abroad in 2008 were China (445,000), India (170,000) and the Republic of Korea (113,000). While most Asian international students go to North America and Europe, many study in other Asia-Pacific countries, such as Australia (183,000), Japan (118,000) and the Russian Federation (34,500).

Tourism

Tourism not only encourages greater interaction between countries and enhances mutual under-standing but is also a major source of employment and foreign exchange. Intraregional tourism is very important in Asia and the Pacific. According to the World Tourism Organization, the number of tourist arrivals originating from the Asia-Pacific region increased between 1980 and 2009, from 14 million to 140 million, which represented 77% of total tourist arrivals that year.

Much of this increase may be traced to easier travel. For instance, entry-visa exemption has been agreed between Cambodia and the Lao People's Democratic Republic, as well as between Cambodia and Viet Nam, resulting in a significant increase in cross-border travel. In the aftermath of the global financial crisis, Asian consumers, whose purchasing power is rising, seem less constrained by debt than their Western counterparts and are now spending some of their savings on travel. Tourists from China, India and other Asian countries appear to be the driving force behind rapid growth in intra-Asian tourism.[48]

Other factors that are contributing to expanding intra-regional tourism are the deregulation of airline services and the development of low cost carriers (LCC) in some countries of the region.[49] The latter is a relatively recent phenomenon. In East and North-East Asia the first LCCs, Skymark Airlines and Air Do, entered the market in 1998, offering limited routes in Japan. A decade later, other 9 airlines started operations in that subregion, including Jeju Air in the Republic of Korea, Spring Air in China and Oasis Hong Kong in Hong Kong. LCCs grew even more rapidly in South-East Asia, the most developed region for low-cost aviation in Asia. Air Asia, based in Malaysia, is the leading LCC in Asia. The development of LCCs was facilitated by deregulation policies. For instance, in 2001 Thailand allowed private airlines to enter any domestic route, and in 2003 airlines were free to charge any price, subject only to an upper limit. Unfortunately, the regulatory environment for intra-Asian routes is much more restrictive, but progress is under way, with ASEAN gradually moving towards a regional open sky policy.

Managing labour migration

Across the region, countries are keen to ensure that labour migration occurs on a legal basis. Some subregions and groups, such as North and Central Asia and ASEAN, have already moved ahead with multilateral agreements. Some countries have established bilateral memorandums of understanding. Although such agreements will not eliminate irregular migration, since many migrants may be deterred by the costs of and controls involved in using official channels, they can offer some protection from abuses.

North and Central Asia. This is the subregion most connected through migration. It is moving towards becoming a common labour market, facilitated by historical ties and a legacy of proficiency in the use of the Russian language. This led, for example, to the 1994 agreement among CIS on cooperation in labour migration and social guarantees for migrant workers. The 1998 agreement between the CIS countries on cooperation in preventing irregular migration, and the 2005 EurAsEc Customs Union

Agreement on visa-free trips between Belarus, Kazakhstan, Kyrgyzstan, the Russian Federation and Tajikistan. There are also bilateral agreements on labour migration, such as between the Russian Federation and Kyrgyzstan and Tajikistan.[50] Since July 2010, migrants from CIS countries can enter the Russian Federation visa-free but they have to obtain licenses. Kazakhstan also grants visa-free entry to nationals of most of the CIS countries, allowing them 90 days to search for work.[51]

ASEAN. In the ASEAN Economic Community Blueprint, the Association foresees a free flow of skilled labour by 2020 and is working to "facilitate the issuance of visas and employment passes for ASEAN professionals and skilled labour who are engaged in cross-border trade and investment-related activities". As a first step, ASEAN has already agreed on a mutual recognition agreement for nurses, dental and medical practitioners, engineering and architectural services, surveying professionals and accountancy services. However, there are likely to be persistent language barriers. In Singapore, for example, migrants from Myanmar and the Philippines find it easier to obtain employment than those from Indonesia and Thailand who often lack proficiency in the English language. On the other hand, for nurses coming to Thailand, the Government requires that they speak Thai.[52] Moreover, the ASEAN framework foresees a free flow only of skilled labour. In reality the majority of migrants within ASEAN are unskilled, attracted by persistent diffferences in real wages across countries, and the majority doing so are irregular migrants.

Pacific. Migration flows in the Pacific are largely shaped by political and other ties between source and destination countries. Migrants from several Polynesian and Micronesian States, for example, have had relatively easy access to Australia, New Zealand or the United States. However, access is more difficult for nationals of island States in Melanesia and therefore only about 1% of Melanesians live abroad.[53] Australia and New Zealand have recently started opening up their borders for seasonal labour migration from all Pacific countries, as well as Asian

countries, to work in agriculture. Although few Pacific islanders have yet benefited from the scheme, it is a step towards connecting all the Pacific countries, not only those with historical ties to Australia and New Zealand.

Key destination economies, such as Hong Kong, China; Macao, China; Malaysia; the Republic of Korea; Singapore; Taiwan Province of China; and Thailand, have points-based application schemes. The Quality Migrant Admission Scheme of Hong Kong, China, facilitates immigration of skilled workers based, among other criteria, on proficiency in the Cantonese or English languages. It also facilitates the migration of domestic helpers. However, neither scheme is open to nationals of Afghanistan, Albania, Cambodia, Cuba, the Democratic People's Republic of Korea, the Lao People's Democratic Republic, Nepal or Viet Nam. In addition, the scheme for domestic helpers does not apply to residents of China; Macao, China; and Taiwan Province of China.

In addition to general admission criteria and multilateral agreements, a number of countries have established memorandums of understanding. Thailand, for example, has entered into such arrangements with Cambodia, the Lao People's Democratic Republic and Myanmar. These cover guidelines and procedures for employment protection and the return of workers. Even so, most migrants continue to move through irregular channels because this is easier and cheaper than doing so legally.

The Republic of Korea in 2004 established an employment permit system that determines yearly quotas for the admission of foreign workers for three-year stays. To administer this scheme it has entered into memorandums of understanding with 15 Asian countries: Bangladesh, Cambodia, China, Indonesia, Kyrgyzstan, Mongolia, Myanmar, Nepal, Pakistan, the Philippines, Sri Lanka, Thailand, Timor-Leste, Uzbekistan and Viet Nam. In addition, it has reserved quotas for persons who are ethnically Korean but holding foreign nationality.[54]

Regional financial cooperation

As mentioned in chapter 1, it is widely recognized that a regional financial architecture could be a useful complement of the international financial architecture. The recognition of this advantage led the members of ESCAP to set up the Asian Development Bank in the mid-1960s as a regional multilateral development bank to provide its member States with development financing. Another institution created in the ESCAP framework was the Asian Clearing Union, which was set up in the mid-1970s to facilitate intraregional trade through the periodic settlement of debits and credits accumulated by each member against the other members, using a unit of account.

The Chiang Mai Initiative

The 1997/98 Asian financial crisis highlighted both the vulnerabilities and the economic interdependence of economies, and stimulated a discussion on the need for a regional crisis-prevention and response mechanism in the form of an Asian monetary fund. While the proposal for such a fund did not go very far, the Chiang-Mai Initiative (CMI), a regional network of bilateral swaps to provide emergency assistance in times of crisis, was set up within the framework of ASEAN+3. In 2010 CMI was "multilateralized", becoming the "Chiang Mai Initiative Multilateralization", or CMIM, with a total pool of $120 billion to supplement the exiting international financing arrangements; 80% of the pool is contributed by the "plus three" countries – China, Japan and the Republic of Korea – while the ASEAN countries provide the remaining 20%. An independent regional surveillance office, ASEAN+3 Macroeconomic Research Office set up in 2010, is responsible for conducting surveillance for CMIM operations.

Development of regional financial markets

Another approach to financial cooperation resulting from policy discussions in the aftermath of 1997 crisis focused on the development of regional bond markets, which provide a relatively more stable source of debt financing than bank loans. Two initiatives have been taken in this regard.

Asian Bond Fund. This fund was established by the Executives Meeting of East Asia-Pacific Central Banks (EMEAP), an association of central banks of several economies in the region (Australia; China; Hong Kong, China; Indonesia; Japan; the Republic of Korea; New Zealand; the Philippines; Singapore; and Thailand). The first stage of the fund was launched in 2003 with voluntary contributions by the members of EMEAP to a $1 billion fund that invested in bonds denominated in the dollars issued by sovereign and quasi-sovereign borrowers from eight EMEAP members, and was managed by the Bank for International Settlements. In the second stage of the fund, launched in 2005, EMEAP created a $2-billion fund to invest in local currency bonds issued by sovereign and quasi-sovereign borrowers from eight EMEAP members. The main goal of the fund has been to enhance further the underdeveloped bond markets of the member economies by enhancing the efficiency of financial intermediation and promoting financial stability.[55]

Asian Bond Market Initiative. Launched by ASEAN+3 in 2003, this initiative is aimed at developing local currency bond markets to make private savings available for regional investment needs. Efforts are being made to promote the demand for and issuance of such bonds. The relevant infrastructure and regulatory framework also need to be put into place. In this connection, ASEAN+3 has recently endorsed the establishment of a $700 million credit guarantee and investment facility that will provide guarantees for local currency denominated bonds issued by companies in the region. It is expected that such initiatives will help to channel money for regional investment needs and reduce the currency and maturity mismatches which made the region more vulnerable to external shocks in the past.

Subregional investment funds

SAARC Development Fund. This fund was set up in Bhutan in 2010 as a part of SAARC financial cooperation with authorized capital of 1 billion special drawing rights (SDRs) and paid up capital of $200 million. The fund will finance infrastructure projects in the subregion, including the preparation of feasibility studies.

ASEAN Infrastructure Fund. Created as a part of an ASEAN initiative to mobilize resources for infrastructure development, this fund has a capital base of $800 million.

Other initiatives

In addition to the above-mentioned initiatives, several other initiatives are taking shape for regional cooperation in the fields of finance and macroeconomic policy. Within the framework of groupings such as ASEAN, SAARC, ASEAN+3, East Asia Summit and Asian Cooperation Dialogue, finance has been identified as an area of cooperation. Cooperation takes the form of periodic meetings of finance ministers and central bank governors, as in ASEAN and SAARC, as well as the exchange of information and expertise. Central banks in the region have formed four groupings or cooperative associations with different permutations of membership, namely South East Asia, Australia and New Zealand, or SEANZA; South East Asian Central Banks, or SEACEN; Network of Central Bank Governors and Finance Secretaries of the SAARC Region, or SAARCFINANCE; and Executives' Meeting of East Asia-Pacific Central Banks, or EMEAP, all of which promote cooperation between members with a focus on capacity-building and sharing expertise. In addition, the Asian Exim Banks Forum was formed in 1996 with membership comprising the export credit agencies of Australia, China, India, Indonesia, Japan, the Republic of Korea, Malaysia, the Philippines and Thailand. Besides sharing information and training resources, the forum has fostered mutual cooperation among its members by facilitating lines of credit on a reciprocal basis. Finally, some countries in the region, such as Japan and India, have instituted bilateral swap arrangements that are not covered under CMI.

Towards a development-friendly regional financial architecture for Asia and the Pacific

Although several initiatives have been taken in the area of financial cooperation in the region, most of them are in their early stages and have limited scope and coverage. CMIM is an important initiative in the direction of developing a regional crisis response facility. However, it should be seen as a work in progress as it has been limited in scale and scope. First, the overall size of the fund is rather small when compared with the scale of bailouts in the recent crises. Second, only 20% of the liquidity available to a country is available without any conditionality, and beyond that threshold IMF conditionality is invoked. This link to IMF conditionality has possibly deterred some countries that needed liquidity support during the 2008/09 crisis from approaching CMI, such as Indonesia, the Republic of Korea and Singapore, which preferred to raise emergency financing from Japan and the United States on a bilateral basis. Finally, the expansion of CMIM membership to cover other key systemically important countries needs to be considered in order to make the initiative truly regional. ABF and the Asian Bond Markets Initiative have also been important initiatives towards developing regional financial markets, but they have been rather modest in scale to make a significant impact in view of the size of the region's economy. The SAARC Development Fund and the ASEAN Infrastructure Fund are also important initiatives for expanding the options for infrastructure financing facilities in the region but currently at a modest scale. Besides enhancing the depth of domestic bond markets in the region, it is important to facilitate cross-border listings to enhance the access of the region's least developed countries to capital markets, among other possibilities.

The region needs a more developed regional financial architecture that not only could assist it in managing the financial crisis but also could provide an adequate supply of development finance to narrow the development gaps. ESCAP analysis

Figure 3.19.   Gaps in infrastructure development in Asia and the Pacific, 2007

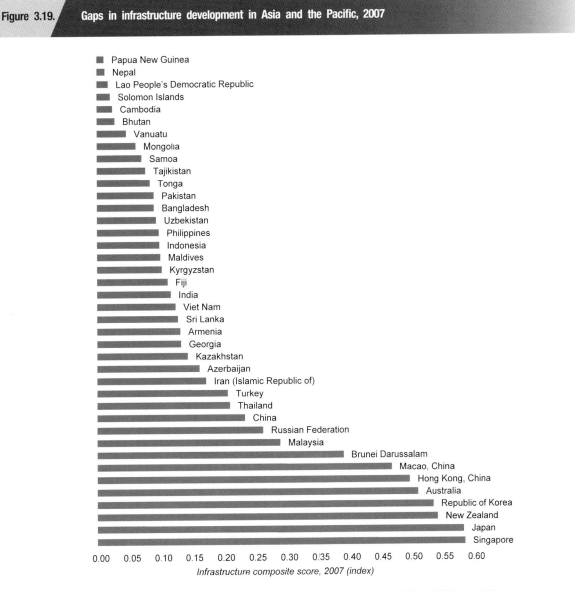

Infrastructure composite score, 2007 (index)

Source: ESCAP, based on data from World Bank, World Development Indicators Database, and ESCAP (2010b, p. 135).

Note: The composite measure of infrastructure development is based on eight physical infrastructure indicators covering 40 ESCAP member countries for 2007. See ESCAP (2010b, p. 143) for details.

shows that the region is characterized by wide infrastructure development gaps (see figure 3.19). There are also similarly wide gaps in social infrastructure and achievement of the Millennium Development Goals, as shown in the *Economic and Social Survey of Asia and the Pacific 2010*.[56] Closing the infrastructure and other development gaps would require huge investments. Available estimates suggest that infrastructure gaps would require $8 trillion in investments over 10 years.[57]

Closing the gaps in achievement of the Millennium Development Goals would require an additional $639 billion in investments. With appropriate mechanisms available for mobilizing the region's savings and channelling into these unmet investment needs through institutional intermediation and catalysing public-private partnerships, it would be possible not only to sustain the region's dynamism for many years but also to make it an anchor of global stability.

The elements of a possible regional financial architecture that need to be developed for supporting the region's development needs include the following:

Crisis prevention and management. In the area of crisis prevention and response, it is important to scale up and build further on the pioneering CMIM to expand its scope and coverage. The expansion of the membership to cover other key systemically important countries, such as Australia, India and the Russian Federation, needs to be considered in order to make the initiative truly regional. Furthermore, with combined foreign exchange reserves of over $5 trillion, the region has the ability to expand considerably the size of the CMIM pool. The goal should be to build CMIM further into a well-endowed, truly regional crisis response facility that could reduce pressure on Governments to build large foreign exchange reserves for protecting their economies against speculative attacks and liquidity crises. Enhanced regional cooperation for crisis response and management, however, should not be regarded as an alternative to full participation in global economic relations. Rather, it should be seen as a complement to it, filling in the gaps and establishing the building blocks for global multilateral cooperation.

In the area of crisis prevention and response, the goal should be to build CMIM further into a well-endowed, truly regional crisis response facility

Development finance and capital markets integration. The region needs to develop further its financial architecture for development financing, which would include systems of intermediation between its large savings and its unmet investment needs. Lack of an appropriate mechanism is the reason why the bulk of the region's foreign exchange reserves has been invested in securities issued by Western Governments, such as United States treasury bills.

One option would be to create a large infrastructure development fund managed by a regional institution, as indicated in chapter 1. If such a fund secured just 5% of the region's reserves of over $5 trillion it could provide start-up capital of $250 billion in addition to its ability to borrow from the central banks. Such a regional institution should be able to issue securities to enable the region's central banks to be able to park their surplus reserves with it. This pooling of reserves could assist the region in meeting some of its investment needs, which are estimated to be on the order of more than $800 billion per annum in transport, energy, water and telecommunications.

The development of regional bond markets and the integration of the region's capital markets would also facilitate investment flows within the region. A framework needs to be developed to enable cross-border listings in the region so that corporate entities in countries with relatively underdeveloped capital markets could raise capital in other regional markets.

The Asia-Pacific region is becoming more economically integrated and has considerable scope for deepening this integration

Exchange rate cooperation. Another area where regional financial architecture could make a positive contribution is in coordination of exchange rates. As economies of the region increasingly trade with each other, they will need a currency management system that facilitates trade and macroeconomic stability and discourages competitive devaluations. One option worthy of consideration is a basket parity relative to a number of reserve currencies, including key currencies of the region instead of the dollar alone, and a set of weights determined on the basis of regional trade shares.

Closer cooperation between central banks and financing institutions. As observed previously, a number of cooperative bodies of central banks have been set up in the region, including South-East Asia, Australia and New Zealand; the Executives' Meeting of East Asia-Pacific Central Banks; the Network of Central Bank Governors and Finance Secretaries of the SAARC Region; and South-East Asian Central Banks, facilitating the coordination, exchange of information and cooperation in training and capacity-building between them. However, there is a need for a broader regional body that could facilitate region-wide information sharing and assist in closing capacity gaps. Similary, the Asian Exim Banks Forum could move forward to create an apex regional trade finance institution, for which it has developed an initial concept, in order to facilitate cooperation in trade finance.

Capacity-building in public-private partnerships. The enormity of resource requirements in Asia and the Pacific for infrastructure development makes it clear that a strong contribution from the private sector is needed, not just to bridge funding gaps but also to overcome the public sector's limited delivery capacity and take advantage of the private sector's efficiency and advanced technology. For this purpose Governments are increasingly turning to public-private partnerships (PPPs) to develop and operate both economic and social infrastructure. Some Governments have made considerable progress in the areas of institutional development, capacity-building, streamlining administrative processes and financing and approving new projects. Important steps have included the following: formulating PPP policy frameworks (Bangladesh, India, Indonesia, the Republic of Korea); enacting new laws or amending existing ones to create a PPP-supportive environment (Cambodia, Fiji, Indonesia, the Philippines, the Republic of Korea, Turkey, Viet Nam and many states in India); establishing institutional mechanisms to furnish government grant/support to PPP projects (Bangladesh, India, the Republic of Korea); establishing special infrastructure financing institutions (Bangladesh, India, Indonesia, the Russian Federation); creating special PPP units in Government (Australia, Bangladesh, Fiji, India, Indonesia, Malaysia, Pakistan, the Republic of Korea, Sri Lanka, Turkey); streamlining administrative processes (India,

the Republic of Korea), among others. As a result there has been a considerable increase in PPPs for infrastructure. Between 2005 and 2009, 826 projects worth about $204 billion reached financial closure. However, a few countries, namely China, India, the Russian Federation and Turkey, accounted for the bulk (82%) of these projects.

In the aftermath of the global financial crisis, some Governments have been reinvigorating PPPs as a part of their stimulus packages, sometimes through policy and fiscal measures, including debt guarantees, direct financial stakes, tax-free bonds, lower-equity capital requirements and sharing interest rate risks. International financing institutions have also considered various measures. For example, the International Finance Corporation, the private sector arm of the World Bank, created a global $300 billion equity fund and a loan financing trust to support PPPs.

Enhancing regional connectivity is a multifaceted task that will require the implementation of bold policy initiatives at the national and regional levels

There is need for building capacity for fuller exploitation of PPPs for infrastructure development in the region. This would include a better understanding of PPPs at the policymaking level, with a clear policy on risk sharing, capacity for developing bankable projects and managing contracts, standardized administrative processes and project documents, clear legal and regulatory regimes and availability of long-term finance. In these areas regional cooperation for sharing development experiences and capacity–building, drawing upon the expertise of countries that started earlier, may be fruitful. Regional organizations, such as ESCAP and ADB, may assist the region in building such capability in the region.

Regional cooperation for the reform of the inter-national financial architecture. The development of a regional financial architecture would also enable the region to develop a regional perspective on the reform of the international financial architecture, including on various proposals such as an SDR-based global reserve currency, a global tax on financial transactions to moderate short-term capital flows, international regulations for curbing excessive risk-taking by the financial sectors, among other issues that are emerging in the G20, United Nations and other forums, as discussed in Chapter 1.

At its sixty-sixth session, held in Incheon, Republic of Korea, in May 2010, the Commission mandated the ESCAP secretariat to assist member countries in elaborating the elements of a regional financial architecture. In line with that mandate the secretariat is engaged in further work on a subject which will feed into the policy agenda of the region in years to come.

Conclusion

The analysis in this chapter suggests that the Asian and Pacific region is becoming more economically integrated and that it has considerable scope for deepening this integration. First, as a result of its higher rates of economic growth vis-à-vis the rest of the world, the region's intraregional trade has increased faster than its total trade – a trend expected to continue into the future. Second, there is a large degree of complementarity in the structures of imports and exports in ESCAP subregions, suggesting large unexploited opportunities for increasing trade both within and across subregions. Third, intra-regional FDI flows are becoming more and more important in the region, providing smaller and poorer countries with much needed capital and technological expertise. Fourth, because the region includes both large energy-importing and energy-exporting countries, it has much to gain from boosting regional cooperation and trade in energy products. Fifth, economic activities that involve the movement of people across borders within the region are increasingly important, with a large share of the region's labour migrants residing in neighbouring countries.

These trends towards a greater degree of regional economic integration suggest that the region is increasing its contribution to supporting its own economic growth and has the potential to contribute even more in the future. However, regional integration does not take place in a vacuum. Exchange activities across borders cannot take place without the physical and institutional infrastructure often referred to as connectivity. Although the region is making progress in boosting its connectivity, much more needs to be done to facilitate the seamless movement of goods, services, energy, capital and people throughout all countries of Asia and the Pacific.

In the area of trade, although the region has a large number of preferential trading arrangements, they are not contributing to the creation of a seamless, broader and unified Asia-Pacific market because of their bilateral and subregional nature. However, initiatives such as CEPEA, which represent about 80% of the region's population and GDP, could constitute the nucleus of an incipient Asia-Pacific-wide free trade area to which other countries in the region could accede in the future.

A major obstacle to the expansion of trade is the high cost of moving goods to the hinterlands of some countries and across countries because of long distances, high vehicle operating costs, high transshipment costs and complex border crossing procedures. The latter in particular have been found to constitute a much more serious obstacle to trade and development of hinterland areas than the lack of physical transport infrastructure. In order to streamline trade procedures, countries are relying more on electronic data interchange and are trying to institute national electronic single windows through which traders can submit required documentation, pay duties and receive clearance. However, for the full benefits of single windows to be realized, the electronic data and documents should be accepted by authorities in all partner countries. For this to happen, it is necessary to develop of an international legal framework. Similarly, to reduce cross-border transport costs it is necessary for landlocked and transit countries to accede to the relevant international conventions in the area of international transport and transit, as recommended by the Almaty Programme of Action.

In the area of physical infrastructure investment, it is important to exploit synergies across various types of infrastructure. For instance, rights of way for roads and railways, such as those established under the intergovernmental agreements on the Asian Highway and the Trans-Asian Railway, could also accommodate telecommunications cabling or base stations. Similarly, those agreements could provide a useful institutional model for identifying missing links and investment needs from a region-wide perspective for other types of infrastructure investment, such as oil and gas pipelines. In the area of energy, the development of a deep, liquid and transparent market for crude oil, petroleum products and gas could also be useful to promote intraregional energy trade.

Finally, in order to fund the large infrastructure investments required to boost its connectivity, the region needs to further develop mechanisms for the financial intermediation between its large savings and its equally large investment needs, estimated to be on the order of $800 billion per year. For that purpose, useful initiatives include deepening the development of bond markets, building on initiatives such as the Asian Bond Fund and the Asian Bond Markets Initiative, integrating capital markets by allowing cross-listings across stock exchanges, expanding the use of public-private partnerships for investment in infrastructure and considering the creation of a large regional infrastructure development fund to channel a small part of the region's foreign exchange reserves into much needed infrastructure investments in the poorer and smaller countries of the region.

In sum, enhancing regional connectivity is a multifaceted task that will require the implementation of bold policy initiatives at the national and regional levels, and in many different areas. However, by facilitating the creation of a seamless and region-wide market, such a task could contribute to sustaining the region's dynamism in decades to come and to reducing the wide disparities in economic opportunities within and across Asia-Pacific countries.

Endnotes

[1]   Association of Southeast Asian Nations, 2011.

[2]   South Asian Association for Regional Cooperation, 2007.

[3]   Rodriguez, 2007; Calderón and Servén, 2004.

[4]   Head, 2000; Santos-Silva and Tenreyro, 2006.

[5]   Head, 2000.

[6]   Asian Development Bank/United Nations, Economic and Social Commission for Asia and the Pacific, 2009.

[7]   Duval and Utokham, 2010.

[8]   United Nations, Economic and Social Commission for Asia and the Pacific, 2010f.

[9]   Japan External Trade Organization, 2009.

[10]   National Development and Reform Commission, 2005; Thai News Agency, 2009.

[11]   Kuroda, Kawai and Nangia, 2007.

[12]   United Nations Conference on Trade and Development, 2010b.

[13]   Dunning and Narula, 1996.

[14]   Aykut and Goldstein, 2007.

[15]   United Nations Conference on Trade and Development, 2006a.

[16]   Akyut and Goldstein, 2007.

[17]   Rajan, 2010.

[18]   Yao, Sutherland and Chen, 2010.

[19]   Kumar, 2008.

[20]   Kumar, 2007a.

[21]   Kumar, 2007b.

[22]   Kawai and Wignaraja, 2010.

[23]   Asian Development Bank, 2010.

[24] United Nations, 2008.

[25] United Nations, Economic and Social Commission for Asia and the Pacific, 2010g.

[26] Australian Agency for International Development, 2008.

[27] Kumagai and others, 2008.

[28] Asian Development Bank/United Nations, Economic and Social Commission for Asia and the Pacific, 2009.

[29] United Nations, 2003.

[30] Rashid and Elder, 2009.

[31] Jensen, 2007.

[32] United Nations, Economic and Social Commission for Asia and the Pacific, 2008b, p. 3.

[33] Secretariat of the Pacific Community, 2010.

[34] TeleGeography, 2009.

[35] International Telecommunication Union, 2010.

[36] Hajela, Tiwaree, and Martinez-Navarrete, 2009.

[37] Association of Southeast Asian Nations, 2011.

[38] ICT Association of Fiji, 2009.

[39] Verisign, 2010, p. 3.

[40] Nicolas, 2009.

[41] Nicolas, 2009.

[42] Association of Southeast Asian Nations, 2011.

[43] Association of Southeast Asian Nations, 2011.

[44] International Energy Agency, 2010b.

[45] Tuli, 2008.

[46] Association of Southeast Asian Nations, 2011, p. 52.

[47] Ratha and Shaw, 2007.

[48] Neumann and Song-yi Kim, 2010.

[49] Zhang and others, 2008.

[50] Ivakhnyuk, 2006.

[51] United Nations, Economic and Social Commission for Asia and the Pacific, 2010h.

[52] Manning and Sidorenko, 2007.

[53] Hayes, 2010.

[54] United Nations, Economic and Social Commission for Asia and the Pacific, 2010b.

[55] Rajan, 2008.

[56] United Nations, Economic and Social Commission for Asia and the Pacific, 2010h and United Nations, Economic and Social Commission for Asia and the Pacific, Asian Development Bank and United Nations Development Programme, 2010.

[57] Asian Development Bank, 2009.

"Technology and know how, innovation and creativity are today key factors for productivity improvement and economic growth. Unfortunately, the international environment presents to the LDCs more challenges than opportunities. We need to address this gap to achieve our MDGs and other development goals."
Sheikh Hasina, Prime Minister of Bangladesh

Building the Productive Capacity of the Least Developed Countries

The previous chapter considered how future growth and development in the region could be achieved through greater regional integration supported by greater connectivity. If the least developed countries are to benefit from regional integration, however, they will need to increase their productive capacity. For this purpose, they must do more than increase the output of existing products; if they are to climb the rungs of the development ladder, they will instead need to produce and trade new and more sophisticated products. This was the development path successfully followed by Japan and, from the early 1960s, by the Republic of Korea, Singapore and Taiwan Province of China.

Table 4.1 summarizes a few indicators that are typically associated with productive capacity for the production and trade of Asia-Pacific least developed countries. It shows that their share in total GDP is less than one tenth of their share in the global population, and for the past 30 years, it has been lower than it was 40 years ago—lower than 0.25% since 1980 compared with 0.43% in 1970. Similarly, their share of global manufacturing value added, which measures the contribution of the manufacturing sector in total production, has also been lower—it was 0.6% in 1970 and declined to about half of that value for most of the past three decades. In terms of trade, least developed countries have been marginal exporters—their share in merchandise exports has been lower than 0.25% throughout a period when total world merchandise exports in current terms has increased 42-fold. In addition, least developed countries have contributed less than 0.2% of manufactured exports and less than 0.01% of world's high-technology products.

The importance of the transformation of productive capacities for development has received growing attention through a series of United Nations Conference on Trade and Development (UNCTAD) least developed country reports,[1] which have argued that national and international policy should focus on developing productive capacities—and the related expansion of productive employment—to achieve sustained development and poverty reduction in the least developed countries (see box 4.1). Such an approach to development presents an alternative to the set of orthodox growth theories that have guided policy discourse over the past three decades, and it brings production and productive employment back to the development agenda. Strategic diversification of production is a key element of this approach.

Anyone from a developing country visiting a supermarket in an industrialized country for the first time will be struck by the amount and variety of products on offer. Wondering how her own country could one day become that rich and match that range, the curious visitor would be told that the country should specialize in the things that it can produce with higher relative efficiency. Hence, if it grows bananas more efficiently than it manufactures cars, computers or airplanes, then it should stick to bananas and acquire the variety of products needed to fill its supermarket shelves through trade.

The inquisitive visitor would certainly note, however, that the developed country also has the advantage of many other kinds of diversity. For example, it has a rich variety of professionals specializing in every imaginable area, along with a wide range of companies producing all manner of goods and services, and farms producing an ever-increasing range of agricultural products. Further, this variety of economic activities and the whole social structure that supports and co-evolves with them emerged not more than few generations ago—a time in which the living standards were comparable with those in her own country. How could her country rapidly achieve something similar by producing bananas? The answer is: it cannot.

| Table 4.1. | Share of Asia-Pacific least developed countries in international production and trade |

(Percentage)

Indicator	1970	1980	1990	2000	2007	2008	2009
Population	3.18	3.21	3.44	3.65	3.83	3.78	3.86
GDP	0.43	0.22	0.18	0.22	0.23	0.24	0.25
Manufacturing, value added	0.60	0.14	0.16	0.16	0.20	0.31	0.58
Merchandize exports	0.11	0.12	0.09	0.17	0.19	0.19	0.24
Manufactured exports	0.01	0.06	0.07	0.16	0.12	0.04	0.01
High-technology exports	..	..	0.00	0.00	0.01	0.00	..

Source: ESCAP, based on data from the World Bank.

Box 4.1. Least developed countries in Asia and the Pacific

The ESCAP region currently has 13 designated least developed countries: Afghanistan, Bangladesh, Bhutan, Cambodia, Kiribati, Lao People's Democratic Republic, Myanmar, Nepal, Samoa, Solomon Islands, Timor-Leste, Tuvalu and Vanuatu. Maldives graduated from that status in January 2011 but it is included in the group of least developed countries analysed in this chapter given that it refers to the period prior to the graduation. The list is reviewed every three years based on three criteria. The first criterion is low income, based on gross national income (GNI) per capita, with a threshold of $905 for addition to the list and $1,086 for graduation from it. The second Is human assets weakness, based on indicators of nutrition, health, school enrolment and literacy. The third is economic vulnerability, based on indicators of exposure and vulnerability to natural and trade shocks. To graduate from least developed country status, a country needs to meet thresholds under at least two criteria in at least two consecutive reviews. Regardless of its performance on the other two criteria, however, a country will be eligible for graduation if it has a GNI per capita of more than double the threshold.[2]

The least developed countries in Asia and the Pacific face a range of problems. They generally suffer from high costs for food, development and transport. In addition, they lack technical skills, have limited domestic savings and are vulnerable to external shocks, including natural disasters.

They also have limited opportunities for realizing economies of scale. For some, such as those in the Pacific, this is because they are remote and have small populations. For others, such as Bangladesh, Cambodia and Nepal, it is because a high proportion of their people live below the poverty line. These limitations have hampered progress towards reducing poverty and hunger and achieving other Millennium Development Goals. Their progress has also been slowed by the food and energy crises of 2008 and 2009, the global financial and economic crisis, and the recent increase in food and oil prices, all of which have increased their vulnerability and further undermined their economic and social development.

Source: ESCAP.

The recent literature has demonstrated that economic development is associated not with producing more of the same goods and services but with expanding the range.[3] As incomes increase, economies become more diversified. Only much later are they likely to specialize.[4] As a result, the rich nations export a wide range of products, including goods also exported by poorer nations, although the rich-country versions have higher unit values.[5]

The importance of diversity may not be evident in current mainstream economic policy discourse, but it has certainly been noticed in the past. One review of the work of seventeenth century economists, for example, concluded: "... it is as if these theorists said: if you wish to estimate the wealth of a city, count the number of professions found within its walls...the larger the number of professions, the wealthier the city".[6]

This chapter reviews the relationship between development, diversity and productive capacities. Instead of the usual approach, which focuses on particular elements of productive capacities, such as productive resources, entrepreneurial capabilities and production linkages, this chapter takes an empirical approach, inferring a country's productive capacity from its mix of actual products (see box 4.2).

Since there are few systematically disaggregated data on each country's production, however, it uses as a proxy the more readily available data on the composition of exports (see box 4.3). It then identifies the opportunities for expanding capacities and take greater advantage of regional integration.

Patterns of diversification

Diversification is the process of expanding the range of goods produced. It may involve producing higher

Box 4.2. Assessing productive capacities

This chapter's assessment of productive capacities seeks to infer the capabilities available in a country by looking at the products that it already produces.[7] The methodology assumes that: (a) products require specific combinations of capabilities; (b) countries have some capabilities but not others; and (c) if they have all the required capabilities, they will produce the corresponding goods.[8]

As illustrated in the figure below, if country C1 has capacities A1, A2 and A3, it can produce all three products P1, P2 and P3. Country C2, however, only has capacity A2 and A3, so it can only produce P2 and P3. The figure also presents a subset of the bipartite network showing Bangladesh, China, Japan and Samoa and all the products they exported. Thus, each country has products that are also produced by other countries, which are indicated in the shared circles, along with other products for which it is the sole producer in this group.

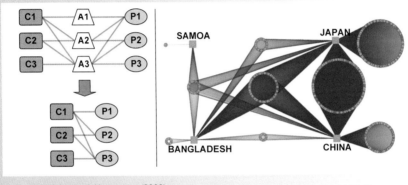

Source: ESCAP, based on Hidalgo and Hausmann (2009).

Box 4.3. Use of trade data to assess productive capacities

To estimate the products that a country can produce, this chapter uses trade data from the United Nations Commodity Trade Statistics Database (COMTRADE),[9] disaggregated at the five-digit level using the Standard International Trade Classification (SITC), Rev. 2, which makes it possible to differentiate products that are otherwise very similar. For example, one can differentiate women's dresses based on their fabric, such as cotton or man-made fibre.

If a country exports a certain product, it is assumed that the country has the capabilities required to produce it. Exports may not, however, fully reflect diversification since some of the production may only be for local consumption. This chapter, however, uses the composition of exports as a proxy for the country's production and uses the terms "exports", "products" and "goods" interchangeably.

One issue to take into account is that, for a given product, one country seldom produces all the constituent parts. Indeed, many developing countries export, with minor value added, products that they have just imported. The analysis in this chapter, however, is able to differentiate between two cases, as can be illustrated by the production of computers. In the first case, a developing country may import from a developed country the microprocessors needed to assemble computers. The analysis considers that the capacities required to produce computers are different from those required to produce microprocessors. The fact that developing countries import sophisticated parts and components of products does not, therefore, increase their productive capacity. A second issue is the degree of sophistication, even of the same product. When developed and developing countries export the same product to the same country, the higher-income country will systematically export one with a higher unit price. In the analysis, we consider computers, for example, of different prices as different products. Hence, the productive capacities available in these countries for these products are inherently different.

Source: ESCAP.

value added versions of the same good: firms can, for example, sell a product at a higher price by incorporating different designs, developing new brands or exploring new ways of marketing. Diversification may also involve producing a wider range of products. Thus, Bangladesh or Cambodia, for example, could diversify to produce more expensive garments or they could diversify into the manufacture of the relevant machinery and other related products.

Diversification leads to increases in total output, as illustrated in figure 4.1, which shows that the countries that export the greatest number of categories of products and those which have more products at different prices within those categories tend to have higher levels of GDP. The patterns of GDP increase differ, though. For diversification towards a wider range of products, the increase tails off at higher levels of GDP – in the figure that happens near the GDP value for Malaysia. This

Figure 4.1.   Diversification and GDP, 2009

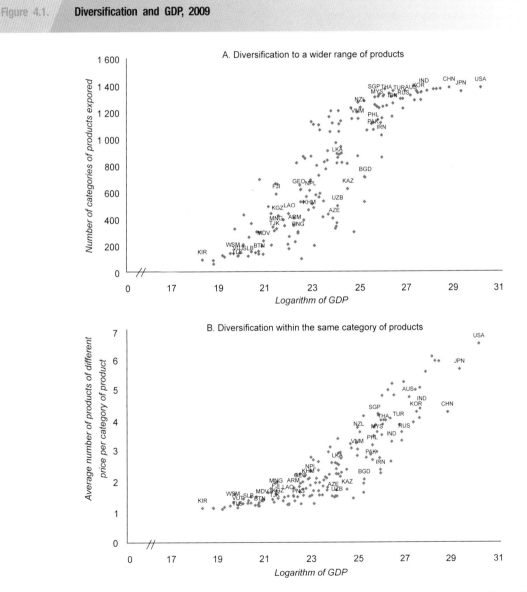

Source: ESCAP, based on data from the World Bank, World Development Indicators Database and the United Nations Commodity Trade Statistics Database (COMTRADE). Available from http://comtrade.un.org/db/default.aspx (accessed November 2010).

Notes: Products are classified using five-digit SITC, Rev. 2 classifications. Products under the same five-digit classification are further differentiated based on their unit value. See Freire (2011) for details. The three-letter codes used in the figure to represent country names are the alpha-3 country codes published in International Organization for Standardization (2006).

observation is consistent with other studies that have used disaggregated export data.[10] For diversification into different varieties of similar goods, however, the increase does not seem to reach an upper limit.

These results suggest that richer countries continue to diversify. Japanese garment firms, for example, diversified into medium- and high-unit-value products beginning in the 1980s. Jane Jacobs noted in 1969 the emergence of the differentiated production of garments, based on much smaller production runs: "This method produces relatively modest amounts of each item as compared with mass production, yet it is not craft manufacturing either.... Thanks to this... kind of garment making, one can look at a crowd of thousands of persons in a large city park... and be hard put to find two women or two children dressed in identical outfits." The richer countries have steadily adopted this differentiated production leaving most of the mass production to poorer nations.[11]

Diversifications within and between categories of products are not mutually exclusive. On the contrary, they occur simultaneously, as illustrated in figure 4.2,

which shows that the countries that produce the larger range of products are also those that produce the larger variety within each category. As the number of product categories rises, however, (for example, to over 1,200 in 2009), the dominant form of diversification is the expansion of production of different varieties within the same category. Given that the two processes are interlinked, the analysis in this chapter will therefore consider diversification to be the sum of the two—both the number of different categories and, within these, the products at different unit values.

Making exports more exclusive

As economies diversify, they tend to export products that are exported by fewer other countries. This will generally mean more exclusive manufactured goods as opposed to more common exports, such as vegetable oils, fish, textiles, garments or mining products. This is illustrated in figure 4.3. Each country's position on this chart is determined by both the number of products it exports and their exclusiveness, as indicated by the number of other countries exporting a similar product mix.

| Figure 4.2. | Simultaneous diversification within and across product categories, 2009 |

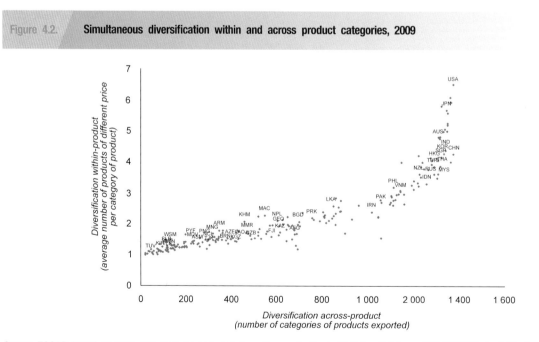

Source: ESCAP, based on trade data from the United Nations Commodity Trade Statistics Database (COMTRADE). Available from http://comtrade.un.org/db/default.aspx (accessed November 2010).

Notes: Products are originally classified using five-digit SITC, Rev. 2 classifications. Products under the same five-digit classification are further differentiated based on their unit value. See Freire (2011) for details. The three-letter codes used in the figure to represent country names are the alpha-3 country codes published in International Organization for Standardization (2006).

Figure 4.3.   **As countries diversify, they produce more exclusive products**

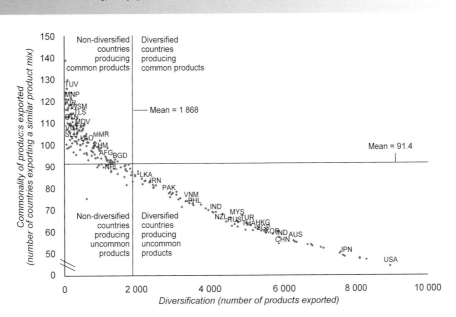

Source: ESCAP, based on trade data from the United Nations Commodity Trade Statistics Database (COMTRADE). Available from http://comtrade. un.org/db/default.aspx (accessed November 2010).

Notes: Products are originally classified using five-digit SITC, Rev. 2 classifications. Products under the same five-digit classification are further differentiated based on their unit value. See Freire (2011) for details. The three-letter codes used in the figure to represent country names are the alpha-3 country codes published in International Organization for Standardization (2006).

Countries that fall in the top left quadrant are the least diversified. This is typical of small island economies in the Pacific. Tuvalu, for example, exported only 75 different types of products in 2009 and was in competition with 126 other economies that exported products of that same export mix. Very different, and diagonally opposite, is the United States, which exported almost 9,000 types of products, which are also less common, being exported, on average, by only 44 other economies. This suggests that, as they diversify, countries do not select new goods at random but rather choose those that are likely to be more exclusive.

Table 4.2 lists countries in the Asia-Pacific region that fall in each quadrant. The countries with more diversified production and more exclusive product mixes are Japan, Australia, China and India, with Japan being the most diversified. In general, the least developed countries are less diversified and produce fairly standard goods. One exception is Nepal: although not yet diversified, it has an above-average

exclusive mix, including medium-priced textile yarn, floor coverings, and apparel and clothing accessories. Similarly, the Democratic People's Republic of Korea and Kazakhstan are not very diversified but they nevertheless have less common products, such as electrical machinery, base metal manufactured goods, and artificial resins and plastics.

All of the Pacific island developing economies are less diversified and tend to produce common goods. The least diversified is Palau, which exported 64 products in 2009 with a mix that is exported by 126 economies, while the most diversified is Fiji, which exported 922 products. Most countries in North and Central Asia also produce relatively common products.

Figure 4.4 highlights the situation of the least developed countries. Here again, the Pacific island countries are in the weakest position. To some extent, this is a result of their small size. Bangladesh, on the other hand, with the largest population, can

Table 4.2.	Economies classified by the diversity of their product mix

Subregion	Economy
Diversified economies producing uncommon products	
ENEA	China; Hong Kong, China; Japan; Republic of Korea
NCA	Russian Federation
PAC	Australia, New Zealand
SEA	Indonesia, Malaysia, Philippines, Singapore, Thailand, Viet Nam
SSWA	India, Iran (Islamic Republic of), Pakistan, Sri Lanka, Turkey
Non-diversified economies producing uncommon products	
ENEA	Democratic People's Republic of Korea
NCA	Kazakhstan
SSWA	Nepal
Non-diversified economies producing common products	
ENEA	Macao, China; Mongolia
NCA	Armenia, Azerbaijan, Georgia, Kyrgyzstan, Tajikistan, Turkmenistan, Uzbekistan
PAC	American Samoa, Cook Islands, Fiji, French Polynesia, Guam, Kiribati, Marshall Islands, Micronesia (Federated States of), Nauru, New Caledonia, Niue, Northern Mariana Islands, Palau, Papua New Guinea, Samoa, Solomon Islands, Tonga, Tuvalu, Vanuatu
SEA	Brunei Darussalam, Cambodia, Lao People's Democratic Republic, Myanmar, Timor-Leste
SSWA	Bangladesh, Bhutan, Maldives

Source: ESCAP, based on trade data from the United Nations Commodity Trade Statistics Database (COMTRADE). Available from http://comtrade.un.org/db/default.aspx (accessed November 2010).

Note: Subregional groupings are as follows: ENEA, East and North-East Asia; NCA, North and Central Asia; PAC, Pacific; SEA, South-East Asia; SSWA, South and South-West Asia.

Figure 4.4.	Diversification in the least developed countries

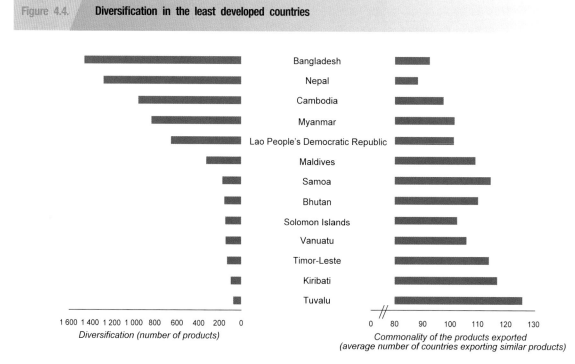

Source: ESCAP, based on trade data from the United Nations Commodity Trade Statistics Database (COMTRADE). Available from http://comtrade.un.org/db/default.aspx (accessed November 2010).

support more diversified production. Overall, a 1.0% increase in population is associated with a 0.3% increase in diversification. This association is statistically significant and explains over 30% of the intercountry variation in diversification. Countries with small populations therefore face an inherent disadvantage in their process of diversification.

Countries wishing to diversify can anticipate competition, since most other countries are aiming to move in a similar direction. Figure 4.5 tracks global progress in diversification. Between 1984 and 2009, average diversification rose from 968 to 1,868 products. The product mix, however, was becoming more standard: for the average country, the number of countries exporting a similar product mix increased from 41 to 91. Given this global trend, countries that do not diversify are likely to fall behind.

Mapping diversification

In order to diversify, firms in poorer countries will need to choose the most appropriate new products.

The easiest will be those for which the required capabilities are similar to those already available. Moving from women's dresses to undergarments, for example, would be quicker than moving to the production of women's shoes, which would not only entail working with new materials, such as leather, plastic, rubber, wood, jute or metal, but also have different environmental and health requirements. New products may need different capabilities, such as machinery or skills, as well as better infrastructure, marketing strategies, standards and regulations.

When considering the most appropriate diversification path, it is therefore useful to get a sense of how products are related. This might be done by analysing the package of resources and skills used for their production, but it is also possible to do so more empirically by observing the positions that the country occupies on the "product space map".[12] Using international export data, it is possible to create a global product space map (see figure 4.6).[13]

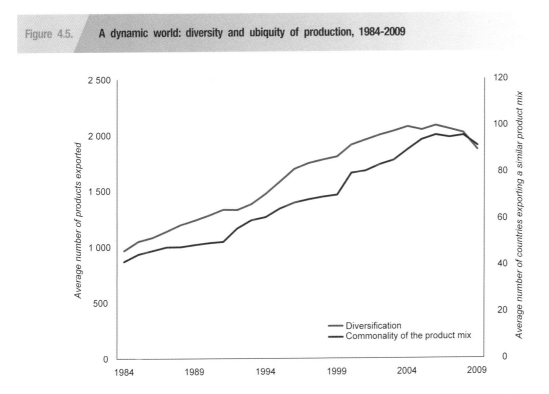

Figure 4.5.   A dynamic world: diversity and ubiquity of production, 1984-2009

— Diversification
— Commonality of the product mix

Source: ESCAP, based on trade data from the United Nations Commodity Trade Statistics Database (COMTRADE). Available from http://comtrade.un.org/db/default.aspx (accessed November 2010).

Figure 4.6. **The global product space map**

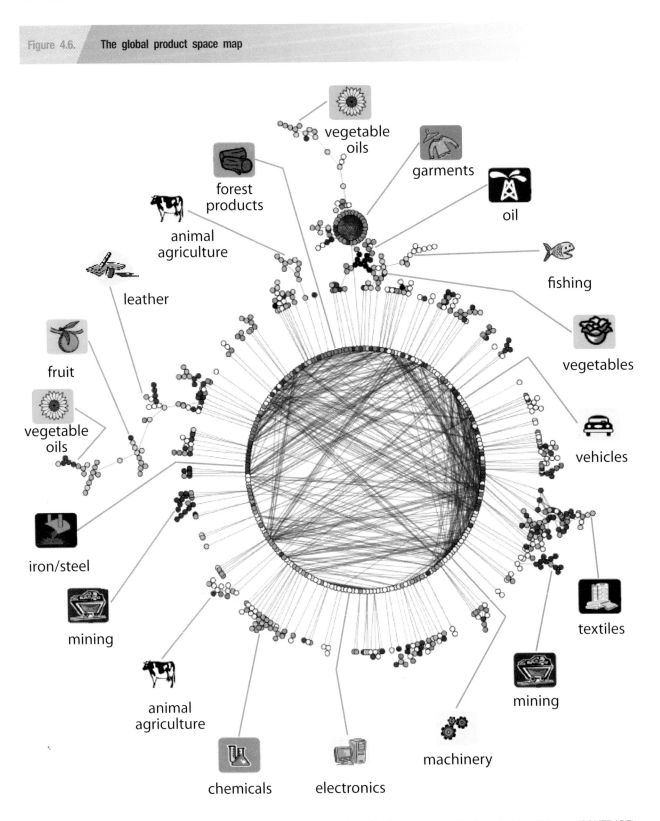

Source: ESCAP, based on Hidalgo and others (2007) and on trade data from the United Nations Commodity Trade Statistics Database (COMTRADE). Available from http://comtrade.un.org/db/default.aspx (accessed November 2010).

Notes: This map indicates clusters and the links between the clusters. The overall shapes they form are arbitrary. For clarity, however, most products are aligned around circles.

In this map, each small circle represents a single product and is coloured according to the broad industry with which it is usually associated. These products are then clustered according to the likelihood that they are part of the same export mix. The grey lines to icons around the edge of the map also indicate the broad industry of clusters. The lines linking the products indicate associations, based on the probability that the export of one is accompanied by the export of the other.

The large circle at the centre of the map represents the core of the space where many products—largely manufactured goods, machinery and transport equipment—are linked by a dense network of lines. Further out, around the periphery, are clusters of less connected products, including some traditional industries of developing countries, such as garments, fish, fruit, vegetable oils and textiles. Of these more peripheral clusters, the largest is that of garments, for which the products, arranged in a circle in the

upper middle of the space, are so closely connected that the lines fill the circle solidly with blue.

One surprising characteristic of the product space map is that goods produced by the same industry can be far apart. For example, the map has two clusters of products under the vegetable oils industry. In addition to the main one at the top, which is linked with garment production, there is another in the middle right, which is associated with the production of fruit.

Each country can consider this product space when assessing the most appropriate opportunities for diversification. If its main products are in the core, it should have the capability to produce many others. If its products are on the periphery, the immediate options are probably more limited, and diversification will require more new capabilities.

It is also possible to use the map to track each country's diversification history, as illustrated in figure 4.7

Figure 4.7.   Cambodia's occupation of the product space map

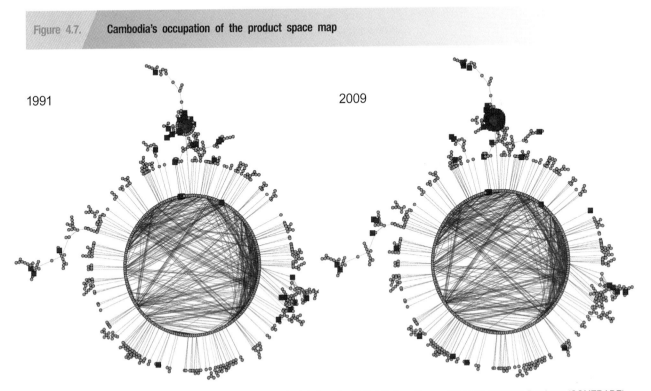

1991

2009

Source: ESCAP, based on Hidalgo and others (2007) and on trade data from the United Nations Commodity Trade Statistics Database (COMTRADE). Available from http://comtrade.un.org/db/default.aspx (accessed November 2010).

Notes: Small circles represent a single product in the product space, which is independent of the country. Red squares represent the effective products of the country depicted in the figure.

for Cambodia in 1991 and 2009. Its "effective products"—those for which the share in national exports is higher than the share in world exports—are highlighted on the map with red squares. In 1991, almost all of Cambodia's effective products were on the periphery: one in the vegetable oils cluster at the top of the map; a few others in the garment, fishing, textiles and mining clusters on the right; and still others in the animal agriculture, fruit and vegetable oils clusters on the left. The only ones at the core were forest products. By 2009, however, Cambodia was exporting almost all the products in the garment cluster. Figure 4.7 shows how Cambodia has steadily occupied

the product space. Some of the notable changes in the product space of other least developed countries during the same period are presented in table 4.3.[14]

The product space presented in figure 4.6 focuses attention on the supply side. When firms are investing in new production, however, they also need to consider potential demand. United Nations Conference on Trade and Development (UNCTAD) has found, for example, that if demand is taken into account, the opportunities for diversification can be greater in commodities than in certain labour-intensive manufacturing industries.[15]

Table 4.3.	Changes in occupation of the product space for least developed countries, 1991-2009
Bangladesh	Exports remain highly concentrated in the garment, fishing and textile clusters. Little diversification towards the core products (see box 4.4).
Bhutan	Less diversified in 2009 than in 1991. Forest products in the core.
Cambodia	Diversification in the garment cluster, which is almost totally occupied in 2009, and to some extent in the textile cluster. No move towards products at the core.
Kiribati	Some diversification in textiles and fishing clusters by 2009. No move towards products at the core.
Lao People's Democratic Republic	Diversification in the garment cluster, which is almost totally occupied in 2009, in vegetable oils, and to some extent in mining and textiles. Reduction of the number of forest products at the core.
Maldives	Concentration in the fishing cluster and reduction of products in the garment cluster. Few new machinery products at the core were exported in 2009.
Myanmar	Diversification in the garment cluster, which is almost totally occupied in 2009, and in the fishing and, to some extent, mining clusters. Few new forest products at the core.
Nepal	Diversification in the periphery and towards the core. Sectors that have diversified are the garment cluster and textiles, which are almost totally occupied by 2009. Most products at the core in 2009 were related to textiles, machinery, iron, paper and forest products.
Samoa	Diversification towards the core. Moved into the textiles cluster and away from the garment cluster. No changes in diversification in the fishing and vegetable oil clusters. Products at the core in 2009 are in the iron, vehicles and machinery industries.
Solomon Islands	Exports remain concentrated in the vegetable oil and fishing clusters in the periphery, with a few forest products at the core. No further move towards core products.
Timor-Leste	Some diversification in the textile cluster and machinery products.
Tuvalu	Some diversification in textiles, mining, and chemicals in the periphery and forest products in the core.
Vanuatu	Further diversification in the fishing cluster and some diversification in textiles, mining and vegetable oils in the periphery.

Source: ESCAP, based on trade data from the United Nations Commodity Trade Statistics Database (COMTRADE). Available from http://comtrade.un.org/db/default.aspx (accessed November 2010).

Box 4.4. Ready-made garments business in Bangladesh

Since the late-1980s, Bangladesh has focused on ready-made garment manufacturing, which has created numerous market opportunities for small, export-oriented enterprises. The industry is highly labour-intensive and employs approximately 2 million workers, 90% of whom are women. The industry imports most of its raw materials, since domestic cotton production is very limited. It exports primarily to the United States and European Union markets. Bangladesh benefited from the abolition of the Multifibre Arrangement. The Government responded proactively and established close ties with China, which included direct air connections and road links through Myanmar.

Most garment companies are located in export processing zones, which account for three quarters of Bangladesh's foreign direct investment in manufacturing. The main foreign investors are China, India, Japan, Malaysia, the Republic of Korea, the United Kingdom and the United States. The most important zone of this type, established in 1993, is the Dhaka Export Processing Zone. Bangladesh's garment production remains highly competitive on the garment market, focusing on labour-intensive, low-value garments based on lower labour costs than in China or India. Domestic firms, however, have little capacity for innovation: lacking design capacity, most simply assemble products according to buyers' specifications.

Source: United Nations Industrial Development Organization, "Bangladesh: sustainable exports of ready-made garments in a new competitive environment", n.d. Available from www.unido.org/index.php?id=953.

The demand situation is analogous to mountain climbing, where products are equivalent to mountains; the higher the mountain, the higher the demand. If one domestic firm starts climbing a mountain that represents a high-demand product, others will follow. This concept is illustrated in figure 4.8. Initially, firms are producing product A but are looking to branch out to a closely-related product that offers an easy path for diversification. Suppose that the most closely-related product is

B. Unfortunately, this mountain is smaller, so it offers fewer incentives. Mountain C is higher, and thus more attractive, but firms cannot jump directly to C because it is too far away—the product requires too many new capabilities. One solution, elaborated in the final section of this chapter, is for the State and the private sector to jointly identify the required supportive policies, incentive structures and institutional arrangements required to travel the distance from A to C.

Figure 4.8.   Demand side of the product space

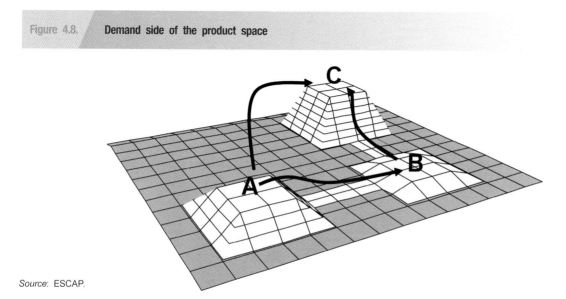

Source: ESCAP.

Assessing productive capacity

If a country is to consider how best to diversify, it will need to assess its current productive capacity. For this purpose, it might consider, for example, current levels of technology, education and skills, along with policies, regulations and infrastructure, as well as how all of these things are related. This is a daunting task.

As previous sections have indicated, however, an alternative is to focus not on the possible components of the productive capacity but on its result—the actual production. The assumption is that the fewest capabilities will be found in the countries that are the least diversified and whose product mixes are similar to those of many other countries. This information on diversification can be combined with other measures to arrive at a composite "productive capacity index".[16]

Figure 4.9.   **Productive capacities, compared with the global mean, 2009**

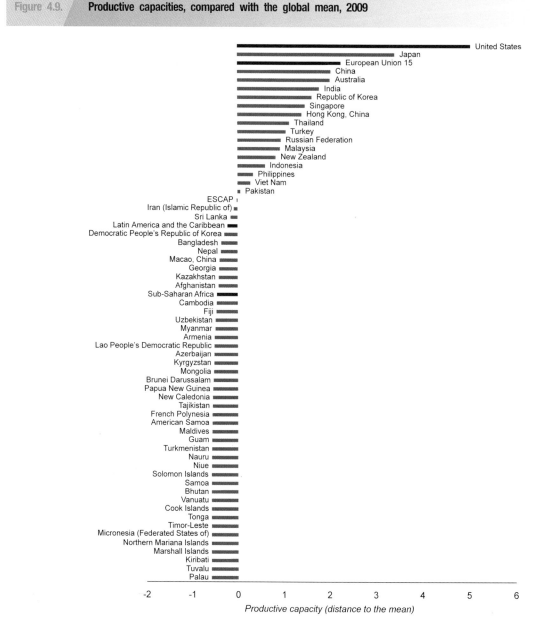

Productive capacity (distance to the mean)

Source: ESCAP, based on trade data from the United Nations Commodity Trade Statistics Database (COMTRADE). Available from http://comtrade. un.org/db/default.aspx (accessed November 2010).

Notes: The unit of measurement is the standard deviation of the distribution of productive capacities. See Freire (2011) for details.

The results for countries of Asia and the Pacific are indicated in figure 4.9, in which each country is compared with the global mean. It shows that most countries in the region are below the global average, and by a similar amount (about half a standard deviation).

Developing countries should aim for a productive capacity that will allow them to reach a GDP per capita similar to that of developed countries

---

Other things being equal, the greatest production capacities, which lead to higher total GDPs, are found in countries with larger populations. This will not necessarily translate into higher standards of living, however, since what matters most is GDP per capita. Singapore, for example, has a lower productive capacity than the United States, but it has a similar GDP per capita, and it also has a comparable standard of living. Developing countries do not, therefore, need to aim for a productive capacity that is above average but rather for one that will allow them to reach a GDP per capita similar to that of developed countries.

Some of the region's larger economies have been moving in this direction, as is depicted for the period 1991-2009 in figure 4.10, which shows that, relative to the global mean, capacities in China and India have been rising while those in the United States and the European Union have remained fairly flat, and those in Japan have been falling. Figure 4.11 shows the corresponding picture for Asia-Pacific subregions. It indicates a slow increase in South-East Asia, mostly in the 1990s, but little change in North and Central Asia and in East and North-East Asia. The situation in the Pacific is disturbing since this subregion has experienced a fall, even though its average level will have been boosted by the rising capacities of Australia and New Zealand.

This information is confirmed in figure 4.12, which shows the pattern in the Asia-Pacific least developed countries. Bangladesh and Nepal have held their positions, while all of the other countries, despite recent rises, have generally lost ground. It is worth noting that this is not because they have lost productive capacity but because they have progressed more slowly than other economies.

Figure 4.10.   **Evolution of average productive capacity, 1991-2009, selected countries**

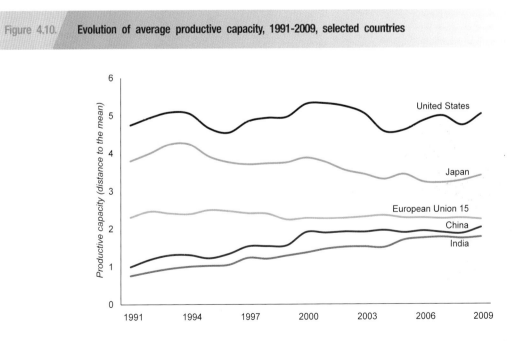

Source: ESCAP, based on trade data from the United Nations Commodity Trade Statistics Database (COMTRADE). Available from http://comtrade.un.org/db/default.aspx (accessed November 2010).

Notes: The unit of measurement is the standard deviation of the distribution of productive capacities. See Freire (2011) for details.

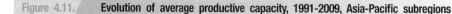

Figure 4.11. Evolution of average productive capacity, 1991-2009, Asia-Pacific subregions

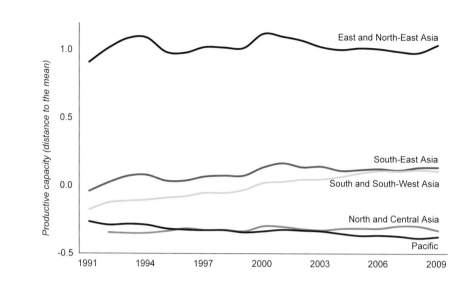

Source: ESCAP, based on trade data from the United Nations Commodity Trade Statistics Database (COMTRADE). Available from http://comtrade.un.org/db/default.aspx (accessed November 2010).

Notes: The unit of measurement is the standard deviation of the distribution of productive capacities. See Freire (2011) for details.

Figure 4.12. Evolution of average productive capacity, 1991-2009, Asia-Pacific least developed countries

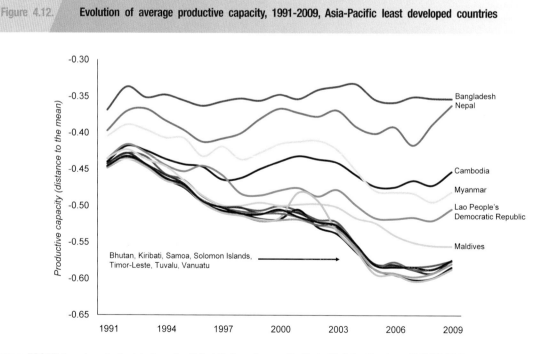

Source: ESCAP, based on trade data from the United Nations Commodity Trade Statistics Database (COMTRADE). Available from http://comtrade.un.org/db/default.aspx (accessed November 2010).

Notes: The unit of measurement is the standard deviation of the distribution of productive capacities. See Freire (2011) for details.

Learning from the transformers of productive capacity

Valuable lessons can be learned from the more successful countries that have transformed themselves while starting from productive capacity levels similar to those of the Asia-Pacific least developed countries. Only four countries have done so. Estonia, Latvia, Lithuania and Viet Nam. Having started far behind, they were able to raise their productive capacity to above the world average (see figure 4.13).

Particularly instructive is the experience of Viet Nam, where diversification took off from 1987 with the shift to free-market reforms known as Dổi Mới (renovation). In 1985, Viet Nam exported only 15 more product categories than in the previous year, but from 1987 to 1990 the annual average increase rose to 34, and during the period 1991-1997, the average number of additional product categories exported annually had reached 77. From 1984 to 2009, the number of product categories exported

increased ninefold: from 125 to 1,143. Since then, the pace has slowed and, particularly in terms of within-product differentiation, it has flattened out (see figure 4.14). Viet Nam has not only diversified, it has also achieved a more exclusive product mix that requires a larger set of capabilities for production and marketing (see box 4.5).

Viet Nam's progress can also be assessed by considering its occupation of the product space map over time (see figure 4.15). In 1984, Viet Nam had only a few effective products, mainly in the vegetable oil, fruit, fishing, textile and mining industries. By 1990, however, it had made inroads into the garment cluster, and by 1995, it had fully occupied the cluster. Since 1990, Viet Nam has also consolidated its position in textiles and fishing. At the same time, it has occupied more of the core of the product space, mainly through manufacturing related to electronics, textiles and forest products, although this was a gradual process, with new products linked to existing ones.

| Figure 4.13. | Evolution of productive capacity: Asia-Pacific least developed countries and successful countries starting at similar levels, 1984-2009 |

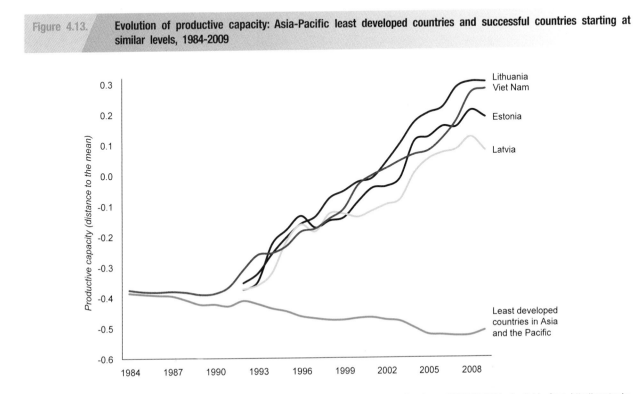

Source: ESCAP, based on trade data from the United Nations Commodity Trade Statistics Database (COMTRADE). Available from http://comtrade.un.org/db/default.aspx (accessed November 2010).

Box 4.5. Complexity of Viet Nam's product mix, 1984-2009

Product complexity can be assessed by analysing how diversified the countries that export a product are and how common the other products that they export are. Products that are exported by diversified countries that export an exclusive product mix are considered to be more complex than products that are exported by less diversified countries that export broadly common products. The figure below shows how the complexity of the product mix exported by Viet Nam has changed over time, shifting to the right towards more complex products.

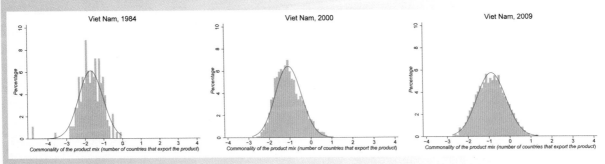

Source: ESCAP, based on trade data from the United Nations Commodity Trade Statistics Database (COMTRADE). Available from http://comtrade.un.org/db/default.aspx (accessed November 2010).

Note: Graphs are normalized so that products with average complexity are in the middle (measured as zero complexity) and the standard deviation from the average is one. See Freire (2011) for details on the calculation of product complexity.

These charts also indicate that there have been no big jumps in product complexity. New products of higher complexity are only slightly more complex than the products that were previously the most complex. The transformations have thus been based not on sudden jumps but on steady increments.

| Figure 4.14. | Evolution of Viet Nam's product diversification, 1984-2009 |

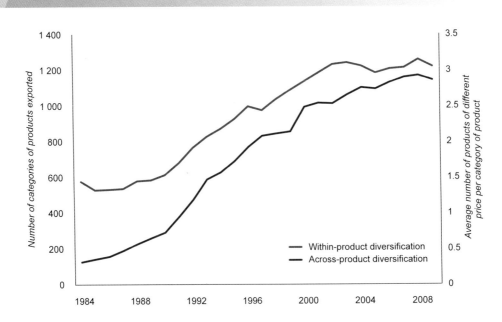

Source: ESCAP, based on trade data from the United Nations Commodity Trade Statistics Database (COMTRADE). Available from http://comtrade.un.org/db/default.aspx (accessed November 2010).

Figure 4.15.	Evolution of Viet Nam's occupation of the product space

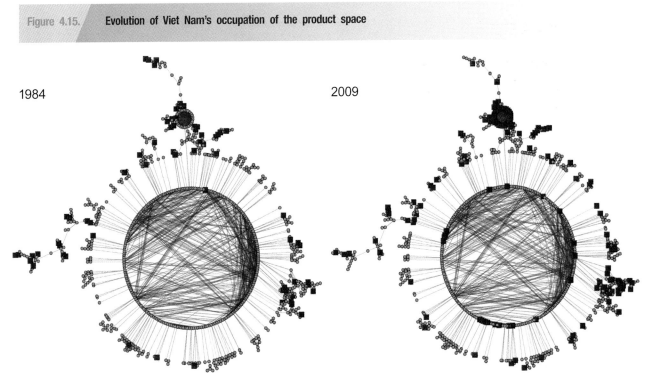

1984

2009

Source: ESCAP, based on Hidalgo and others (2007) and on trade data from the United Nations Commodity Trade Statistics Database (COMTRADE). Available from http://comtrade.un.org/db/default.aspx (accessed November 2010).

Notes: Small circles represent a single product in the product space, which is independent of the country. Red squares represent the effective products of the country depicted in the figure.

Graduating from least developed country status

Can Asia-Pacific least developed countries make similar progress? How can Tuvalu, for example, with a population of around 10,000, sufficiently increase its productive capacity and produce a wider range of goods and services? The prospect is not as daunting as it might seem since countries with small populations do not have to increase productive capacity as much as Viet Nam to boost their GDP per capita above the threshold required to graduate from least developed country status.

Table 4.4 presents estimates of the increase in the number of products that the less populated least developed countries would need in order to graduate. For example, Bhutan exported 158 products in 2009, and to graduate from least developed country status, it would need to increase that number to 260. This

is a sizeable increase, but by no means impossible; this total number has already been reached by some other small developing economies, such as the Central African Republic, Grenada and Guam.

It should also be emphasized that small least developed countries can boost their per capita GDPs, and thus their prospects of graduation, through means other than expanding their productive capacities. They can, for example, exploit and expand tourism. In fact, the only two countries that have graduated so far—Botswana and Cape Verde—have taken different paths, as indicated in figure 4.16. Botswana does have a higher productive capacity, mainly due to diversification within the mining industry, but Cape Verde has had a capacity trajectory similar to that of less populated countries in Asia and the Pacific. It was able to graduate largely by boosting tourism, from less than 6% in 1995 to 28% of its GDP in 2008. Analysis suggests that, after controlling for

Table 4.4. **Diversification required to graduate from least developed country status, 2009**

Country	Current number of products	Number of products required	Percentage increase require	Countries with diversification similar to the desired level
Bhutan	158	260	64	Central African Republic, Grenada, Guam
Kiribati	99	210	112	Rwanda, Somalia
Solomon Islands	149	330	121	Bermuda, Maldives
Timor-Leste	133	470	253	Guyana, Suriname, Togo
Tuvalu	75	100	33	Montserrat, Northern Mariana Islands
Vanuatu	146	220	50	Eritrea, Nauru, Turks and Caicos Islands

Source: ESCAP, based on trade data from the United Nations Commodity Trade Statistics Database (COMTRADE). Available from http://comtrade.un.org/db/default.aspx (accessed November 2010).

Figure 4.16. **Evolution of productive capacity: Asia-Pacific least developed countries and other graduating countries, 1984-2009**

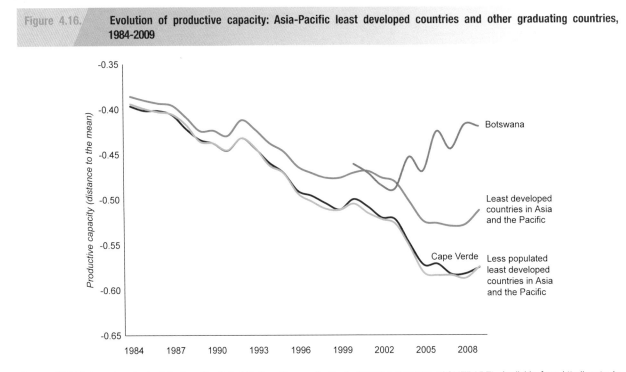

Source: ESCAP, based on trade data from the United Nations Commodity Trade Statistics Database (COMTRADE). Available from http://comtrade.un.org/db/default.aspx (accessed November 2010).

population size and the level of productive capacity, a 1.00% increase in tourism revenue increases the total output of a country by around 0.25%. The two Asia-Pacific countries already recommended for graduation could follow a similar path. For Maldives, which graduated in January 2011, tourism contributes 50% of GDP. For Samoa, which is set to graduate in 2014, tourism represents 21% of GDP.

Tourism can and does promote development in less populated countries. It is self-evident, however, that such activity has inherent limits. In the long run, an increase in productive capacity and the associated increase in diversification through the production of more complex goods is the most viable way to attain sustainable development in all countries, regardless of their size. For less populated least developed countries to reduce their economic vulnerability and promote sustainable development, they ultimately have to steer their development towards enhancement of their production capabilities.

The benefits of regional integration

Chapter 3 indicated how countries in Asia and the Pacific can facilitate the movement of goods, services, people and finances across the region and overcome market constraints through greater regional integration. How could such integration also help least developed countries increase their productive capacity?

Over the past two decades, as globalization has intensified, the region has been redirecting its output to the rest of the world, as illustrated in figure 4.17. Between 1985 and 2008, the productive capacity that the region directed exclusively to itself fell from 40% to 14%, while that used to service exports both within and beyond the region rose from 22% to 48%. This suggests that countries initially produce for the region and later direct these products to global markets.

Trade within the Asia-Pacific region can serve as a training ground for economies to increase their productive capacities

Does the outside market promote an increase in productive capacities or is the regional market a better training ground for firms to upgrade their production? To try to answer this question, this chapter assesses the level of complexity of new exports directed to economies both inside and outside the region. New products are defined here as products that were not exported in the previous two years, and products are considered more complex if they are commonly exported by more diversified countries producing more exclusive goods.

For the majority of the economies in the region, the new products directed to the regional market are more complex than the new products directed to the outside market. This is illustrated in figure 4.18, which shows the list of Asia-Pacific countries for which 2009 trade data are available ordered by the difference between the average product complexity of

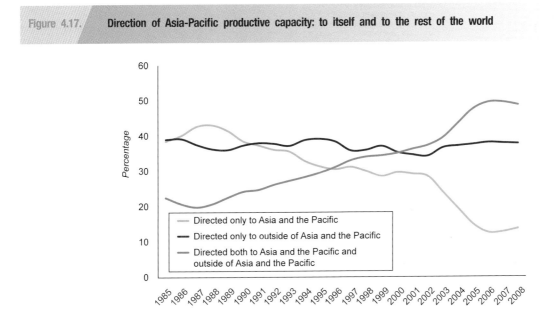

Figure 4.17.   **Direction of Asia-Pacific productive capacity: to itself and to the rest of the world**

Source: ESCAP, based on trade data from the United Nations Commodity Trade Statistics Database (COMTRADE). Available from http://comtrade.un.org/db/default.aspx (accessed November 2010).

Figure 4.18. **Trade within Asia and the Pacific is a training ground for increasing productive capacity**

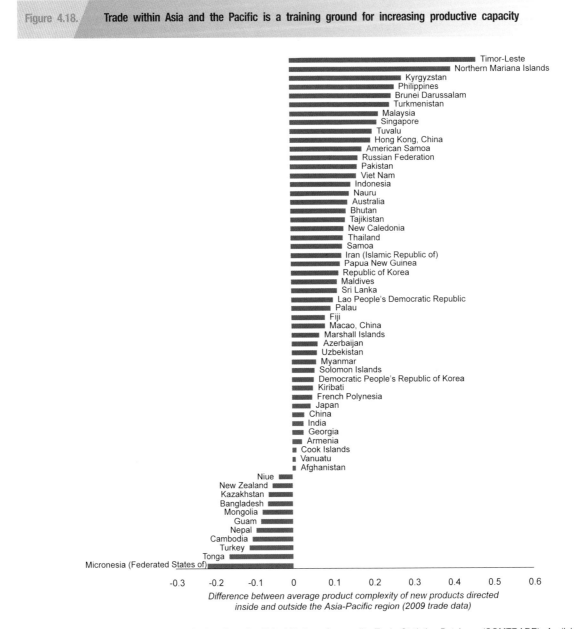

Difference between average product complexity of new products directed
inside and outside the Asia-Pacific region (2009 trade data)

Source: ESCAP secretariat based on trade data from the United Nations Commodity Trade Statistics Database (COMTRADE). Available from http://comtrade.un.org/db/default.aspx (accessed November 2010).

Note: The unit of measurement is the standard deviation of the distribution of product complexity.

new exports directed inside and outside the region, with positive values for this difference represented by positive values on the horizontal axis (right side). The fact that there are more positive values than negative values reflects the fact that the new products directed to the regional market are more complex than the new products directed to the outside market for the majority of the economies in the region. This, in turn, suggests that trade within the Asia-Pacific region can serve as a training ground for economies to increase their productive capacities, thereby facilitating the production of more complex goods.

In summary, although the outside market is undoubtedly very important for the sustainability of current levels of productive capacity of the economies in the region, the intraregional market is the one that generally provides the opportunities for product upgrades that lead to the production of more complex products. Therefore, regional integration that facilitates intraregional trade has the potential to increase the productive capacities of the economies in the region.

Strategy for increasing the productive capacities of least developed countries

The discussions in the previous sections suggest that the increase in productive capacities is not a matter of the efficient exploitation of the existing comparative advantages. It requires the exploration of new economic activities and a strategic sense of direction towards building up the capabilities to produce goods that are more exclusive and only produced by countries that are more diversified.

Least developed countries, however, are constrained by several structural factors, such as small market size, along with other handicaps, such as their status as landlocked countries or small islands, a high degree of vulnerability to natural disasters and the effects of climate change, a poor base of domestic savings and entrepreneurship, skills and technological capability and infrastructure, and the lack of well-developed capital markets and financial and other institutions that foster industrialization. Least developed countries were at the tail end of the ESCAP infrastructure index, which captured a composite measure of infrastructure development as summarized in figure 3.19.[17] Their process of industrialization has also been adversely affected in a number of cases by the reduction in policy space resulting from the policies adopted under the structural adjustment programmes pursued since the mid-1980s by the international financial institutions, which focused on liberalization and privatization as a part of the Washington Consensus. Premature liberalization of trade and investment regimes exposed relatively fragile fledgling industries to international competition, leading to their sickness and the closure of whatever capabilities had been built up while FDI inflows that were expected to assist in building productive capacities failed to turn up.

Productive capacities can be generated as part of the process of strategic diversification through the combined efforts of the State and the private sector with a supportive role played by development partners

This section discusses some elements of a strategy that countries with special needs, in particular the least developed countries, should consider to increase their productive capacities. In the past, the mainstream approach to expanding productive capacity has been to try to identify and strengthen some contributing factors, such as levels of human capital and the quality of infrastructure, along with good governance and the rule of law. The development experience of industrialized and newly industrializing countries, however, has demonstrated the critical role played by strong and active intervention by the "development State" in fostering their industrialization and building up productive capacities in the early stages.[18] Such a State would adopt macroeconomic policies oriented towards growth, investment and employment, while also creating fiscal space for the delivery of key services and long-term public investment in infrastructure, agriculture and human skills. It would also have a proactive industrial policy that would involve selective investment financing, along with a strategic trade policy to promote diversification and value addition. At the same time, it would encourage innovation and entrepreneurship. The State would also need to encourage local demand in order to encourage the further development of productive capacities and thus drive a virtuous circle.

The analysis presented in the previous sections suggests that economies build their productive capacities through a path-dependent diversification process that expands their production bases by including products that are increasingly more complex, thus facilitating even further diversification in the future. The idea is to let the productive capacities be generated or acquired as a part of the process of such strategic diversification through the combined efforts of the State and the private sector with a supportive role played by development partners.

The strategy for increasing the productive capacities comprises three main processes for discovering, acquiring and spreading the productive capacities required for developing economies to catch up

---

Such a strategy is related to models in which new capabilities emerge as combinations of previous capabilities through an evolutionary process.[19] The evolutionary strategy comprises three main processes that, when set in motion, can act as an algorithm for discovering, acquiring and spreading the productive capacities required for developing economies to catch up to more developed economies.

The first process is differentiation through strategic product innovation—the identification and production of products that are new to the firms or farms in the economy and that are more complex and facilitate further diversification. The second process is the selection of the business models of those firms and farms that were successful in the differentiation process. Here, the qualifier "successful" implies a judge and criteria for judgement. Invariably, the best judge is the market and the ultimate criterion is the demand for the products. The third process is the amplification of the successful business models and the exploitation of the new market. It is important to the strategy that these processes be repeated continuously (see figure 4.19).

The objective of the strategy is not to outsmart the evolutionary process of the economy, but to better understand how it happens and to harness its power to benefit the least developed countries.

Differentiation

During the differentiation process, possible new activities that could be added to the economy are

Figure 4.19. An evolutionary strategy: differentiation, selection and amplification

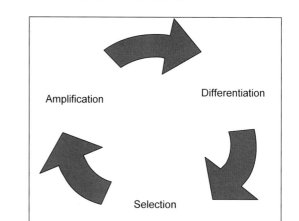

Source: ESCAP, based on Beinhocker (2007).

explored. This process is the same as product innovation—the production of new products—as opposed to process innovation, in which the use of new technologies (physical or managerial) is employed to increase the scale of the production of existing products. Such products are not necessarily new to the world and, in the context of developing countries, they rarely are. In fact, the discussion in the previous sections presented the stylized fact that countries develop by diversifying towards products that are produced by fewer and more diversified countries. That empirical regularity highlights an important element of the strategy that countries follow while developing: they emulate the countries that are more developed than they are. Emulation of the production of richer countries seems to be a constant characteristic of the process of catching up.[20]

The first process is differentiation through strategic product innovation

---

The State and the private sector should jointly identify a strategic direction for differentiation. Without a strategic direction, differentiation may lead to products that are less complex or to products that, although more complex, do not serve as an easy platform for further diversification in the future, in which case the short-term progress will be doomed to grind to a halt. Having a strategic direction helps to avoid this problem.

> *A pragmatic way to look for potential new products is by emulating the production pattern of countries that have higher productive capacities*

Each economy can estimate this potential for incremental innovation by comparing its existing output with that of other economies producing similar products. This suggests that each of the least developed countries in Asia and the Pacific could produce about 400 new products closely related to existing ones. Only around 10% to 15% of them, however, would be both more complex and better connected to other products, thereby helping the country move forward and position itself for future innovation (see table 4.5). It is therefore important to focus on those products which yield the highest social benefit.

A pragmatic way to look for potential new products is by emulating the production pattern of countries that have higher productive capacities, even if they do not have higher per capita GDPs. Bhutan, for example, might look to India, which has a lower per capita GDP but, thanks to its larger population, is producing a more diverse range of goods. Ideally, the country to be followed should not be too far ahead so that emulating it does not entail too great a leap.

> *The State and the private sector should jointly identify a strategic direction for differentiation*

New products need not be restricted to exportables; they should also replace some of the current imports of the country. Products that are imported, if they have levels of complexity similar to the products domestically produced, help domestic firms to discover new possibilities for the recombination of existing productive capacities; they show the frontier

Table 4.5.   **Potential new products related to those already produced by Asia-Pacific least developed countries**

Country	Total	Product that are more complex and better positioned for future diversification	
		Number	Percentage
Bangladesh	439	43	10
Bhutan	498	51	10
Cambodia	468	47	10
Kiribati	343	42	12
Lao People's Democratic Republic	493	74	15
Maldives	423	75	18
Myanmar	481	62	13
Nepal	514	58	11
Samoa	561	63	11
Solomon Islands	434	39	9
Timor-Leste	464	48	10
Tuvalu	340	35	10
Vanuatu	446	47	11

Source: ESCAP, based on trade data from the United Nations Commodity Trade Statistics Database (COMTRADE). Available from http://comtrade.un.org/db/default.aspx (accessed November 2010).

of possibilities available for the use of the productive capacities that they already have. That increases the chances for new combinations of the productive capacities, replacing some of the imports or creating new products altogether. Trade decreases the cost of discovering such possibilities.

In the process of strategically identifying potential new areas of differentiation, other factors should be taken into consideration, such as the potential for employment creation in the new economic activities and the ecological sustainability of the production process. It is important for the State to lead the process, to function as a catalyst that facilitates the interests of new businesses to overcome the expected resistance to change of traditional businesses.

The second process is the selection of the business models of those firms and farms that were successful in the differentiation process

---

After setting such a strategic direction for differentiation, the State should establish a process designed to find areas where policy actions are most likely to make a difference—a process whereby the State and the private sector jointly come up with the required supportive policies, incentive structure and institutional arrangements to ensure the flow of private investment in the identified niche.[21] The implementation of such strategic differentiation therefore requires the selective promotion of certain economic activities over others through the use of industrial policy. In this case, the policy would promote new economic activities/products that are more complex and allow for further diversification in the future, regardless of whether they are located within industry or manufacturing, per se. Such policies would be much more focused than most current policies, which provide incentives for any new investment regardless of its potential to spawn new economic activities.

Selection

As in any entrepreneurial venture, some of these new activities and business models will fail. For example, entrepreneurs may try to start the production of a new good for which there is not enough demand, or the costs of production may end up being higher than was planned and the resulting profits may therefore not justify the investment. Ideally, clear benchmarks for success should be set and the market is invariably in a better position than the State to establish them.

Perhaps the most pragmatic measure of success is progress in foreign markets, which was the measure used by East Asian countries during their industrialization process. In the case of import-substituting products, though, the State needs a sunset plan for the removal of protection. When the State provides supportive incentives to ensure private investment to new activities, as is the case with the industrial policies required for the differentiation process, corruption and rent-seeking can slow down the process of economic evolution or even bring it to a halt by allowing business failures to continue.

An important element of the selection process is choosing the time frame for the assessment of performance. Different economic activities require different periods to come to fruition. The greater the jump in complexity from existing to new products, the longer it will take the private sector and the State to acquire the necessary capabilities.

Amplification

When business models leading to new production are successful, they need to be further promoted and replicated by attracting sufficient capital. It should be noted that this amplification need not take place in the original companies: the aim is not to scale up particular firms but to replicate the model. In Bangladesh and Cambodia, for example, successful models in the garment sector were initially implemented in a few companies before being replicated by many other firms.

Amplification will also depend on sufficient demand. The opportunities for boosting domestic demand may well be limited if the country is too small or too poor. One option for small developing economies is for them to pool their demand by providing preferential access to other small economies. Economies in the South usually import many goods from the North that are available, under competitive conditions, in other developing economies, often in the same region.[22]

The third process is the amplification of the successful business models and the exploitation of the new market

---

Repetition

The three processes described above should be put into perpetual motion for least developed countries to catch up with the frontier countries. In this process, it is essential to strengthen national institutions and good governance in order to provide a stable environment for the evolution of the economy, the curbing of capitalist cronyism and the promotion of development goals.

Implementing the strategy: national effort and international partnership

In what follows, we outline a policy agenda for national action and a supportive global partnership for implementing the strategy to increase the productive capacities of least developed countries, drawing upon the outcome of the High-level Asia-Pacific Policy Dialogue on the Brussels Programme of Action for the Least Developed Countries organized by ESCAP in collaboration with the Government of Bangladesh in Dhaka in January 2010.[23]

National policy framework

Stable investment-friendly macroeconomic policy framework

Least developed countries need to maintain strong macroeconomic fundamentals aimed at increasing productive investments, which are critical for strong and sustained economic growth leading to expanding employment opportunities with macroeconomic stability, including low and stable inflation, and sustainable domestic and external imbalances. Countries need to utilize the full scope of appropriate countercyclical policies to maintain economic and financial stability in the face of domestic and external shocks in order to avoid abrupt economic fluctuations. The international community and the G20 should aim to assist least developed countries in their development processes by providing a stable and benign external environment for development and by fostering the flow of long-term development financing.

Least developed countries need to maintain strong macroeconomic fundamentals aimed at increasing productive investment

---

Industrial policy and infrastructure development

In addition to a stable macroeconomic policy framework, the fostering of productive capacities requires more active public intervention aimed at creating infrastructure, including industrial estates and economic zones, capacity-building in entrepreneurship development, support services to small and medium-sized enterprises (SMEs) in technology, marketing and export market development and other promotional measures that are covered under industrial policy. An important aspect of industrial policy has been infant industry protection provided to domestic industry in the early stages of development. Infant industry protection was extensively employed as a policy tool by most developed countries and newly industrialized countries in the early stages of their development.[24] Least developed countries have every right to use infant industry protection to diversify their productive capacities in new areas and provide fledgling productive capacities some space to grow.

Public investment could play a proactive role in infrastructure development and act as a catalyst for public-private partnerships by creating a virtuous cycle of investment and spurring inclusive growth. For that reason, countries need to implement fiscal and tax reforms, improve budgetary processes, improve the quality of public expenditure, promote financial inclusion through creative monetary policies and enhance the transparency of public financial management.

Domestic resource mobilization

It is vital for the Asia-Pacific least developed countries to create a financial architecture that provides access to a variety of financial services and products, especially for SMEs and microenterprises, with particular emphasis on women, the poor and those in rural areas. This requires a diversified, well-regulated and inclusive financial system that promotes savings and channels them to productive investments, especially in rural areas. The domestic supply of long-term capital also needs to be increased by developing domestic capital markets, venture capital funds, term lending institutions and industrial development banks to provide the finances required for the creation of new productive capacities. Microfinance, including microcredit, is an effective tool in generating employment, especially self-employment, improving the well-being of poor households, including women, in the Asia-Pacific least developed countries, empowering individuals

Least developed countries have every right to use infant industry protection to diversify their productive capacities in new areas and provide fledgling productive capacities some space to grow

and communities, and initiating social development. Governments should provide appropriate and coordinated support to meet the rising demand for microfinance, including capacity-building for microfinance institutions and the creation of the necessary regulatory framework. Effective domestic resource mobilization and institution-building by least developed countries have to be supported by development-oriented FDI and targeted ODA, as well as trade policies of development partners that create favourable conditions for productive capacity-building. Support is also needed to foster the growth of the scale and scope of indigenous enterprises and their ability to partner with global enterprises and with production and retail chains and networks.

Least developed countries need to foster a diversified, well-regulated and inclusive financial system that promotes savings and channels them to productive investments

Technological upgrading

It is important to upgrade and further diffuse technology in the least developed countries in order to strengthen productive capacities. The scientific and technological and research and development capacities of these countries need to be built up through national programmes and supported by international institutions and programmes. It is timely to consider setting up a technology bank for least developed countries, which could promote the transfer of key technologies, including pro-poor, green, agricultural and renewable energy-related technologies. In order to address the development challenges facing the Asia-Pacific least developed countries, it is vital to take specific measures to support creative, inventive and innovative activities, including the involvement of universities and research institutions, across all economic sectors and to emphasize the need for the commercialization of research outputs. Least developed countries should be fully assisted in meeting all of their technological development and adaptation objectives.

The creation of an enabling national environment for technological capacity-building should be supported by all organizations and development partners. Least developed countries should be fully supported in the formulation of national innovation strategies and their access to technological and scientific information for development should be ensured. Article 66.2 of the World Trade Organization (WTO) Agreement on Trade-related Aspects of Intellectual Property Rights (TRIPS Agreement) requires developed countries to facilitate technology transfer to least developed countries. It remains rather a statement of intent, however, as it defines neither technology transfer nor the mechanisms for encouraging it; it has therefore remained ineffective. In the new programme of action for least developed countries, transfer of technology should be a critical component of the global partnership if such countries are to develop productive capacities and exploit the potential of green industry, in particular.

Least developed countries should be fully assisted in meeting all of their technological development and adaptation objectives

Supportive global partnership for building productive capacities in least developed countries

Financing for development: foreign direct investment and official development assistance

FDI can help least developed countries to expand their production structure into more modern and knowledge-intensive areas that are characterized by higher value added production. Asia-Pacific least developed countries, however, continue to remain rather minor recipients of FDI, with their share of global inflows at a negligible 0.23% in 2009. The bulk of this FDI is concentrated in their traditional sectors, such as mining, textiles and garments, and they have not been successful in attracting

high quality investments that would help them to build diversified and complex production capacities.[25] Policies aimed at harnessing the potential of FDI should be oriented towards stimulating productive investment, building technological capacities, developing infrastructure and strengthening linkages within and across sectors and between different enterprises. The strengthening of domestic productive

Policies aimed at harnessing the potential of FDI should be oriented towards stimulating productive investment, building technological capacities, developing infrastructure and strengthening linkages within and across sectors and between different enterprises

capacities should also be aimed at producing a wider range of more sophisticated products. Given that many least developed countries have not been able to attract FDI despite liberalization and reform, in order to enhance private capital flows, there is a need to strengthen national, bilateral and multilateral efforts to overcome structural and other constraints that limit their attractiveness as destinations for private capital and FDI. Bilateral and multilateral partners can provide technical, financial and other forms of assistance; share best practices; promote and strengthen partnerships and cooperation arrangements; provide political risk cover and guarantees; leverage aid resources, business development services and funding for feasibility studies; and support national efforts to create a stable and predictable investment climate. Promoting investment proactively by developing projects and then inviting key international players in the sectors to undertake these projects may also help. In addition, least developed countries could adopt associated policies, such as performance requirements and incentives for the promotion of inter-firm linkages, to facilitate the transfer and diffusion of technologies that are introduced through FDI. The emergence of outward FDI from developing countries is enhancing options for least developed countries in terms of sources of FDI, especially FDI that brings with it more appropriate technologies for the geo-climatic conditions and market sizes of least developed countries. South-South FDI flows have been rising faster and now account for over a third of FDI flows received by least developed countries, as observed in chapter 3.

Efforts need to be made to continue to improve the quality of ODA and increasing its development impact

---

ODA has a potential catalytic role to play in helping least developed countries to promote sustainable and inclusive development; enhancing social, institutional and physical infrastructure; promoting FDI; adapting trade and technological inventions and innovations; improving health and education; fostering gender equality; ensuring food security; and reducing poverty. Despite a significant increase in ODA to least developed countries in recent years, only the 9 smallest countries out of the 22 donors on the OECD Development Assistance Committee met the target of providing at least 0.15% of their gross national income in ODA to least developed countries in 2008. While it is important that the internationally agreed targets for ODA be met, there is also a need to match the assistance provided to the priorities set by the least developed countries, which include economic infrastructure-building, skills development and the necessary social infrastructure to enable universal access to essential services and aid for leapfrogging into green production, food security and rural development. Aid for "new" purposes, such as aid for trade and financing for adaptation to climate change, needs to be truly additional and should not divert resources from other internationally agreed goals. Efforts need to be made to continue to improve the quality of ODA and increase its development impact by building on the fundamental principles agreed in the 2005 Paris Declaration on Aid Effectiveness and the 2008

Accra Agenda for Action, which include aligning aid with country priorities, untying aid to least developed countries and increasing the predictability of aid. There is a need to set up special purpose thematic funds dedicated to and earmarked for least developed countries, such as a commodity stabilization fund, a technology fund, a diversification fund and environment-related funds. Least developed countries themselves should be able to determine the terms of access to these funds and they should have equitable representation in their governance. Commitments to provide additional resources to least developed countries made at the G8 and G20 summits should be implemented expeditiously and monitored by the international community.

Least developed countries need to be provided with enhanced and predictable market access, support for the establishment of export supply capacities and new trade-related infrastructure

---

Market access and aid for trade

In order for the least developed countries to substantially increase their contribution to world trade, which would, in turn, enhance their development, they need to be provided with enhanced and predictable market access by their partners, support for the establishment of export supply capacity that is competitive in both cost and quality, and new trade-related infrastructure. Tariff and non-tariff barriers and subsidies in developed countries adversely affect the export earnings of the Asia-Pacific least developed countries. Although developed countries generally levy lower overall tariffs, tariff peaks and tariff escalation are applied to agricultural and labour-intensive products, which are typically exported by least developed countries. As a result, these countries face higher average tariffs than their developed country counterparts. Most least developed countries enjoy preferential access to industrial country markets under the Generalized System of

Preferences (GSP), but experience suggests that the benefits of many GSP schemes are limited due to stringent rules of origin, small preference margins

> *Least developed countries should be granted greater preferential treatment than other countries to enable them to offset some of their disadvantages*

and intense competition among the beneficiary countries. More transparent and simplified rules of origin, allowing for cumulation of origin, at least at the regional level, could improve the use and value of preferences, as would more comprehensive product coverage. Least developed countries should be granted greater preferential treatment than other countries to enable them to offset some of their disadvantages. Few of the least developed countries in the Asia-Pacific region have been granted preferential schemes similar to those that benefit such countries in Africa and the Caribbean, such as the African Growth and Opportunity Act and the Caribbean Basin Initiative of the United States and the benefits for African, Caribbean and Pacific States granted by the European Union under the Lomé Convention. Even though the WTO agreements include special and differential treatment for least developed countries, most of the provisions are best endeavour clauses lacking specific targets and legal enforcement mechanisms and they sometimes provide a few additional years for implementation. Furthermore, a number of least developed countries are not yet able to benefit from the multilateral trade rules. In the Asia-Pacific region, Bangladesh, Cambodia, Myanmar, Nepal and Solomon Islands are WTO members and Afghanistan, Bhutan, the Lao People's Democratic Republic, Samoa and Vanuatu are undergoing the accession process, while Kiribati, Timor-Leste and Tuvalu have yet to initiate the accession process. Concerns have been raised about the arduous conditions imposed on the least developed countries in the process of their accession, which make them undertake

obligations far beyond those justified by their level of development. To enable them to benefit from the multilateral framework, the accession process should be simplified and made less onerous.

For the Asia-Pacific least developed countries, the full implementation of duty-free, quota-free market access by developed countries and developing countries in a position to do so, as agreed in the Hong Kong Ministerial Declaration, is critical to integrating beneficially into the global trading system. Notable initiatives in this direction include the expansion of the European Union GSP scheme for least developed countries to the "Everything but Arms" initiative in 2001. Similar initiatives have been adopted by Australia, Canada, Iceland, Norway, Switzerland and Turkey. The Republic of Korea's presidential decree of 2008 granted preferential tariffs, including duty-free access, to least developed countries on 75% of tariff lines,[26] and the harmonized system of preferences adopted by the Eurasian Economic Community, whose membership included Kazakhstan, Kyrgyzstan, the Russian Federation, Tajikistan and Uzbekistan, entered into force in May 2001 and offered preferential tariff rates to least developed countries on 100% of tariff lines.[27] What is more encouraging is the initiative of some developing countries to announce their own preferential schemes for least developed countries. They include India's duty-free preference scheme announced in 2008 for least developed countries on 85% of tariff lines within a five-year time frame, in addition to unilateral tariff exemptions on all products for Bhutan and Nepal and tariff reductions on 38 lines for Afghanistan; and China's special preference tariff for Afghanistan, Maldives, Samoa, Vanuatu and Yemen on 288 categories of products.[28] China and India have also offered special preferences to least developed country partners in the South Asian Association for Regional Cooperation and ASEAN under different agreements with these groupings and the Asia-Pacific Trade Agreement.

The focus of aid for trade and the Enhanced Integrated Framework should be to assist the least developed countries in building productive infrastructure and trade capacities to enable them to participate effectively in the multilateral trading system. They also need to build their capacity to comply with international product and safety standards. Aid for trade should be aligned with the national development strategies of individual countries to support them in specific areas, such as trade policy and regulations, trade development, the building of productive capacities, trade-related infrastructure and trade-related adjustments. Although total aid for trade commitments increased to $42 billion in 2008, least developed countries received only 25% of the allocations, and Afghanistan and Bangladesh were the only Asia-Pacific least developed countries among the top 20 recipients.[29] Least developed countries should receive priority attention for the disbursement of funds from aid for trade.

Focus of aid for trade should be to assist the least developed countries in building productive infrastructure and trade capacities to enable them to participate effectively in the multilateral trading system

South-South, triangular and regional cooperation

With the rise of emerging countries in the region as the growth poles of the world economy, South-South cooperation and regional economic cooperation have become viable strategies for development. An increasing number of countries, including China, India, Malaysia, the Russian Federation, Singapore and Thailand, have well-developed programmes for assisting other developing countries, especially the least developed countries, in their neighbourhoods. The bulk of South-South cooperation is directed at the capacity-building programmes through which emerging countries share their expertise with least developed countries to enhance education and vocational skills, thereby developing infrastructure that can be critical for increasing production capabilities. Given that developing countries may sometimes possess technologies and skills that are appropriate for other developing countries, triangular cooperation,

in which a traditional partner supports South-South cooperation projects, also has a significant potential. In the Asia-Pacific region, Japan supports triangular cooperation as a modality for fostering development.[30]

With the rise of emerging countries in the region, South-South cooperation and regional economic cooperation have become viable strategies for development

The emergence of South-South FDI flows is also helping least developed countries to build productive capacities, as observed earlier. In addition, emerging countries, such as China and India, have announced their own duty-free-quota-free schemes for exports from least developed countries, as described above. Given the dynamism of Asian economies, regional economic integration complemented by stronger connectivity provides valuable opportunities for mutually beneficial cooperation and the sharing of dynamism across the region, as discussed in chapter 3. As observed earlier in the present chapter, regional markets provide opportunities for venturing into more complex areas. The Global System of Trade Preferences among Developing Countries is another framework for cooperation that makes use of the exchange of trade preferences, especially between regions. It needs to be strengthened, taking into account the special trade and economic needs and prospects of Asia-Pacific least developed countries.

Choosing the diversification path

As this chapter has indicated, countries develop not by producing more of the same products but by diversifying to more complex products. The process of diversification is path-dependent: products that a country produces today affect those it will be able to produce tomorrow. As a result, diversifying to include certain products would increase the range of possibilities for further diversification.

Based on market forces alone, least developed countries may not diversify along the path that will bring them the highest possible future returns. Nor does the current WTO international trade regime encourage the most effective improvement of their productive capacities. As a result, over the past 25 years, the least developed countries have lagged behind world averages. This chapter argues that a pragmatic strategy for increasing productive capacity is to move towards increasingly more complex products that would serve as better platforms for further diversification.

This would require the State and the private sector to coordinate their efforts to steer innovation and replicate successful business models. Least developed countries will therefore need to pursue macroeconomic, trade, finance and infrastructure policies that promote strategic diversification and the evolution of their economies. All of this needs to be supported by enhanced and targeted development assistance, financing, preferential market access, and South-South and regional cooperation.

Endnotes

1   United Nations Conference on Trade and Development, 2006b, 2007 and 2010c.

2   United Nations, Economic and Social Council, 2004; United Nations Conference on Trade and Development, 2010c.

3   Imbs and Wacziarg, 2003.

4   Klinger and Lederman, 2004; Carrère, Strauss-Kahn and Cadot, 2007.

5   Schott, 2004.

6   Reinert, 2007.

7   Hidalgo and Hausmann, 2009.

8   Hausmann and Hidalgo, 2010.

9   Available from http://comtrade.un.org/db/default.aspx (accessed November 2010).

10   Klinger and Lederman, 2004; Carrère, Strauss-Kahn and Cadot, 2007.

11   Jacobs, 1969, pp. 236-238.

12   Hausmann and Klinger (2007); Hidalgo and others, 2007.

13   For the creation of the product space maps shown in this chapter, the software created by César Hidalgo was used to generate the information regarding the product space network. The software is available from www.chidalgo.com/productspace. The networks created were then reformatted using a circular layout using the program Cytoscape, which is available from www.cytoscape.org.

14   Corresponding product space maps are available from www.unescap.org/pdd/publications/survey2011/additional/index.asp.

15   United Nations Conference on Trade and Development, 2002.

16   See Freire, 2011 for details on the calculation of the productive capacity index.

17   United Nations, Economic and Social Commission for Asia and the Pacific, 2010b, figure 61.

18   See Bairoch, 1993; Chang, 2002; Wade, 2003.

19   Hausmann and Hidalgo, 2010; Weitzman, 1998; Kauffman, 1993; Beinhocker, 2007.

20   Reinert, 2007.

21   Rodrik, 2004; Hausmann and Rodrik, 2006.

22   Roelofsen, 1999.

23   United Nations, Economic and Social Commission for Asia and the Pacific, 2010i.

24   For examples see Bairoch, 1993; Wade, 2003; Akyüz, 2005; Chang, 2002; and Reinert, 2007.

25   See Kumar, 2002 for a discussion on quality of FDI and their distribution.

26   United Nations, 2010b.

27   United Nations Conference on Trade and Development, 2010c.

28   World Trade Organization, 2010a; United Nations Conference on Trade and Development, 2010b, pp. 60-61; United Nations, 2010b.

29   United Nations, 2010b.

30   Kumar, 2009.

REFERENCES AND FURTHER READINGS

Agence France-Presse (2008). World needs new Bretton Woods, says Brown, 13 October. Available from http://afp. google.com/article/ALeqM5iqbjATskwxNr2tyDViM7bbz8J_rg.

Aizenman, Joshua and Jaewoo Lee (2007). International reserves: precautionary versus mercantilist views, theory and evidence. *Open Economies Review*, vol. 18, No. 2, pp.191-214.

Akyüz, Yilmaz (2005). *Trade, Growth and Industrialisation: Issues, Experiences and Policy Challenges*. TWN Trade & Development Series 28. Penang: Third World Network. Available from www.twnside.org.sg/title2/t&d/tnd28.pdf.

Akyüz, Yilmaz (2011). Capital flows to developing countries in a historical perspective: Will the current boom end in a bust? South Centre Research Paper, 37. Available from www.southcentre.org/index.php?option=com_docman&task=doc_download&gid=1974&Itemid=182&lang=es.

Asian Development Bank and Asian Development Bank Institute (2009). *Infrastructure for a Seamless Asia*. Tokyo: ADB/ADBI. Available from www.adbi.org/files/2009.08.31.book.infrastructure.seamless.asia.pdf.

_____ (2010). The rise of Asia's middle class. In *Key Indicators for Asia and the Pacific 2010*. Manila. Available from www.adb.org/documents/books/key_indicators/ 2010/pdf/Key-Indicators-2010.pdf.

Asian Development Bank and United Nations, Economic and Social Commission for Asia and the Pacific (2009). *Designing and Implementing Trade Facilitation in Asia and the Pacific*. Manila: ADB. Available from http://aric.adb.org/pdf/Trade_Facilitation_Reference_Book.pdf.

Association of Southeast Asian Nations (2010). ASEANWEB: Foreign Direct Investment Statistics. Available from www.aseansec.org/18144.htm. Accessed 28 October 2010.

_____ (2011). *Master Plan on ASEAN Connectivity: One Vision, One Identity, One Community*. Jakarta: ASEAN Secretariat. Available from www.aseansec.org/documents/MPAC.pdf.

Australia, Commonwealth of Australia (2008). *Pacific Economic Survey: Connecting the Region*. Canberra: Australian Agency for International Development (AusAID). Available from www.ausaid.gov.au/publications/pdf/pacific_economic_survey08.pdf.

Aykut, Dilek and Andrea Goldstein (2007). Developing country multinationals: South-South investment comes of age. In *Industrial Development for the 21st Century: Sustainable Development Perspectives*. New York: United Nations, Department of Economic and Social Affairs. Available from www.un.org/esa/sustdev/publications/ industrial_development/full_report.pdf.

Bairoch, P. (1993). *Economics & World History. Myths and Paradoxes*. Chicago: University of Chicago Press.

Bangladesh, Bangladesh Bank (2010). *Major Economic Indicators: Monthly Update*. Dhaka, October. Available from www.bangladesh-bank.org.

Barclays Capital (2010). Barclays Commodities Weekly, 20 August. Available from www.scribd.com/doc/36315961/ Barclays-Commodities-Weekly-20100820.

Beinhocker, Eric D. (2007). *The Origin of Wealth: Evolution, Complexity and the Radical Remaking of Economics*. London: RH Business Books.

Bjerga, Alan (2010). U.S. ethanol tax credit needed for now, Broin says, *Bloomberg*, 10 December. Available from www.bloomberg.com/news/2010-12-09/u-s-ethanol-tax-credit-necessary-for-now-poet-s-broin-says.html.

Calderón, César and Luis Servén (2004). The effects of infrastructure development on growth and income distribution. Central Bank of Chile Working Papers No. 270, September. Available from www.bcentral.cl/eng/studies/working-papers/pdf/dtbc270.pdf.

Calvo, Guillermo A., Leonardo Leiderman, and Carmen M. Reinhart (1994). The capital inflows problem: concepts and issues. *Contemporary Economic Policy*, vol. 12, No. 3 (July), pp. 54-66.

Capannelli, Giovanni and Jayant Menon, eds. (2010). *Dealing with Multiple Currencies in Transitional Economies: the Scope for Regional Cooperation in Cambodia, the Lao People's Democratic Republic, and Viet Nam.* Mandaluyong City, Philippines: Asian Development Bank. Available from www.adb.org/documents/books/dealing-with-currencies/dealing-with-currencies.pdf. Accessed 21 March 2011.

Capital Economics (2011). Who is most vulnerable to high oil prices? 24 February. Available by subscription from www.capitaleconomics.com/.

Carrère, Céline, Vanessa Strauss-Kahn, and Olivier Cadot (2007). Export diversification: what's behind the hump? CEPR Discussion Papers No. 6590, September. London: Centre for Economic Policy Research. Available from http://r0.unctad.org/ditc/tab/events/emstrade/Speakers/Cadot_doc.pdf.

Cetorelli, Nicola and Linda S. Goldberg (2010). Global banks and international shock transmission: evidence from the crisis. Staff Reports 446. Federal Reserve Bank of New York. Available from www.ny.frb.org/research/economists/goldberg/IMF-BOF-PSG_121409all.pdf.

Chang, Ha-Joon (2002). *Kicking Away the Ladder: Development Strategy in Historical Perspective.* London: Anthem.

Chang, Ha-Joon and Ilene Grabel (2004). *Reclaiming Development: An Alternative Economic Policy Manual.* New York, New York: Zed Books.

Chatterjee, Neil (2011). Indonesia to boost rice stocks amid global food fears. *Reuters*, 9 February. Available from www.reuters.com/article/2011/02/09/us-asia-rice-idUSTRE7186NU20110209. Accessed 21 March 2011.

Chen, Wen and Saholian Liao (2005). *China-ASEAN Trade Relation: A Discussion on Complementarity and Competition.* Singapore: Institute of Southeast Asian Studies.

China, National Development and Reform Commission (2005). Implementing scientific development and promoting sustainable, rapid and healthy development of China's modern logistics industry. Speech given by Ms. Ou Xinqian, Deputy Director of NDRC. 22 September. Available from www.ndrc.gov.cn/jjyx/xdwl/ t20051013_46261.htm (in Chinese only).

Cooks, Robert (2010). Renminbi deposits jump at HK banks. *Financial Times*, 31 August. Available from www.ft.com/cms/s/0/7af4ea7e-b51d-11df-9af8-00144feabdc0.html. Accessed 10 November 2010.

Crawley, John (2009). Japanese, Koreans gain most from cash for clunkers. *Reuters*, 26 August. Available from www.reuters.com/article/2009/08/26/retire-us-usa-clunkers-sales-idUSTRE57P5C220090826. Accessed 21 March 2011.

De Gregorio, José, Sebastian Edwards, and Rodrigo Valdés (2000). Controls on capital inflows: do they work? *Journal of Development Economics*, vol. 63, No. 1, pp. 59-83.

Der Spiegel (2010). The dangers of agricultural speculation. Interview with Prof. Joachim von Braun, 25 August. Available from www.spiegel.de/international/business/0,1518,713456,00.html.

Dunning, John H. and Rajneesh Narula (1996). The investment development path revisited: some emerging issues. In *Foreign Direct Investment and Governments: Catalysts for Economic Restructuring*, John H. Dunning and Rajneesh Narula, eds. London: New York: Routledge.

Duval, Yann and Chorthip Utoktham (2010). Intraregional trade costs in Asia: a primer. Trade and Investment Division, Staff Working Paper 01/10, December. Bangkok: UNESCAP. Available from www.unescap.org/tid/publication/swp110.pdf.

Earth Systems (2010). *Pacific Green Growth Framework Partnership: Interim Report*. Report commissioned by the ESCAP Pacific Office, Suva. September.

Eichengreen, Barry J. (2009). Out of the box thoughts about the international financial architecture. IMF Working Papers 09/116. Washington, D.C.: International Monetary Fund. Available from papers.ssrn.com/sol3/papers.cfm?abstract_id=1415173.

Eurostat (2011). Euro area GDP up by 0.3% and EU27 GDP up by 0.2% Euro area GDP up by 0.3% and EU27 GDP up by 0.2%. *News Release*, 15 February 2011. Available from http://epp.eurostat.ec.europa.eu/cache/ITY_PUBLIC/2-15022011-AP/EN/2-15022011-AP-EN.PDF.

Farchy, Jack (2010). Dollar faces gathering headwinds. *Financial Times*, 4 August. Available from www.ft.com/cms/s/0/d0fee1fa-9fe6-11df-8cc5-00144feabdc0.html.

Ferguson, Niall (2008). *The Ascent of Money: A Financial History of the World*. New York: Penguin Press.

Food and Agriculture Organization of the United Nations (2008). Soaring food prices: facts, perspectives, impacts and actions required. Document for High-Level Conference on World Food Security: The Challenges of Climate Change and Bioenergy, 3-5 June. Available from ftp://ftp.fao.org/docrep/fao/meeting/013/k2414e.pdf.

_____ (2009). *The State of Food Insecurity in the World: Economic Crises – Impacts and Lessons Learned*. Rome. Available from ftp://ftp.fao.org/docrep/fao/012/i0876e/i0876e00.pdf.

Frankel, Jeffrey A. and Andrew K. Rose (2009). Determinants of agricultural and mineral commodity prices. In *Inflation in an Era of Relative Price Shocks*, Renée Fry, Callum Jones, and Christopher Kent, eds. Proceedings of a Conference held at the H.C. Coombs Centre for Financial Studies, Kirribilli, 17-18 August. Sydney: Reserve Bank of Australia. Available from www.rba.gov.au/publications/confs/2009/conf-vol-2009.pdf.

Freire, Clovis (2011). Productive capacity in Asia and the Pacific. MPDD Working Papers, forthcoming. Bangkok: UNESCAP.

Freire, Clovis and Alberto Isgut (2011). High food prices and its impact on the achievement of MDG 1 in Asia and the Pacific. MPDD Working Papers, forthcoming. Bangkok: UNESCAP.

G20 Seoul Summit Leaders' Declaration (2010). 11-12 November. Available from www.g20.org/Documents2010/11/seoulsummit_declaration.pdf.

G20 Toronto Summit Declaration (2010). 27 June. Available from www.g20.org/Documents/g20_declaration_en.pdf.

Ghosh, Jayati (2010). Commodity speculation and the food crisis. World Development Movement Briefing, October, p. 2. Available from www.wdm.org.uk/sites/default/files/Commodity%20speculation%20and%20food%20crisis.pdf.

Goyal, Ashima (2011). Inflationary pressures in South Asia. MPDD Working Papers, WP/11/14, January. Bangkok: UNESCAP. Available from www.unescap.org/pdd/publications/workingpaper/wp_10_14.pdf.

Griffith-Jones, Stephany and Kevin P. Gallagher (2011). Curbing hot capital flows to protect the real economy. *Economic and Political Weekly*, January, pp. 12-14. Available from http://ase.tufts.edu/gdae/Pubs/rp/Griffith-Jones_GallagherEPWJan11.pdf.

Griffith-Jones, Stephany, José Antonio Ocampo, and Joseph E. Stiglitz (2010). *Time for a Visible Hand: Lessons from the 2008 World Financial Crisis*. Oxford; New York, N.Y.: Oxford University Press.

Gupta, Ashish (2011). Foreign investments in 2011 to exceed 2010's record inflows: analysts. *Economic Times*, 2 January. Available from http://articles.economictimes.indiatimes.com/2011-01-02/news/28426558_1_fii-inflows-lakh-crores-foreign-funds.

Hajela, Mukesh, Ram Tiwaree, and Jorge Martinez-Navarrete (2009). Regional progress and strategies towards building the information society in Asia and the Pacific. UNESCAP Technical Paper IDD/TP-09-12, December.

Hang Seng Bank (2011). Mainland China's Economy Grew 10.3% in 2010. Economic Flash. 20 January. Available from www.hangseng.com/cms/tpr/eng/analyses/PDF/ecflash_e_2011jan.pdf.

Hausmann, Ricardo and Bailey Klinger (2007). The structure of the product space and the evolution of comparative advantage. CDI Working Paper No. 146, April. Cambridge, MA: Harvard University, Center for International Development. Available from www.hks.harvard.edu/var/ezp_site/storage/fckeditor/file/pdfs/centers-programs/centers/cid/publications/faculty/wp/146.pdf.

Hausmann, Ricardo and César A. Hidalgo (2010). Country diversification, product ubiquity, and economic divergence. CID Working Paper No. 201, October. Cambridge, MA: Harvard University, Center for International Development. Available from www.hks.harvard.edu/var/ezp_site/storage/fckeditor/file/pdfs/centers-programs/centers/cid/publications/faculty/wp/201.pdf.

Hausmann, Ricardo and Dani Rodrik (2006). Doomed to choose: industrial policy as predicament. 2 September (first draft). Paper prepared for the first Blue Sky seminar organized by the Center for International Development at Harvard University on 9 September. Cambridge, MA: Harvard University, John F. Kennedy School of Government. Available from http://reut-institute.org/data/uploads/Articles and Reports from other organizations/hausmann_doomed_0609.pdf.

Hayes, Geoffrey (2010). Migration in the Pacific. Background paper for the Meeting on Strengthening National Capacities to Deal with International Migration, Bangkok, 22-23 April. ESCAP. Available from www.unescap.org/ESID/Meetings/Migration10/MigrationPacific.pdf.

Head, Keith (2000). Gravity for beginners. Material presented at Rethinking the Line: The Canada-U.S. Border Conference, Vancouver, British Columbia, 22 October. Available from www.unescap.org/tid/artnet/mtg/gravity10_reading1.pdf.

Hernandez, Manuel A., Miguel Robles, and Maximo Terero (2010). Fires in Russia, wheat production, and volatile markets: reasons to panic? International Food Policy Research Institute, 6 August. Available from www.ifpri.org/sites/default/files/wheat.pdf.

Heyzer, Noeleen (2010). Social Protection Agenda in Asia-Pacific. In *Enhancing Social Protection in Asia and the Pacific,* Sri Wening Handayani, ed. Manila: Asian Development Bank, pp. 30-34.

Hidalgo, César A., B. Klinger, A.L. Barabási and R. Hausmann (2007). The product space conditions the development of nations. *Science*, vol. 317, No. 5837, pp. 482-487. Available from http://arxiv.org/ftp/arxiv/papers/0708/0708.2090.pdf.

Hidalgo, César A. and Ricardo Hausmann (2009). The building blocks of economic complexity. *PNAS*, vol. 106, No. 26, pp. 10570-10575. Available from www.chidalgo.com/Papers/HidalgoHausmann_PNAS_2009_PaperAndSM.pdf.

Hornby, Catherine (2011). FAO sees record food prices heading even higher. *Reuters*, 5 January. Available from http://uk.reuters.com/article/2011/01/05/uk-food-fao-index-idUKTRE7041D220110105. Accessed 29 March 2011.

Hui, Tai (2010). India, China and ASEAN Economic Growth. *Jakarta Globe*, 25 March. Available from www.thejakartaglobe.com/opinion/india-china-and-asean-economic-growth/365812.

ICT Association of Fiji (2009). Fiji's world-class facility lured global call centre. Available from www.ictfiji.org.fj/pages.cfm/about/news/fijis-world-class-facility-lured-global-call-centre.html. Accessed 24 June 2009.

Imbs, Jean and Romain Wacziarg (2003). Stages of diversification. *American Economic Review*, vol. 93, No. 1, pp. 63-86. Available from www.anderson.ucla.edu/faculty_pages/romain.wacziarg/downloads/stages.pdf.

India, Reserve Bank of India (2010). *Annual Report 2009-10*. Mumbai, August. Available from http://rbi.org.in/scripts/AnnualReportPublications.aspx?year=2010.

International Financial Services London Research (2009). *Fund Management 2009*, October. Available from www.altassets.com/pdfs/ifsl_fundmanagement_2009.pdf.

International Energy Agency (2010a). *Natural Gas Information 2010.* Available from www.iea.org/publications/free_new_Desc.asp?PUBS_ID=2044.

_____ (2010b). *World Energy Outlook 2010.* Paris.

International Organization for Standardization (2006). *Codes for the representation of names of countries and their subdivisions -- Part 1: Country codes* (ISO 3166-1: 2006).

International Labour Organization (2010a). *Global Employment Trends Model.* October.

_____ (2010b). Building a sustainable future with decent work in Asia and the Pacific. Report of the Director-General, 15th Asia and the Pacific Regional Meeting Report. Geneva: ILO. Available from www.ilo.org/wcmsp5/groups/public/@ed_norm/@relconf/documents/meetingdocument/wcms_151860.pdf.

_____ (2010c). *Labour and Social Trends in ASEAN 2010: Sustaining Recovery and Development through Decent Work.* Bangkok: ILO Regional Office for Asia and the Pacific. Available from www.ilo.org/wcmsp5/groups/public/---asia/---ro-bangkok/documents/publication/wcms_127957.pdf.

_____ (2010d). *Global Wage Report 2010/11: Wage Policies in Times of Crisis.* Geneva. Available from www.ilo.org/wcmsp5/groups/public/@dgreports/@dcomm/@publ/documents/publication/wcms_145265.pdf.

_____ (2011a). *Asia-Pacific Labour Market Update*, March, Bangkok.

_____ (2011b). *Global Employment Trends 2011: The Challenge of a Jobs Recovery.* Geneva. Available from www.ilo.org/wcmsp5/groups/public/@dgreports/@dcomm/@publ/documents/publication/wcms_150440.pdf.

International Monetary Fund (2010a). *Regional Economic Outlook: Europe Building Confidence.* October. Available from www.imf.org/external/pubs/ft/reo/2010/eur/eng/ereo1010ex.pdf.

_____ (2010b). *Regional Economic Outlook: Asia and Pacific - Leading the global recovery: rebalancing for the medium term* (April). Washington, D.C. Available from www.imf.org/external/pubs/ft/reo/2010/apd/eng/areo0410.pdf.

_____ (2010c). The Fund's role regarding cross-border capital flows. 15 November. IMF Staff Paper. Washington, D.C. Available from www.imf.org/external/np/pp/eng/2010/111510.pdf.

_____ (2011). IMF develops framework to manage capital inflows. *IMF Survey.* 5 April 2011. Available from http://ftalphaville.ft.com/blog/2011/03/28/529131/more-on-uncertainty -and-capital-controls/.

International Telecommunication Union (2010). *Trends in Telecommunication Reform 2009: Hands-on or Hands-off? Stimulating Growth Through Effective ICT Regulation: Summary.* Geneva: ITU. Available from www.itu.int/dms_pub/itu-d/opb/reg/D-REG-TTR.11-2009-SUM-PDF-E.pdf.

Isgut, Alberto (2011). Actual and estimated intraregional trade flows in Asia and the Pacific, 1993-2009. MPDD Working Papers, forthcoming. Bangkok: UNESCAP.

Ivakhnyuk, Irina (2006). Migration in the CIS region: common problems and mutual benefits. Paper contributed at the International Symposium on International Migration and Development, Turin, Italy, 28-30 June. UN/POP/MIG/SYMP/2006/10. Available from www.un.org/esa/population/migration/turin/Symposium_Turin_files/P10_SYMP_Ivakhniouk.pdf.

Jacobs, Jane (1969). *The Economy of Cities*. New York: Vintage Books.

Japan External Trade Organization (2009). *ASEAN Logistics Network Map*. 2nd ed. Tokyo: JETRO.

Jeanne, Olivier (2007). International reserves in emerging market countries: too much of a good thing? Brookings Papers on Economic Activity, vol. 38, issue 2007-1, pp. 1-78.

Jeanne, Olivier and Anton Korinek (2010). Excessive volatility in capital flows: a Pigouvian taxation approach. *American Economic Review*, vol. 100, No. 2 (May), pp. 403-407.

Jensen, Robert (2007). The digital provide: information (technology), market performance, and welfare in the South Indian fisheries sector. *Quarterly Journal of Economics*, vol. 122, No. 3, pp. 879-924.

Kauffman, Stuart A. (1993). *The Origins of Order: Self-organization and Selection in Evolution*. New York: Oxford University Press.

Kawai, Masahiro and Ganeshan Wignaraja (2010). Asian FTAs: trends, prospects, and challenges. ADB Economics Working Paper Series No. 226, October. Manila: Asian Development Bank. Available from www.adb.org/ documents/Working-Papers/2010/Economics-WP226.pdf.

Kelegama, Saman (2011). *Migration, Remittances and Developments in South Asia*. Institute of Policy Studies. Delhi, India: SAGE Publications Pvt. Ltd.

Khalik, Abdul (2011). ASEAN agrees on rice reserve, discusses Middle East. *Jakarta Post*, 28 February 2011. Available from www.thejakartapost.com/news/2011/02/28/asean-agrees-rice-reserve-discusses-middle-east.html.

Klinger, Bailey and Daniel Lederman (2004). Discovery and development: an empirical exploration of 'new' products. World Bank Policy Research Working Paper 3450, November. Washington, D.C.: World Bank. Available from www-wds.worldbank.org/external/default/WDSContentServer/WDSP/IB/2004/12/01/000160016_20041201114215/ additional/310436360_20050014111839.pdf.

Knight, Frank (2010). Global house price recovery loses steam; over half of all countries see negative growth in Q3 2010. Knight Frank Global House Price Index, Q3 2010 results, 22 December. Available from www.knightfrank.com/news/ Global-house-price-recovery-loses-steam;-over-half-of-all-countries-see-negative-growth-in-Q3-2010-0480.aspx.

Koo, Chung Mo (2006). Green tax shift in Europe and its implications for East Asian countries. Presentation given at the Second Roundtable Workshop: Prospects of Green Tax and Budget Reform. Bangkok, 14-15 December.

Kose, M. Ayhan, Eswar Prasad, Kenneth Rogoff, and Shang-Jin Wei (2006). Financial globalization: a reappraisal. NBER Working Paper No. 12484. Cambridge, Massachusetts: National Bureau of Economic Research. Available from www.nber.org/papers/w12484.pdf.

Kumagai, S., T. Gokan, I. Isono, and S. Keola (2008). Geographical simulation model for ERIA: predicting the long-run effects of infrastructure development projects in East Asia. In *International infrastructure development in East Asia: towards a balanced regional development and integration*, Nagesh Kumar, ed. ERIA Research Project Report 2007, No. 2. Available from www.eria.org/research/images/pdf/PDF%20No.2/No.2-part3-12.GEOGRAPHICAL.pdf.

Kumar, Nagesh (2002). *Globalization and the Quality of Foreign Direct Investment*, New Delhi: Oxford University Press.

_____(2007a). Investment provisions in regional trading arrangements in Asia: relevance, emerging trends, and policy implications. Artnet Working Papers No. 46. UNESCAP. Available from www.unesacp.org/tid/artnet/pub/wp4607.pdf.

_____ (2007b). Towards broader regional cooperation in Asia. RCC Discussion Paper Series, December. Colombo, Sri Lanka: UNDP Regional Centre in Colombo. Available from http://hdru.aprc.undp.org/resource_centre/pub_pdfs/ P1059.pdf.

_____ (2008). Internationalization of Indian enterprises: patterns, strategies, ownership advantages, and implications. *Asian Economic Policy Review*, vol. 3, No. 2 (December), pp. 242-261.

_____ (2009). South-South and triangular cooperation in Asia-Pacific: towards a new paradigm in development cooperation. UNESCAP Working Paper, WP/09/05, December. Bangkok: UNESCAP. Available from www.unescap.org/pdd/publications/workingpaper/wp_09_05.pdf.

_____ (2010). Capital flows and development: lessons from South Asian experiences. MPDD Working Papers, WP/10/11, November. Bangkok: UNESCAP. Available from www.unescap.org/pdd/publications/workingpaper/wp_10_11.pdf

Kuroda, Haruhiko, Masahiro Kawai, and Rita Nangia (2007). Infrastructure and regional cooperation. ADB Institute Discussion Paper No. 76, September. Tokyo: ADBI. Available from http://adbi.org/files/dp76.infrastructure.regional.cooperation.pdf.

Leaders' Statement: The Pittsburgh G20 Summit (2009). 24-25 September. Available from www.pittsburghsummit.gov/mediacenter/129639.htm.

Li, Muqun, Wei Liu, and Shunfeng Song (2010). Export relationships among China, Japan, and South Korea. *Review of Development Economics*, vol. 14, No. 3 (August), pp. 547-562.

Manning, Chris and Alexandra Sidorenko (2007). The regulation of professional migration in ASEAN - insights from the health and IT sectors. *World Economy*, vol. 30, No. 7, pp. 1084-1113 (July). Available from http://onlinelibrary.wiley.com/doi/10.1111/j.1467-9701.2007.01013.x/pdf.

Mohapatra, Sanket, Dilip Ratha, and Ani Silwal (2010). Outlook for remittance flows 2011-12: recovery after the crisis, but risks lie ahead. Migration and Development Brief 13, 8 November. Washington, D.C.: World Bank. Available from http://siteresources.worldbank.org/INTPROSPECTS/Resources/334934-1110315015165/MigrationAndDevelopment Brief13.pdf.

Myanmar, Central Statistical Organization (n.d.). Foreign investment of permitted enterprises by country of origin. Available from www.csostat.gov.mm/s25MA0201.asp. Accessed 21 March 2011.

Neumann, Frederic and Song-yi Kim (2010). The Chinese are coming. *HSBC Global Research*. 15 October. Available from www.research.hsbc.com/midas/Res/RDV?p=pdf&%24sessionid%24=JBg_HzKbazdftKAaqHQBxO1&key=pw PUHwjjrK&n=280297.PDF.

New Zealand, Reserve Bank of New Zealand (n.d.). Official Cash Rate (OCR) decisions and current rate. Available from www.rbnz.govt.nz/monpol/statements/0090630.html.

Nicolas, Françoise (2009). ASEAN energy cooperation: an increasingly daunting challenge. Paris: Institut Française the Relations Internationales (IFRI). Available from www.ifri.org/files/Energie/FNicolas.pdf.

Nomura Global Economics (2010). The coming surge in food prices. September. Available from www.nomura.com/research/getpub.aspx?pid=390252.

Obstfeld, Maurice, Jay C. Shambaugh, and Alan M. Talyor (2008). Financial stability, the trilemma, and international reserves. NBER Working Paper 14217, August. Available from www.nber.org/papers/w14217.pdf.

Organization for Economic Cooperation and Development (2005). *Paris Declaration on Aid Effectiveness: Ownership, Harmonisation, Alignment, Results and Mutual Accountability* in OECD (2005/2008) *The Paris Declaration on Aid Effectiveness and the Accra Agenda for Action*. Paris. Available from www.oecd.org/dataoecd/11/41/34428351.pdf.

Pacific Islands Forum Secretariat (2010). *Forum Economic Ministers' Meeting: Forum Economic Action Plan 2010*. Alofi, Niue, 27-28 October.

Pakistan, Ministry of Finance (2010). *Pakistan Economic Survey 2010*. Islamabad, June.

_____ State Bank of Pakistan (2010). *Annual Report 2009-2010*. Karachi, October.

Parker, George, Tony Barber, and Daniel Dombey (2008). Senior figures call for new Bretton Woods ahead of Bank/Fund meetings, 9 October. Available from www.eurodad.org/whatsnew/articles.aspx?id=2988.

Philippines, Bureau of Labor and Employment Statistics (2010). *Current Labor Statistics* (October). Available from www.bles.dole.gov.ph.

Prasad, Biman C. (2010). Global crisis, domestic crisis and crisis of confidence: which way forward for Fiji? *Pacific Economic Bulletin*, vol. 25, No.2 (June), pp. 1-24.

Prasad, Biman C., R. Singh, and G. Chand (2010). Labour mobility and Pacific economic integration. In *Population and Development in the Pacific Islands: Accelerating the ICPD Program of Action*, Narsey et.al, eds. Proceedings, Suva: UNFPA; USP.

Rajan, Raghuram (2010). *Fault Lines: How Hidden Fractures Still Threaten the World Economy*. Princeton, N.J.; Oxford: Princeton University Press.

Rajan, Ramkishen (2008). Money and financial cooperation in Asia. In *Asia's New Regionalism and Global Role: Agenda for the East Asia Summit*, Nagesh Kumar, K. Kesavapany, and Yao Chaocheng, eds. New Delhi: RIS and Singapore: ISEAS.

_____ (2010). South-South foreign direct investment flows: Focus on Asia. *Global Studies Review*, vol. 6, No. 3 (Fall). Available from www.globality-gmu.net/archives/2248.

Rashid, Ahmed T. and Laurent Elder (2009). Mobile phones and development: an analysis of IDRC-supported projects data sheet. *Electronic Journal on Information Systems in Developing Countries*, vol. 36, No. 2, pp. 1-16. Available from www.mobileactive.org/files/file_uploads/ICDT%20projects%20review.pdf.

Ratha, Dilip and William Shaw (2007). South-South migration and remittances. World Bank Working Paper No. 102. Available from http://siteresources.worldbank.org/ INTPROS PECTS/Resources/334934-1110315015165/SouthSouthMigrationandRemittances.pdf.

Reinert, Erik S. (2007). *How Rich Countries Got Rich and Why Poor Countries Stay Poor*. London: Constable.

Reuters (2008). Italy queries dollar's role in Bretton Woods reform, 16 October. Available from www.reuters.com/article/euMergersNews/idUSLG34287520081016.

Reuters Analysis, Global Investing (2010). Shock! Emerging capital controls may just be working, 30 July.

Rodriguez, Francisco (2007). Have collapses in infrastructure spending led to cross-country divergence in per capita GDP? DESA Working Paper No. 52, July. Available from www.un.org/esa/desa/papers/2007/wp52_2007.pdf.

Rodrik, Dani (2004). Industrial policy for the twenty-first century. September. Cambridge: John F. Kennedy School of Government, Harvard University. Available from http://citeseerx.ist.psu.edu/viewdoc/download?doi=10.1.1.111.7348&rep=rep1&type=pdf.

_____ (2006). The social cost of foreign exchange reserves. *International Economic Journal*, vol. 20 (3 September).

_____ (2010). Making room for China in the world economy. *American Economic Review*, vol. 100, No. 2 (May), pp. 89-93.

Roelofsen, Henrik (1999). South-South trade: a strategic alternative in global marketing. Paper prepared for the 1999 International Trade Centre Executive Forum on National Export Strategies, "Re-defining Trade Promotion: The Need for a Strategic Response", Annecy, France, 26-29 September. Available from www.intracen.org/wedf/ef1999/sup_p_7.pdf.

Samoa (2009). SAMOA: *Post-Disaster Needs Assessment Following the Earthquake and Tsunami of 29th September 2009*. World Bank, Government of Samoa and Global Facility for Disaster Reduction and Recovery. Available from www.reliefweb.int/rw/RWFiles2009.nsf/FilesByRWDocUnidFilename/EGUA-89JR6N-full_report.pdf/$File/full_report.pdf.

Santos-Silva, J. M. C. and S. Tenreyro (2006). The Log of Gravity. *Review of Economics and Statistics*, vol. 88, No. 4 (November), pp. 641-658.

Schott, P. (2004). Across-product versus within-product specialization in international trade. *Quarterly Journal of Economics*, vol. 119, No. 2, pp. 647-678.

Secretariat of the Pacific Community (2010). *Framework for Action on ICT for Development in the Pacific*. Available from http://e-pic.info/resources/ict-meetings/item/download/23.

Shirotori, Miho and Ana Cristina Molina (2009). *South-South Trade: The Reality Check*. Geneva: UNCTAD. UNCTAD/DITC/TAB/2008/1. Available from http://r0.unctad.org/ditc/tab/publications/DITC-TAB-2008-1-final-17MARCH2009.pdf.

South Asian Association for Regional Cooperation (2007). Declaration of the 14th SAARC Summit, New Delhi, 4 April. Government of India, Ministry of External Affairs. Available from www.satp.org/satporgtp/countries/india/document/papers/sarc14ind.htm.

Sri Lanka, Central Bank of Sri Lanka (2010). *Recent Economic Developments: Highlights of 2010 and Prospects for 2011*. Colombo, November.

Stiglitz , Joseph E. (2010). *Freefall: America, Free Markets, and the Sinking of the World Economy*, New York: W.W. Norton.

Sundaram, Jomo Kwame (2010). Lessons from the 2008 world food crisis. *Economic & Political Weekly*, vol. XLV, No. 12, pp. 35-40.

TeleGeography Research (2009). Review of 2009: Telecoms during a global recession, executive summary. Globalcomms Insight, December. Washington, D.C.: PriMetrica. Available from http://tinyurl.com/3thncex.

Thai News Agency (2009). Thailand to invest Bt676 billion to improve logistics infrastructures. MCOT English News, 26 February 2009. Available from http://enews.mcot.net/view.php?id=8782.

Theparat, Chatrudee (2010). Stimulus spending pays off. *Bangkok Post*, 24 December. Available from www.bangkokpost.com/business/economics/212901/stimulus-spending-pays-off.

Tuli, Vipul (2008). Regional cooperation for Asian energy security. In *Asia's New Regionalism and Global Role: Agenda for the East Asia Summit*, Nagesh Kumar, K. Kesavapany and Yao Chaocheng, eds. New Delhi: RIS and Singapore: ISEAS.

United Kingdom, Department for Environment, Food and Rural Affairs (2010). Food and Farming Brief, Annex A - 2009/10 Sugar Price Spike, June. Available from www.defra.gov.uk/evidence/statistics/foodfarm/general/monthlybrief/documents/FarmFoodBrief-June2010-AnnexA.pdf.

United Nations (2003). Report of the International Ministerial Conference of Landlocked and Transit Developing Countries and Donor Countries and International Financial and Development Institutions on Transit Transport Cooperation, Almaty, Kazakhstan. 28-29 August. A/CONF.202/3.

_____ (2008). Intergovernmental Agreement on the Asian Highway Network, Bangkok, 18 November 2003. *Treaty Series*, vol. 2323, No. 41607.

_____ (2009). Reforms of the International Monetary and Financial System. Report of the Experts of the President of the United Nations General Assembly, 21 September. New York. Available from www.un.org/ga/econcrisissummit/docs/FinalReport_CoE.pdf.

_____ (2010a). Food commodities speculation and food price crises - Regulation to reduce the risks of price volatility. United Nations Special Rapporteur on the Right to Food Briefing Note No. 2, by Olivier de Schutter, September 2010. Available from www.srfood.org/images/stories/pdf/otherdocuments/20102309_briefing_note_02_en_ok.pdf.

_____ (2010b). *The Global Partnership for Development at a Critical Juncture: MDG Gap Task Force Report 2010.* Sales No. E.10.I.12. Available from www.un.org/millenniumgoals/pdf/10-43282_MDG_2010 (E) WEBv2.pdf.

United Nations Conference on Trade and Development (2002). *Trade and Development Report 2002: Developing Countries in World Trade.* Sales No. E.02.II.D.2. Available from www.unctad.org/en/docs/tdr2002_en.pdf.

_____ (2006a). *World Investment Report 2006 – FDI from Developing and Transition Economies: Implications for Development.* Sales No. E.06.II.D.11. New York: United Nations. Available from www.unctad.org/en/docs/ wir2006_en.pdf.

_____ (2006b). *The Least Developed Countries Report 2006: Developing Productive Capacities.* Sales No. E.06. II.D9. Available from www.unctad.org/en/docs/ldc2006_en.pdf.

_____ (2007) *The Least Developed Countries Report 2007: Knowledge, Technological Learning and Innovation for Development.* Sales No. E.07.II.D.8. Available from www.unctad.org/en/docs/ldc2007_en.pdf.

_____ (2009). *The Global Economic Crisis: Systemic Failures and Multilateral Remedies.* New York; Geneva: United Nations. Available from www.unctad.org/en/docs/gds20091_en.pdf.

_____ (2010a). *Public Symposium - Responding to Global Crises: New Development Paths.* Report of the Public Symposium, 10-11 May. UNCTAD/OSG/CIO/2010/2. Available from www.unctad.org/en/docs/osgcio20102_ en.pdf.

_____ (2010b). *World Investment Report 2010: Investing in a Low-carbon Economy.* Sales No. E.10.II.D.2. New York and Geneva. Available from www.unctad.org/en/docs/wir2010_en.pdf.

_____ (2010c). *The Least Developed Countries Report 2010: Towards a New International Development Architecture for LDCs.* Sales No. E.10.II.D.5. Available from www.unctad.org/en/docs/ldc2010_en.pdf.

_____ (2011). *Global Investment Trends Monitor,* No. 5, 17 January 2011. Geneva. Available from www.unctad.org/en/docs// webdiaeia20111_en.pdf.

United Nations, Department of Economic and Social Affairs (2007). *Industrial Development for the 21st Century: Sustainable Development Perspectives.* New York. Available from www.un.org/esa/sustdev/publications/industrial_ development/full_report.pdf.

_____ (2010) *Trends in Sustainable Development: Small Island Developing States.* Sales No. E.10.II.A.12. Available from www.un.org/esa/dsd/resources/res_pdfs/publications/trends/trends_sids/Trends_in_Sustainable_Development_ SIDS.pdf.

_____ (2011). *World Economic Situation and Prospects 2011.* Sales No. E.11.II.C.2. Available from www.un.org/en/ development/desa/policy/wesp/wesp_current/2011wesp.pdf

United Nations, Economic and Social Commission for Asia and the Pacific (2008a) *Economic and Social Survey of Asia and the Pacific 2008.* Sales No. E.08.II.F.7.

_____ (2008b) *Enhancing Pacific Connectivity: The Current Situation, Opportunities for Progress.* Sales No. E.08. II.F.14. Available from www.unapcict.org/ecohub/resources/enhancing-pacific-connectivity-the-current.

_____ (2009a). *Asia-Pacific Trade and Investment Report 2009.* Sales No. E.09.II.F.19.

_____ (2009b). *Sustainable Agriculture and Food Security in Asia and the Pacific.* Sales No. E.09.II.F.12.

_____ (2009c). *Low Carbon Green Growth: Integrated Policy Approach to Climate Change for Asia-Pacific Developing Countries.* Available from www.greengrowth.org/download/2010/LCGG_web.version.pdf.

_____ (2010a). The European debt crisis: implications for Asia and the Pacific. MPDD Policy Brief, 27 June. Available from http://www.unescap.org/pdd/publications/me_brief/mpdd-pb-4.pdf.

_____ (2010b). *Economic and Social Survey of Asia and the Pacific 2010: Sustaining Recovery and Dynamism for Inclusive Development.* Sales No. E.10.II.F.2. Available from www.unescap.org/pdd/publications/survey2010/download/Survey2010.pdf.

_____ (2010c). Chairperson's Summary of the High-level Consultation on Perspectives from Asia and the Pacific on the G20 Seoul Summit. Available from www.unescap.org/pdd/calendar/HLC_G20/papers/outcome%20document_edited.pdf.

_____ (2010d). UNESCAP Secretariat Background Paper for UNESCAP-Republic of Korea High-level Consultation on the G20 Seoul Summit: Perspectives from Asia-Pacific. United Nations Conference Centre, Bangkok, 25-26 October. Available from www.unescap.org/pdd/calendar/HLC_G20/papers/Secretariat1_22Oct10.pdf.

_____ (2010e). Global partnership for strong, sustainable and balanced growth: an agenda for the G20 summits. MPDD Working Papers, WP/10/12, November. Bangkok: UNESCAP. Available from www.unescap.org/pdd/publications/workingpaper/wp_10_12.pdf.

_____ (2010f). *Asia-Pacific Trade and Investment Report 2010: Recent Trends and Developments.* ST/ESCAP2590. Available from www.unescap.org/tid/publication/ aptir2590.pdf.

_____ (2010g). *Statistical Yearbook for Asia and the Pacific 2009.* Sales No. E.10.II.F.1. Available from www.unescap.org/stat/data/syb2009/ESCAP-SYB2009.pdf.

_____ (2010h). *Financing an Inclusive and Green Future: A Supportive Financial System and Green Growth for Achieving the Millennium Development Goals in Asia and the Pacific.* Sales No. E.10.II.F.4. Available from www.unescap.org/66/documents/Theme-Study/st-escap-2575.pdf.

_____ (2010i). Asia-Pacific regional review of the Brussels Programme of Action for the Least Developed Countries for the Decade 2001-2010: Dhaka Outcome Document, Sixty-sixth session, Incheon, 13-19 May. E/ESCAP/66/6. Available from www.un.org/ga/search/view_doc.asp?symbol=E/ESCAP/66/6.

_____ (2011a). Rising food prices and inflation in the Asia-Pacific region: causes, impact and policy response. MPDD Policy Briefs. No. 7, March 2011. Available from www.unescap.org/pdd/publications/me_brief/mpdd-pb-7.pdf.

_____ (2011b). Towards a global currency for a global economy. MPDD Policy Briefs. No. 8, April 2011. Available from www.unescap.org/pdd/publications/me_brief/mpdd-pb-8.pdf.

_____ Asian Development Bank and United Nations Development Programme (2010). *Path to 2015: MDG Priorities in Asia and the Pacific, Asia-Pacific MDG report 2010/11.* Bangkok: Sales No. E.10.II.F.20.

_____ and United Nations International Strategy and Disaster Reduction (2010). *Asia Pacific Disaster Report 2010.* Bangkok. Available from www.unescap.org/idd/pubs/Asia-Pacific-Disaster-Report%20-2010.pdf.

United Nations, Economic Commission for Africa (2010). African Economic Conference 2010: Agenda for Africa's Economic Recovery and Long Term Growth. Statement by Mr. Abdoulie Janneh, United Nations Under-Secretary-General and Executive Secretary of ECA, Tunis, Tunisia, 27 October 2010. Available from www.uneca.org/eca_resources/Speeches/Janneh/2010/101027_speech_janneh.html.

United Nations, Economic and Social Council (2004). Official Records of the Economic and Social Council, 2004, Supplement No. 13 (E/2004/33). Available from www.un.org/ga/search/view_cod.asp?symbol=E/2004/33/SUPP).

United Nations, Economic Commission for Latin America and the Caribbean (2010). *Latin America and the Caribbean in the World Economy 2009-2010: A crisis Generated in the Centre and a Recovery Driven by the Emerging Economies.* Sales No. E.10.II.G.5. Available from www.eclac.org/publicaciones/xml/6/40696/crisis_generated_in_the_centre_and_a_recovery_driven_by_the_emerging_economies.pdf.

United Nations, Economic Commission for Latin America and the Caribbean (2011). International merchandise trade in Latin America and the Caribbean. Statistical Bulletin No.2, First quarter. Available from www.eclac.org/cgi-bin/getProd.asp?xml=%20publicaciones/xml/0/43090/P43090.xml&xsl=/comercio/tpl/p9f.xsl%20&base=/tpl/top-bottom.xslt.

VeriSign (2010). The VeriSign Domain Report. *Domain Name Industry Brief*, vol. 7, No. 3 (September). Available from www.verisigninc.com/assets/domain-name-report-sept10.pdf.

Wade, Robert Hunter (2003). What strategies are available for developing countries today? The World Trade Organization and the shrinking of 'development space'. *Review of International Political Economy*, vol. 10, No. 4 (November), pp. 621-644.

Wang, Jing and John Whalley (2010). The trade performance of Asian economies during and following the 2008 financial crisis. NBER Working Paper 16142. Available from www.nber.org/papers/w16142.pdf.

Weitzman, Martin L. (1998). Recombinant growth. *Quarterly Journal of Economics*, vol. 113, No. 2 (May), pp. 331-360.

World Bank (2000). *East Asia: Recovery and Beyond*. Washington, D.C.

World Bank (2010). Food price watch, December. Available from http://siteresources.worldbank.org/INTPOVERTY/Resources/FoodPriceWatchDec2010.pdf.

World Trade Organization (2005). Doha work programme: Ministerial declaration, adopted on 18 December 2005 (WT/MIN(05)/DEC). Available from www.wto.org/english/thewto_e/minist_e/min05_e/final_text_e.pdf.

_____ (2010a). Market access for products and services of export interest to least-developed countries. Sub-Committee on Least-Developed Countries. (WT/COMTD/LDC/W/46/REV.1). Available from www.mdg-trade.org/LDCW48 E.pdf.

_____ (2010b). Transparency mechanism for preferential trade arrangements set for approval, WTO: 2010 News Items, 4 October. Available from www.wto.org/english/news_e/news10_e/devel_04oct10_e.htm. Accessed January 2011.

Xin, Chen (2010). Chinese workers take home larger pay packets. *China Daily*, 19 August. Available from http://www.chinadaily.com.cn/bizchina/2010-08/19/content_11173835.htm.

Yao, Shujie, Dylan Sutherland, and Jian Chen (2010). China's outward FDI and resource-seeking strategy: a case study on Chinalco and Rio Tinto. *Asia-Pacific Journal of Accounting & Economics*, vol. 17, pp. 313-326. Available from www.cb.cityu.edu.hk/research/apjae/document/17-3/07.pdf.

Yoon, Al (2010). Global stock fund inflows gain, bonds slow: source, *Reuters*, 31 December 2010. Available from www.reuters.com/article/2010/12/31/funds-flows-idUSN3113990220101231.

Yu, Yongding (2010). Asia: China's policy response to the global financial crisis. *Journal of Globalization and Development*, vol. 1, issue 1.

Zhang, Anming, Shinya Hanaoka, Hajime Inamura, and Tomoki Ishikura (2008). Low-cost carriers in Asia: Deregulation, regional liberalization and secondary airports. *Research in Transportation Economics,* vol. 24, issue 1, pp. 36–50.

STATISTICAL ANNEX

List of tables

Table 1. Real gross domestic product growth rates

(Percentage)

	1999	2000	2001	2002	2003	2004	2005	2006	2007	2008	2009	2010
East and North-East Asia	3.5	5.3	3.0	3.9	4.4	5.5	5.3	5.9	6.7	2.8	-1.0	6.4
China	7.6	8.4	8.3	9.1	10.0	10.1	11.3	12.7	14.2	9.6	9.1	10.3
Democratic People's Republic of Korea	6.1	0.4	3.8	1.2	1.8	2.1	3.8	-1.0	-1.2	3.1	..	..
Hong Kong, China	2.6	8.0	0.5	1.8	3.0	8.5	7.1	7.0	6.4	2.2	-2.8	6.8
Japan	-0.1	2.9	0.2	0.3	1.4	2.7	1.9	2.0	2.4	-1.2	-6.3	3.9
Macao, China	-2.4	5.7	2.9	10.1	14.2	27.3	6.9	16.5	26.0	12.9	1.3	35.0
Mongolia	3.2	1.1	0.9	4.7	7.0	10.6	7.3	8.6	10.2	8.9	-1.3	6.1
Republic of Korea	10.7	8.8	4.0	7.2	2.8	4.6	4.0	5.2	5.1	2.3	0.2	6.1
North and Central Asia	6.2	9.5	5.9	5.3	7.5	7.5	7.7	9.1	9.1	5.9	-5.4	4.6
Armenia	3.3	5.9	9.6	13.2	14.0	10.5	13.9	13.2	13.7	6.9	-14.2	2.6
Azerbaijan	7.4	11.1	9.9	10.6	11.2	10.2	26.4	34.5	25.0	10.8	9.3	5.0
Georgia	2.9	1.8	4.8	5.5	11.1	5.9	9.6	9.4	12.3	2.1	-3.9	5.3
Kazakhstan	2.7	9.8	13.5	9.8	9.3	9.6	9.7	10.7	8.9	3.3	1.2	7.0
Kyrgyzstan	3.7	5.4	5.3	0.0	7.0	7.0	-0.2	3.1	8.5	8.4	2.3	-1.4
Russian Federation	6.4	10.0	5.1	4.7	7.3	7.2	6.4	7.7	8.1	5.6	-7.9	4.0
Tajikistan	3.7	8.3	9.6	10.8	11.0	10.3	6.7	7.0	7.8	7.9	3.4	6.5
Turkmenistan	16.5	5.5	4.3	0.3	3.3	5.0	13.0	11.4	11.6	10.5	6.1	8.0
Uzbekistan	4.3	3.8	4.2	4.0	4.4	7.7	7.0	7.3	9.5	9.0	8.1	8.5
Pacific	4.2	3.3	2.6	4.0	3.4	3.8	3.1	2.6	4.5	2.3	1.2	2.6
Pacific island developing economies	2.8	-1.8	0.1	1.8	3.6	2.3	2.9	2.6	5.1	4.3	2.2	4.3
Cook Islands	2.7	13.9	4.9	2.6	8.2	4.3	0.0	0.7	9.5	-1.2	-0.1	0.5
Fiji	8.7	-1.7	1.9	3.2	0.8	5.4	-1.3	1.9	-0.5	-0.1	-3.0	0.1
Kiribati	-1.2	7.6	-5.1	6.1	2.3	2.2	3.9	1.9	0.4	-1.1	-0.7	0.5
Marshall Islands	..	..	..	..	..	4.0	0.7	2.4	3.3	-2.0	0.0	0.5
Micronesia (Federated States of)	-2.1	4.7	0.1	0.9	2.9	-3.3	3.0	-0.4	-0.1	-2.9	-1.0	0.5
Nauru	..	..	..	..	..	..	-14.5	6.3	-27.3	1.0	0.0	0.0
Palau	-5.4	0.3	1.3	-3.5	-1.3	6.0	5.9	4.8	-0.5	-4.9	-2.1	2.0
Papua New Guinea	1.9	-2.5	-0.1	2.0	4.4	0.6	3.9	2.3	7.2	6.6	5.5	7.1
Samoa	-0.6	4.8	8.0	6.2	3.8	4.2	7.0	2.2	2.3	5.0	-4.9	0.0
Solomon Islands	-1.6	-14.2	-8.0	-2.8	6.5	4.9	5.4	6.9	10.3	7.3	-1.2	4.0
Tonga	4.2	3.2	3.5	3.6	2.6	1.0	-1.0	0.5	-1.2	2.0	-0.4	-1.2
Tuvalu	2.4	-12.8	13.2	5.5	-3.2	-1.3	-4.1	6.6	4.9	1.3	-1.7	0.0
Vanuatu	0.4	5.8	-3.3	-4.2	3.7	4.4	5.1	7.2	6.8	6.3	3.8	3.0
Developed economies	4.3	3.4	2.7	4.1	3.4	3.8	3.1	2.6	4.5	2.2	1.2	2.6
Australia	4.3	3.3	2.7	4.0	3.3	3.8	3.1	2.6	4.6	2.6	1.3	2.7
New Zealand	4.7	3.8	2.5	4.5	4.3	4.0	3.1	2.1	3.4	-0.8	0.1	1.5
South and South-West Asia	3.6	5.1	2.6	4.7	7.1	7.6	8.6	8.3	7.6	4.7	3.9	7.5
Afghanistan			-3.5	81.1	14.3	9.4	14.5	11.2	16.2	3.4	22.5	8.9
Bangladesh	4.9	6.0	5.3	4.4	5.3	6.3	6.0	6.6	6.4	6.2	5.7	5.8
Bhutan	7.7	7.2	8.2	10.8	4.0	8.0	8.8	6.8	17.9	4.7	6.7	6.8
India	6.4	4.4	5.8	3.8	8.5	7.5	9.5	9.7	9.2	6.7	8.0	8.6
Iran (Islamic Republic of)	1.9	5.1	3.3	7.5	6.8	4.8	5.7	6.2	6.9	2.5	1.5	3.0
Maldives	7.2	4.8	3.5	6.5	8.5	9.5	-4.6	18.0	7.2	5.8	-2.3	4.8
Nepal	4.3	5.9	4.7	0.2	3.8	4.4	3.2	3.7	2.8	5.8	4.0	3.5
Pakistan	4.2	3.9	2.0	3.1	4.7	7.5	9.0	5.8	6.8	4.1	1.2	4.1
Sri Lanka	4.3	6.0	-1.4	4.0	5.9	5.4	6.2	7.7	6.8	6.0	3.5	8.0
Turkey	-3.4	6.8	-5.7	6.2	5.3	9.4	8.4	6.9	4.7	0.7	-4.7	8.1
South-East Asia	4.0	6.6	2.0	5.0	5.5	6.6	5.8	6.2	6.6	4.2	1.0	8.1
Brunei Darussalam	3.1	2.8	2.7	3.9	2.9	0.5	0.4	4.4	0.2	-1.9	-1.8	1.1
Cambodia	12.6	8.4	7.7	7.0	8.5	10.3	13.2	10.8	10.2	6.7	-2.0	6.0
Indonesia	0.8	4.9	3.6	4.5	4.8	5.0	5.7	5.5	6.3	6.0	4.5	6.1
Lao People's Democratic Republic	7.3	6.3	4.6	6.9	6.2	7.0	6.8	8.7	7.8	7.2	7.6	8.0
Malaysia	6.1	8.9	0.5	5.4	5.8	6.8	5.3	5.8	6.5	4.7	-1.7	7.2
Myanmar	10.9	13.7	11.3	12.0	13.8	13.6	13.6	13.1	11.9	3.6	4.9	5.5
Philippines	3.4	6.0	1.8	4.4	4.9	6.4	5.0	5.3	7.1	3.7	1.1	7.3
Singapore	7.2	10.1	-2.4	4.1	3.8	9.3	7.3	8.4	7.8	1.8	-0.8	14.5
Thailand	4.4	4.8	2.2	5.3	7.1	6.3	4.6	5.2	4.9	2.5	-2.2	7.8
Timor-Leste	-35.5	13.7	16.5	2.4	0.1	4.4	6.5	-5.9	9.1	11.0	11.6	7.9
Viet Nam	4.8	6.8	6.9	7.1	7.3	7.8	8.4	8.2	8.5	6.3	5.3	6.8
Memorandum items:												
Developing ESCAP economies	6.2	7.2	4.8	6.8	7.3	8.2	8.6	9.3	9.9	6.1	4.7	8.8
(excluding China and India)	4.8	6.9	1.1	5.5	4.5	6.6	5.7	6.0	6.0	2.7	-0.5	7.4
East and North-East Asia (excluding China and Japan)	7.8	7.8	1.8	5.8	3.2	6.0	4.8	5.7	5.8	2.0	-0.9	7.7
North and Central Asia (excluding Russian Federation)	5.3	7.6	9.0	7.5	8.2	8.7	12.5	14.4	12.7	7.0	4.0	6.6
South and South-West Asia (excluding India)	0.1	5.9	-1.2	5.7	5.5	7.6	7.5	6.6	5.7	2.4	-1.0	6.1
Developed ESCAP economies	0.3	2.9	0.5	0.7	1.6	2.8	2.0	2.1	2.6	-0.8	-5.5	3.8

Source and table notes appear in the technical notes at the end of the annex.

Table 2. Gross domestic savings rates

(Percentage of GDP)

	1999	2000	2001	2002	2003	2004	2005	2006	2007	2008	2009	2010
East and North-East Asia												
China	38.0	38.0	39.0	40.4	43.0	45.2	46.4	47.9	50.5	51.5	52.0	51.1
Hong Kong, China	30.1	32.0	29.8	31.1	31.2	30.7	33.0	33.1	31.8	30.6	29.7	28.5
Japan	26.2	26.4	24.3	23.6	23.8	24.0	24.6	24.2	24.1	21.9	18.9	20.2
Macao, China	42.9	47.4	47.9	51.6	56.7	63.5	63.6	67.3	70.7	70.3	67.3	61.1
Mongolia	14.6	10.4	5.7	3.4	12.2	19.5	32.0	39.8	37.2	35.7	24.7	34.5
Republic of Korea	35.1	33.3	31.3	30.7	32.2	34.1	32.3	31.0	30.9	30.0	29.7	30.9
North and Central Asia												
Armenia	-8.3	-8.9	-4.8	0.9	6.5	7.4	14.0	17.7	18.2	18.2	6.1	4.7
Azerbaijan	8.6	20.4	24.9	24.7	27.6	31.3	47.5	54.4	56.9	58.1	43.9	46.6
Georgia	8.2	0.9	10.9	12.4	17.9	12.7	15.7	5.9	7.4	-2.7	-7.1	-5.0
Kazakhstan	16.0	26.0	28.7	33.8	34.3	34.9	38.9	44.1	43.8	46.3	41.6	45.5
Kyrgyzstan	3.2	14.3	17.7	13.8	5.3	5.8	-2.1	-13.1	-4.6	-10.8	-10.2	-8.4
Russian Federation	31.9	38.7	34.6	30.8	32.1	33.1	33.7	34.1	32.9	34.9	25.3	32.0
Tajikistan	19.4	0.6	1.8	6.4	9.3	14.2	4.3	6.0	6.9	3.1	-15.3	..
Turkmenistan	12.3	49.3	36.2	43.2	31.1	25.2	40.5	58.0	55.0	40.0	41.0	40.7
Uzbekistan	17.3	19.4	20.0	21.8	26.9	31.9	32.7	26.6	30.2	29.8	28.9	..
Pacific												
Pacific island developing economies												
Cook Islands	22.0	23.2	27.5	25.5	24.2	21.8	24.7	24.1	21.1	18.7	21.3	..
Fiji	22.4	12.2	8.1	17.3	13.6	2.5	2.9	-5.6	-4.2	-5.5	-4.0	..
Kiribati	7.9	7.5	4.8	4.3	-9.5	-11.0	-67.8	-64.5	-60.3	-59.9	-59.4	..
Papua New Guinea	26.6	38.8	36.0	27.9	35.7	31.0	35.9	36.1	33.1	40.8	22.9	23.0
Samoa	-13.0	-9.2	-14.1	-14.5	-14.0	-14.1	-14.0	-13.9	-14.1	-14.4	-13.7	..
Solomon Islands	-0.2	-7.9	-12.7	-5.5	4.1	0.0	-6.8	-6.5	..	..	..	..
Tonga	-8.3	-9.8	-8.0	-6.1	-8.9	-11.5	-18.7	-17.9	-18.8	-19.1	-19.2	..
Tuvalu	6.5	-21.3	5.2	-61.5	-64.2	-72.2	-69.7	-81.9	-68.8	-71.3	-72.8	..
Vanuatu	19.2	19.3	17.9	9.4	12.7	16.4	20.2	23.8	24.9	25.5	23.7	..
Developed economies												
Australia	23.6	24.1	23.4	24.1	23.7	24.4	24.7	26.4	27.0	27.5	27.1	29.5
New Zealand	21.3	23.0	24.4	23.9	23.6	23.8	22.5	21.8	23.1	21.4	20.4	21.2
South and South-West Asia												
Bangladesh	17.7	17.9	18.0	18.2	18.6	19.5	20.0	20.2	20.4	20.3	20.1	19.2
Bhutan	28.9	30.3	33.9	36.4	35.6	34.6	36.6	38.8	42.7	42.3	42.0	41.2
India	24.8	23.7	23.5	26.3	29.8	32.2	33.1	34.4	36.4	32.5	30.4	32.1
Iran (Islamic Republic of)	25.4	26.8	38.4	38.5	38.6	39.6	39.3	37.7	37.0	37.6	39.1	38.0
Maldives	44.2	44.2	44.9	46.3	48.8	42.7	28.0	36.8	35.8	33.5	35.4	..
Nepal	12.6	14.1	11.7	9.5	8.6	11.7	11.6	9.0	9.8	9.8	9.7	9.4
Pakistan	14.0	16.0	15.9	16.5	17.3	17.6	15.2	14.2	15.4	11.0	11.4	10.6
Sri Lanka	18.1	15.4	16.5	16.0	16.0	16.4	17.9	17.0	17.6	13.9	18.0	19.0
Turkey	19.3	17.8	19.2	19.2	16.6	16.8	16.5	17.1	15.9	17.3	13.7	14.2
South-East Asia												
Brunei Darussalam	36.9	49.4	44.3	47.2	48.6	51.4	59.1	62.1	57.3	65.2	61.5	57.2
Cambodia	7.6	8.1	11.6	8.5	9.1	8.5	9.9	13.8	16.1	30.3	..	..
Indonesia	19.5	31.8	30.0	25.1	23.7	24.9	27.5	28.7	28.1	31.0	31.8	34.1
Lao People's Democratic Republic	2.5	14.2	17.9	19.3	21.1	16.4	18.8	22.5	23.1	25.5	17.9	..
Malaysia	47.4	46.1	41.8	42.0	42.5	43.4	42.8	43.1	42.1	42.3	36.0	39.1
Myanmar	13.0	12.3	11.5	10.2	11.0	12.3	13.1	15.2	14.9	16.9	16.6	17.2
Philippines	14.3	17.3	17.1	19.1	19.7	21.2	21.0	20.1	20.8	19.3	15.6	21.0
Singapore	49.0	47.4	44.2	40.5	43.6	47.1	49.4	51.0	53.0	50.6	48.3	52.6
Thailand	32.5	32.5	31.4	31.7	32.0	31.7	30.9	32.4	34.4	32.5	31.7	33.2
Viet Nam	24.6	27.1	28.8	28.7	27.4	28.5	30.3	30.6	29.2	26.5	27.2	27.5

Source and table notes appear in the technical notes at the end of the annex.

Table 3. Gross domestic investment rates

(Percentage of GDP)

	1999	2000	2001	2002	2003	2004	2005	2006	2007	2008	2009	2010
East and North-East Asia												
China	36.7	35.1	36.3	37.9	41.2	43.3	42.1	43.0	41.7	44.0	47.7	48.8
Hong Kong, China	24.8	27.5	25.3	22.8	21.9	21.8	20.6	21.7	20.9	20.4	22.6	22.6
Japan	24.8	25.4	24.8	23.1	22.8	23.0	23.6	23.8	23.7	23.6	20.4	20.3
Macao, China	17.7	11.6	10.3	11.0	14.6	17.0	27.5	35.4	36.8	29.2	18.6	10.0
Mongolia	37.0	36.2	36.1	39.6	35.5	34.5	37.0	35.1	40.2	52.2	49.0	47.5
Republic of Korea	28.9	30.6	29.2	29.2	29.9	29.9	29.7	29.6	29.4	31.2	25.9	29.4
North and Central Asia												
Armenia	18.4	18.6	19.8	21.7	24.3	24.9	30.5	35.9	37.8	40.9	33.8	34.2
Azerbaijan	26.5	20.7	20.7	34.6	53.2	58.0	41.5	29.9	21.5	18.7	18.3	17.4
Georgia	26.5	26.6	30.3	28.5	31.3	31.9	33.5	30.9	32.1	27.0	12.1	17.0
Kazakhstan	17.8	18.1	26.9	27.3	25.7	26.3	31.0	33.9	35.5	27.5	29.6	27.6
Kyrgyzstan	18.0	20.0	18.0	17.6	11.8	14.5	16.4	24.2	26.6	24.8	19.0	24.4
Russian Federation	14.8	18.7	21.9	20.0	20.8	20.9	20.1	21.4	24.3	25.4	18.7	22.5
Tajikistan	17.3	9.4	9.7	9.4	10.0	12.2	11.6	16.0	24.6	26.5	25.0	24.2
Turkmenistan	39.7	34.7	31.7	27.6	25.4	23.1	22.9	23.8	23.3	23.3	..	..
Uzbekistan	17.1	19.6	21.1	21.2	20.8	23.9	23.0	18.5	21.8	21.1	20.5	..
Pacific												
Pacific island developing economies												
Cook Islands	13.0	12.4	11.0	12.1	13.8	14.7	13.2	13.7	14.5	14.1	14.1	..
Fiji	22.8	17.3	16.1	19.7	22.0	19.2	19.4	28.6	24.7	23.8	23.7	22.2
Kiribati	48.3	48.3	49.7	50.1	57.2	58.0	87.7	86.0	83.8	83.6	83.3	..
Papua New Guinea	16.1	21.9	23.0	25.0	21.4	21.4	17.5	15.7	15.1	15.9	17.3	19.2
Samoa	14.1	14.2	14.3	13.1	12.3	11.2	10.4	9.8	9.1	8.7	9.2	..
Solomon Islands	6.2	6.6	6.8	5.4	9.4	11.4	13.8	14.6	13.3	13.9	13.9	..
Tonga	21.3	21.7	24.7	30.8	25.7	23.5	22.4	19.5	19.7	26.3	26.1	26.2
Tuvalu	54.8	52.0	77.3	35.5	36.6	3.3	8.1	0.9	15.6	12.9	8.2	..
Vanuatu	20.3	22.2	20.0	21.1	19.4	21.2	21.5	23.9	25.8	23.4	22.2	21.2
Developed economies												
Australia	25.9	26.1	23.2	24.0	25.7	26.9	27.2	27.9	28.2	29.6	28.3	27.7
New Zealand	22.0	21.3	22.1	22.0	23.2	24.4	24.7	23.2	23.9	22.4	18.2	18.7
South and South-West Asia												
Bangladesh	22.2	23.0	23.1	23.1	23.4	24.0	24.5	24.7	24.5	24.2	24.4	23.8
Bhutan	39.4	48.2	59.2	59.2	56.8	64.1	50.8	47.3	36.6	40.5	37.9	39.5
India	25.9	24.3	22.8	25.2	27.6	32.5	34.3	35.5	37.7	34.9	35.0	35.7
Iran (Islamic Republic of)	26.0	27.1	32.6	33.9	35.1	35.7	35.8	35.0	36.4	38.9	40.8	42.7
Maldives	34.0	26.0	28.0	26.0	27.0	35.0	53.0	..	..	..	..	..
Nepal	19.0	22.6	22.3	20.2	21.4	24.5	26.5	26.9	28.7	30.3	31.9	38.2
Pakistan	15.6	17.2	17.0	16.6	16.8	16.6	19.1	22.1	22.5	22.1	19.0	16.6
Sri Lanka	25.6	25.4	22.2	22.0	21.6	24.7	26.1	27.4	27.3	27.1	24.4	24.8
Turkey	19.1	20.8	15.1	17.6	17.6	19.4	20.0	22.1	21.5	21.8	14.8	17.5
South-East Asia												
Brunei Darussalam	21.4	13.1	14.4	21.3	15.1	13.5	11.4	10.4	13.0	13.7	14.7	15.1
Cambodia	16.7	16.9	18.5	18.1	20.1	16.2	18.5	20.6	20.8	16.6	22.5	21.8
Indonesia	11.4	22.2	22.5	21.4	25.6	24.1	25.1	25.4	24.9	27.8	31.0	30.7
Lao People's Democratic Republic	22.7	20.5	21.0	24.0	21.4	21.1	17.5	21.4	22.0	24.0	..	..
Malaysia	22.4	26.9	24.4	24.8	22.8	23.0	20.0	20.5	21.6	19.3	14.5	20.0
Myanmar	13.4	12.4	11.6	10.1	11.0	12.2	13.2	13.7	14.7	14.4	14.9	15.5
Philippines	18.8	21.2	19.0	17.7	16.8	16.8	14.6	14.5	15.4	15.3	14.6	15.0
Singapore	32.0	32.5	26.0	23.7	16.0	21.8	20.0	20.8	21.2	29.9	27.2	28.5
Thailand	20.5	22.8	24.1	23.8	25.0	26.8	31.4	28.3	26.4	28.9	21.8	25.5
Viet Nam	27.6	29.6	31.2	33.2	35.4	35.5	35.6	36.8	43.1	39.7	38.1	39.0

Source and table notes appear in the technical notes at the end of the annex.

Table 4. Inflation rates

(Percentage)

	1999	2000	2001	2002	2003	2004	2005	2006	2007	2008	2009	2010
East and North-East Asia	-0.6	-0.1	0.1	-0.6	0.4	1.6	0.8	0.9	2.2	3.7	-0.2	1.2
China	-1.4	0.4	0.7	-0.8	1.2	3.9	1.8	1.5	4.8	5.9	-0.7	3.3
Democratic People's Republic of Korea												
Hong Kong, China	-4.0	-3.8	-1.6	-3.1	-2.5	-0.4	0.9	2.1	2.0	4.3	0.5	2.4
Japan	-0.3	-0.7	-0.8	-0.9	-0.3	0.0	-0.3	0.2	0.1	1.4	-1.4	-0.7
Macao, China	-3.2	-1.6	2.0	-2.6	-1.6	1.0	4.4	5.1	5.6	8.6	1.2	2.8
Mongolia	7.5	11.6	6.3	0.9	5.1	8.2	12.7	5.1	9.0	25.1	6.3	10.1
Republic of Korea	0.8	2.3	4.1	2.8	3.5	3.6	2.8	2.2	2.5	4.7	2.8	3.0
North and Central Asia	70.4	19.1	19.5	14.7	12.2	10.0	11.8	9.7	9.6	14.5	10.8	7.1
Armenia	0.7	-0.8	3.1	1.1	4.8	7.0	0.6	2.9	4.4	9.0	3.4	8.2
Azerbaijan	-8.5	1.8	1.5	2.8	2.1	6.8	9.7	8.4	16.6	20.8	1.5	5.7
Georgia	19.1	4.0	4.7	5.6	4.8	5.7	8.2	9.2	9.2	10.0	1.7	7.1
Kazakhstan	8.3	13.2	8.4	5.9	6.4	6.9	7.6	8.6	10.8	17.2	7.3	7.1
Kyrgyzstan	36.0	18.7	6.9	2.1	3.1	4.1	4.4	5.6	10.2	24.5	6.8	8.0
Russian Federation	85.7	20.8	21.5	15.8	13.7	10.9	12.7	9.7	9.0	14.1	11.7	6.9
Tajikistan	26.0	24.0	36.5	10.2	17.1	6.8	7.8	11.9	21.5	20.4	6.5	6.5
Turkmenistan	23.5	8.0	11.6	8.8	5.6	5.9	10.7	8.2	6.3	13.0	10.0	12.0
Uzbekistan	29.1	25.0	27.3	27.3	11.6	6.6	10.0	14.2	12.3	12.7	14.1	9.3
Pacific	1.4	4.4	4.2	3.0	2.8	2.3	2.7	3.5	2.3	4.4	1.9	2.7
Pacific island developing economies	9.8	9.7	7.0	7.9	10.0	3.0	2.8	3.2	2.7	10.3	6.7	4.7
Cook Islands	1.3	3.2	8.7	3.4	2.0	0.9	2.5	3.4	2.5	7.8	6.6	3.5
Fiji	2.0	1.1	4.3	0.8	4.2	2.8	2.4	2.5	4.8	7.7	6.8	4.0
Kiribati	1.8	0.4	6.0	3.2	1.9	-1.0	-0.3	-1.5	4.2	11.0	8.4	0.8
Marshall Islands	1.7	1.6	1.7	1.3	-2.8	2.2	4.4	4.3	2.6	14.7	0.5	1.0
Micronesia (Federated States of)	..	2.2	0.5	-0.1	0.1	2.3	4.3	4.4	3.6	6.8	7.4	3.5
Nauru	..	..	..	..	..	2.3	2.7	3.5	2.3	4.5	2.2	-0.5
Palau	..	..	-1.8	-1.3	0.9	5.0	3.9	4.5	3.2	11.3	5.2	3.8
Papua New Guinea	14.9	15.6	9.3	11.8	14.7	2.1	1.8	2.4	0.9	10.8	7.0	6.0
Samoa	0.8	-0.2	1.9	7.4	4.3	7.8	7.8	3.2	4.5	11.5	6.6	1.0
Solomon Islands	7.9	6.8	7.4	9.5	10.5	6.9	7.0	11.1	7.7	17.3	7.1	3.0
Tonga	4.5	6.2	8.3	10.4	11.6	11.0	9.9	7.3	5.1	9.8	5.0	2.0
Tuvalu	4.0	1.3	1.3	8.0	3.3	2.8	3.2	3.8	2.2	10.4	0.0	-1.9
Vanuatu	3.1	2.1	3.5	2.1	1.1	3.2	1.2	2.6	4.1	4.8	4.5	3.4
Developed economies	1.3	4.3	4.2	3.0	2.7	2.3	2.7	3.5	2.3	4.4	1.8	2.7
Australia	1.5	4.5	4.4	3.0	2.8	2.3	2.7	3.5	2.3	4.4	1.8	2.7
New Zealand	-0.1	2.6	2.6	2.7	1.8	2.3	3.0	3.4	2.4	4.0	2.1	2.3
South and South-West Asia	19.8	16.1	15.9	14.4	9.8	6.2	6.5	8.2	8.3	11.4	11.0	10.3
Afghanistan						13.2	12.3	5.1	13.0	26.8	-8.3	0.4
Bangladesh	7.0	2.8	1.9	2.8	4.4	5.8	6.5	7.2	7.2	9.9	6.7	7.3
Bhutan	6.8	4.0	3.4	2.5	2.1	4.6	5.3	5.0	5.2	8.8	3.0	6.1
India	4.7	4.0	3.8	4.3	3.8	3.8	4.4	6.7	6.2	9.1	12.4	11.0
Iran (Islamic Republic of)	20.1	12.6	11.4	15.8	15.6	15.2	12.1	13.6	18.4	25.4	10.8	12.0
Maldives	3.0	-1.2	0.7	0.9	-2.9	6.4	3.3	3.5	7.4	12.3	4.0	6.0
Nepal	11.4	3.4	2.4	2.9	4.8	4.0	4.5	8.0	6.4	7.7	13.2	10.7
Pakistan	5.7	3.6	4.4	3.5	3.1	4.6	9.3	7.9	7.8	12.0	20.8	11.7
Sri Lanka	4.7	6.2	14.2	9.6	6.3	9.0	11.0	10.0	15.8	22.6	3.4	5.9
Turkey	64.9	54.9	54.4	45.1	25.3	8.6	8.2	9.6	8.8	10.4	6.3	8.6
South-East Asia	7.9	2.3	5.0	4.8	3.3	4.2	6.1	6.7	4.0	8.8	2.3	4.0
Brunei Darussalam	-0.1	1.2	0.6	-2.3	0.3	0.9	1.1	0.2	0.3	2.7	1.8	1.8
Cambodia	4.0	-0.8	-0.6	3.2	1.2	3.9	6.3	6.1	7.7	25.0	-0.7	4.1
Indonesia	20.5	3.7	11.5	11.9	6.6	6.2	10.5	13.1	6.3	10.1	4.8	5.1
Lao People's Democratic Republic	128.4	25.1	7.8	10.6	15.5	10.5	7.2	6.8	4.5	7.6	0.0	5.4
Malaysia	2.7	1.5	1.4	1.8	1.0	1.5	3.0	3.6	2.0	5.4	0.6	1.7
Myanmar	10.9	-1.7	34.5	58.1	24.9	3.8	10.7	26.3	32.9	22.5	8.0	7.9
Philippines	5.9	4.0	6.8	3.0	3.5	6.0	7.7	6.3	2.8	9.3	3.2	3.8
Singapore	0.0	1.4	1.0	-0.4	0.5	1.7	0.5	1.0	2.1	6.6	0.6	2.8
Thailand	0.3	1.6	1.6	0.7	1.8	2.8	4.5	4.6	2.2	5.5	-0.8	3.3
Timor-Leste	..	63.6	3.6	4.7	7.2	3.2	1.1	3.9	10.3	9.1	0.7	6.5
Viet Nam	4.1	-1.7	-0.4	3.8	3.2	7.8	8.3	7.4	8.3	23.1	6.9	9.0
Memorandum items:												
Developing ESCAP economies	5.2	4.5	5.2	4.0	3.6	4.2	3.6	3.9	5.0	7.3	2.9	4.9
(excluding China and India)	11.4	8.5	9.7	8.3	5.7	4.5	5.1	5.3	4.9	8.1	3.6	4.6
East and North-East Asia	-0.2	0.9	1.9	0.9	1.4	2.3	2.4	1.8	2.3	4.4	1.4	2.3
(excluding China and Japan)												
North and Central Asia	12.4	12.6	11.9	10.4	6.7	6.6	8.5	9.7	11.7	16.0	7.6	7.8
(excluding Russian Federation)												
South and South-West Asia	37.6	30.4	30.2	26.5	16.8	9.1	9.1	9.9	10.8	14.2	9.4	9.6
(excluding India)												
Developed ESCAP economies	-0.1	-0.2	-0.2	-0.5	0.0	0.2	0.0	0.6	0.3	1.7	-1.1	-0.3

Source and table notes appear in the technical notes at the end of the annex.

Table 5. Budget balance

(Percentage of GDP)

	1999	2000	2001	2002	2003	2004	2005	2006	2007	2008	2009	2010
East and North-East Asia												
China	-3.0	-2.8	-2.5	-2.6	-2.2	-1.3	-1.2	-0.8	0.6	-0.4	-2.2	-2.2
Hong Kong, China	0.8	-0.6	-4.9	-4.8	-3.2	1.7	1.0	4.1	7.7	0.2	1.1	2.9
Japan	-7.3	-6.4	-5.9	-6.7	-6.7	-5.2	-6.2	-1.0	-2.6	-2.6	-7.2	-7.5
Mongolia	-11.6	-7.7	-4.5	-5.8	-3.7	-1.8	2.6	3.3	2.9	-4.9	-5.4	0.0
Republic of Korea	-2.4	1.1	1.1	3.1	1.0	0.6	0.4	0.4	3.5	1.2	-1.7	-1.9
North and Central Asia												
Armenia	-5.2	-4.9	-4.3	-2.6	-1.3	-1.7	-1.9	-1.5	-1.5	-0.7	-4.7	-5.2
Azerbaijan	-2.4	-1.0	-0.4	-0.4	-0.2	0.3	-0.7	0.4	-0.3	0.0	-0.7	-2.3
Georgia	-6.7	-3.7	-1.8	-3.7	-2.9	-3.2	-1.1	-3.0	-4.7	-6.3	-9.2	-6.6
Kazakhstan	-3.5	-0.1	-0.4	-0.3	-0.9	-0.3	0.6	0.8	-1.7	-2.1	-3.1	-3.0
Kyrgyzstan	-2.0	-2.2	0.4	-1.0	-0.8	-0.5	0.2	-0.2	0.1	0.8	-1.5	-9.0
Russian Federation	-1.2	2.4	3.1	1.7	2.4	4.8	7.5	7.5	5.4	4.1	-5.9	-4.1
Tajikistan	-2.4	-5.7	-3.1	-2.4	-1.8	-2.4	-1.6	0.4	1.7	1.6	-0.5	-1.2
Turkmenistan	0.0	-0.3	0.6	0.2	-1.3	1.4	0.8	5.3	3.9	11.3	7.7	5.0
Uzbekistan	-1.7	-1.0	-1.0	-1.5	0.6	1.2	2.8	3.8	2.7	1.5	0.2	0.2
Pacific												
Pacific island developing economies												
Cook Islands	-2.4	-1.8	1.3	-4.2	-0.8	-1.0	2.1	2.6	0.1	-0.8	-11.7	-0.8
Fiji	-0.3	-3.2	-6.5	-5.7	-5.8	-3.1	-3.4	-2.8	-1.7	-3.2	-3.8	-3.6
Kiribati	37.5	41.8	9.8	3.7	9.6	11.9	7.5	-1.7	2.7	1.8	1.7	0.6
Papua New Guinea	-2.6	-2.0	-3.4	-3.8	-0.9	1.7	0.1	3.1	2.4	-2.2	-0.2	0.0
Samoa	0.3	-0.7	-2.2	-2.0	-0.6	-0.8	0.3	-0.5	0.6	-1.9	-3.9	-8.1
Solomon Islands	-3.7	-7.5	-12.3	-10.3	0.2	5.1	2.5	1.5	1.3	-0.3	2.2	2.4
Tonga	-0.2	-0.3	-0.1	2.6	1.3	4.6	3.1	-4.8	1.6	1.8	-1.0	-0.6
Tuvalu	-3.5	-1.9	-43.0	33.0	-32.8	-14.3	-7.6	-15.8	-19.0	0.2	-0.3	-27.9
Vanuatu	-0.5	-6.1	-3.5	-3.5	-1.4	0.9	2.8	0.4	-1.4	2.2	1.0	-2.1
Developed economies												
Australia	0.6	1.9	0.9	-0.4	0.7	0.7	1.3	1.7	1.5	1.8	-2.4	-4.1
New Zealand	0.1	2.1	1.9	3.7	4.0	4.2	5.0	5.7	4.1	0.4	-3.7	-5.3
South and South-West Asia												
Bangladesh	-4.6	-6.1	-5.2	-4.7	-4.2	-4.2	-4.4	-3.9	-3.7	-6.1	-4.1	-4.5
Bhutan	-1.7	-3.9	-10.6	-4.6	-9.8	1.9	-6.7	-0.8	0.6	0.8	2.0	-6.7
India	-5.4	-5.7	-6.2	-5.9	-4.5	-3.9	-4.0	-3.3	-2.6	-5.9	-6.6	-5.1
Iran (Islamic Republic of)	-0.2	-0.2	-0.4	-4.1	-3.4	-3.0	-3.7	-7.2	-3.5	-5.0	-4.0	-1.8
Maldives	-4.1	-4.4	-4.7	-4.9	-3.4	-1.6	-10.9	-6.8	-4.7	-16.9	-29.4	-20.9
Nepal	-4.9	-4.3	-5.5	-5.0	-3.3	-2.9	-3.1	-3.8	-4.1	-4.1	-5.0	-3.9
Pakistan	-6.1	-5.4	-4.3	-4.3	-3.7	-2.3	-3.3	-4.3	-4.4	-7.6	-5.2	-6.3
Sri Lanka	-7.3	-9.7	-10.6	-8.6	-7.7	-7.9	-8.4	-8.0	-7.7	-7.7	-9.9	-8.0
Turkey	-6.4	-5.6	-11.9	-12.0	-8.7	-5.3	-1.5	-0.6	-1.6	-1.8	-5.5	-3.3
South-East Asia												
Cambodia	-3.8	-4.8	-6.3	-7.0	-6.1	-3.5	-2.6	-2.7	-2.7	-2.5	-5.7	-5.3
Indonesia	-2.5	-1.1	-2.5	-1.5	-1.8	-1.0	-0.6	-0.9	-1.3	-0.1	-1.6	-0.8
Lao People's Democratic Republic	-2.6	-4.6	-4.5	-3.4	-5.7	-2.6	-4.5	-3.1	-2.6	-2.2	-3.3	-3.0
Malaysia	-3.2	-5.5	-5.2	-5.3	-5.0	-4.1	-3.6	-3.3	-3.2	-4.8	-7.0	-5.6
Myanmar	-0.3	0.7	..	..	..	..	..	..	..	..	..	..
Philippines	-3.8	-4.0	-4.0	-5.3	-4.6	-3.8	-2.7	-1.1	-0.2	-0.9	-3.9	-3.9
Singapore	0.5	2.0	1.6	-1.1	-1.6	-1.1	-0.3	0.5	3.1	1.4	-1.0	-0.7
Thailand	-3.3	-2.2	-2.4	-1.4	0.4	0.1	-0.6	1.1	-1.7	-1.1	-4.4	-0.7
Timor-Leste	..	2.0	1.0	4.0	14.0	46.0	102.0	174.0	284.0	384.0	178.0	..
Viet Nam	-4.4	-5.0	-4.9	-4.8	-4.9	-4.9	-4.9	-5.0	-4.9	-4.5	-6.9	-6.2

Source and table notes appear in the technical notes at the end of the annex.

Table 6. Current account balance

(Percentage of GDP)

	1999	2000	2001	2002	2003	2004	2005	2006	2007	2008	2009	2010
East and North-East Asia												
China	1.9	1.7	1.3	2.4	2.8	3.6	7.2	9.5	11.0	9.8	6.1	5.2
Hong Kong, China	6.3	4.1	5.9	7.6	10.4	9.5	11.4	12.1	12.3	13.6	8.7	8.4
Japan	2.6	2.6	2.1	2.9	3.2	3.7	3.6	3.9	4.8	3.2	2.8	3.2
Macao, China	..	..	..	39.8	39.9	40.5	28.4	19.2	30.1	26.6	36.9	..
Mongolia	-5.8	-5.0	-12.0	-8.6	-7.1	1.3	1.3	7.0	6.7	-14.0	-9.8	-15.0
Republic of Korea	5.5	2.3	1.6	0.9	1.9	3.9	1.8	0.6	0.8	-0.6	5.1	3.5
North and Central Asia												
Armenia	-16.6	-14.6	-9.4	-6.2	-6.7	-0.5	-1.1	-1.8	-6.4	-11.8	-16.0	-14.2
Azerbaijan	-13.1	-3.2	-0.9	-12.3	-27.8	-29.8	1.3	17.7	27.3	33.7	23.7	31.3
Georgia	-10.0	-7.9	-6.4	-6.4	-9.6	-6.9	-11.1	-15.1	-19.7	-22.7	-11.7	-10.9
Kazakhstan	-1.0	2.0	-6.5	-4.4	-0.9	0.8	-1.8	-2.5	-8.1	4.6	-3.2	4.5
Kyrgyzstan	-20.1	-9.0	-3.4	-3.8	-3.2	0.2	-2.4	-10.6	-6.9	-14.6	-6.6	-3.6
Russian Federation	12.6	18.0	11.0	8.5	8.2	10.1	11.1	9.6	6.1	6.2	4.0	4.5
Tajikistan	-0.9	-1.6	-4.9	-3.5	-1.3	-3.9	-2.7	-2.8	-8.6	-7.7	-4.9	-3.6
Turkmenistan	-14.8	8.2	1.7	6.7	2.7	0.6	5.1	15.7	15.5	18.7	17.8	30.0
Uzbekistan	-0.7	1.6	-1.6	1.2	8.7	10.1	14.2	17.2	19.4	14.2	11.0	17.9
Pacific												
Pacific island developing economies												
Fiji	-1.1	-3.9	-6.6	2.5	-6.4	-12.6	-9.9	-18.8	-13.6	-17.9	-8.1	-2.3
Kiribati	11.9	-0.8	16.1	7.6	-19.5	-11.1	-18.5	-2.9	-1.0	-0.6	-4.1	-7.1
Papua New Guinea	4.2	10.1	8.8	-4.2	3.8	2.9	12.5	8.0	2.9	9.9	-7.3	-26.6
Samoa	-9.6	-1.9	-4.6	-8.9	-8.3	-8.4	-9.6	-11.1	-15.9	-6.2	-2.0	-8.0
Solomon Islands	3.1	-7.6	-6.4	-4.3	6.3	16.3	-7.0	-1.6	-8.2	-16.4	-21.1	-20.0
Tonga	-0.8	-5.2	-8.1	4.0	-2.4	3.2	-2.2	-7.8	-8.3	-8.9	-9.2	-5.6
Vanuatu	-4.4	1.7	1.8	-4.6	-5.7	-6.0	-8.4	-5.3	-6.9	-5.9	-2.2	-2.4
Developed economies												
Australia	-5.1	-3.7	-2.0	-3.7	-5.3	-5.9	-5.6	-5.3	-6.1	-4.6	-4.4	-2.7
New Zealand	-6.0	-5.0	-2.7	-3.9	-4.2	-6.1	-8.2	-8.4	-7.9	-8.7	-3.2	-3.4
South and South-West Asia												
Bangladesh	-0.9	0.0	-1.7	0.5	0.4	0.9	-0.6	1.2	1.4	1.5	2.8	3.2
Bhutan	2.2	5.4	-8.8	-14.9	-21.8	-17.6	-29.2	-4.3	12.2	-2.2	-1.7	-13.3
India	-1.0	-0.6	0.7	1.3	2.4	-0.4	-1.2	-1.0	-1.3	-2.4	-2.8	-3.0
Iran (Islamic Republic of)	6.3	13.0	5.2	3.1	0.6	0.6	8.8	9.2	11.9	7.3	3.6	4.2
Maldives	-13.4	-8.2	-9.8	-5.6	-4.5	-15.8	-36.4	-33.0	-41.5	-51.4	-30.8	-27.0
Nepal	4.0	2.9	4.5	4.2	2.4	2.7	2.0	2.2	-0.1	2.9	4.2	-2.3
Pakistan	-2.6	-0.3	0.4	3.9	4.9	1.8	-1.4	-3.9	-4.8	-8.5	-5.7	-2.0
Sri Lanka	-3.5	-6.3	-1.1	-1.4	-0.4	-3.1	-2.5	-5.3	-4.3	-9.8	-0.5	-3.7
Turkey	-0.4	-3.7	1.9	-0.3	-2.5	-3.7	-4.6	-6.0	-5.9	-5.7	-2.3	-5.9
South-East Asia												
Cambodia	-5.0	-2.7	-1.1	-2.3	-3.6	-2.2	-3.6	0.4	-2.8	-7.3	-5.1	-7.3
Indonesia	4.1	4.8	4.3	4.0	3.5	0.6	0.1	3.0	2.4	0.1	2.0	1.3
Lao People's Democratic Republic	-8.3	-0.5	-3.8	0.5	-1.5	-7.1	-6.1	2.2	3.4	2.2	0.2	-0.4
Malaysia	15.9	9.0	7.9	7.1	12.1	12.1	14.5	16.7	15.7	17.5	16.5	13.4
Myanmar	-0.1	-0.1	-0.03	0.01	0.00	0.01	0.00	0.03	..	..	..	..
Philippines	-3.8	-2.9	-2.4	-0.4	0.4	1.9	2.0	4.5	4.9	2.2	5.3	5.4
Singapore	17.0	10.8	12.8	12.9	22.8	17.1	21.3	24.2	26.7	18.5	17.8	19.7
Thailand	10.1	7.6	4.4	3.7	3.3	1.7	-4.3	1.1	6.3	0.4	7.7	3.9
Timor-Leste	..	-6.7	-12.2	-15.6	-15.1	21.1	78.8	165.5	295.8	405.4	231.0	203.0
Viet Nam	4.1	3.5	2.1	-1.7	-4.9	-2.1	-1.1	-0.3	-9.8	-11.8	-7.7	-5.6

Source and table notes appear in the technical notes at the end of the annex.

Table 7.	Change in money supply

(Percentage)

	1999	2000	2001	2002	2003	2004	2005	2006	2007	2008	2009	2010
East and North-East Asia												
China	14.7	12.3	15.0	13.1	19.2	14.9	16.7	22.1	16.7	17.8	28.4	18.9
Hong Kong, China	8.3	9.3	-0.3	0.5	6.3	7.3	3.5	16.2	18.8	4.2	5.2	7.4
Japan	2.8	1.3	-17.1	0.9	0.5	0.6	0.5	-0.7	0.7	0.7	2.1	2.3[a]
Macao, China				8.1	12.3	8.9	12.2	24.5	9.8	2.3	11.8	14.6
Mongolia	31.6	17.6	27.9	42.0	49.6	20.4	34.6	34.8	56.3	-5.5	26.9	62.5
Republic of Korea	27.4	25.4	13.2	11.0	6.7	-0.6	3.1	4.4	0.3	15.9	12.2	14.9
North and Central Asia												
Armenia	14.0	38.6	4.3	34.0	10.4	22.3	27.8	32.9	42.3	2.4	16.4	10.6
Azerbaijan	20.1	73.4	-11.3	14.5	29.7	47.5	22.1	86.8	71.7	44.0	-0.3	24.3
Georgia	20.6	39.2	17.6	17.9	22.8	42.4	26.5	39.7	49.7	6.9	8.2	34.8
Kazakhstan	84.4	45.0	40.2	30.1	34.2	68.2	26.3	78.1	25.9	35.4	19.5	14.1
Kyrgyzstan	33.7	11.7	11.3	33.9	33.4	32.1	10.0	51.5	33.2	12.6	20.4	18.6
Russian Federation	56.7	58.0	36.3	33.8	38.5	33.7	36.3	40.6	44.2	14.6	16.4	28.5
Tajikistan	24.6	63.3	35.0	40.5	40.9	9.8	113.3	65.4	108.7	-3.6	..	..
Turkmenistan	75.7	83.3	23.8	1.5	40.9	13.4	27.2	17.7	..	..	..	..
Uzbekistan	32.7	37.1	54.3	29.7	27.1	47.8	54.3	36.8	46.1	31.8	31.4	33.7
Pacific												
Pacific island developing economies												
Cook Islands	16.7	4.8	14.4	3.2	9.9	9.6	-5.2	22.4	-5.8	4.0	65.9	..
Fiji	13.6	-1.5	-3.1	7.8	25.0	10.5	15.1	20.2	10.3	-6.7	7.4	3.9
Kiribati	..	..	..	..	..	..	..	..	..	..	..	..
Micronesia (Federated States of)	3.4	-1.0	6.0	-12.0	-3.7	-0.1	1.6	-8.5	4.6	3.2	16.3	-0.1
Papua New Guinea	9.2	5.0	6.2	7.3	-4.4	14.8	29.5	38.9	27.8	7.8	21.9	10.0
Samoa	15.7	16.3	6.1	10.2	14.0	8.3	15.6	13.7	11.0	5.8	9.1	7.1
Solomon Islands	..	..	..	6.4	23.8	17.7	46.1	26.4	21.7	8.0	16.8	16.6
Tonga	15.6	15.3	15.5	8.3	14.5	13.9	22.1	5.4	13.5	0.7	0.3	6.3
Tuvalu	..	..	..	..	..	..	..	..	..	..	..	..
Vanuatu	-9.2	5.5	5.5	-1.6	-0.9	9.9	11.6	7.0	16.1	13.2	0.5	-6.0
Developed economies												
Australia	11.7	3.7	13.2	5.7	12.8	11.4	8.6	15.0	29.9	14.2	0.5	9.3
New Zealand	7.1	1.5	9.1	0.2	9.5	3.5	9.5	11.3	11.1	10.4	-0.6	2.1
South and South-West Asia												
Bangladesh	12.8	18.6	16.6	13.1	15.6	13.8	16.7	19.3	17.1	17.6	19.2	22.4
Bhutan	32.0	17.4	7.9	26.9	1.8	19.9	11.9	13.0	13.0	31.2	43.2	26.6[a]
India	17.1	15.2	14.3	16.8	13.0	16.7	15.6	21.6	22.3	20.5	18.0	17.5
Iran (Islamic Republic of)	21.5	22.4	27.6	24.9	24.5	23.0	22.8	29.1	30.6	7.9	27.7	..
Maldives	3.5	4.2	7.8	21.6	17.2	31.4	10.6	18.9	24.1	21.8	12.5	16.4
Nepal	20.8	21.8	15.2	4.4	9.8	12.8	8.3	15.6	13.8	25.2	27.7	14.0
Pakistan	4.3	12.1	11.7	16.8	17.5	20.3	17.5	14.5	19.7	5.7	14.7	15.0
Sri Lanka	13.4	12.9	13.6	13.4	15.5	19.6	19.0	17.9	16.5	8.4	18.7	14.4[b]
Turkey	96.1	42.5	48.0	31.0	33.7	31.2	120.0	24.7	15.7	26.7	13.0	15.7[a]
South-East Asia												
Brunei Darussalam	..	38.0	-16.7	1.9	4.1	15.8	-4.5	2.1	6.7	9.6	9.7	4.8
Cambodia	17.3	26.9	20.4	31.1	15.4	28.3	15.8	40.5	61.8	5.4	35.6	21.3
Indonesia	11.9	15.6	13.0	4.7	8.1	8.2	16.3	14.9	19.3	14.9	13.0	15.3
Lao People's Democratic Republic	78.4	46.0	13.7	37.6	20.1	21.6	7.9	26.7	38.7	18.3	31.2	23.8
Malaysia	14.2	5.3	2.3	6.0	11.1	25.4	15.4	16.6	11.0	13.3	9.5	7.1
Myanmar	29.5	42.5	43.9	34.7	1.4	32.4	27.3	27.2	30.0	14.8	30.6	36.9[b]
Philippines	16.9	8.1	3.6	10.4	3.6	9.9	9.6	21.8	10.5	15.3	7.5	13.1
Singapore	8.5	-2.0	5.9	-0.3	8.1	6.2	6.2	19.4	13.4	12.0	11.3	8.6
Thailand	1.8	4.0	5.8	1.3	6.2	5.8	6.1	8.2	6.3	9.2	6.8	10.9
Timor-Leste					41.1	6.9	18.3	28.2	43.9	34.1	39.3	9.9
Viet Nam	66.5	35.4	27.3	13.3	33.1	31.0	30.9	29.7	49.1	20.7	26.2	25.4[b]

Source and table notes appear in the technical notes at the end of the annex.

Table 8.   Merchandise export growth rates

(Percentage)

	1999	2000	2001	2002	2003	2004	2005	2006	2007	2008	2009	2010
East and North-East Asia												
China	6.1	27.9	7.0	22.1	34.6	35.4	28.4	27.2	25.7	17.3	-15.9	32.0
Hong Kong, China	0.0	16.1	-5.9	5.4	11.8	15.8	11.6	9.4	8.8	5.3	-12.2	22.5
Japan	8.1	14.3	-15.9	3.4	13.1	19.9	5.2	8.7	10.4	9.5	-25.7	32.5
Macao, China	2.8	16.3	-9.4	2.4	9.5	9.0	-11.9	3.3	-0.6	-21.4	-51.9	-9.5
Mongolia	3.8	49.6	11.3	-12.1	17.5	41.2	22.4	44.9	26.3	30.1	-25.6	59.5[a]
Republic of Korea	8.6	19.9	-12.7	8.0	19.3	31.0	12.0	14.4	14.1	13.6	-13.9	28.8
North and Central Asia												
Armenia	5.1	29.1	14.1	48.2	35.4	5.5	34.8	1.1	17.0	-8.3	-34.0	43.9[a]
Azerbaijan	51.3	81.3	11.9	10.9	13.9	42.6	104.4	70.1	63.4	43.8	-69.2	56.8[a]
Georgia	24.4	35.6	-1.6	8.9	33.4	40.2	33.8	8.2	31.6	21.4	-23.8	38.9
Kazakhstan	-7.5	63.2	-5.2	12.3	33.5	55.0	38.6	37.3	24.8	49.1	-39.3	32.8
Kyrgyzstan	-13.5	10.4	-6.1	3.8	18.5	24.2	-6.3	31.9	47.6	38.1	-6.6[b]	-2.5[c]
Russian Federation	2.2	41.4	-3.0	6.7	25.2	35.9	32.9	24.8	16.8	32.9	-35.5	29.6
Tajikistan	..	..	-22.3	7.0	14.5	14.7	-0.7	54.0	4.9	-4.2	-28.3	14.0[a]
Turkmenistan	93.3	111.1	4.5	9.0	22.5	11.2	28.3	44.7	12.9	52.7[b]	-45.4[b]	44.0[c]
Uzbekistan	-3.4	5.2	-6.6	-8.4	29.1	31.6	11.6	18.0	43.0	28.3[b]	4.2[b]	22.3[c]
Pacific												
Pacific island developing economies												
Fiji	12.5	-4.1	-6.4	-2.7	19.0	19.8	-1.2	8.7	7.7	12.4	-11.2	9.6[a]
Papua New Guinea	18.3	0.8	-6.6	1.5	37.5	16.3	22.8	24.8	15.0	21.0	-13.3	20.8[a]
Samoa	-12.2	6.2	2.6	10.3	34.6	-7.9	138.4	-43.3	23.2	-5.9	-22.1	5.5[a]
Solomon Islands	-14.6	-37.5	-12.9	12.8	28.7	41.4	16.8	14.8	36.7	14.9	-24.3	40.1[a]
Tonga	66.7	41.1	34.7	16.7	11.9	9.2	-42.9	14.7	-17.2	0.1	-23.7	-12.2[a]
Vanuatu	14.1	-5.0	-33.6	1.2	32.2	163.4	12.5	-4.4	53.5	51.0	-65.2	18.7[a]
Developed economies												
Australia	0.3	13.6	-0.8	2.8	8.3	23.0	22.3	16.6	14.5	31.9	-17.2	37.6
New Zealand	3.7	6.6	3.2	4.8	14.9	23.1	6.8	3.2	20.1	13.5	-18.5	25.8
South and South-West Asia												
Afghanistan[d]	..	..	..	46.8	43.6	111.1	26.5	8.5	9.6	19.9	..	..
Bangladesh[d]	2.9	8.3	12.4	-7.4	9.4	16.1	13.8	21.6	15.7	15.9	10.3	4.1
Bhutan[d]	-5.9	9.2	-12.9	4.1	8.9	39.7	34.5	47.2	83.7	4.4	-23.7	..
India[d]	20.8	5.3	4.6	-5.1	10.8	21.0	-1.6	20.3	21.1	30.8	23.4	26.7[e]
Iran (Islamic Republic of)[d]	60.3	35.3	-16.0	18.1	20.4	29.0	47.2	18.1	28.2	3.0	-13.0	40.5[f]
Maldives	-4.3	18.8	1.4	20.2	14.8	19.1	-10.7	39.4	1.2	45.3	-49.0	18.3
Nepal[d]	18.2	37.4	4.5	-19.0	5.1	13.8	11.5	2.2	1.1	8.2	-4.0	-8.9[a]
Pakistan[d]	-10.7	8.8	9.1	2.3	19.1	13.8	16.8	14.3	4.4	18.2	-6.4	2.7
Sri Lanka	0.0	19.8	-12.8	-2.4	9.2	12.2	10.2	8.4	11.6	5.9	-12.9	17.3
Turkey	-1.4	4.5	12.8	15.1	31.0	33.7	16.3	16.4	25.4	23.1	-22.6	11.8
South-East Asia												
Brunei Darussalam	28.9	23.9	5.5	3.1	28.6	2.0	24.9	26.0	0.9	42.8	-36.9	17.4[a]
Cambodia	11.4	7.9	15.4	15.0	18.9	23.5	37.8	18.2	13.7	26.6	-2.8	-10.2[g]
Indonesia	1.7	27.6	-12.3	3.1	8.4	12.6	19.5	18.3	16.8	16.9	-14.2	31.9
Lao People's Democratic Republic	24.7	-15.4	-4.0	2.8	13.3	22.3	30.1	69.2	12.4	21.1	-5.2	39.2[a]
Malaysia	15.3	16.1	-10.4	6.9	11.3	21.0	11.4	13.4	10.0	13.3	-21.0	25.9
Myanmar	22.4	42.1	32.6	4.8	0.5	14.1	17.4	20.9	7.0	38.3	-21.9	..
Philippines	18.8	8.7	-15.6	9.5	2.9	9.5	4.0	14.9	6.4	-2.8	-21.7	33.7
Singapore	4.4	20.2	-11.7	2.8	27.8	24.2	15.6	18.4	10.1	13.0	-20.2	30.4
Thailand	7.4	19.3	-6.6	4.6	17.4	20.6	15.0	16.9	18.6	15.5	-14.3	28.1
Timor-Leste	..	..	230.8	48.8	21.9	6.4	10.8	12.5	-22.2	100.0	-28.6	..
Viet Nam	23.3	25.5	3.8	11.2	19.0	30.8	24.0	22.9	22.2	29.5	-8.9	25.5

Source and table notes appear in the technical notes at the end of the annex.

Table 9. **Merchandise import growth rates**

(Percentage)

	1999	2000	2001	2002	2003	2004	2005	2006	2007	2008	2009	2010
East and North-East Asia												
China	18.2	35.8	8.2	21.2	39.9	35.8	17.7	19.9	20.8	18.4	-11.3	38.9
Hong Kong, China	-2.7	18.6	-5.4	3.2	11.8	16.7	10.5	11.6	10.0	5.6	-10.6	24.7
Japan	11.0	22.0	-8.0	-3.3	13.5	18.8	13.4	12.2	7.4	22.6	-27.6	25.4
Macao, China	4.5	11.4	5.8	6.0	8.9	26.2	12.5	16.6	17.5	0.0	-13.9	19.3
Mongolia	1.9	19.8	3.8	8.3	14.6	28.9	15.3	21.8	43.7	57.2	-33.4	66.7[a]
Republic of Korea	28.4	34.0	-12.1	7.8	17.6	25.5	16.4	18.4	15.3	22.0	-25.8	31.8
North and Central Asia												
Armenia	-11.4	10.3	-6.2	19.8	28.1	5.7	31.7	24.1	49.6	34.9	-25.3	19.2[a]
Azerbaijan	-16.9	7.4	-4.8	24.5	49.3	31.5	21.4	21.1	14.7	25.3	-14.0	3.8[a]
Georgia	-21.9	2.9	6.2	5.6	43.4	61.7	34.9	47.7	41.8	20.9	-30.6	16.4
Kazakhstan	-52.4	37.0	26.0	2.0	29.3	52.3	35.8	36.4	38.3	15.7	-25.0	-14.1
Kyrgyzstan[b]	-27.1	-8.2	-11.3	27.2	26.6	25.0	22.3	62.0	47.1	42.4	-20.4[c]	2.9[d]
Russian Federation	-30.5	11.9	23.6	10.2	24.2	31.8	30.6	39.6	45.0	33.7	-37.3	35.8
Tajikistan	..	..	-20.0	0.0	28.2	56.0	-3.3	29.5	42.5	33.2	-21.4	-0.4[a]
Turkmenistan[b]	..	..	..	..	40.8	22.1	-6.4	-13.2	41.5	54.8[c]	-26.6[c]	19.3[d]
Uzbekistan[b]	-4.8	-5.6	4.6	-14.4	10.0	27.3	8.1	16.0	65.0	46.4[c]	-2.7[c]	4.6[d]
Pacific												
Pacific island developing economies												
Fiji	23.7	-23.1	-1.0	12.0	17.8	23.7	17.9	9.9	-1.5	20.7	-27.0	17.3[a]
Papua New Guinea	-6.2	-2.6	-8.6	6.3	13.2	18.6	25.8	17.0	25.2	18.0	10.6	26.3[a]
Samoa	10.4	69.5	1.1	-35.3	42.4	12.9	122.1	-50.5	8.4	9.0	-9.1	51.1[a]
Solomon Islands	16.1	-30.0	-7.6	-12.0	36.4	16.3	30.0	23.4	36.0	0.5	-13.1	22.2[a]
Tonga	5.9	13.6	-10.7	17.8	16.5	20.0	4.9	8.6	15.1	1.1	-7.7	36.6[a]
Vanuatu	38.1	-36.6	40.4	-23.8	59.6	8.5	16.6	1.3	16.8	39.0	4.6	-11.2[a]
Developed economies												
Australia	7.8	3.3	-10.2	14.3	22.0	22.5	14.2	11.9	18.9	20.9	-16.6	21.6
New Zealand	14.4	-2.7	-4.3	13.1	23.3	25.0	13.1	0.7	16.9	11.3	-25.6	19.7
South and South-West Asia												
Afghanistan[e]	..	..	..	36.9	-8.8	1.5	14.9	11.1	10.1	5.7	..	..
Bangladesh[e]	6.5	4.6	11.5	-8.5	13.1	12.9	20.6	12.2	16.3	26.1	4.1	5.5
Bhutan[e]	19.3	14.0	1.1	8.6	1.6	27.3	75.5	-5.6	21.1	27.4	-10.4	..
India[e]	28.0	6.7	6.0	2.2	17.2	1.7	1.7	19.4	27.3	42.7	33.8	22.6[f]
Iran (Islamic Republic of)[b, e]	-6.0	12.3	20.2	21.6	34.1	31.1	11.9	15.2	16.5	17.7	-2.8	17.2[g]
Maldives	13.6	-3.4	1.3	-0.4	20.2	36.3	16.1	24.4	18.3	26.6	-30.3	13.2
Nepal[e]	-10.3	22.0	-0.3	-10.9	14.4	15.5	12.3	15.8	14.9	23.6	8.4	44.7[a]
Pakistan[e]	-6.7	-0.1	6.2	-7.5	20.1	20.0	39.6	31.6	8.0	31.2	-10.3	-2.2
Sri Lanka	..	17.4	-14.9	2.2	9.3	19.9	10.8	15.7	10.2	23.9	-27.1	32.0
Turkey	-11.4	34.0	-24.0	24.5	34.5	40.7	19.7	19.5	21.8	18.8	-30.2	31.6
South-East Asia												
Brunei Darussalam	-43.1	7.5	-7.9	23.9	-17.7	22.2	1.9	17.4	98.2	-32.6	-2.2	2.1[a]
Cambodia	10.1	14.5	2.2	15.2	3.4	19.7	22.9	17.2	118.7	-32.3	-12.0	134.5[h]
Indonesia	-5.6	30.8	-13.9	2.1	10.3	29.9	26.7	14.6	15.4	37.7	-26.8	40.6[h]
Lao People's Democratic Republic	25.5	-14.7	4.3	0.4	12.0	30.5	20.3	30.1	27.6	34.0	2.4	24.0[a]
Malaysia	11.9	25.3	-10.0	8.2	4.4	26.3	8.3	14.0	12.6	7.0	-20.7	32.6
Myanmar	7.2	20.3	-12.4	11.5	8.7	7.1	3.5	9.4	43.1	24.6	1.5	39.3[a]
Philippines[b]	3.6	12.3	-4.2	18.7	3.1	8.8	7.7	9.2	7.2	2.2	-24.1	26.9
Singapore	9.3	21.1	-13.8	0.4	17.0	27.4	15.2	19.3	10.2	21.5	-23.1	26.5
Thailand	17.7	24.6	-0.7	4.0	16.8	25.3	25.7	9.0	8.7	28.0	-25.4	36.5
Timor-Leste	..	..	13.5	-16.8	-10.8	-16.1	-16.0	-9.8	74.3	100.6	24.6	..
Viet Nam	2.1	33.2	3.7	21.7	26.7	26.1	17.0	20.4	37.0	32.7	-13.3	20.1

Source and table notes appear in the technical notes at the end of the annex.

Table 10. Inward foreign direct investment

| | FDI inward stock | | | | | FDI net inflows | | | | |
| | Millions of US dollars | Percentage of GDP | | | | Millions of US dollars | Percentage of GDP | | | |
	2009	91-95	96-00	01-05	06-09	2009	91-95	96-00	01-05	06-09
East and North-East Asia	1 713 362	5.6	9.0	11.9	16.0	163 974	0.5	1.3	1.4	1.7
China	473 083	10.3	16.0	13.5	9.4	95 000	3.9	4.1	3.3	2.3
Democratic People's Republic of Korea	1 437	7.1	9.4	10.6	10.4	2	0.3	0.6	0.7	0.0
Hong Kong, China	912 166	180.8	188.5	253.8	443.3	48 449	4.4	14.8	13.8	25.2
Japan	200 141	0.4	0.8	1.9	3.4	11 939	0.0	0.1	0.2	0.3
Macao, China	13 381	50.8	44.5	43.8	52.9	2 303	0.0	0.0	6.3	12.2
Mongolia	2 383	1.7	9.3	27.5	39.4	437	0.6	2.5	6.6	10.1
Republic of Korea	110 770	1.9	4.6	11.4	11.8	5 844	0.2	1.2	0.8	0.6
North and Central Asia	356 693	0.7	8.1	24.6	25.6	55 619	0.4	1.6	2.5	4.3
Armenia	3 628	2.9	18.4	30.2	31.8	838	0.9	5.8	5.0	8.6
Azerbaijan	9 044	1.5	62.9	107.0	27.0	473	0.8	14.3	24.6	-3.3
Georgia	7 547	0.4	13.7	34.3	56.1	764	0.1	4.8	7.0	12.7
Kazakhstan	72 333	5.0	33.8	52.9	48.9	12 649	2.5	6.3	7.7	10.7
Kyrgyzstan	1 075	2.1	21.7	27.1	21.6	60	1.5	3.6	2.4	4.4
Russian Federation	252 456	0.4	5.6	21.4	23.6	38 722	0.2	1.1	1.7	3.8
Tajikistan	870	1.1	9.3	13.3	25.2	8	0.4	1.8	4.9	8.0
Turkmenistan	6 103	5.2	22.3	26.4	31.7	1 355	3.2	3.3	4.5	6.6
Uzbekistan	3 638	0.4	3.2	9.0	10.4	750	0.2	0.8	1.1	2.4
Pacific										
Pacific island developing economies	12 209	21.8	25.1	28.3	35.5	1 863	2.4	2.9	1.7	6.1
American Samoa										
Cook Islands	41	18.0	66.2	25.4	20.0	1	0.1	4.8	0.1	0.7
Fiji	2 163	25.4	25.4	27.2	56.1	238	2.8	2.8	4.4	9.9
French Polynesia	340	4.0	4.8	5.4	6.8	34	0.3	0.3	0.4	0.8
Guam										
Kiribati	143	1.6	50.6	131.6	114.1	2	0.2	20.0	15.2	1.8
Marshall Islands						8	-1.6	36.9	-5.2	5.0
Micronesia (Federated State of)						8	0.0	-6.8	0.0	3.0
Nauru						0	-0.3	0.9	3.6	0.9
New Caledonia	4 184	2.8	2.7	6.2	30.0	955	0.2	-0.2	1.2	11.1
Niue	7					0				
Northern Mariana Islands										
Palau	126	0.0	57.4	87.3	68.6	2	0.4	17.0	3.3	1.1
Papua New Guinea	3 071	35.0	43.2	57.4	35.9	396	4.8	6.0	1.3	1.6
Samoa	81	14.2	20.9	16.7	14.2	1	2.6	2.1	0.0	1.3
Solomon Islands	873	118.2	101.8	108.2	106.6	173	3.9	1.3	0.5	14.6
Tonga	99	3.0	5.0	10.7	24.3	15	0.9	0.6	2.4	4.6
Tuvalu	34	0.9	1.0	111.0	118.3	2	0.4	-1.2	28.4	8.3
Vanuatu	1 046	117.5	147.2	160.3	165.9	27	11.6	8.2	5.0	6.1
Developed economies	394 724	26.2	29.9	37.3	35.7	22 920	2.1	2.0	1.9	3.6
Australia	328 090	24.9	26.7	35.7	33.9	22 572	1.8	1.8	1.9	3.8
New Zealand	66 634	35.6	51.7	48.2	50.2	348	4.3	3.3	1.8	2.8
South and South-West Asia	295 399	3.2	4.7	7.1	11.0	49 016	0.3	0.5	1.1	2.3
Afghanistan	1 550	0.4	0.4	4.4	11.4	185	0.0	0.0	2.3	2.3
Bangladesh	5 139	1.6	3.8	5.5	6.2	716	0.1	1.1	0.9	1.1
Bhutan	167	1.0	1.0	1.7	9.4	36	0.1	0.1	0.5	3.2
India	163 959	1.0	3.0	5.1	9.8	34 613	0.3	0.7	0.9	2.6
Iran (Islamic Republic of)	23 984	2.1	2.2	6.6	6.4	3 016	0.0	0.1	1.8	0.6
Maldives	231	15.2	17.3	22.4	19.0	10	2.4	2.1	1.8	1.1
Nepal	166	0.3	1.2	1.8	1.2	39	0.0	0.2	0.1	0.1
Pakistan	17 789	5.5	10.8	8.5	12.8	2 387	0.8	0.7	1.2	3.1
Sri Lanka	4 687	9.4	11.5	10.1	10.7	404	1.1	1.4	1.1	1.6
Turkey	77 729	6.3	6.8	11.3	15.7	7 611	0.4	0.3	1.2	2.7
South-East Asia	689 980	20.7	36.6	42.4	46.6	36 806	3.5	4.5	3.8	4.0
Brunei Darussalam	10 672	4.0	52.3	105.1	84.3	311	2.9	12.9	15.7	2.6
Cambodia	5 169	6.4	35.4	41.2	43.7	533	2.5	6.3	3.6	7.1
Indonesia	72 841	8.3	15.9	7.9	14.9	4 877	1.3	0.5	0.6	1.4
Lao People's Democratic Republic	1 564	6.7	29.9	29.5	27.2	157	3.0	4.5	1.1	4.9
Malaysia	74 643	28.9	49.0	35.3	36.8	1 381	7.2	5.2	2.6	3.1
Myanmar	5 869	12.4	41.2	44.9	32.5	323	2.8	7.1	2.3	1.9
Philippines	23 559	12.7	19.2	14.8	14.0	1 948	1.9	2.1	1.2	1.6
Singapore	343 599	76.5	104.0	152.1	182.3	16 809	10.4	14.3	14.0	13.7
Thailand	99 000	10.8	17.3	32.4	36.7	5 949	1.5	3.4	3.8	3.6
Timor-Leste	238	21.3	25.2	46.4	39.7	18	5.8	0.0	5.4	3.6
Viet Nam	52 825	30.2	56.1	66.5	55.4	4 500	8.1	6.4	3.7	6.9
Memorandum items:										
Developing ESCAP economies	2 510 809	17.6	23.8	24.8	26.0	239 720	2.1	3.2	2.8	2.9
(excluding CIS)										
Central Asia	104 237	3.0	23.6	46.3	38.1	16 896	1.5	4.9	7.9	6.8
East and North-East Asia	1 040 138	42.2	50.4	59.4	87.6	57 035	1.1	4.5	3.5	5.1
(excluding China and Japan)										
South and South-West Asia	131 440	4.8	6.2	9.1	12.0	14 403	0.3	0.4	1.3	2.0
(excluding India)										
Developed ESCAP economies	594 865	2.6	3.7	6.6	9.6	34 858	0.2	0.3	0.4	0.9

Source and table notes appear in the technical notes at the end of the annex.

Table 11. Official development assistance and workers' remittances

	ODA received						Workers' remittances received					
	Millions of US dollars			Percentage of GNI			Millions of US dollars			Percentage of GNI		
	1990	2000	2009	1990	2000	2009	1990	2000	2009	1990	2000	2009
East and North-East Asia												
China	2 030	1 712	201	0.5	0.1	0.0	124	556	13 693	0.0	0.0	0.3
Democratic People's Republic of Korea	8	73	14	0.0	0.7	0.1						
Hong Kong, China	38			0.1								
Japan								1	1		0.0	0.0
Macao, China	0			0.0					65			0.3
Mongolia	13	217	143	1.0	20.0	3.3		12	192		1.1	4.5
Republic of Korea	52			0.0			488	63	373	0.2	0.0	0.0
North and Central Asia												
Armenia		216	176		11.4	2.1		9	86		0.5	1.0
Azerbaijan		139	92		2.7	0.2		57	1 182		1.1	3.1
Georgia		169	248		5.3	2.3		95	317		3.0	3.0
Kazakhstan		189	39		1.1	0.0		64	56		0.4	0.1
Kyrgyzstan		215	58		16.7	1.3		2	983		0.2	22.0
Russian Federation									775			0.1
Tajikistan		124	81		11.7	1.2			1 742			26.2
Turkmenistan		31	4		0.8	0.0						
Uzbekistan		186	89		1.4	0.3						
Pacific												
Pacific island developing economies	..			..								
American Samoa												
Cook Islands	12	4	3	20.7	5.3	1.5						
Fiji	50	29	4	3.7	1.6	0.1		26	104		1.4	3.4
French Polynesia	260			11.2					16			0.3
Guam												
Kiribati	20	18	6	60.1	20.2	3.5	3			7.6		
Marshall Islands		57	0		42.7	0.1						
Micronesia (Federated State of)		102	0		43.5	0.1						
Nauru	0	4	1	0.3	13.9	2.2						
New Caledonia	302			12.0					6			0.1
Niue	7	3	6									
Northern Mariana Islands												
Palau		39	0		31.3	0.1						
Papua New Guinea	412	275	65	15.5	8.2	0.9			2			0.0
Samoa	48	27	13	28.9	11.7	2.5	43		122	26.1		24.0
Solomon Islands	46	68	27	35.4	20.2	3.9			0			0.0
Tonga	30	19	9	24.7	9.9	2.5	23			19.1		
Tuvalu	5	4	1	53.0	32.9	5.2						
Vanuatu	50	46	15	26.8	19.8	2.6	7	11		3.7	4.7	
Developed economies												
Australia												
New Zealand							254			0.6		
South and South-West Asia	7 265	4 570	4 310	1.0	0.5	0.2						
Afghanistan	122	136	1 010	3.4	3.8	7.9						
Bangladesh	2 093	1 172	381	7.3	2.5	0.4	779	1 958	10 510	2.7	4.2	10.6
Bhutan	46	53	57	17.6	12.1	4.7			3			0.2
India	1 399	1 373	1 006	0.4	0.3	0.1	2 352	12 738	48 596	0.7	2.8	3.8
Iran (Islamic Republic of)	105	130	59	0.1	0.1	0.0						
Maldives	21	19	3	11.1	3.2	0.2						
Nepal	423	386	268	11.4	6.7	2.1		111	2 858		1.9	22.1
Pakistan	1 127	700	1 247	2.2	1.0	0.8	2 006	1 075	8 701	4.0	1.5	5.3
Sri Lanka	728	275	227	9.1	1.7	0.5	401	1 142	3 330	5.0	7.0	7.9
Turkey	1 202	327	50	0.6	0.1	0.0	3 246	4 560	934	1.6	1.7	0.2
South-East Asia	4 782	5 659	2 502	1.4	1.2	0.2						
Brunei Darussalam	4			0.1								
Cambodia	41	396	193	3.3	12.6	2.1		100	140		3.2	1.5
Indonesia	1 716	1 651	399	1.4	1.1	0.1	166	1 190	6 618	0.1	0.8	1.4
Lao People's Democratic Republic	148	281	123	17.1	17.7	2.3			10			0.2
Malaysia	468	45	18	1.1	0.1	0.0						
Myanmar	161	106	52	3.0	1.5	0.3	6	77		0.1	1.1	
Philippines	1 271	572	100	2.9	0.7	0.1	262	5 161	15 141	0.6	6.4	8.2
Singapore	-3			0.0								
Thailand	796	697	42	0.9	0.6	0.0						
Timor-Leste	0	231	28	0.1	71.6	1.3						
Viet Nam	181	1 681	1 548	3.0	5.5	1.7						
Memorandum items:												
Developing ESCAP economies (excluding CIS)	15 493	12 927	7 319	0.8	0.5	0.1						
Central Asia		1 268	786		2.7	0.4						
East and North-East Asia (excluding China and Japan)	111			0.0								
South and South-West Asia (excluding India)	5 866	3 197	3 304	1.5	0.6	0.3						
Central Asia		1 268	786		2.7	0.4						
Developed ESCAP economies												

Source and table notes appear in the technical notes at the end of the annex.

Table 12. International migration

| | Stock of foreign population | | | | | | Net migration rate | | | |
| | Thousands | | | Percentage of total population | | | Per 1 000 populaiton | | | |
	1990	2000	2005	1990	2000	2005	90-95	95-00	00-05	05-10
East and North-East Asia	4 484	5 716	6 185	0.3	0.4	0.4	-0.1	-0.1	-0.3	-0.2
China	376	508	590	0.0	0.0	0.0	-0.1	-0.1	-0.3	-0.3
Democratic People's Republic of Korea	34	36	37	0.2	0.2	0.2				
Hong Kong, China	2 218	2 669	2 721	38.9	40.0	39.5	10.1	9.3	3.3	3.3
Japan	1 076	1 687	1 999	0.9	1.3	1.6	0.8	0.1	0.1	0.2
Macao, China	200	240	278	53.9	54.5	57.0	7.8	7.1	17.2	19.3
Mongolia	7	8	9	0.3	0.3	0.4	-15.4	-4.3	1.4	-0.8
Republic of Korea	572	568	551	1.3	1.2	1.2	-2.9	-0.3	-0.3	-0.1
North and Central Asia	19 510	18 214	18 078	9.1	8.4	8.3	-1.2	-0.6	-0.5	-0.8
Armenia	659	574	493	18.6	18.7	16.1	-29.6	-14.3	-6.5	-4.9
Azerbaijan	361	348	255	5.0	4.3	3.0	-3.1	-3.2	-2.4	-1.2
Georgia	338	219	191	6.2	4.6	4.3	-20.7	-15.9	-13.4	-11.5
Kazakhstan	3 619	2 871	2 974	21.9	19.2	19.6	-18.6	-17.1	-2.7	-1.3
Kyrgyzstan	623	373	288	14.2	7.5	5.5	-12.2	-1.1	-2.9	-2.8
Russian Federation	11 525	11 892	12 080	7.8	8.1	8.4	3.0	3.0	1.3	0.4
Tajikistan	426	330	306	8.0	5.4	4.7	-10.7	-11.2	-10.9	-5.9
Turkmenistan	307	241	224	8.4	5.4	4.6	2.5	-2.3	-1.1	-1.0
Uzbekistan	1 653	1 367	1 268	8.1	5.5	4.8	-3.1	-3.4	-3.1	-3.0
Pacific										
Pacific island developing economies	259	301	320	4.0	3.7	3.5	-6.4	-8.7	-7.7	-8.7
American Samoa	21	25	27	45.2	43.2	42.3				
Cook Islands	3	3	3	14.6	15.9	14.6				
Fiji	14	16	17	1.9	2.0	2.1	-9.3	-10.7	-10.3	-8.3
French Polynesia	26	30	32	13.2	12.9	12.7	-0.5	1.4	1.5	
Guam	70	74	76	52.1	47.8	45.4	-4.6	-6.4	1.0	
Kiribati	2	2	2	3.0	2.4	2.2				
Marshall Islands	2	2	2	3.3	3.1	2.9				
Micronesia (Federated State of)	4	3	3	3.8	2.9	2.6	-4.4	-25.4	-17.9	-16.3
Nauru	4	5	5	42.9	45.4	48.7				
New Caledonia	38	50	54	22.0	23.1	23.2	5.8	5.5	4.3	4.5
Niue	0	0	0	20.0	21.8	23.7				
Northern Mariana Islands	27	45	51	61.6	65.0	63.4				
Palau	3	6	6	19.2	32.7	30.0				
Papua New Guinea	33	26	25	0.8	0.5	0.4				
Samoa	3	6	7	2.0	3.2	4.0	-15.8	-16.3	-20.8	-18.4
Solomon Islands	5	6	6	1.5	1.4	1.4				
Tonga	3	2	1	3.2	1.6	1.1	-18.0	-19.5	-15.9	-17.5
Tuvalu	0	0	0	3.6	2.3	1.9				
Vanuatu	2	1	1	1.4	0.7	0.5	-1.1	-7.9		
Developed economies	4 105	4 713	5 193	20.0	20.5	21.2				
Australia	3 581	4 027	4 336	21.0	21.0	21.3	4.2	5.0	6.5	4.8
New Zealand	523	685	858	15.5	17.7	20.9	8.1	2.3	5.1	2.4
South and South-West Asia	21 346	16 933	15 181	1.7	1.1	0.9	-0.4	-0.4	-0.5	-0.3
Afghanistan	58	76	86	0.5	0.4	0.4	42.6	-3.8	7.2	7.5
Bangladesh	882	988	1 032	0.8	0.7	0.7	-0.8	-0.8	-1.0	-0.7
Bhutan	24	32	37	4.3	5.7	5.7	-38.2	0.1	11.6	2.9
India	7 493	6 411	5 887	0.9	0.6	0.5	-0.2	-0.3	-0.3	-0.2
Iran (Islamic Republic of)	4 292	2 804	2 062	7.6	4.2	2.9	-3.9	-0.2	-2.9	-1.4
Maldives	3	3	3	1.2	1.1	1.1				
Nepal	431	718	819	2.3	2.9	3.0	-1.0	-0.9	-0.8	-0.7
Pakistan	6 556	4 243	3 554	5.7	2.9	2.1	-4.2	-0.1	-1.6	-1.6
Sri Lanka	459	395	366	2.7	2.1	1.9	-2.9	-4.3	-4.6	-3.0
Turkey	1 150	1 263	1 334	2.1	1.9	1.9	-0.2	0.0	-0.2	-0.1
South-East Asia	3 060	4 838	5 624	0.7	0.9	1.0	-0.9	-0.7	-0.5	-0.5
Brunei Darussalam	73	104	124	28.5	31.2	33.6	2.6	2.2	2.0	1.8
Cambodia	38	237	304	0.4	1.9	2.2	2.8	1.3	0.2	-0.1
Indonesia	466	292	136	0.3	0.1	0.1	-0.8	-0.9	-0.9	-0.6
Lao People's Democratic Republic	23	22	20	0.5	0.4	0.3	-1.3	-3.4	-4.1	-2.4
Malaysia	1 014	1 554	2 029	5.6	6.7	7.9	3.0	4.5	1.2	1.0
Myanmar	134	98	93	0.3	0.2	0.2	-0.6	0.0	-4.2	-2.0
Philippines	159	323	375	0.3	0.4	0.4	-2.7	-2.4	-2.2	-2.0
Singapore	727	1 352	1 494	24.1	33.6	35.0	15.4	19.6	6.7	22.0
Thailand	387	792	982	0.7	1.3	1.5	-0.1	-1.5	4.4	0.9
Timor-Leste	9	9	12	1.2	1.1	1.2		-40.9	9.1	1.8
Viet Nam	29	56	55	0.0	0.1	0.1	-2.4	-0.5	-0.5	-0.5
Memorandum items:										
Developing ESCAP economies (excluding CIS)	28 074	26 101	25 311	1.0	0.8	0.7				
Central Asia	7 985	6 322	5 998	12.0	8.9	8.1	-10.4	-8.2	-4.3	-3.1
East and North-East Asia (excluding China and Japan)	3 032	3 522	3 596	4.2	4.5	4.4				
South and South-West Asia (excluding India)	13 853	10 521	9 294	3.5	2.2	1.7				
Developed ESCAP economies	5 180	6 399	7 192	3.6	4.3	4.7				

Source and table notes appear in the technical notes at the end of the annex.

Table 13.   Primary, secondary and tertiary education

	Net enrolment ratio in primary education (Percentage of primary school-aged children)			Net enrolment ratio in secondary education (Percentage of secondary school-aged children)				Gross enrolment ratio in tertiary education (Percentage of tertiary school-aged children)			
	1999	2000	2009	1999	2002	2004	2009	1999	2002	2004	2009
East and North-East Asia											
China								6.6	12.8	17.6	22.7 (08)
Democratic People's Republic of Korea											
Hong Kong, China			93.5		73.9	74.6	74.6			31.2	56.6
Japan	100.0	100.0	100.0 (08)	99.4	99.6	99.4	98.3 (08)	45.2	51.0	54.2	58.0 (08)
Macao, China	84.7	85.4	87.4	62.2	71.6	75.6	75.9	27.8	64.3	67.0	62.9
Mongolia	93.0	93.6	90.5	57.7	73.2	82.9	82.4	26.9	34.9	39.4	52.7
Republic of Korea	98.2	99.1	98.8 (08)	97.4	89.7	91.9	95.5 (08)	72.5	86.9	90.5	98.1 (08)
North and Central Asia											
Armenia			84.1 (07)		83.1	83.6	87.2	23.7	26.5	26.2	50.1
Azerbaijan	88.7	89.5	96.0 (08)	75.3	77.8	80.7	98.3 (08)	15.7	15.9	14.9	15.8 (08)
Georgia			99.6	75.8			80.8 (07)	36.0	40.9	41.3	25.5
Kazakhstan		87.2	89.0		87.9	90.7	88.5	24.5	38.8	47.2	41.1
Kyrgyzstan	88.0	86.7	83.5			82.1	79.1	29.0	42.9	39.6	50.8
Russian Federation								51.1	66.4	69.7	77.2 (08)
Tajikistan		95.9	97.3 (08)	62.9	76.5	79.9	82.5 (08)	13.6	14.0	16.4	19.8
Turkmenistan											
Uzbekistan			87.3				91.7	12.8	13.8	14.1	9.8
Pacific											
Pacific island developing economies											
American Samoa											
Cook Islands	84.8	92.7	96.8 (07)	59.0			78.8 (07)				
Fiji	98.7	97.5	89.5 (08)	78.6	77.0	81.1				15.5	
French Polynesia											
Guam											
Kiribati	96.6	97.0				70.3					
Marshall Islands			80.0 (07)		60.2		52.4 (07)		16.4		
Micronesia (Federated State of)								14.1			
Nauru											
New Caledonia											
Niue	98.5			93.4							
Northern Mariana Islands											
Palau	96.8	96.4							37.9		
Papua New Guinea								2.0			
Samoa	91.9	90.0	92.8	71.8	64.7	64.2	70.6	11.5			
Solomon Islands			80.6 (07)	23.0	27.6		30.2 (07)				
Tonga	88.1			71.7		71.2		3.4	5.6	6.4	
Tuvalu											
Vanuatu	91.4	93.9		29.6	36.2	38.1		4.0	5.0	4.8	
Developed economies											
Australia	94.1	94.5	96.9 (08)		87.8	85.8	88.0 (08)	65.4	76.3	72.2	77.0 (08)
New Zealand	98.7	98.2	99.5 (08)		90.8			64.1	68.5	84.8	78.5 (08)
South and South-West Asia											
Afghanistan							26.8 (07)			1.3	
Bangladesh			85.5 (08)	39.6	43.8	41.1	41.5 (07)	4.9	5.5	5.1	7.9
Bhutan	55.6	58.4	87.4	16.7	24.2		47.5	2.7			6.6 (08)
India		79.4	91.4 (08)						10.4	11.3	13.5 (07)
Iran (Islamic Republic of)	92.9	92.6						17.5	18.1	21.2	36.5
Maldives	97.6	98.5	96.2 (08)	30.7	50.5		69.4 (07)				
Nepal	65.2	71.2							4.9	5.6	
Pakistan			66.4	22.2		29.6	32.7		2.5	3.1	6.4
Sri Lanka			99.5 (08)								
Turkey		92.2	94.7 (08)		69.1	70.4	73.9 (08)	21.6	24.5	29.2	38.4 (08)
South-East Asia											
Brunei Darussalam			92.9				89.1	12.3	13.7	14.9	17.1
Cambodia	83.2	87.3	88.6 (08)	15.4	22.2	25.9	34.0 (07)		2.5	3.0	7.0 (08)
Indonesia		94.3	95.7 (08)			57.9	68.4 (08)		15.5	17.1	21.3 (08)
Lao People's Democratic Republic	77.5	78.6	82.4 (08)	25.9	30.5	35.9	36.0 (07)	2.4	4.2	5.7	13.4 (08)
Malaysia	97.7	96.8	96.1 (07)	65.1	65.4	72.0	67.9 (07)	23.0	28.0	30.6	32.1 (07)
Myanmar				30.8	36.9	42.0	49.2 (08)				10.7 (07)
Philippines	90.0		91.7 (08)	49.8	55.1	59.6	60.7 (08)	28.4	29.9	28.2	28.7 (08)
Singapore											
Thailand			90.1				72.2	34.1	42.4	42.9	44.6
Timor-Leste			82.0				31.4 (07)		9.8		15.2
Viet Nam	95.7	95.1		58.8				10.8			

Source and table notes appear in the technical notes at the end of the annex.

Table 14. Poverty and malnutrition

	Population living below $1.25 (2005 PPP) per day				Undernourished population		Prevalence of underweight children	
	Percentage				Percentage		Percentage of children under 5	
	1990	1996	2002	2007	1991	2005	Earliest	Latest
East and North-East Asia								
China	60.2	36.4	28.4	15.9 (05)	15	10	19 (90)	7 (05)
Democratic People's Republic of Korea					21	32	60 (98)	23 (04)
Hong Kong, China								
Japan					5	5		
Macao, China								
Mongolia		18.8 (95)	15.5	2.2 (08)	30	29	12 (92)	6 (05)
Republic of Korea					5	5		
North and Central Asia								
Armenia		17.5	15.0	3.7		23	4 (98)	4 (05)
Azerbaijan		15.6 (95)	6.3 (01)	2.0 (05)		11	10 (96)	10 (06)
Georgia		4.5	15.1	13.4 (05)		12		2 (05)
Kazakhstan	4.2 (93)	5.0	5.2	2.0		5	8 (95)	4 (06)
Kyrgyzstan	18.6 (93)	15.5 (99)	34.0	3.4		5	11 (97)	3 (06)
Russian Federation	2.8 (93)	3.5	2.0	2.0		5	3 (95)	
Tajikistan		44.5 (99)		21.5 (04)		26		18 (07)
Turkmenistan	63.5 (93)	24.8 (98)				6		11 (05)
Uzbekistan		32.1 (98)	42.3	46.3 (03)		13	19 (96)	5 (06)
Pacific								
Pacific island developing economies								
American Samoa								
Cook Islands							10 (97)	
Fiji					8	5	8 (93)	
French Polynesia					5	5		
Guam								
Kiribati					8	5		
Marshall Islands								
Micronesia (Federated State of)							15 (97)	
Nauru								
New Caledonia					8	9		
Niue								
Northern Mariana Islands								
Palau								
Papua New Guinea		35.8						26 (05)
Samoa					9	5		
Solomon Islands					25	9		
Tonga								
Tuvalu								
Vanuatu					10	6		16 (07)
Developed economies								
Australia					5	5		
New Zealand					5	5		
South and South-West Asia								
Afghanistan							48 (97)	39 (04)
Bangladesh	66.8 (92)	59.4	57.8 (00)	49.6 (05)	36	26	67 (92)	46 (07)
Bhutan				26.2 (03)				
India		49.4 (94)		41.6 (05)	24	22	53 (93)	48 (05)
Iran (Islamic Republic of)	3.9	2.0 (98)		2.0 (05)	5	5	16 (95)	5 (04)
Maldives					9	7	39 (94)	30 (01)
Nepal		68.4		55.1 (04)	21	16	49 (95)	45 (06)
Pakistan	64.7 (91)	48.1 (97)	35.9	22.6 (05)	22	23	40 (91)	38 (02)
Sri Lanka	15.0 (91)	16.3	14.0		27	21	38 (93)	
Turkey		2.1 (94)	2.0	2.6 (06)	5	5	10 (93)	3 (08)
South-East Asia								
Brunei Darussalam					5	5		
Cambodia		48.6 (94)		25.8	38	25	40 (93)	36 (05)
Indonesia				29.4	19	16	34 (95)	28 (03)
Lao People's Democratic Republic	55.7 (92)	49.3 (97)	44.0		27	19	44 (93)	37 (06)
Malaysia	2.0 (92)	2.1 (95)		2.0 (04)	5	5	23 (93)	8 (05)
Myanmar					44	17	32 (90)	32 (03)
Philippines	30.7 (91)	28.1 (94)	22.0 (03)	22.6 (06)	21	15	34 (90)	28 (03)
Singapore								
Thailand	5.5 (92)	2.0	2.0	2.0 (04)	29	17	19 (93)	9 (05)
Timor-Leste			52.9 (01)	37.2	18	23		49 (07)
Viet Nam	63.7 (93)	49.7 (98)	40.1	21.5 (06)	28	13	45 (94)	20 (06)

Source and table notes appear in the technical notes at the end of the annex.

Table 15.   Unemployment

	Total unemployment rate			Total unemployment rate, female			Total unemployment rate, male			Youth unemployment rate		
	Percentage of labour force			Percentage of female labour force			Percentage of male labour force			Percentage of labour force		
	1995	2000	2009	1995	2000	2009	1995	2000	2009	1995	2000	2009
East and North-East Asia												
China	2.9	3.1										
Democratic People's Republic of Korea												
Hong Kong, China	3.2	4.9	5.2	2.9	4.0	4.3	3.4	5.6	6.0	6.9	11.2	12.6
Japan	3.2	4.8	5.0	3.3	4.5	4.7	3.1	5.0	5.3	6.1	9.2	9.1
Macao, China	3.6	6.7	3.6	3.0	4.6	2.8	4.1	8.6	4.3		9.9	7.5
Mongolia												
Republic of Korea	2.1	4.4	3.6	1.7	3.6	3.0	2.3	5.0	4.1	6.3	10.8	9.8
North and Central Asia												
Armenia												
Azerbaijan												
Georgia		10.8			10.5			11.1			21.1	
Kazakhstan	11.0	12.8	6.6			7.5			5.6			6.7
Kyrgyzstan		7.5										
Russian Federation	9.5	10.6	8.2	9.2	10.4	7.9	9.7	10.7	8.4	18.7	20.5	18.3
Tajikistan												
Turkmenistan												
Uzbekistan												
Pacific												
Pacific island developing economies												
American Samoa		5.1			6.0			4.9				
Cook Islands												
Fiji	5.4											
French Polynesia												
Guam		15.3										
Kiribati												
Marshall Islands												
Micronesia (Federated State of)												
Nauru												
New Caledonia												
Niue												
Northern Mariana Islands		3.8			3.3			4.4				
Palau												
Papua New Guinea					1.3			4.3			5.3	
Samoa												
Solomon Islands												
Tonga												
Tuvalu												
Vanuatu												
Developed economies												
Australia	8.5	6.3	5.6	8.1	6.1	5.4	8.8	6.5	5.7	15.4	12.1	11.6
New Zealand	6.5	6.2	6.1	6.5	6.0	6.1	6.4	6.3	6.1	12.3	13.6	16.6
South and South-West Asia												
Afghanistan												
Bangladesh		3.3			3.3			3.2			10.7	
Bhutan												
India	2.2	4.3		1.7	4.1		2.4	4.4			10.1	
Iran (Islamic Republic of)												
Maldives	0.8	2.0		1.3	2.7		0.6	1.6		1.9	4.4	
Nepal												
Pakistan	5.0	7.2		14.0	15.8		3.7	5.5		8.9	13.3	
Sri Lanka	12.2	7.7	7.6	18.7	11.4	8.1	9.0	5.9	7.2	35.2	23.6	21.3
Turkey	7.6	6.5	14.0	7.3	6.3	14.3	7.8	6.6	13.9	15.6	13.1	25.3
South-East Asia												
Brunei Darussalam												
Cambodia		2.5			2.8			2.2				
Indonesia		6.1	7.9		6.7	8.5		5.7	7.5		19.9	22.2
Lao People's Democratic Republic	2.6			2.6			2.6			5.0		
Malaysia	3.1	3.0	3.7	3.8	3.1		2.8	2.9			8.3	
Myanmar												
Philippines	8.4	11.2	7.5	9.4	11.5	7.4	7.7	11.0	7.5	16.1	21.2	17.4
Singapore	2.7	6.0	5.9	2.8	6.6	6.5	2.6	5.6	5.4	5.0	8.8	12.9
Thailand		2.4	1.2		2.3	1.1		2.4	1.2		6.6	4.3
Timor-Leste												
Viet Nam		2.3			2.1			2.4			4.8	

Source and table notes appear in the technical notes at the end of the annex.

Table 16. Telecommunications

	Fixed and mobile phones						Internet					
	Number of dedicated fixed telephone lines			Number of mobile cellular subscriptions			Number of internet users			Fixed broadband internet subscribers		
	Per 100 population		per annum (%)	Per 100 population		per annum (%)	Per 100 population		per annum (%)	Per 100 population		per annum (%)
	2005	2009	05-09	2005	2009	05-09	2005	2009	05-09	2005	2009	05-09
East and North-East Asia	28.8	25.0	-2.9	35.4	59.7	14.6	15.5	34.3	22.5	4.9	9.9	19.9
China	26.7	23.3	-2.7	30.0	55.5	17.4	8.5	28.9	36.6	2.8	7.7	29.2
Democratic People's Republic of Korea	4.3	4.9	4.2	0.0	0.3		0.0	0.0		0.0	0.0	
Hong Kong, China	55.1	60.9	3.1	124.1	179.4	10.2	56.9	69.4	5.6	24.1	29.2	5.4
Japan	45.6	34.1	-7.0	75.7	91.5	4.8	66.9	78.0	3.8	18.3	24.9	8.0
Macao, China	35.8	31.7	-0.6	109.3	192.8	18.1	34.9	50.2	12.3	13.9	23.4	16.7
Mongolia	6.1	7.1	4.9	21.9	84.2	41.7	10.5	13.1	6.9	0.1	1.4	112.5
Republic of Korea	50.3	53.7	2.1	80.6	100.7	6.1	73.5	81.5	3.0	25.6	33.8	7.6
North and Central Asia	22.1	25.3	3.5	60.2	132.2	21.8	11.4	26.5	23.5	0.7	6.4	71.3
Armenia	19.4	20.4	1.5	10.4	85.0	69.4	5.3	6.8	6.6	0.1	0.2	31.6
Azerbaijan	12.9	15.9	6.4	26.5	87.8	36.4	8.0	27.4	37.4	0.0	1.1	159.7
Georgia	12.8	14.6	2.1	26.3	66.6	24.7	6.1	30.5	47.9	0.1	3.5	181.2
Kazakhstan	17.8	24.7	9.2	35.5	107.9	33.0	3.0	33.9	85.2	0.0	3.7	272.4
Kyrgyzstan	8.4	9.1	3.1	10.4	81.8	69.6	10.5	40.0	41.3	0.0	0.3	60.6
Russian Federation	28.0	32.2	3.1	83.8	163.6	17.7	15.2	29.0	17.0	1.1	9.2	68.8
Tajikistan	4.3	4.2	0.9	4.1	70.5	107.4	0.3	10.1	144.8	0.0	0.1	
Turkmenistan	8.2	9.4	4.7	2.2	29.4	94.4	1.0	1.6	13.6	0.0	0.1	
Uzbekistan	6.8	6.8	0.9	2.7	59.7	118.5	3.3	17.1	51.9	0.0	0.3	80.8
Pacific												
Pacific island developing economies	5.2	5.4	3.2	8.4	25.2	33.2	4.8	6.4	9.5	0.3	1.0	31.6
American Samoa	16.6	15.4	0.0	3.5						0.0		
Cook Islands	34.6	34.8	1.1	21.0	35.3	15.0	26.2	30.3	4.7	0.5	7.6	96.8
Fiji	13.6	16.1	5.0	24.8	75.4	32.9	8.5	13.4	13.0	0.8	2.5	31.6
French Polynesia	20.9	20.2	0.4	47.0	77.4	14.8	21.5	44.6	21.5	4.3	11.2	28.5
Guam	38.9	36.9	0.0	58.1			38.6	50.6	8.5	1.1	1.7	13.6
Kiribati	4.6	4.1	-1.2	0.7	1.0	13.6	4.0	8.0	20.5	0.0	0.0	
Marshall Islands	7.8	7.1	0.0	1.2	4.8	43.9	3.9	3.5	0.0	0.0	0.0	
Micronesia (Federated State of)	11.3	7.9	-8.5	12.9	34.3	28.1	11.9	15.4	6.9	0.0	0.1	
Nauru	17.8	18.6	1.4	14.8			3.0					
New Caledonia	23.5	27.0	5.1	57.2	83.8	11.8	32.4	34.0	2.8	4.1	13.2	36.3
Niue	60.8	74.5	2.4	36.5			48.7	74.5	8.3	0.0	0.0	
Northern Mariana Islands	29.1	28.9	1.9	25.6						0.0	0.0	
Palau	39.8	34.7	-2.9	30.3	64.5	21.3	26.8			0.5	1.0	18.9
Papua New Guinea	1.0	0.9	-1.5	1.2	13.4	86.1	1.7	1.9	4.5	0.0	0.0	
Samoa	10.9	17.8	13.1	13.4	84.4	58.4	3.4	5.0	10.7	0.1	0.1	18.9
Solomon Islands	1.6	1.6	2.6	1.3	5.7	49.5	0.8	1.9	25.7	0.1	0.4	49.5
Tonga	13.4	29.8	22.6	29.3	51.0	15.4	4.9	8.1	13.8	0.6	1.0	13.6
Tuvalu	9.2	17.1	17.2	13.3	20.1	11.4	25.6	43.3	14.5	2.0	4.0	18.9
Vanuatu	3.2	3.0	1.7	5.9	52.8	77.7	5.1	7.1	11.5	0.0	0.2	49.5
Developed economies	48.4	42.6	-2.1	89.6	113.1	7.1	63.0	75.2	5.6	9.5	24.2	27.5
Australia	49.6	42.4	-2.8	90.3	113.7	7.1	63.0	74.3	5.3	9.9	24.4	26.7
New Zealand	42.1	43.8	2.0	85.9	110.2	7.4	62.7	79.7	7.2	7.8	23.0	32.2
South and South-West Asia	5.9	5.0	-2.3	10.2	46.3	48.4	3.3	6.9	21.6	0.2	0.9	50.0
Afghanistan	0.4	0.5	6.6	4.9	42.6	77.8	1.2	3.5	35.1	0.0	0.0	49.5
Bangladesh	0.7	0.9	9.2	5.9	32.3	55.4	0.2	0.4	13.7	0.0	0.0	
Bhutan	5.1	3.8	-5.5	5.5	48.6	75.2	3.8	7.2	18.9	0.0	0.4	
India	4.4	3.1	-7.3	8.0	43.8	55.4	2.4	5.1	22.8	0.1	0.6	54.8
Iran (Islamic Republic of)	28.7	34.8	6.1	12.0	70.8	57.6	8.1	11.1	9.4	0.0	0.5	388.9
Maldives	11.0	15.8	11.0	69.6	147.9	22.5	6.9	27.9	44.0	1.1	5.8	52.4
Nepal	1.8	2.8	13.8	0.8	19.1	122.8	0.8	2.0	26.6	0.0	0.1	
Pakistan	3.2	1.9	-9.4	7.7	52.2	64.9	6.3	11.3	18.1	0.0	0.2	113.4
Sri Lanka	6.4	17.0	28.9	17.2	69.6	43.1	1.8	8.8	50.1	0.1	0.8	68.6
Turkey	26.7	22.1	-3.4	61.3	83.9	9.5	15.5	36.4	25.4	2.2	8.5	41.6
South-East Asia	8.4	12.5	11.8	26.8	79.5	32.9	8.7	15.2	16.3	0.3	1.8	57.9
Brunei Darussalam	22.7	20.1	-1.0	62.9	103.3	15.4	36.5	78.8	23.6	2.2	5.0	25.4
Cambodia	0.2	0.4	13.2	7.7	42.3	55.9	0.3	0.5	15.6	0.0	0.2	134.0
Indonesia	6.2	14.8	25.9	21.4	69.2	35.7	3.6	8.7	26.2	0.0	0.7	99.1
Lao People's Democratic Republic	1.5	2.1	9.8	11.2	51.2	48.9	0.9	4.7	56.5	0.0	0.1	130.0
Malaysia	17.0	17.6	2.5	76.2	109.7	11.4	48.6	55.9	5.3	1.9	6.1	36.4
Myanmar	1.0	1.1	2.3	0.3	1.0	40.5	0.1	0.2	36.7	0.0	0.0	194.3
Philippines	3.9	7.4	19.1	40.7	100.3	27.6	5.4	9.0	15.7	0.1	1.9	93.4
Singapore	43.2	40.7	1.1	102.8	145.2	11.9	61.0	68.3	5.6	15.4	24.7	15.6
Thailand	10.7	10.6	0.6	47.2	97.3	20.6	15.0	25.8	15.3	0.2	1.5	75.4
Timor-Leste	0.2	0.2	1.1	3.3	29.1	77.7	0.1	0.2	20.4	0.0	0.0	
Viet Nam	18.8	19.8	2.4	11.4	111.5	78.9	12.7	26.6	21.6	0.2	3.6	97.8
Memorandum items:												
Developing ESCAP economies	14.5	13.4	-0.8	21.0	55.4	28.9	7.1	17.0	26.0	1.5	3.9	27.6
(excluding CIS)												
Central Asia	10.6	12.5	5.1	14.5	74.7	52.0	4.1	22.0	53.3	0.0	1.2	161.4
East and North-East Asia	35.8	38.5	2.3	59.2	78.4	7.7	48.5	54.4	3.4	17.2	22.5	7.5
(excluding China and Japan)												
South and South-West Asia	8.9	9.1	2.2	14.8	51.6	39.0	5.4	10.5	20.4	0.3	1.3	45.7
(excluding India)												
Developed ESCAP economies	46.0	35.5	-6.1	77.9	95.1	5.2	66.3	77.5	4.1	16.9	24.8	10.3

Source and table notes appear in the technical notes at the end of the annex.

Table 17. Infrastructure and transport

	Road density (Km per 1 000 km²)			Paved roads (Percentage of total roads)			Railway density (Km per 1 000 km²)			Passenger cars (Per 1 000 population)		
	1990	2000	2007	1990	2000	2007	1990	2000	2007	2002	2005	2007
East and North-East Asia	198	239	432			44	7	7	8	50.9	48.4	55.2
China	110	150	384			50	6	6	7	8.0	15.0	22.5
Democratic People's Republic of Korea	231	259		6	6							
Hong Kong, China				100		100						53.7
Japan	3 057	3 200	3 284	69	77	79	56	55	55	428.0		324.6
Macao, China				100	100					118.0		143.2
Mongolia	27	32		10	4		1	1	1	26.0		42.2
Republic of Korea	574	881	1 053	72	75	78	31	32	35	205.0	230.0	248.1
North and Central Asia	62	41		72			5	5	5	132.2		175.5
Armenia	270		264	99		90	30	30				96.3
Azerbaijan	630	332						26		43.0	57.0	
Georgia	311	293		94			23	22	22	55.0		94.6
Kazakhstan	59		34	55		90	5	5	5	72.0	93.0	141.0
Kyrgyzstan	98	96	177	90	91				2	38.0	39.0	43.9
Russian Federation	54	32		74			5	5	5	156.0		205.8
Tajikistan	213	198		72								28.6
Turkmenistan	45	51		74	81				7			81.4
Uzbekistan	170	192		79	87			9	9			
Pacific												
Pacific island developing economies	51	54		5	6							20.0
American Samoa												
Cook Islands												
Fiji	167	188		45	49					85.0		113.1
French Polynesia												
Guam												
Kiribati		827										99.4
Marshall Islands												
Micronesia (Federated State of)		343		16	18							16.0
Nauru												
New Caledonia												
Niue												
Northern Mariana Islands												
Palau												
Papua New Guinea	41	43		3	4							6.0
Samoa											45.5	
Solomon Islands	43	50		2	2							
Tonga		944			27							
Tuvalu												
Vanuatu		88		22	24							
Developed economies	114	114	114	36			1	2	2		552.9	557.0
Australia	105	106	106	35			1	1	1		542.0	545.4
New Zealand	352	350	356	57	63	65	15			613.0	607.0	614.8
South and South-West Asia	415	623	639		47		14	14	14	9.9		
Afghanistan	32	32		13	13							15.3
Bangladesh	1 444	1 594			10		21	21	22			1.0
Bhutan	50			77						12.0		29.9
India	673	1 115	1 115		47		21	21	21	7.0		
Iran (Islamic Republic of)	80						3	4	4	24.0		13.0
Maldives												10.0
Nepal	48	92		38						3.0		3.1
Pakistan	219	311		54	56		11	10	10	7.0		8.9
Sri Lanka	1 483						23			13.0	15.8	18.1
Turkey	477						11	11	11	66.0	80.0	87.6
South-East Asia	173	234		37								40.1
Brunei Darussalam	192	218		31	35					330.0		649.1
Cambodia	203			8			3	3				
Indonesia	159	196		45	57							42.1
Lao People's Democratic Republic	61	94		24								2.2
Malaysia	164	202		70	76		5	5	5	211.0		
Myanmar	38	43		11	11		5				4.0	5.6
Philippines	538	676					2	2		10.0	9.0	10.7
Singapore	4 176	4 584	4 744	97	100	100				97.0	101.0	112.7
Thailand	141			55	99		8	8		52.0		
Timor-Leste												
Viet Nam	295	693	516	24		48	9	10	10			13.5
Memorandum items:												
Developing ESCAP economies (excluding CIS)	212	306	411				8	8	8	16.2		
Central Asia	93	76		64				6	7			
East and North-East Asia (excluding China and Japan)	72	94		13	8	8						214.6
South and South-West Asia (excluding India)	233	274					8	8	8	16.0		17.9
Developed ESCAP economies	243	249	253	37	41	41	4	4	4	445.4		362.8

Source and table notes appear in the technical notes at the end of the annex.

Table 18. Energy and water use

	Energy use						Water withdrawal					
	Consumption of electricity for domestic purposes			Energy use per $ 1 000 GDP [2005 PPP]			Share of total renewable water resources			Withdrawal for domestic purposes		
	Kilowatt-hours per capita			Kilograms of oil equivalent			Percentages			Cubic metres per capita		
	1990	2000	2008	1990	2000	2008	1992	1997	2002	1992	1997	2002
East and North-East Asia	194	325	522	276	224	218						
China	42	132	329	691	325	280	17.6	18.5	21.8	29.9	20.4	
Democratic People's Republic of Korea									11.7			77.2
Hong Kong, China	927	1 343	1 476	65	67	50						
Japan	1 495	2 035	2 260	136	143	124	21.3		20.6	137.0		136.9
Macao, China												
Mongolia	213	216	335	695	486	363		1.2	1.3		36.9	36.7
Republic of Korea	413	799	1 168	191	211	183		34.0	36.5		136.8	141.0
North and Central Asia	598	803	695	502	517	342						
Armenia	577	507	582	740	284	174	45.1	37.7	22.3		275.9	168.9
Azerbaijan	236	1 389	853	759	571	190	44.9	36.1	29.0		28.0	61.0
Georgia	532	561	664	411	259	151	5.5					
Kazakhstan	478	319	478	628	501	432	33.4	29.5	30.7		37.7	39.5
Kyrgyzstan	224	474	424	676	325	265	53.4	43.7	43.7		63.7	63.1
Russian Federation	722	959	828	470	491	328	1.8	1.7	1.5		96.6	92.2
Tajikistan	245	527	454	327	347	207	75.2	74.3	74.8		69.4	69.7
Turkmenistan	278	272	364	1 428	1 388	605	100.1	96.2	99.7		80.6	90.6
Uzbekistan	173	291	272	1 129	1 261	753	124.0	115.2	115.7		108.8	109.0
Pacific												
Pacific island developing economies												
American Samoa												
Cook Islands												
Fiji								0.2				12.3
French Polynesia												
Guam												
Kiribati												
Marshall Islands												
Micronesia (Federated State of)												
Nauru												
New Caledonia												
Niue												
Northern Mariana Islands												
Palau												
Papua New Guinea								0.0				7.0
Samoa												
Solomon Islands												
Tonga												
Tuvalu												
Vanuatu												
Developed economies	2 383	2 609	2 791	209	190	174						
Australia	2 255	2 544	2 761	211	190	176			4.9			179.1
New Zealand	3 032	2 930	2 939	195	193	158			0.6			257.5
South and South-West Asia	56	107	154	236	222	190						
Afghanistan									35.8			19.2
Bangladesh	11	39	65	162	148	142			6.6	14.1	30.2	
Bhutan									0.5			33.5
India	37	73	105	301	255	195	26.3		34.0	27.8		48.5
Iran (Islamic Republic of)	306	467	722	201	243	269		60.4	65.2		93.5	71.9
Maldives												
Nepal	14	22	32	426	367	333			4.8		10.8	11.7
Pakistan	81	154	182	237	239	214	69.1		75.2	20.5		21.1
Sri Lanka	38	110	165	160	145	105	18.5		23.9	11.0		15.8
Turkey	162	359	536	120	122	112	14.8		19.7	89.5		93.6
South-East Asia	88	182	267	233	229	203						
Brunei Darussalam	1 300	1 568	3 077	139	155	197	0.9	1.1				
Cambodia	7	17	51	432	309	199			0.9			4.5
Indonesia	48	149	221	281	278	237	2.6		2.9	25.8		31.4
Lao People's Democratic Republic									0.9			23.2
Malaysia	561	487	718	183	198	205	1.7		1.6	42.9	61.9	62.7
Myanmar	15	28	37						2.8			8.7
Philippines	90	166	184	185	204	140		5.8	6.0		58.4	
Singapore	793	1 425	1 462	160	122	80						
Thailand	143	312	427	187	208	213			21.2	25.7		
Timor-Leste												
Viet Nam	35	142	299	407	299	267	6.1		8.1	29.0		68.5
Memorandum items:												
Developing ESCAP economies	63	140	251	340	256	229						
(excluding CIS)												
Central Asia	321	481	449	725	691	420						
East and North-East Asia	462	839	1 167	168	186	159						
(excluding China and Japan)												
South and South-West Asia	100	185	262	173	185	184						
(excluding India)												
Central Asia	321	481	449	725	691	420						
Developed ESCAP economies	1 621	2 123	2 348	145	150	133						

Source and table notes appear in the technical notes at the end of the annex.

Technical notes

Table 1. Real gross domestic product growth rates

Sources: ESCAP, based on national sources; International Monetary Fund, International Financial Statistics online database. Available from www.imfstatistics.org/imf (accessed 16 February 2011); Asian Development Bank, Key *Indicators for Asia and the Pacific 2010* (Manila, 2010); CEIC Data Company Limited, data available from http://ceicdata.com (accessed 25 March 2011); and the website of the Interstate Statistical Committee of the Commonwealth of Independent States, www.cisstat. com (accessed 16 February 2011). Historical data are based on the National Accounts Main Aggregates Database of the United Nations Statistics Division, with updates from national and local sources. The data for 2010 are generally ESCAP estimates and calculations, although some projections are in line with the economic programmes/projections of the governments concerned.

Notes: Real annual percentage changes in GDP are reported in this table at constant market prices in national currencies. GDP is defined as the total cost of all finished goods and services produced within the country in a given year. Most countries use constant market price values. The growth rates of some countries, including Fiji, India, the Islamic Republic of Iran and Pakistan, are shown at factor cost, while that of Bhutan is at purchasers' prices and that of Nepal is at producers' prices. In the case of Timor-Leste, the data refer to real non-oil GDP, including the locally paid compensation of United Nations peacekeeping mission staff. Data and estimates for countries relate to fiscal years, defined as follows: 2009 refers to the fiscal year spanning 21 March 2009 to 20 March 2010 in the Islamic Republic of Iran; 1 April 2009 to 31 March 2010 in India; 1July 2008 to 30 June 2009 in Bangladesh and Pakistan; and 16 July 2008 to 15 July 2009 in Nepal. Developing ESCAP economies refer to developing Asian and Pacific economies, excluding those of North and Central Asia. Developed ESCAP economies refer to Australia, Japan and New Zealand.

Table 2. Gross domestic savings rates

Sources: Most historical data are generated by ESCAP, based on Asian Development Bank, Key *Indicators for Asia and the Pacific 2010* (Manila, 2010), with updates and estimates from national and local sources. The data for 2010 are obtained from input supplied by national authorities and ESCAP calculations and estimates. Data for the Islamic Republic of Iran and Nepal are based on national sources. Data for Macao, China, the Lao People's Democratic Republic, the Russian Federation, Solomon Islands, Turkmenistan and Turkey are based on World Bank, World Development Indicators online. Available from http://data.worldbank.org/data-catalog/world-development-indicators (accessed 14 January 2011). Data for the Cook Islands, Kiribati, Maldives, Samoa and Tuvalu are calculated based on United Nations Statistics Division databases.

Notes: Gross domestic savings are calculated as the difference between GDP and total consumption expenditure in the national accounts statistics. All figures used in computing gross domestic savings as a percentage of GDP are in current prices.

Table 3. Gross domestic investment rates

Sources: Historical data are mostly generated by ESCAP, based on Asian Development Bank, Key *Indicators for Asia and the Pacific 2010* (Manila, 2010), with updates and estimates from national and local sources. The data for 2010 are obtained from input supplied by national authorities and ESCAP calculations and estimates. Data for the Islamic Republic of Iran, the Lao People's Democratic Republic and Nepal are based on national sources. Data for Macao, China, Maldives and the Russian Federation are based on World Bank, World Development Indicators online. Available from http://data.worldbank.org/data-catalog/world-development-indicators (accessed 14 January 2011). Data for the Cook Islands, Kiribati, Samoa, Solomon Islands and Tuvalu are calculated based on United Nations Statistics Division databases.

Notes: Gross domestic investment is the sum of gross fixed capital formation and changes in inventories. Gross fixed capital formation is measured by the total value of a producer's acquisitions, minus disposals of fixed assets in a given accounting period. Additions to the value of non-produced assets, such as land, form part of gross fixed capital formation. Inventories are stocks of goods held by institutional units to meet temporary or unexpected fluctuations in production and sales. All figures used in computing gross domestic investment as a percentage of GDP are in current prices.

Table 4. Inflation rates

Sources: Historical data are based on International Monetary Fund, International Financial Statistics online database. Available from www.imfstatistics.org/imf (accessed 16 February 2011) and the World Economic Outlook Database. Available from www.imf.org/external/pubs/ft/weo/2010/02/weodata/index.aspx (accessed 28 November 2010), with updates and estimates from national sources, statistical publications and secondary publications. The figures for 2010 are generally estimates based on ESCAP calculations. Projections/estimates are also provided by country authorities. Data are also drawn from Asian Development Bank, Key *Indicators for Asia and the Pacific 2010* (Manila, 2010); CEIC Data Company Limited, data available from http://ceicdata.com (accessed 25 March 2011); the website of the Interstate Statistical Committee of the Commonwealth of Independent States, www.cisstat.com (accessed 16 February 2011). Figures for 2010 are estimates.

Notes: Rates of inflation in this table refer to changes in the consumer price index (CPI) and reflect changes in the cost of acquiring a fixed basket of goods and services by an average consumer. Data and estimates for countries relate to fiscal years defined as follows: 2009 refers to the fiscal year spanning 21 March 2009 to 20 March 2010 in the Islamic Republic of Iran; 1 April 2009 to 31 March 2010 in India; 1July 2008 to 30 June 2009 in Bangladesh and Pakistan; and 16 July 2008 to 15 July 2009 in Nepal. Developing ESCAP economies refer to developing Asian and Pacific economies, excluding those of North and Central Asia. Developed ESCAP economies refer to Australia, Japan and New Zealand. Consumer price inflation data for the following countries are for a given city or group of consumers: data on Cambodia are for Phnom Penh; data on India refer to the industrial workers index; data on Nepal are for urban consumers; data on Sri Lanka are for Colombo; and data on Timor-Leste are for Dili.

Table 5. Budget balance

Sources: ESCAP, based on national sources; Asian Development Bank, *Key Indicators for Asia and the Pacific 2010* (Manila, 2010); International Monetary Fund, Article IV Consultations, various issues; and ESCAP estimates.

Notes: The government fiscal balance (surplus or deficit) is the difference between central government total revenues (including grants) and total expenditures as a percentage of GDP. This provides a picture of the changes in the government's financial position each year. When the difference is positive, the fiscal position is in surplus; otherwise, it is in deficit. Government revenue is the sum of current and capital revenues. Current revenue is the revenue accruing from taxes, as well as all current non-tax revenues, except for transfers received from other (foreign or domestic) governments and international institutions. Major items of non-tax revenue include receipts from government enterprises, rents and royalties, fees and fines, forfeits, private donations and the repayments of loans properly defined as components of net lending. Capital revenue consists of the proceeds from the sale of non-financial capital assets. Government expenditure is defined as the sum of current and capital expenditure. Current expenditure comprises purchases of goods and services by the central government, transfers to non-central government units and to households, subsidies to producers and the interest on public debt. Capital expenditures, on the other hand, cover outlays for the acquisition or construction of capital assets and for the purchase of land and intangible assets, as well as capital transfers to domestic and foreign recipients. Loans and advances for capital purposes are also included. Grants are excluded in Bangladesh, Cambodia, China, Hong Kong, China, Indonesia, Kiribati, Malaysia, Pakistan, the Republic of Korea, Singapore, Sri Lanka, Thailand, Turkmenistan and developed countries. In the case of Timor-Leste, the budget balance was computed as a share of non-oil GDP. The budget surplus/deficit of Singapore was computed from government operating revenue minus government operating expenditure and minus government development expenditure, while the budget balance of Thailand refers to a government cash balance comprising the budgetary balance and non-budgetary balance. In the case of Australia, budget balance refers to data on a cash basis and are based on national sources.

Table 6. Current account balance

Sources: Historical data are mainly generated by ESCAP based on International Monetary Fund, International Financial Statistics online database. Available from www.imfstatistics. org/imf (accessed at various times in October 2010) and the World Economic Outlook Database. Available from www.imf. org/external/pubs/ft/weo/2010/02/weodata/index.aspx (accessed 27 November 2010), with updates and estimates from national and local sources. The 2010 data are estimates and are derived from projections supplied by national authorities and ESCAP estimates. The current account balances of Samoa and Tonga for 2006-2010 are based on International Monetary Fund, *2010 Article IV Consultations*.

Notes: The current account balance refers to the sum of the balance on goods, services and income. It also includes current transfers crossing national borders. A positive (or negative) balance shows that the foreign currencies flow into (or out of) the domestic economy. The figures are reported as a percentage of GDP at current prices (in the national currency) to allow for cross-country comparisons. In the case of Cambodia, current account includes official transfers. For Timor-Leste, the current account balance includes international assistance and is represented as a percentage of non-oil GDP.

Table 7. Changes in money supply

Sources: Historical data for M2 are mainly obtained from International Monetary Fund, International Financial Statistics online database. Available from www.imfstatistics.org/imf (accessed 16 December 2010), with updates and estimates from national and local sources. Data for 2010 are computed by ESCAP on the basis of IMF data and estimates based on national sources. For the Cook Islands, Turkmenistan and Uzbekistan, data are based on Asian Development Bank, *Key Indicators for Asia and the Pacific 2010* (Manila, 2010).

Notes:
[a] November, compared with the corresponding period of the previous year.
[b] October, compared with the corresponding period of the previous year.

The table depicts annual growth rates of broad money supply (at the end of a given period), as represented by M2. M2 is defined as the sum of currency in circulation plus demand deposits (M1) and quasi-money, which consists of time and savings deposits, including foreign currency deposits.

Table 8. Merchandise export growth rates

Sources: ESCAP calculations based on data from national sources; International Monetary Fund, Statistics Department, *Direction of Trade Statistics* (February 2011), CD-ROM; Economist Intelligence Unit, *Country Reports*; CEIC Data Company Limited, data available from http://ceicdata.com (accessed 30 March

2011); and the website of the Interstate Statistical Committee of the Commonwealth of Independent States, www.cisstat.com (accessed 25 March 2011). Historical data and figures for 2010 on exports are mainly obtained from country sources, statistical publications, and secondary publications.

Notes:

[a] Refers to first 9 months.

[b] Estimate.

[c] Forecast.

[d] Fiscal year.

[e] Refers to first 8 months.

[f] Refers to first 3 months.

[g] Refers to first 10 months.

The annual growth rates of exports, in terms of merchandise goods only, are shown in the table. Calculations are based on data expressed in millions of United States dollars. Data are primarily obtained from the balance-of-payments accounts of each country. Exports, in general, are reported on a free-on-board (f.o.b.) basis. In this case, exports are valued at the customs frontier of the exporting country plus export duties and the costs of loading the goods onto the carriers unless the latter is borne by the carrier. It excludes the cost of freight and insurance beyond the customs frontier.

Table 9. Merchandise import growth rates

Sources: ESCAP calculations based on data from national sources; International Monetary Fund, Statistics Department, *Direction of Trade Statistics* (February 2011), CD-ROM ; Economist Intelligence Unit, *Country Reports*; CEIC Data Company Limited, data available from http://ceicdata.com (accessed 30 March 2011); and the website of the Interstate Statistical Committee of the Commonwealth of Independent States, www.cisstat.com (accessed 25 March 2011). Historical data and figures for 2010 on imports are mainly obtained from country sources, statistical publications, and secondary publications.

Notes:

[a] Refers to first 9 months.

[b] f.o.b. value.

[c] Estimate.

[d] Forecast.

[e] Fiscal year.

[f] Refers to first 8 months.

[g] Refers to first 3 months.

[h] Refers to first 10 months.

The annual growth rates of imports, in terms of merchandise goods only, are shown in the table. Calculations are based on data expressed in millions of United States dollars. Data are primarily obtained from the balance-of-payments accounts of each country. Data for imports are reported either on an f.o.b. or c.i.f. (cost, insurance, freight) basis. On a c.i.f. basis,

the value of imports includes the cost of international freight and insurance up to the customs frontier of the importing country. It excludes the cost of unloading the goods from the carrier unless it is borne by the carrier.

Table 10. Inward foreign direct investment

Source: Calculated by ESCAP using data from United Nations Conference on Trade and Development, "Foreign direct investment", UNCTADstat database. Available from http://unctadstat.unctad.org/ReportFolders/reportFolders.aspx (accessed 23 July 2010); and United Nations Statistics Division, National Accounts Main Aggregates Database. Available from http://unstats.un.org/unsd/snaama/selbasicFast.asp (accessed 11 January 2011).

Notes: *FDI stock* represents the value of the share of capital and reserves (including retained profits) attributable to the parent enterprise, plus the net indebtedness of affiliates to the parent enterprise. *Inward stock* is the value of the capital and reserves in the economy attributable to a parent enterprise resident in a different economy. Aggregates are calculated by ESCAP as the sum of FDI inward stock of a country (value in millions of United States dollars) and as the sum of FDI inward stock divided by GDP (percentage of GDP). *FDI flows* comprise capital provided (either directly or through related enterprises) by a foreign direct investor to an FDI enterprise, or capital received by a foreign direct investor from an FDI enterprise. *FDI inflows* comprise capital provided (either directly or through related enterprises) by a foreign direct investor to an FDI enterprise in the reporting economy. Aggregates are calculated by ESCAP as the sum of FDI inflows to an economy (value in millions of United States dollars), and as the sum of FDI inflows divided by GDP (percentage of GDP).

Table 11. Official development assistance and workers' remittances

Sources: Figures on official development assistance (ODA) are calculated by ESCAP using data from the Organization for Economic Cooperation and Development, Development Database on Aid from Development Assistance Committee Members. Available from www.oecd.org/maintopic/0,3348,en_ 2649_201185_1_1_1_1_1,00.html (accessed 14 October 2010); and United Nations Statistics Division, National Accounts Main Aggregates Database. Available from http://unstats.un.org/unsd/ snaama/selbasicFast.asp (accessed 11 January 2011). Figures on workers' remittances are calculated by ESCAP using data from the International Monetary Fund, Balance of Payment Statistics (CD-ROM, January 2011) and United Nations Statistics Division, National Accounts Main Aggregates Database. Available from http://unstats.un.org/unsd/snaama/selbasicFast.asp (accessed 11 January 2011).

Notes: The amount of *ODA* received in grants and loans during the reporting period is provided in the table. Aggregates are calculated by ESCAP as the sum of ODA received by an economy (value in millions of the dollars), and as the sum of ODA received divided by GNI (percentage of GNI). *Workers' remittances* received represent current transfers from abroad by migrants who are employed or intend to remain employed for more than a year in another economy in which they are considered residents.

Table 12.   International migration

Sources: The figures on foreign population are drawn from United Nations Department of Economics and Social Affairs, World Migrant Stock: The 2008 Revision Population Database. Available from http://esa.un.org/migration/ (accessed 25 August 2009). The net migration rate figures are drawn from World Population Prospects: The 2008 Revision Population Database. Available from http://esa.un.org/unpp/ (accessed 28 April 2009).

Notes: The *foreign population* represents the estimated number of international immigrants, male and female, in the middle of the indicated year. Generally, this represents the number of persons born in a country other than where they live. The number of international immigrants divided by the total population is expressed as a percentage in the middle of the indicated year. Where data on the place of birth are unavailable, the number of non-citizens is used as a proxy for the number of international immigrants. In either case, the migrant stock includes refugees, some of whom may not be foreign-born. The *net migration rate* is the number of immigrants minus the number of emigrants over a period, divided by the average population of the country over that period.

Table 13.   Primary, secondary and tertiary education

Source: United Nations Educational, Scientific and Cultural Organization (UNESCO) Institute for Statistics, Data Centre. Available from http://stats.uis.unesco.org/unesco/TableViewer/document.aspx?ReportId=136&IF_Language=eng&BR_Topic=0 (accessed 11 January 2011).

Notes: The *net enrolment ratio in primary education* is the enrolment rate of children in the official age group for primary education expressed as a percentage of the primary school-aged population. The *net enrolment ratio in secondary education* is the enrolment rate of children in the official age group for secondary education expressed as a percentage of the secondary school-aged population. The *gross enrolment ratio in tertiary education* represents the total enrolment in tertiary education, regardless of age, expressed as a percentage of the eligible official school-aged population corresponding to tertiary education in a given school year. For the tertiary level, the population used is that of the five-year age group following the end of secondary school. Numbers in parentheses indicate the year for which data are available.

Table 14.   Poverty and malnutrition

Source: United Nations Millennium Development Goals Indicators. Available from http://mdgs.un.org/unsd/mdg/Data.aspx (accessed

12 January 2011).

Notes: The poverty rate at $1.25 per day is the proportion of *the population living on less than $1.25 per day*, measured at 2005 international prices, adjusted for purchasing power parity (PPP). The purchasing power parity conversion factor is the number of units of a country's currency required to buy the same amounts of goods and services in the domestic market as the United States dollar would buy in the United States. The *undernourished population* is the proportion of the population receiving less than the minimum level of dietary energy consumption as a percentage of the total population. The *prevalence of underweight children* is the percentage of children aged 0-59 months whose weights for their age are less than two standard deviations below the median weight of the international reference population. The international reference population, often referred to as the NCHS/WHO reference population, was formulated by the United States National Center for Health Statistics (NCHS) as a national reference and later adopted by the World Health Organization (WHO). Numbers in parentheses indicate the year for which data are available.

Table 15.   Unemployment

Sources: Figures for total unemployment are calculated by ESCAP using data from International Labour Organization, *Key Indicators of the Labour Market*, 6th ed. Interactive software CD-ROM. Figures on youth unemployment are drawn from United Nations Millennium Development Goals Indicators. Available from http://mdgs.un.org/unsd/mdg/Data.aspx (accessed 4 August 2010).

Notes: The *total unemployment rate* is the number of persons of working age who, during the reference period, were without work, currently available for work and seeking work, divided by the total labour force. National definitions and coverage of unemployment may vary. Data are disaggregated by sex. The *youth unemployment rate* represents the number of young persons aged 15-24 who are without work, currently available for work and seeking work, divided by the total labour force of that age group.

Table 16.   Telecommunications

Sources: Calculated by ESCAP using data from International Telecommunication Union, ICT Statistics Database. Available from www.itu.int/ITU-D/ICTEYE/Indicators/Indicators.aspx (accessed 11 January 2011); and World Population Prospects: The 2008 Revision Population Database. Available from http://esa.un.org/unpd/wpp2008/index.htm (accessed 28 April 2009).

Notes: *Fixed telephone lines* refer to telephone lines that have been active during the past three months, that connect a subscriber's terminal equipment to the public switched telephone network (PSTN) and that have a dedicated port on a telephone exchange. They include the active number of analogue fixed telephone lines (112a), ISDN channels (28c), fixed wireless (WLL), public payphones (1112) and VoIP subscriptions (112IP).

Aggregates are calculated by ESCAP using total population as weight. The *number of mobile cellular subscriptions* refers to subscriptions to a public mobile telephone service that provides access to the public switched telephone network (PSTN) using cellular technology, including pre-paid subscriber identity module (SIM) cards that were active during the past three months. It includes both analogue and digital cellular systems IMT-2000 (third generation/3G), fourth generation/4G subscriptions and all mobile cellular subscriptions that offer voice communications, but excludes mobile broadband subscriptions via data cards or Universal Serial Bus (USB) modems. Subscriptions to public mobile data services, private trunked mobile radio, telepoint or radio paging, and telemetry services is also excluded. Aggregates are calculated by ESCAP using total population as weight. The estimated *number of Internet users* out of total population includes those using the Internet from any device (including mobile phones) in the last 12 months. Aggregates are calculated by ESCAP using total population as weight. The number of *fixed broadband Internet subscribers* refers to the number of subscriptions to high-speed access to the public Internet (a TCP/IP connection) at downstream speeds equal to, or greater than, 256 kbit/s. It includes, for example, cable modem, DSL, fibre-to-the-home/-building and other fixed (wired) broadband subscriptions. It excludes subscriptions to data communications (including the Internet) via mobile cellular networks. Aggregates are calculated by ESCAP using total population as weight. `Missing data are assumed to be zero when calculating aggregates.

Table 17. Infrastructure and transport

Sources: Data for all topics in the table are drawn from World Bank, World Development Indicators online. Available from http://data.worldbank.org/data-catalog/world-development-indicators (accessed 10 January 2011). Additional data for road and railway density are drawn from Food and Agriculture Organization of the United Nations, FAOSTAT database. Available from http://faostat.fao.org/site/348/default.aspx (accessed 20 October 2010).

Notes: *Road density (km per 1,000 km²)* represents the total length of the road network divided by the land area. The total road network includes motorways, highways, and main or national roads; secondary or regional roads; and all other roads in a country or area, measured in kilometres. Aggregates are calculated by ESCAP using land area as weight. Missing data for some countries and years have been imputed. *Paved roads (percentage of total roads)* comprise the share of roads surfaced with crushed stone (macadam) and hydrocarbon binder or bituminized agents, concrete or cobblestones. Aggregates are calculated by ESCAP using land area as weight. Missing data for some countries and years have been imputed. *Railway density (km per 1,000 km²)* is the length of rail lines divided by the land area. The length represents railway routes available for train service, measured in kilometres, irrespective of the number of parallel tracks. Aggregates are calculated by ESCAP using land area as weight. Missing data for some countries and years have been imputed. *Passenger cars (per 1,000 population)* refer to road motor vehicles, other than two-wheelers, intended for the

carriage of passengers and designed to seat no more than nine people (including the driver). Aggregates are calculated by ESCAP using total population as weight. Missing data for some countries and years have been imputed.

Table 18. Energy and water use

Sources: Data on both categories of energy use are drawn from International Energy Agency, World Energy Statistics and Balances online database. Available from www.oecd-ilibrary.org/content/datacollection/enestats-data-en (accessed 19 and 20 January 2011). Additional data on the consumption of electricity for domestic purposes are drawn from United Nations Department of Economic and Social Affairs, Population Division, World Population Prospects: The 2008 Revision Population Database. Available from http://esa.un.org/unpp/ (accessed 28 April 2009). Additional data on energy use per $1,000 GDP are drawn from World Bank, World Development Indicators online. Available from http://data.worldbank.org/data-catalog/world-development-indicators (accessed 20 January 2011). Data on water withdrawals are obtained from Food and Agriculture Organization of the United Nations, AQUASTAT database. Available from www.fao.org/nr/water/aquastat/data/query/index.html?lang=en (accessed 10 January 2011).

Notes: The *consumption of electricity for domestic purposes (kilowatt-hours per capita)* is annual electricity consumption divided by total population. Aggregates are calculated by ESCAP using total population as weight. *Energy use per $1,000 GDP (2005 PPP) (kilograms of oil equivalent)* is the energy use per gross domestic product converted to 2005 constant international dollars using purchasing power parity rates. Energy use refers to use of primary energy before transformation to other end-use fuels, which is equal to indigenous production plus imports and stock changes, minus exports and fuels supplied to ships and aircraft engaged in international transport. Aggregates are calculated by ESCAP using GDP (2005 PPP dollars) as weight. *Water withdrawals* represent the gross amount of water extracted in a day from any source, either permanently or temporarily. Water can be withdrawn from surface water, groundwater or produced (non-conventional) water sources, such as treated wastewater and desalinated water.

Since the 1957 issue, the *Economic and Social Survey of Asia and the Pacific* has, in addition to a review of the current situation of the region, contained a study or studies of some major aspect or problem of the economies of the Asian and Pacific region, as specified below:

1957: Postwar problems of economic development
1958: Review of postwar industrialization
1959: Foreign trade of ECAFE primary exporting countries
1960: Public finance in the postwar period
1961: Economic growth of ECAFE countries
1962: Asia's trade with western Europe
1963: Imports substitution and export diversification
1964: Economic development and the role of the agricultural sector
1965: Economic development and human resources
1966: Aspects of the finance of development
1967: Policies and planning for export
1968: Economic problems of export-dependent countries. Implications of economic controls and liberalization
1969: Strategies for agricultural development. Intraregional trade as a growth strategy
1970: The role of foreign private investment in economic development and cooperation in the ECAFE region. Problems and prospects of the ECAFE region in the Second Development Decade
1971: Economic growth and social justice. Economic growth and employment. Economic growth and income distribution
1972: First biennial review of social and economic developments in ECAFE developing countries during the Second United Nations Development Decade
1973: Education and employment
1974: Mid-term review and appraisal of the International Development Strategy for the Second United Nations Development Decade in the ESCAP region, 1974
1975: Rural development, the small farmer and institutional reform
1976: Biennial review and appraisal of the International Development Strategy at the regional level for the Second United Nations Development Decade in the ESCAP region, 1976
1977: The international economic crises and developing Asia and the Pacific
1978: Biennial review and appraisal at the regional level of the International Development Strategy for the Second United Nations Development Decade
1979: Regional development strategy for the 1980s
1980: Short-term economic policy aspects of the energy situation in the ESCAP region
1981: Recent economic developments in major subregions of the ESCAP region
1982: Fiscal policy for development in the ESCAP region
1983: Implementing the International Development Strategy: major issues facing the developing ESCAP region
1984: Financing development
1985: Trade, trade policies and development
1986: Human resources development in Asia and the Pacific: problems, policies and perspectives
1987: International trade in primary commodities
1988: Recent economic and social developments
1989: Patterns of economic growth and structural transformation in the least developed and Pacific island countries of the ESCAP region: implications for development policy and planning for the 1990s
1990: Infrastructure development in the developing ESCAP region: needs, issues and policy options
1991: Challenges of macroeconomic management in the developing ESCAP region
1992: Expansion of investment and intraregional trade as a vehicle for enhancing regional economic cooperation and development in Asia and the Pacific
1993: Fiscal reform. Economic transformation and social development. Population dynamics: implications for development
1995: Reform and liberalization of the financial sector. Social security
1996: Enhancing the role of the private sector in development. The role of public expenditure in the provision of social services
1997: External financial and investment flows. Transport and communications
1998: Managing the external sector. Growth and equity
1999: Social impact of the economic crisis. Information technology, globalization, economic security and development
2000: Social security and safety nets. Economic and financial monitoring and surveillance
2001: Socio-economic implications of demographic dynamics. Financing for development
2002: The feasibility of achieving the Millennium Development Goals in Asia and the Pacific. Regional development cooperation in Asia and the Pacific
2003: The role of public expenditure in the provision of education and health. Environment-poverty nexus revisited: linkages and policy options
2004: Poverty reduction strategies: tackling the multidimensional nature of poverty
2005: Dynamics of population ageing: how can Asia and the Pacific respond?
2006: Emerging unemployment issues in Asia and the Pacific: rising to the challenges
2007: Gender inequality continues – at great cost
2008: Unequal benefits of growth – agriculture left behind
2009: Triple threats to development: food, fuel and climate change policy challenges
2010: Multiple imbalances and development gaps as new engines of growth. A regional policy agenda for regaining the dynamism

This publication may be obtained from bookstores and distributors throughout the world. Please consult your bookstore or write to any of the following:

Sales Section
Room DC2-0853
United Nations Secretariat
New York, NY 10017
USA

Tel: (1) (212) 963-8302
Fax: (1) (212) 963-4116
E-mail: publications@un.org

Sales Section
United Nations Office at Geneva
Palais des Nations
CH-1211 Geneva 10
Switzerland

Tel: (41) (22) 917-1234
Fax: (41) (22) 917-0123
E-mail: unpubli@unog.ch

Chief
Conference Management Unit
Conference Services Section
Administrative Services Division
Economic and Social Commission for
    Asia and the Pacific (ESCAP)
United Nations Building
Rajadamnern Nok Avenue
Bangkok 10200, Thailand

Tel: (662) 288-1976
Fax: (662) 288-1000
E-mail: rizvis@un.org

For further information on publications in this series, please address your enquiries to:

Director
Macroeconomic Policy and Development Division
Economic and Social Commission for
    Asia and the Pacific (ESCAP)
United Nations Building
Rajadamnern Nok Avenue
Bangkok 10200, Thailand

Tel: (662) 288-2063
Fax: (662) 288-1000, 288-3007
E-mail: escap-mpdd@un.org

READERSHIP SURVEY

The Macroeconomic Policy and Development Division of ESCAP is undertaking an evaluation of this publication, **Economic and Social Survey of Asia and the Pacific 2011**, with a view to making future issues more useful for our readers. We would appreciate it if you could complete this questionnaire and return it, at your earliest convenience, to:

Director
Macroeconomic Policy and Development Division
ESCAP, United Nations Building
Rajadamnern Nok Avenue
Bangkok 10200, THAILAND

QUESTIONNAIRE

	Excellent	Very good	Average	Poor
1. Please indicate your assessment of the *quality* of the publication on:				
• Presentation/format	4	3	2	1
• Readability	4	3	2	1
• Timeliness of information	4	3	2	1
• Coverage of subject matter	4	3	2	1
• Analytical rigour	4	3	2	1
• Overall quality	4	3	2	1
2. How *useful* is the publication for your work?				
• Provision of information	4	3	2	1
• Clarification of issues	4	3	2	1
• Its findings	4	3	2	1
• Policy suggestions	4	3	2	1
• Overall usefulness	4	3	2	1

3. Please give examples of how this publication has contributed to your work:

....
....
....
....

4. Suggestions for improving the publication:

....

....

....

....

5. Your background information, please:

Name: ....

Title/position: ....

Institution: ....

Office address: ....

....

**Please use additional sheets of paper, if required, to answer the questions.
Thank you for your kind cooperation in completing this questionnaire.**

'IE